THE SUFFERING
SAVIOUR

THE SUFFERING SAVIOUR

F. W. Krummacher

THE BANNER OF TRUTH TRUST

THE BANNER OF TRUTH TRUST
3 Murrayfield Road, Edinburgh EH12 6EL, UK
P.O. Box 621, Carlisle, PA 17013, USA

*

First English edition, Edinburgh, 1856
First Banner of Truth edition 2004

ISBN 0 85151 856 7

*

Typeset in 12 /14 pt Goudy Old Style BT
by Initial Typesetting Services, Dalkeith
Printed and bound in Great Britain
at the University Press,
Cambridge

Contents

PART TWO: THE HOLY PLACE (continued)

PART THREE: THE MOST HOLY PLACE

Biographical Introduction

Friedrich Wilhelm Krummacher, perhaps the greatest preacher on the continent of Europe in the middle years of the nineteenth century, was born on 28 January 1796, at Mörs, on the River Rhine, the first son of Friedrich Adolf Krummacher, a minister of the Reformed Church. When Friedrich was four, his father accepted a call to be Professor of Theology and Eloquence at the University of Duisburg, and it was in Duisburg that Friedrich spent his childhood years, up to the age of 13.

In 1807 Friedrich's father received a call to Kettwig on the Ruhr, where the family spent the next five years. In his autobiography,[1] Krummacher gives details of his father's ministry and his own gradual advance in the knowledge of God in Christ. The first deep and enduring religious impression made on Friedrich was occasioned by the death of a relative. At this time an uncle said to Friedrich and his brother Emil:

> Yes, dear young friends, as we all, so you too, must one day lie on a dying bed. We are born to die. See that you learn early to believe in the Lord Jesus Christ, for without Him we are the most miserable of all creatures.

[1] Second edition, Edinburgh: T. & T. Clark, 1871.

These words made an impression which was never to be erased.

In 1811 Friedrich's father was invited to become the superintendent of the Duchy of Anhalt-Bernburg, so the family moved once more, this time to the town of Bernburg on the banks of the Saale, in Saxony. During their first year there, they saw a large part of the 'grand army' of Napoleon pass on its march to Russia, 'with imposing pomp and with an overbearing haughtiness as if already the whole world were subject to it'. Only a few months later the defeated remains of the army were in full retreat, 'now reduced by the judgment of God which overtook them on the snowy plains of Russia to a few tattered fragments', and Friedrich and his school-friends saw Napoleon himself pass in his carriage, not many months before his defeat at the Battle of Leipzig.

Friedrich was still in his teens when Germany was delivered from the yoke of Napoleon and experienced an upsurge of patriotic and religious fervour:

> The people again rendered to God, after having long forgotten Him, the honour which was His due. The churches were filled anew with worshippers as they had not been for many years before, and again they resounded with the songs of praise and thankfulness. 'The Lord has been our helper', men were heard frequently to say – men from whose lips such a pious utterance was never heard before . . . Even the cold, hard Rationalism which then, from almost every pulpit in the land, cast down the chopped straw and chaff of its poor ideas to scanty and spiritually famished congregations, felt itself breathed upon and irradiated by the general religious spirit which hovered in the very air; and its God . . . became the Living God, and came near to men as the Hearer of prayer and the Director of battles.

From 1815 to 1817 Friedrich attended the University of Halle. Most of the theological teaching was decidedly rationalistic. Of the teaching of one professor, he says:

> We saw the Lord of Glory stripped of His supernatural majesty, shrivelled into the rank of a mere rabbi, noble indeed, and highly gifted, but yet always entangled by the prejudices of His time, He had never performed a real miracle and had neither risen from the dead nor ascended up into heaven. We saw also the whole contents of the gospel, after being stripped of its particularistic and mythic veilings, reduced to a mere moral system for the manifestation of which no divine revelation was at all needed . . . From Wegscheider's *Dogmatics* I learned more about rationalism than I did about Christianity and I know that it was so also with many others of my fellow-students who, at the most, were pleased only with the logical frame in which his caricature of the gospel was set. Thousands indeed there were who carried away with them from Wegscheider's classroom more than the frame, and many congregations are to this day doomed to spiritual famine because they have presented to them only the husks and chaff which were there gathered and stored up by his students.

From Halle, Krummacher went on to Jena, where he spent two years. Some of Germany's most distinguished theologians were teaching there at that time.

While Krummacher was studying at Jena, he was influenced by a work of his father's, *The Spirit and Form of the Gospels*, which helped to maintain a love of the truth in his own heart, despite the rationalistic atmosphere he was breathing. At his examination before the Anhalt consistory, when asked, as a trial discourse, to expound the miracle of the loaves and fishes, he presented it as a symbol of the inexhaustible goodness of God toward the suffering children of men; but his father interrupted the discussion to ask whether he regarded the gospel narrative as historically true or as a mere allegory. He comments:

> This question, which had never before in the same form pressed itself on my attention, filled me at once with perplexity and confusion. It was some time before I had the power of composing myself to answer that I did not at all deny that the miracles of Jesus were true, but that I regarded their chief value as consisting in the religious and moral truths which they represented. But at the same moment when I thus answered, a light broke in upon my mind convincing me how miserably this notion harmonized with my supposed belief of the historical verity of the miracles and making it manifest to me that my whole Christianity consisted as yet more in undefined sentimentality than in firm conviction; more in the hazy vision of the imagination than in the possession of truth won as the result of warfare against error or as gained from experience.

Soon after successfully passing his theological examination he was invited to become assistant preacher to the Reformed congregation at Frankfurt-on-Main, where he remained for nearly five happy years, 1819–23. Some of the friendships which he made there had a significant influence on him for the rest of his life. Among those also ministering in the town was a pastor from Lausanne, Manuel, minister of the French Reformed congregation. Krummacher says of him:

> In spirit I anoint the tombstone of this distinguished man whose life came too soon to an end. His was a character out and out pure and genuine as gold . . . oh, the never-to-be-forgotten delightful days spent in fellowship with each other! I bless the man whom the Lord used as the principal instrument in leading me to know the depths of my own heart

better, in revealing to me the barren deserts which were there, in vivifying and making distinctly felt in my heart my need of salvation, and in heightening the earnestness of my prayers. He has often made me despair of myself, but under his encouragement I always again was able to compose myself and gain courage. Tempted by doubts – historical, critical or philosophical – we sought in common their solution and rested not till it was found. We read together Latin, Greek, and German, with which languages he was perfectly acquainted, and also French. We engaged in a constant intercourse of thoughts, if not about some portion of God's Word, about some one of the reformers or church fathers, or about some distinguished theological work of recent date.

From 1823 to 1825 Krummacher was pastor at Ruhrort, where he had a congregation which delighted him. 'How incomparably happy was the time which was granted to me in dear Ruhrort,' he writes. 'I felt myself as if borne up by the affections and by the prayers of considerable circles of experienced and well-informed Christians who gathered around me, and I thought that I saw very soon my constant and yet very imperfect instruction honoured with the rich blessing of fruitfulness among the old, and especially among the young.'

After nine years of ministry at Barmen, where, he says, 'Great crowds of hearers were everywhere thronging the churches, and it was a common thing to hear the sound of choral singing in which many voices were united proceeding from the workshops and factories and echoing from the woods and hills around on the Sabbath afternoons', Krummacher went on to Elberfeld, where his fame began to grow. So powerful in fact was his ministry in Elberfeld that his next post was as Court Preacher in Berlin. At Elberfeld, he believed, the preachers were borne up by the spiritual vigour of the people to a degree known nowhere else in Germany.

There was, for a brief time, a mighty upsurge of evangelical fervour, in which Krummacher was a notable instrument. 'From the pulpits', he said, 'there is heard more and more in new and distinct utterances the proclamation of the old good Word; there are flourishing mission schools under the shelter of the gentle royal sceptre; Bible societies in full and unwearied activity; institutions aiming at the promotion of the welfare of the neglected and the criminal, and what is yet more than all this, there are considerable bands of men continually in-creasing in number in all districts of the land who have sworn that they will never more bow the knee to Baal; a company of praying men encompassing the land as a chain, diffusing blessings all around.'

While he was minister at Elberfeld, during a visit to Bremen, Krummacher 'threw the torch of war into the midst of the church life' of Bremen by a sermon on Galatians 1:8–9. Many rationalists concluded that he had them personally in mind, and a vehement controversy was ignited.

Still at Elberfeld, Krummacher received an invitation to take up a professorship in the theological seminary of Mercersburg, U.S.A. He felt led to decline the invitation, but recommended to the seminary a man who was to become a most distinguished church historian, Philip Schaff, then a student in Berlin. From his association with Krummacher, Schaff gives a vivid picture of the older man as a preacher:

> Krummacher does not make a pleasing impression at first sight. He is not good looking. He is built like a lion, and his eloquence corresponds with his build. An imposing, strong figure, massive facial features, a wild confused head of hair, grey eyes, the man vanishes, so to speak, in the pulpit orator. The solemn bass voice which pours itself forth like thunder upon his congregation, the rushing torrent of his figures, the bold but controlled gestures, the tossing of the head from side

to side, the contents of the sermon itself, which is always original and, clothed in splendid garb, unlocks the depths of sin and grace, now breaking to pieces the fabric of the old man and the pleasures of the world, now comforting and with magic softness, wooing to the source of salvation.

In 1847 Krummacher was called to the pulpit of Trinity Church in Berlin, occupied, some years before, by Friedrich Schleiermacher. Here he found an atmosphere altogether different from the one he had enjoyed in western Germany.

He was in close association with the most distinguished thinkers of his day, and describes them in his autobiography. Particularly delightful was his fellowship with the stalwart defender of the faith, the Hebraist, E. W. Hengstenberg, and the distinguished church historian, August Neander, at whose grave he later delivered the funeral oration. He could not fail to be aware, however, of the accelerating drift of the German church into infidelity and rationalism. At a great meeting of the Evangelical Alliance held in Freemason's Hall, London, in the summer of 1851, Krummacher read a paper on 'The Religious State of Germany and Its Infidelity'. Despite the prevailing climate, he still held out hope regarding a turning of the tide against Germany's rationalism. Sadly, this hope was not to be fulfilled.

So great was the influence of Krummacher throughout all Germany that he was called in 1853 to be the court chaplain at Potsdam, and here he remained until his death, sixteen years later. Specially interesting among his later correspondence is a letter from the king, Friedrich Wilhelm, written on 27 November 1853: 'That advent sermon which you preached surpassed all I have ever heard. May the Lord of the church with a thousand-fold blessing make it fruitful! I have the confidence that this blessing, dear Krummacher, will not fail to descend upon your head, and also on the labours of your ministry, though you may have long and patiently to wait for it . . . Do not let the impression made by your advent sermon at Potsdam die with this Sabbath. Multiply it by the press and send to me a hundred copies of it. He who has through you begun the good work will also carry it to a completion!'

Krummacher was by many reckoned the greatest evangelical preacher in all Europe at that time. Philip Schaff wrote an eloquent tribute following Krummacher's death on 19 December 1868. He spoke of him as 'endowed with every gift that constitutes an orator, a most fertile and brilliant imagination, a vigorous and original mind, a glowing heart, an extraordinary facility and felicity of diction, perfect familiarity with the Scriptures, an athletic and commanding presence, and a powerful and melodious voice, which, however, in later years underwent a great change, and sounded like the rolling of the distant thunder or like the trumpet of the last judgment . . . He was full of the fire of faith and the Holy Ghost. In the pulpit he was as bold and fearless as a lion, at home as gentle and amiable as a lamb. Like all truly great men, he had a childlike disposition.'

Krummacher was the author of numerous books, perhaps the best-known of which are *Elijah the Tishbite* and the present volume. The work here reprinted appeared originally in 1854 and was immediately translated into English by Samuel Jackson. The first two editions appeared in Edinburgh in 1856, and by 1875 an eighth edition had appeared. It has frequently been republished since. C. H. Spurgeon believed that Krummacher's name was 'a sufficient guarantee' of the value of any book he wrote. Certainly, the value of this moving series of meditations is not in doubt. It has instructed and comforted successive generations of Christians, and deserves a wide modern readership.

THE PUBLISHER
Edinburgh, January 2004

Part One

~~~

THE OUTER
COURT

Chapter 1

The Announcement

The history of our Saviour's passion is about to display before us its bleeding mysteries and its awful vicarious scenes. The 'Lamb of God, which taketh away the sin of the world' approaches the altar of burnt-offering. Bonds, the scourge, the crown of thorns, and the cross, present themselves to our view in the distance; and the 'seven words' uttered by Jesus on the cross, sound in our ears, like the funeral knell of the kingdom of Satan, and like intimations of liberty and joy to the sinful race of man.

O what wonders are we about to approach in our meditations! From the most appalling scene the world ever witnessed, a paradise of peace springs forth. From the most ignominious sufferings, we see the most glorious triumph emerge; and from the most dreadful of deaths, a divine and never-fading life arise!

May devotion, humbleness of mind, and child-like faith accompany us in our meditations, and penitential tears become our eye-salve! But do Thou, who hast the key of David, unlock for us the gates to the sanctuary of Thy sacred passion, and in the awful scenes of Thy sufferings, enable us to discover the mystery of our eternal redemption!

Almost immediately after our blessed Lord had performed perhaps the most stupendous of His miracles, in raising

Lazarus from the grave, after he had been dead four days, we are informed by the Evangelist that 'the chief priests and the Pharisees took counsel together to put him to death.' What a humbling view does this circumstance give us of the depravity of human nature as exemplified in these men, who, while obliged to confess the fact of the miracles which Jesus wrought, not only refused to accept Him as the Messiah, but even conspired together to rid themselves of Him by condemning Him to death! 'Neither will they be persuaded though one rose from the dead.'

'Jesus therefore,' we are told, 'walked no more openly among the Jews, but went thence unto a country near to the wilderness, into a city called Ephraim, and there continued with his disciples.' But 'when the time was come that he should be received up, he steadfastly set his face to go to Jerusalem.'

With this object in view, the Lord takes His twelve disciples aside. He has matters of importance to disclose to them. Destined, as they were, to lay the foundations of His Church, they soon perceive His intention, and hang upon His lips with increasing eagerness. They probably reckon on some cheering intelligence, and expect to hear that the triumphant development of His kingdom is at hand. But what short-sightedness and simplicity do they display! O the mighty chasm which intervenes between their thoughts and God's thoughts! As though the restoration of fallen man were a thing of such easy accomplishment! As if sin had caused only a transient disturbance in the relations between God and man, and occasioned a breach which could be healed, either by a voluntary declaration of mercy from on high, or by a confession of sin on the part of the fallen!

The Lord opens His mouth, and to the astonishment of the disciples, announces to them in plain terms His approaching sufferings, and at the same time His subsequent victory.

'Behold,' says He, 'we go up to Jerusalem, and all things that are written by the prophets concerning the Son of man shall be accomplished.'

Observe, first of all, how these words convey our Lord's fixed resolution. His heart, under the impulse of love, is firmly and immutably bent on taking the way to the cross. You well remember with what impressive earnestness He rejected the advice of Simon Peter to spare Himself, and not to go up to Jerusalem. 'Get thee behind me, Satan,' was His reply; 'thou art an offence unto me; for thou savourest not the things that be of God, but those that be of man.' So evident was it to Him that the sufferings He was going to meet were the express will and counsel of His heavenly Father, that in the contrary advice of His disciple, He could recognize nothing but a temptation from the bottomless pit, and Simon as the unconscious instrument of it.

No affectionate entreaty restrains Him in His course; no menace dictated by hatred deters Him from it. The blood-thirsty council has already assembled at Jerusalem, and is concocting its plan of treachery and murder. But the watch-word of Jesus continues to be 'Behold we go up!' and though another Red Sea were foaming at His feet, and though a hundred deaths awaited Him, yet the only sentiment of His heart is, 'We go up.' For it is His Father's will, and the path to the great and ardently longed-for aim of the world's redemption. O what resignation, what obedience, what love to sinners is here exemplified by our adorable Immanuel!

'Behold,' says our Lord, 'we go up to Jerusalem, and all things that are written by the prophets concerning the Son of man shall be accomplished.' Here we are informed what was His staff and His stay on the road to His sufferings. He found it in the 'sure word of prophecy,' in which He read what was recorded of Himself, and the counsel of God respecting Him. And if any one still requires a definite

authority for the divine inspiration of the Holy Scriptures, it
is here presented to him. Christ, the King of Truth, recognizes
in the Scriptures nothing less than the infallible record of
the revelation of His heavenly Father; He bears it, day and
night, on His heart; He decides according to its statutes, as
the Canon Law, which puts an end to all strife respecting
the vital questions of human life, and directs His steps wither-
soever it points the way. It is to Him the infallible guiding-
star of His life. Whether the voice of His heavenly Father is
heard direct from heaven, or sounds to Him from this venerable record: it is the same to Him. The one is as important as
the other; and He reverently bows to every tittle and iota of
it. It is thus His ways are established; and every moment's
experience seals it to Him, that He is actually obeying a divine
command. Every thing that the Word enjoins becomes reality.

'Certainly,' some one may say, 'it ought to strengthen our
determination to proceed upon the path prescribed for us by
the Word of God, when, like Christ, we are aware that our
way through life is not only divinely ordered and superin-
tended, generally speaking, but also when we can survey it,
from step to step, in the light of an infallible and divine
revelation, even to its glorious termination.' But is not this
really the case, if thou hast believingly and sincerely given
thyself up to God? For can there be any situation in which
the divine Word, with its counsel, leaves thee at a loss? Is it
not also written respecting thee, 'The Lord will not suffer
thee to want any good thing?' 'Through much tribulation
thou must enter into the kingdom of heaven.' But 'when thou
passest through the waters, they shall not overflow thee; and
through the fire, the flame shall not kindle upon thee, for
the Lord is with thee.' It may indeed be the case that men
will revile and persecute thee; but if thou faithfully endure,
thy reward shall be great. The light shall always rise upon
thee after the darkness; and after sorrow, joy shall again visit

thy threshold. Nor shall any one be able to snatch thee out of the Lord's hands; but after having fought the good fight, thou shalt finally receive the crown of righteousness, shalt not see death, but pass from death unto life, and triumph eternally.

Does not all this, and manifold more stand written of thee; and is not therefore thy path pointed out? Mayest thou not also say, in thy measure, with the Lord Jesus, 'Behold, we go up to Jerusalem, and all shall be accomplished, that stands written by the finger of God, respecting me, a poor sinner, since I am no longer my own, but belong to Christ?' O certainly thou mayest say this! How ought we not, therefore, with such a consciousness, to put on a cheerful courage, during our pilgrimage, and feel as if heavenly triumphal music preceded us on our path through life!

My dear readers, let us place a firm reliance on the Word of truth and, in its light, ascend the precipitous road; according to its instructions, proceed forward with firm and steady steps, unmindful of the tumult of the world, and not deviating a hand-breadth from the way prescribed. Let us meet him who would direct us otherwise, with a voice of thunder, and exclaim, 'Get thee behind me, Satan, for thou savourest not the things that be of God, but those that be of man!' The Almighty will then be favourable to us; we shall then carry the peace of God in our bosoms; and literal accomplishments of the divine promises, which we have taken for our compass, and for a lamp unto our feet, will daily fall upon our path, like lights from heaven.

The Lord's face is toward Jerusalem; and we have already seen for what purpose. His intention is to suffer and to die. O there must be something of immense importance connected with His passion! It appears as the crisis of the work for the accomplishment of which He left His Father's bosom, and came down to earth! Were this not the case, it would have been tempting God, thus to rush to meet death after having completed His prophetic office in Jerusalem; and the overruling Majesty on high would have exposed His justice to well-founded reproach, in giving up the Holy One, who had fulfilled His commands, to the horrible fate of a male-factor and reprobate. But the Eternal Father had included in His counsels the scourge, the crown of thorns, and the cross, long before the sons of Belial thought of having recourse to these instruments of torture; and all His prophets, however reluctantly, were compelled in spirit to interweave these horrid emblems along with the majestic image of the Messiah, which they portrayed. Thus the Lord could say with profound truth, 'All things that are written by the prophets concerning the Son of man shall be accomplished; for he shall be de-livered unto the Gentiles, and shall be mocked, and spitefully entreated, and spitted on, and they shall scourge him and put him to death.'

Such were the ingredients which filled the cup that Satan, in accordance with the counsels of eternal wisdom, was to present to the Son of the Most High. These counsels went far, very far, beyond all that we understand by martyrdom, chastisement, purification, or trial. The immaculate and righteous Saviour did not require correction as for Himself; and if a purification had been salutary for Him, it needed not to have come upon the Holy One of Israel in the form of such degrading infamy, unheard-of reproach and humiliation, and such unparalleled suffering. The passion of our Lord has an infinitely more profound significancy; and it requires only a cursory glance at the narrative to discover that this was the case. Observe what the Evangelist informs us respecting the way and manner in which the twelve received their Master's communication. He states that 'they understood none of these things, and this saying was hidden from them, neither knew they the things which were spoken.'

How striking is this circumstance! Who can resist inquiring what it was they did not understand? They could not possibly have mistaken what their Master said respecting His suffering and dying at Jerusalem. Yet Luke assures us that 'they understood none of those things, and knew not what it was that was spoken.' Is it not obvious that the Evangelist's meaning is that he who would only apprehend the history of Christ's sufferings, and regard His passion as a martyrdom, not essentially different from the bloody testimony borne by other saints, does not understand its true signification? We have here an evident reference to an infinitely deeper cause of the tragical termination of our Saviour's life before us.

It is confessedly true that the eternal Father, by an almighty decree, might have annihilated the fallen race, in which sin had taken root, and thus have put an end to evil. But we were to live and not die. And thus He has not only caused the sin of man to act as a foil for the display of the full radiance of His attributes, and especially of His love, but has also, by the offering up of His Son, provided a means of salvation by which we might attain to a much higher stage of glory and relationship to God than we once possessed in our progenitor, or than we should ever have attained if we had not fallen. Our fall afforded Him the opportunity of showing that in the destruction of sin He could not only manifest His justice, but also glorify His mercy in remitting and forgiving sin, without infringing upon His righteousness.

We sinned, and were exposed to the curse. The Word that was with God, and was God, then was made flesh. The eternal Son became our brother; took upon Himself our sin, in the way of a mysterious imputation; paid our debt to the majesty of the inviolable law; covered our nakedness with His righteousness; presented us, as those in whose stead He appeared, unblamable and acceptable to the Father; excited the hallelujahs of angels at our exaltation; elevated us to a participation of His own riches, blessedness, and privileges; pitched tents of peace for us around the throne of God; and connected us with Himself by the bonds of eternal gratitude and affection. Such is the edifice which the Almighty reared upon the ruins of sin; and of which the disciples, at that time, had not the remotest idea. In the sequel, they recognized the divine method of salvation and of peace; and how happy were they, subsequently, in the knowledge of this 'great mystery of godliness!'

Chapter 2

The Anointing

S ix days before the Passover, and, consequently, four before
the awful day of crucifixion, we find our Lord in the
peaceful village of Bethany, on the other side of the Mount
of Olives, where He was wont so willingly to stay. We meet
with Him this time in the house of a man named Simon,
where His followers had prepared Him a feast. He appears
before us in the unassuming form of a guest, invited with
others; but look a little more narrowly, and you will see Him,
even there, as John afterward saw Him in vision, only in a
somewhat different sense, as 'walking amid the candlesticks.'

The Lord Jesus has no need to testify of Himself; for
those who are present bear witness of Him in the most
eloquent manner. Look, first, at Mary and her sister Martha.
They are women possessing true nobility of soul, respected
by all sensible, clear-sighted, and sober-minded. Martha,
cheerful, active, and busy; Mary, thoughtful and contemplative. Both, however, rest all their hopes on Jesus. He
is, to both, the living pillar which supports their heaven;
their prospects of a blissful futurity arises solely from His
mediation; and the peace and comfort, which refreshes
them in life and death, they derive from Christ alone as
the source. What a high idea must this fact alone afford
us of the Man of Nazareth.

Look around you further. There are the disciples, Peter, Andrew, John, James, Nathanael, Thomas, and the rest. You formerly saw them listening to the Baptist in the wilderness, like a flock of scattered and helpless sheep. You learned to know them as people who were incited to seek for help, by a very different motive than a mere thirst for knowledge. You found them to be men whose hearts were grievously burdened by sin, and by the anticipation of 'the wrath to come,' and whose inward peace was entirely at an end, after having seen God in the fiery splendour of His law, with its requirements and threatenings. Neither man nor angel was able to comfort them; but since they had found Jesus, their thoroughly humbled souls were like the sparrow which has found a house, and the swallow, a nest, where they may drop their weary wings. They are now elevated above all anxiety. What bright rays of light does this fact also shed upon Jesus! How highly does it exalt Him above the idea of being a mere mortal!

But alas! among the disciples we still find Judas, the child of darkness, the son of perdition. He, indeed, was never, in his own eyes, a helpless sinner; he had never thirsted after God; he was never truly devout; nor had ever set his affections on things above. It may be asked what induced him to force himself into the immediate vicinity of Jesus? Assuredly, first, the irresistible and overpowering impression of the superhuman greatness and dignity of the Son of David, and then doubtless, also, an ambitious desire of being called to act some important part in the new kingdom, to establish which Jesus had evidently come. Thus the presentiment of the traitor aided in glorifying the person of the Lord. The divine majesty of Immanuel shone so powerfully through His human form that its rays penetrated even into the darkness of Iscariot's soul.

But let us further inspect the circle of guests. Who is the master of the house? He is called Simon, and bears the surname of 'the Leper.' He bears it to the honour of Jesus; for the name betokens what he was, before the Lord pronounced over him the almighty words, 'Be clean!' Simon had once been infected with that horrible disease which no earthly physician was able to heal, and which He alone could remove who had inflicted it – the Almighty, He who could testify, saying, 'I and my Father are one.'

Simon, stand forward, and show thyself to every sceptic as a living monument of the divine fullness which dwelt in Christ! All Bethany knows that he had prepared this feast for the Lord Jesus, solely from feelings of gratitude for the marvellous cure which he had experienced through Him; and even His enemies can not deny that, in this man, a monument is erected to the Lord Jesus, which speaks louder and more effectually than any inscription is able to do.

But look! Who is it that sits next to Jesus? – the young man with piercing eye and sunny countenance. Oh, do you not recognize him? Once you saw him lying shrouded on the bier. You were present when his corpse was carried out, followed by his weeping sisters and a mourning crowd. You looked down into the gloomy vault into which it was lowered. But you were equally witnesses of that which took place four days after, when One approached the grave who called Himself 'the Resurrection and the Life,' and then commanded the stone to be taken away from its mouth. You heard the words of Martha, 'Lord, by this time he stinketh,' and the majestic reply, 'Said I not unto thee that if thou wouldst believe thou shouldst see the glory of God?' and then, after the stone had been removed, how the Lord, lifting up His eyes toward heaven, over the putrifying corpse, exclaimed, 'Father, I thank thee that thou hast heard me. And I knew that thou hearest me always; but because of the people which stand by, I said it, that they may believe that thou hast sent me!' and then how, with a loud, commanding, and creating voice, he called down into the sepulchre, 'Lazarus, come forth!' and you know what followed.

He that was once dead, now sits among the guests, having escaped from the adamantine prison of the tomb. He lives, and is vigorous and happy; and it never occurs, either to friend or foe, to deny that Lazarus once lay as a corpse in the grave, and now lives again at the omnipotent word of Jesus. We find abundant traces that the Pharisees were beside themselves with rage and envy at this miracle, but not the smallest that any one ventured to deny or even to doubt the fact itself. There he sits, and completes the row of lights amid which Jesus walks.

Oh, then, go to Jesus, my dear readers, as the Lord from heaven, the Prince of Life, the Conqueror of Death, for such He is, when regarded even in the light that streams upon Him from the circle which surrounds Him at Bethany. And He is still something more than all this.

He is staying at Bethany. He has now accomplished His public ministry. Several times has He given His disciples of late to understand that such is the case. He has told them and revealed to them as much as they were able to bear. The Comforter, who is to succeed Him, will instruct them further. We do not see Him now retiring into silence, nor returning to His heavenly Father; but saying, on the contrary, 'I have a baptism to be baptised with, and how am I straitened till it is accomplished!' He knows that the principal task assigned Him has still to be performed. He is on the road to Jerusalem, with the full consciousness of all that is passing and concerting there; that His enemies are now in earnest to seize Him, and get rid of Him; that the chief priests and Pharisees have already 'given a commandment, that if any man knew where he were, he should show it, that they might take him.'

All this was known to Him; but far from seeking to escape the snare which was laid for Him, He goes directly toward it.

He was now – according to His own words – to be delivered to the heathen, crucified, and slain; and there was a necessity for it. 'The Lamb of God which taketh away the sin of the world,' was not yet sacrificed. His assertion, that 'the Son of man came not to be ministered unto, but to minister, and to give his life a ransom for many,' was not yet fulfilled. The blood, to which the whole of the Old Testament had pointed as the procuring cause of all remission of sin, had not yet stained the fatal tree, but still flowed through His veins. And for this He prepared Himself on the evening He spent at Bethany.

Above all things, therefore, let us draw nigh to Jesus as our sole and everlasting High Priest, as our Mediator, Surety, and Ransom. 'Without shedding of blood there is no remission.' 'The blood of Jesus Christ cleanseth us from all sin.' The saints above 'have washed their robes and made them white in the blood of the Lamb.' O delay no longer, therefore, to follow their example! Jesus, in His crown of thorns and bleeding wounds, must be the object of your love and the ground of your hope, or else He is nothing to you, and you are in danger of eternal perdition.

The Lord has just placed Himself at the table, when Mary approaches, deeply affected by gratitude, veneration, love, and with a foreboding of what is about to befall Him. She feels impelled to display to Him her inmost soul once more, and to manifest her reverential and devout attachment to Him. But how is she to do this? Words seem to her too poor. Presents she has none to make. But what she has that is valuable – possibly a legacy left by her mother – is an alabaster vessel of pure oil of spikenard, much valued in the East, and used only on peculiarly festive occasions. She brings it with her. She does not intend to pour out a few drops only, but that it should be wholly an emblem of her profound devotion to the Lord of Glory. With the utmost reverence she approaches her divine Friend, breaks unobservedly behind Him the well-closed vessel, sheds the spikenard upon His head and feet, then humbly bends herself down and wipes the latter with her loosened tresses.

'And the whole house was filled with the ointment.' Yes, we may well believe that this odour ascended up even into the throne-room of heaven, and was inhaled with delight by the holy angels. In this affectionate and symbolical act, a degree of devotedness was manifested such as is rarely exhibited. Mary desires to belong to Christ for time and eternity; to cleave to Him by faith, like the ivy to the tree, round which it entwines itself. She wishes to live in His light, like a dark planet in the beams of the sun which lends it its radiance. Mary knows no anchor of hope, no ground of consolation, no way to heaven, except through His mediation; and were she to imagine existence without Him, she could only think of herself as in the jaws of despair, and irrecoverably lost. He is her last resource, but at the same time all-sufficient for her eternal salvation. Hence she cleaves to Him with all her soul, and nothing is able to divide her from Him. He is always in her thoughts her sole delight, and the supreme object of her affections – all which she expresses in the act of anointing.

The whole circle of the guests at Bethany are deeply touched by Mary's significant act. Only in the case of one does its sweet harmony sound as discord; only one of them with repugnance rejects the grateful odour. Ah, we imagine who it is! No other than the unhappy Judas, the child of darkness. Never, probably, has frigid self-love stood in such horrible contrast with warm and sacred affection, as was the case here, in the cold and really offensive expression, 'Why this waste? Why was not this ointment sold for three hundred pence, and given to the poor?' Alas, how deeply is the miserable man already fallen! 'The poor?' O thou hypocrite! As if the reason were unknown to his Master why he would rather have the ointment sold. 'For three hundred pence!' He knows how to value the spikenard, but is unable to appreciate the love that provided it, for he is wholly destitute of such a feeling.

Observe how the Lord Jesus appreciates the act of Mary. Like a faithful advocate, He immediately enters the lists on her behalf, against Judas and the transient impression made by his dark spirit upon the disciples, and says, while intimating to Judas that He was well aware of the cause of his displeasure, 'Why trouble you the woman? Let her alone; she has wrought a good work on me. The poor ye have always with you, but me ye have not always. Against the day of my burying hath she kept this' (or, according to another Evangelist, 'She is come aforehand to anoint my body to the burying.') 'Verily, I say unto you, wheresoever this gospel shall be preached throughout the whole world, this also that she hath done shall be spoken of for a memorial of her.'

Do but notice how He who was otherwise so spare in commending human works, mentions with a particular emphasis Mary's work as good. All the world is to know that such devotedness as Mary shows Him is considered valuable, and how highly He estimates this feeling as being the source of Mary's act. And that every one may know it, He has caused Mary's deed to be recorded. What He predicted has taken place; wherever this gospel is preached in the world, that which she did is mentioned as a memorial of her, even to this day.

Scarcely had our Lord ended this remarkable speech, when, as Matthew relates, 'One of the twelve, called Judas Iscariot, went unto the chief priests, and said unto them, What will ye give me, and I will deliver him unto you? And they covenanted with him for thirty pieces of silver. And from that time, he sought opportunity to betray him.' Where, in all the world, can we meet with a contrast so striking, so appalling, and beyond measure dreadful, as is here presented to us in Mary's tender and affectionate act, and the horrible procedure of this unhappy son of perdition? He is already so far gone that words of compassion, which might have tended to his eternal salvation, completely pervade the unhappy man as with a mortal poison. 'He went out.' He turns his back upon the Saviour, because he now feels that He sees through him. He rushes out into the night, to which as a child of darkness, he belongs – nay, he rushes out into a more awful night than the natural one; and the divine 'Woe!' follows him upon his way.

We shudder. We shrink from the idea of accompanying the wretched man, and return with increased fervour to Jesus. 'Against the day of my burial hath she kept this,' says our Lord. We understand His meaning. He sees His death and resurrection at one glance. An embalming of His body was to take place while He was still alive, since there was no time afforded for it after His death. It is not to be supposed that Mary had any idea of this; but a presentiment of His approaching departure certainly affected her heart; and anticipations of its saving significance fanned the holy glow of her love to a brilliant flame, and contributed to impel her to that effusion of affection in Simon's house which we have been just contemplating. Her Master's love, which was even unto death, excited hers in the highest degree; even as the love of His people is wont to be enkindled, most of all, by the remembrance of Christ's sufferings.

But wherever the love of Jesus finds room, there will never be a want of activity in relieving the distress of others. 'The poor,' says our Lord, while casting the words like an arrow into the soul of Judas, 'the poor ye have always with you,' by which He means that Mary will not be deficient in her charity to them. 'But me,' He adds, in conclusion, 'ye have not always,' and these words are addressed to all my readers, who can not yet call Jesus their Saviour.

O take them to heart, my friends! Him you have no longer, when the wings of death suddenly overshadow you, or when your senses depart under the influence of disease, and the message of salvation no longer penetrates through the crowd of unbridled imaginations. You have Him no longer, when God, the righteous judge, gives you up at length to 'strong delusions,' and permits them to take up their permanent abode in your minds, because you have long enough hardened yourselves against His calls to repentance. You have Him no longer, when the last great 'hour of temptation,' with its infernal delusions, as well as with its persecuting horrors, shall break in upon you, and when – to use the prophet's words – 'Your feet shall stumble upon the dark mountains.' You have Him no longer, if, in the abundance of your prosperity, you are ready to exclaim, with the man in the Gospel, 'Soul, thou hast much goods laid up for many years: eat, drink, and be merry!' to whom the horrifying announcement was made, 'Thou fool! this night shall thy soul be required of thee.' Therefore 'flee from the wrath to come!' Hasten to save yourselves. Stay not in all the plain. Let nothing hinder you from immediately repairing to the blessed Saviour, who has so graciously assured us, that whosoever cometh unto Him, He will in no wise cast out.

Chapter 3

The Entry into Jerusalem

'Art thou he that should come, or do we look for another?' Questions like this lie heavily on the hearts of many whose intentions, in other respects, are honest and sincere. 'Is He the Lord from heaven? Is He the King of Israel?' 'No!' is the response of an apostatizing world; and, alas! the lamentable condition of His Church on earth seems only to confirm this negative assertion. For if He fills the throne of omnipotence and glory, why do the people rage? If He governs all things, why does Satan so frequently triumph? If His arm reaches from heaven to earth, why does He not close the mouths of blasphemers? If He wields the sword of divine justice, why does He not immolate those who defy Him and lay waste His vineyard? If all power is at His command, why does He not compel, by signs and wonders, the glory which is His due? And if He only need put forth His breath to reanimate the dead and refresh the wilderness, why have not the wastes of the heathen world long ago flourished, and the deserts blossomed as the rose?

O how often do these and similar questions urge themselves even upon believers; and how inclined they are to doubt whether He is that which they think Him to be! But doubt is the worst enemy to peace; and hence nothing is more acceptable to those who are sincere than that which disables and destroys the former. To such, the narrative of our Lord's triumphant entry into Jerusalem will be, therefore, extremely welcome, since it scatters every cloud of uncertainty, displays a divinely sealed attestation of the Messiahship and kingly dignity of Christ, and again loosens our tongue-tied hearts, reanimates our faith, and causes us joyfully to exclaim, 'Yes, Thou art the Christ! Blessed art Thou who comest in the name of the Lord! Hosanna in the highest!'

That He is the Christ, the Son of God, and that we have every reason to trust in Him, is confirmed to us by His own consciousness of being so. We find Him proceeding to Jericho on His last visit to Jerusalem. On arriving at the Mount of Olives, He requests two of His disciples to go into the village over against them, where they would find an ass tied, and a colt with her. These they were to loose and bring to Him.

Observe here that He sees the animals He is in want of at a greater distance than the eye could reach. Even in this circumstance we see something superhuman breaking through the lowliness of the Saviour's form. He then gives instructions respecting the ass and her colt, with a decision which betrays to us the Governor of all things. He tells them, 'If any man say aught unto you, ye shall say, the Lord hath need of them, and straightway he will send them.' He says, 'the Lord,' and not 'the Master' only, or 'Jesus of Nazareth'. This is a title of majesty, a name of dignity, by which He elevates Himself high above every creature, and declares Himself to be Jehovah. 'The Lord hath need of them.' As the mere Son of man, He never could have spoken this of Himself without being guilty of blasphemy. But He knows who He is, and how He may call and entitle Himself, and He utters the words with firmness and dignity.

But will the owner feel induced, at the mere expression of the disciples – 'The Lord hath need of them' – to resign the animals to them? Assuredly he will. The Lord has no doubt of it, but is perfectly confident that, as the Lord from heaven, there was nothing which was not His, that He had power over all things, and that His eternal Father would grant such a power with His words that, as He expressly says, the owner would 'straightway' send them. Oh, let us revive from our state of despondency by the consideration of our Lord's self-consciousness, as here manifested, which substantiates His superhuman glory.

The ass's colt is led away with its parent. The disciples lay their garments upon it as a covering, and the Lord seats Himself upon the animal in order to ride into Jerusalem. This seems a trifling feature in the case, and scarcely worthy of notice; but look a little deeper, and its importance will increase. Our Lord by this act, testifies something infinitely greater respecting Himself than would have been the case had He suddenly placed Himself upon a royal throne, or had made His entry into the Holy City beneath a gilded canopy, and arrayed in a purple robe. It is evident, and the Scriptures expressly inform us, that our Lord had in view, at that moment, an ancient divine prophecy. You will read it in Zechariah 9:8, 9. Jehovah there says – predicting the future – 'Rejoice greatly, O daughter of 'Zion! shout, O daughter of Jerusalem! Behold thy king cometh unto thee; he is just, and having salvation, lowly, and riding upon an ass, and upon a colt, the foal of an ass.'

This is a delightful prediction, at which the whole world of sinners ought to rejoice. It is a gracious star of hope in the hemisphere of the Old Testament, greeted for centuries by the saints of God with tears of ardent longing. More than four hundred years had elapsed after these words had been uttered, when, on the summit of the Mount of Olives, the Man of Nazareth appears, and calls to mind this ancient prophecy. On the point of approaching Jerusalem, He orders an ass and its colt to be brought Him, seats Himself upon one of them, and publicly enters Jerusalem upon it, in the presence of assembled multitudes.

But what does He testify by this mute but significant action? What else than that the prophet's words are being fulfilled in His own person? What else than that He is the promised King of glory, just, and having salvation, and bringing peace to His people? What else than as if He had said, 'It is I, whose dominion shall extend from sea to sea, and from the river to the ends of the earth? It is I; therefore rejoice, O daughter of Zion! and shout, O daughter of Jerusalem!' Yes, He announces this as loudly as with a voice of thunder. No other meaning can lie at the bottom of that scene. If Jesus were not the promised King of Peace, with what epithet should we be compelled to designate that act? But He knew what He did, and how far He was justified in it; and hence, in His entry into Jerusalem, we have a new, powerful, and actual proof that Christ was the true Messiah announced by the prophets, and at the same time, the only-begotten Son of the Father, our Mediator, and eternal High Priest.

The passage on which we are meditating has never been sufficiently appreciated from this point of view. The disciples, and even many of the people after this event, had no doubt whatever that He was no other than the mighty Prince of Peace so long before predicted. Observe how He is attended. A more than regal entry is prepared for Him. The people cast their garments in the way, bestrew the road with verdure, and precede and follow Him with palm-branches in their hands, as in a triumphal procession, and there is no end to their exulting hosannas. 'Hail,' they cry, 'to the Son of David! Blessed be he that cometh in the name of the Lord! Hosanna in the highest!'

Only think of such homage being paid to a simple individual, devoid of all regal insignia! But it explains itself.

The rider on the lowly beast of burden was seen, in part at least, by the ancient prophets, surrounded by this homage. It could not fail that Zechariah, in particular, whose prophetic vision of the King of Glory enabled him to describe the scene as minutely as if he had really witnessed it, fully dispelled from their minds any remains of obscurity, which might still envelop the person of Him who was thus entering Jerusalem. But that which elevated their ideas of Him to perfect certainty was the stupendous miracle which He had performed at Bethany, in raising Lazarus from the dead. After such an occurrence, how could they be silent, or cease exultingly to exclaim, 'Hosanna to the Son of David!'

The Pharisees heard the rejoicing with secret indignation, and morosely said to Him who was thus applauded, 'Master, rebuke thy disciples.' But why did not they rebuke the rejoicing multitude themselves? Why did they not accuse them of being under a delusion? Why did they not adduce proof that the raising of Lazarus was only a tale, as well as that one born blind had been restored to sight by Him? O had they been able to do so they certainly would not have refrained! But this was out of their power. The facts were too generally known and acknowledged. In despair, therefore, they ask the Master Himself to rebuke His followers. O how does this significant trait tend also to strengthen our faith!

But does the Saviour comply with their wishes, and reprove the enthusiastic crowd? On the contrary, He rides on, surrounded by a thousand hosannas; thus letting the ancient prophecy of Zechariah develop itself in all its aspects in His procession, and calmly receives the homage as His due, while remarking to the Pharisees, 'I tell you that if these should hold their peace, the stones would immediately cry out.' My friends, what more can you desire? Nothing under heaven is more fully proved than that the Lord Jesus knew Himself to be the God-man, who had been promised and expected for thousands of years; and this is in itself a sufficient weapon for us victoriously to repel and overthrow all objections which might be raised against our belief in Him.

The whole scene of the entrance of Jesus into Jerusalem has both its typical and prophetic side. The progress of our Lord, so destitute of pomp, neither clothed in purple, nor on a gaily caparisoned war-horse, nor accompanied by ribboned magnates or dignitaries, but in the simplest attire, on the foal of an ass, and surrounded by poor fishermen and trades-people, gives us a hint in what manner Christ, for centuries together, will manifest Himself on earth until His second coming. And the expressly quoted, and now accomplished prophecy of Zechariah, confirms and attests this, in the words, 'Behold, thy king cometh unto thee *lowly*' – a word which implies at the same time the idea of an entire absence of display, pomp, and dignity; and this is the attribute which is peculiar to His government to this hour.

'But where do we discover Him?' O descend into the base-ments of human society; become initiated into the privacy of experimental religion in the cottage; listen to the narratives of 'the quiet in the land.' Read the missionary records, which, like Noah's dove, fly toward us with the green olive leaf of refreshing intelligence from the regions of home and foreign missions. Inquire of the many thousands, who, in every quar-ter, and in quiet concealment at Jesus's feet, are healed of their heartfelt maladies, or else, already comforted, fall asleep in His name to awaken to life eternal. Do this, and you will no longer ask, Where is Christ, the King? Truly He is still among you, with the same power, love, and miraculous grace by which He was formerly accompanied. The 'Hosanna to the Son of David,' has not yet ceased upon earth, and never will.

'But will His kingdom prosper in the world?' O be not anxious on this account! The passage we have been con-

sidering affords a powerful panacea against such apprehensions. Observe, first, what our Lord commissions His disciples to say to the owner of the ass and its colt: 'Say to him,
that the Lord hath need of them, and straightway he will
send them ... The Lord hath need of them' – more is not
necessary. If He requires them, all must be at His command.
He speaks, and it is done; He commands, and it stands fast.
'The Lord hath need of them!' What a glorious encouragement for missionaries, what valuable consolation for the
Church, when fears are entertained for the supply of faithful
witnesses! What an incomparable assurance that He can
never be deficient of means for the accomplishment of His
plans! Hide these words in your spiritual treasury, my friends,
and refresh yourselves with them as often as you feel your
courage fail.

Observe, further, how the Lord, while fulfilling to the letter
the prediction of Zechariah by the manner of His entrance
into the Holy City, confirms at the same time, the whole of
the prophecies respecting Him. You know what these passages
predict. According to them His foes shall eventually become
His footstool; the ends of the earth shall be His inheritance.
Jerusalem, cleansed and purified, shall become a praise in the
earth; and there shall be one fold, and one Shepherd; and
whatever else the eternal Father may have sworn to give Him.
As infallibly as the one was accomplished, so surely will not
the other remain a mere type and shadow. The literal ful-
fillment of Zechariah's prophecy is a most striking pledge of
the eventual accomplishment of the vision of John in the
Revelation. 'Behold, a white horse, and he that sat upon him
is called Faithful and True, and hath on his vesture and on
his thigh a name written, King of kings, and Lord of lords.'
And in like manner shall be fulfilled that other vision in
which he beheld, around the throne of the Lamb, that host
of adoring saints 'which no man could number.'

Finally, consider another expression of Immanuel's, which Luke records. When enraged at the loud rejoicings of His disciples and the people, the Pharisees called upon the Lord Jesus to reprove them, He uttered the following significant and ever memorable words: 'I tell you that if these should hold their peace, the stones would immediately cry out.' The Lord, in these words, could not have more clearly evinced His inmost conviction of the invaluable blessing the world enjoyed in Him, and the object of His mission. For what else do they imply than that 'I am such a Saviour and bring you such aid, and offer you such felicity, that if it produced no exultation and rejoicing among mankind, the Almighty would animate the lifeless creation to celebrate His love and compassion!' The Lord, in these words, gives us also the assurance, that earth shall never be silent concerning Him and His salvation; for should Israel and Christendom be silent, He would animate the sons of the desert, the dead heathen world, to sing hosannas to Him.

This He has done, is still doing, and will continue to do. Earth's whole population shall eventually spread their garments on His path, and strew it with palm branches, even as the people did on this occasion. As thousands did then, millions will hereafter shout, 'Hosanna to the Son of David! Blessed is he that cometh in the name of the Lord! Hosanna in the highest!' O let us mingle with the adoring crowd, and once more take our Lord's assertion to heart, that the salvation which God has prepared for us in Him is so infinitely great that if we could keep silence, the very stones would cry out.

Chapter 4

Christ Washing His Disciples' Feet

We are approaching, in our meditations, a very solemn section of our Lord's history. Jesus has completed His sojourn on earth, and the eve of the great and awful day of atonement has arrived. He assembles His followers around Him once more, in the social chamber of a friend's house in Jerusalem. Once more they are permitted to look into their Master's faithful heart, and to feel how much God has given them in Him. Never was the recollection of the affecting circumstances which took place that evening erased from their memory. The tranquil majesty displayed by their Lord and Master – the astonishing degree of ardent affection which manifested itself in every look, and every word – the heavenly peace which shone forth in His whole deportment – His cheerful and filial resignation to the will and counsel of God; and with all His dignity, such amiable condescension, while in every expression of His lips, and in all His actions and conduct, there was something divinely profound, consoling, and mysterious. The whole scene was overpowering and heart-cheering in a manner they had never before experienced. They felt themselves translated, as it were, into an outer court of heaven, and would have felt infinitely greater blessedness than even in the glory of Mount Tabor, had it not been for the anticipation of their Master's approaching departure, which threw a melancholy gloom over their joy.

The evangelist John informs us that 'before the Feast of the Passover, when Jesus knew that his hour was come that he should depart out of this world unto the Father, having loved his own which were in the world, he loved them to the end.' What a wonderful style of writing is this! Does it not seem as if the Evangelist's heart beat audibly through the whole passage? But that which so powerfully affects his heart above every thing else, is the fact that the Lord Jesus, although He was then clearly conscious that His hour of return to the bosom of the Father was near at hand, and although He had already lived more above than on the earth, and heard from a distance the hymns of praise, amid whose echoes He was soon to reascend the throne of divine Majesty – yet He did not forget His followers, but still retained so much room for these pilgrims in this vale of death, in His affectionate solicitude and recollection.

And yet how much sorrow of heart had these very disciples occasioned Him only a short time before, by their lamentable strife for precedence, and especially by their conduct, when Mary poured the costly ointment upon Him. You remember the mild and gentle reply which our Lord then gave them; but so far was it from humbling them, and causing them to acknowledge their fault, that it created discordant feelings within them and even closed and estranged their hearts from Him for a season. And yet – O comprehend this depth of fidelity and compassion! and yet – the Evangelist writes as if the tears were bursting from his eyes – and yet 'having loved his own which were in the world, he loved them to the end.' For it was to this end – is the Apostle's meaning – that He associated with sinners, that He might bear them eternally on His heart. Those whom His Father had given Him were more the objects of His affection than the holy angels around the throne of God, and His love to them increased as the end drew near. O how He loved them, when He took their sins with Him into judgment, and cast Himself into the fire which their transgressions had kindled! How He loved them, when His own blood did not seem to Him too dear a price to be paid for them, although it was they who were the transgressors; He loved them to the end; and to this day He loves them that are His in a similar manner. If a feeling of heavenly rapture thrilled through the apostle John at such a thought; let our hearts vibrate in like manner! Whatever may befall us, His love continues the same; 'For the mountains shall depart and the hills be removed; but my kindness shall not depart from thee, neither shall the covenant of my peace be removed, saith the Lord, that hath mercy on thee' (*Isa.* 54: 10).

We return to the chamber at Jerusalem, and find the company already reclining around the paschal meal. It would seem that at the commencement, little was spoken. But when the Lord is silent, His disciple speaks. Unveiling the heart of the incomparable Redeemer, like a sanctuary, he says, 'Jesus, knowing that the Father had given all things into his hands, and that he was come from God, and went to God.' What a knowledge is this! Had such an idea sprung up in the heart of any one who was a mere man, though he were the most excellent of his kind, he must either have been an idiot, or the worst of blasphemers that ever called down the curse of the Almighty upon his guilty head. We see the Lord Jesus, sitting at table, in the consciousness of His eternal majesty and Godhead, of His being the King of kings and the Lord of lords, as well as the Mediator, to whose hands, for His work's sake, the Father has committed all things, including the divine authority to forgive sins; and, regarding the shedding of His blood as having already taken place, to whom nothing more stands in the way of His acting as the high priest and intercessor of His people, at the bar of the Thrice Holy in the heavens.

In this sublime and twofold consciousness, we see Him unexpectedly rising up from supper; and for what purpose? To appear in His dignity? To display the splendour of His divine glory? To constrain His disciples to bow the knee in the dust before Him? One might imagine so; but no, He has something very different in view. Look, what means that? He lays aside His upper garments, takes a towel and girds Himself with it; pours water into a basin, bends down to the feet of the disciples, and begins to wash them in their turn, and then to wipe them with the towel. What a spectacle! It is enough to make one start, and to hold one's breath with astonishment! Are we not ready to exclaim aloud, 'Lord, Lord, what art thou doing?' Think of the Holy One, who came down from heaven, thus engaged with sinners; the majestic Being, whom angels adore, abasing Himself to the occupation of a menial servant! No, we should never be able to make such an action agree with His high dignity, were we not acquainted with His wonderful and peculiar sentiment. He no longer knows His followers 'after the flesh'; He sees in them those whom His Father has given Him – those whom God so loved, that He gave His only-begotten Son for them – the objects of an eternal and paternal counsel of mercy – beings, who, notwithstanding the sin which still cleaves to them, carry in their bosoms the work of the Holy Spirit, and in it the seed of God; and still more than all this does He behold in them. They are to Him the spiritual bride, clothed with the sun; for they stand before Him arrayed in the royal robe of His righteousness.

O great and significant symbol! O powerful exposition of the words 'I came not to be ministered unto, but to minister!' O important testimony to that which is of value in His

kingdom, and to that which is not! O impressive condemnation of all selfishness and self-exaltation in the children of
men! O deeply affecting commendation of humility and self-
denial, as the characteristics of His children, and amiable and
ennobling instance of that love, which ought to animate us!
And how much more than all this is there not comprised in
this act of our Lord's? It testifies of the sweetest, most
glorious, and most exalted things in store for us, as will now
be exposed to our view.

The disciples continue motionless and lost in mute astonishment. And how are they now ashamed of ever having
striven among themselves as to who should be the greatest!
They could almost bury themselves in the earth for confusion
and regret. How humbled do they feel, and what tenderness
and love pervade their hearts! With feelings of blissful
astonishment, they suffer their Lord to act as He pleases with
them.

The work of unheard-of condescension proceeds in silence,
until the turn comes to Simon Peter. Here, as might be
expected, resistance is offered and a stand is made. When
the Master approaches him, his face flushes with a fiery
excitement. He hastily draws back his feet, and, as on a
former occasion, he exclaimed, 'Depart from me, for I am a
sinful man, O Lord!' so now he cries in the violence of his
feelings, 'Lord, dost thou wash my feet?' He can not comprehend how any thing so unseemly should take place. The
glory of the Lord and the worthlessness of the creature
contrast too strongly. How deeply does Peter abase himself
in this expression of his feelings, and how highly does he
elevate his Lord and Master! 'Thou, the Holy One,' is the
language of his heart – 'I, a worm of the dust! It can not be.'

But however commendable may have been such a feeling
in Simon's soul, it was nevertheless, in other respects, culpable and improper. He ought to have remembered his

Master's own words: 'I came not to be ministered unto, but to minister.' It is His peculiar office to cleanse the polluted and to purify the unclean. What would have become of us had He not condescended to the depth of that depravity in which He found us? Simon thought it would be more befitting for him to wash his Master's feet. Yes, do not cease to wash them with penitential tears; but in other respects let Him wash and cleanse thee, otherwise how wilt thou escape eternal perdition? But Simon does not understand his Lord, and has no idea of his error. Jesus, therefore, replies to him in the well-known words, 'What I do, thou knowest not now, but thou shalt know hereafter.'

But will not this remark of our Lord's induce Simon to resign himself wholly to Him? On the contrary, Simon thinks he ought to preserve his Master's dignity, and therefore exclaims, in a very decided tone, 'Thou shalt never wash my feet!' Simon, however, forgot that obedience is better than sacrifice. O, my friends, if you wish to honour Jesus, do so by submitting to His Word! He says, 'I am come to seek and to save that which is lost.' 'No,' you reply, 'I can not imagine that His divine Majesty will trouble Himself about the prayers of such a worm as I!' O unreasonable zeal for the divine dignity! It is the will of God that we should glorify Him in this very particular, that we believe Him to be the hearer of prayer.

'Thou shalt never wash my feet!' said the mistaken disciple. But listen to the Saviour's reply, 'If I wash thee not, thou hast no part with me.' What an important declaration is this! You perceive how the more profound and mystic meaning of our Lord's act shines forth in these words – namely, as having reference to the blood of atonement, to forgiveness, justifi-cation, and purification from sin. You know how much lies concealed in this passage, and how every syllable has its profound signification. 'If I wash thee not.' Yes, Thou, Lord

Jesus, must do it; for who ever purified himself from sin? 'If I do not *wash* thee.' Yes, Thou must wash us; for teaching, instructing, and setting us an example, is not sufficient. 'If *I* wash thee not.' Certainly, what does it avail me, if Peter or Paul is cleansed, and I remain defiled? I must be forgiven, and it remains eternally true, that he who is not washed in the blood of Christ has no part with Him, nor the blessings of His kingdom.

It may easily be supposed that our Lord's words excited in Simon a degree of astonishment he had never before experienced; and the idea of having no part with Jesus humbles him unspeakably. Resigning himself therefore, without reserve, he says, 'Lord, not my feet only, but also my hands and my head' – that is, the whole man. When Jesus makes it appear that He is about to depart from us, it then becomes evident how closely and deeply we are connected with Him, though for a time He may have been forgotten by us in the bustle of daily life. When it would seem that He is willing to leave us to walk again in our own ways, it becomes manifest how valueless is all beside compared with Him. The anxious doubt, whether we have any feeling for Him, disappears, and the 'bond of perfectness,' which inseparably binds us to Him in our inmost being, is again brought to light, and we feel, with renewed vitality and force, how suddenly the curse, death, hell, and Satan, would again break in upon us, were we no longer permitted to trust and hope in Him. Experience of this kind gives 'songs in the night,' and encourages us in a time of darkness, even as King David was cheered by the remembrance of his former hymns of praise.

'Lord, not my feet only, but also my hands and my head.' Excellent, but again not altogether correct. Simon now oversteps the line to the right, as he had before transgressed to the left. He had previously rejected that which was indispensable; he now requires what is superfluous. He does not yet comprehend the whole of the matter clearly; and probably the full meaning of Christ's reply became evident to him only in the sequel; 'He that is washed need not save to wash his feet, but is clean every whit: and ye are clean, but not all.' It is clear that the last words have reference to the traitor.

But what is the meaning of this mysterious speech? I believe it to be as follows: he is washed, who, as a poor sinner, enters by faith into fellowship with Jesus. Such a one is then purified from sin, in consequence of being justified by grace. The blood of the Lamb was shed for him. The payment of all his debts was made. He is clean in the sight of God, for the merits of the Surety are imputed to him, and he continues to be thus regarded; for 'the gifts and calling of God are without repentance.' He ought daily and hourly to rejoice in this his purified state. Peter, in his second epistle, admonishes us not to forget that we are 'cleansed from our old sins.' But the individual is also pure as regards his sanctification; since, in consequence of being born again of water and the Spirit, he has forever renounced all that is sinful, and by reason of his new nature, though still assaulted and tempted in various ways by the flesh, he desires that the will of God may be accomplished in him, and that whatsoever he does may be well-pleasing in His sight.

But what is wont to happen in the progress of the life of faith? Unguarded moments occur, in which the man again sins in one way or other. He incautiously thinks, speaks, or does that which is improper, and is again guilty of unfaithfulness, although against his will; for only the devil and his seed sin wilfully; while he that is born of God, saith the apostle, *can not practise* sin. The man's walk is polluted; his feet, with which he comes in contact with the earth, are defiled. What is now to be done? Two by-paths present themselves, and not unfrequently one of them is taken. The individual either gives himself up to an excessive feeling of his guilt; openly cries out, 'Unclean, unclean!' like one who is excluded from the fellowship of the pure; regards himself as fallen from grace; considers the bond of union with the Lord as rent asunder, and cries out with Peter, 'Lord, not my feet only, but also my hands and my head!' Or else the man takes his trangressions too easily; persuades himself that the faults he has committed are of no importance; soothes his conscience with the rash and vain idea that the iniquity belongs to the multitude of sins which have been atoned for and annihilated by the blood of Christ, and thus unconcernedly proceeds on his way.

In each of these cases there is a deviation, the one to the right, and the other to the left of the line of truth. In the former, the man gives way unnecessarily to an excessive idea of the fault he has committed, and ascribes to it an influence over his entire state of grace, which according to the Word of God it does not exercise. The individual transgressions which a Christian may be induced to commit are by no means to be compared to an apostasy from Christ. In the single advantages which the flesh gains over the spirit, the regeneration which has been experienced is no more lost than divine grace is withdrawn. In the other case, the sin committed is too lightly esteemed; and by an arbitrary act of the understanding, the man forgives himself, instead of letting himself be forgiven. But the little faults, as they are termed, are not thereby rendered less; and so far from being erased from the conscience, in consequence of our persuading ourselves that they belong to the multitude of those for which the atoning blood was shed, they remain in it, on the contrary, as a secret evil which gnaws the peace of our hearts like a cancer, and gradually robs us of filial boldness in our approaches to the throne of grace.

What, then, ought to be our conduct, according to the Scriptures, in situations like the foregoing? First, beware of despondency, by which we only prepare a feast for Satan. Next, withdraw not from the presence of the Lord, as if His heart were closed against us. Thirdly, think not that it is necessary to make a fresh beginning of a religious life. The seed of the new birth remains within us; and the child of the family of God is not suddenly turned out of doors, like a servant or a stranger. 'He that is washed,' says our Lord, 'is clean every whit; and ye are clean, but not all.'

Who does not now understand this speech? Its meaning is, he that is become a partaker of the blood of sprinkling and of the baptism of the Spirit – that is, of the twofold grace of absolution from the guilt of sin, and of regeneration to newness of life, is, as regards the inmost germ of his being, a thoroughly new man, who has eternally renounced sin, and whose inmost love, desire, and intention is directed to God and things divine. When such a one, from weakness, is overtaken by a fault, he has no need of an entirely new transformation but only of a *cleansing*. He must let his feet be washed. Let this be duly considered by those who are in a state of grace, and let them resist the infernal accuser, lest he gain an advantage over them by his boundless accusations. Hold up the blood of the Lamb as a shield against him, and do not suffer your courage and confidence to be shaken.

The other danger which menaces us here, must be equally cautiously avoided; and we must beware of cloaking or underestimating any act of unfaithfulness we may have committed. No fault is too trifling or inconsiderable. We must suffer the judge in our breasts to perform his office without hindrance and not refuse to listen to his convictions. We must draw near to God and sincerely confess our faults. Let our language be, 'O Lord, my God, I have sinned against Thee afresh, and am grieved at it. I judge and condemn myself; but Thy mercy

is great, and therein do I trust. Sprinkle my conscience with
the blood of atonement, and enable me, by faith, to appropriate for this my fault, the suffering Thou hast endured for
me!'

Let the humbled and contrite heart pray thus, and the Lord
will graciously incline to it, and impart forgiveness to the soul
by His Holy Spirit, and the peace of the heart with the consciousness of adoption will then remain undisturbed in the
blood of the Lamb. And O, how do we feel ourselves again
united to the Lord, and strengthened anew to fight against
Satan, the world, and our own flesh; and how does the joyful
confidence bloom afresh in our minds, that we really possess
a Saviour, after such a renewed experience of His faithfulness!
Then we arrive again at Peniel, and exultingly say with Jacob,
'I have seen the Lord face to face, and my life is preserved;'
and join, with deep emotion, in the words of David, 'Return
unto thy rest, O my soul! for the Lord hath dealt bountifully
with thee!'

This is letting our feet be washed, in the sense intended by
our Lord; and you will observe how blissful, refreshing, and
reviving is the act. And in the eyes of him who is possessed
of true simplicity, this daily renewed repentance, and the fresh
experience of salvation which attends it, is nothing legal, but
the real gospel, and an exercise which is unspeakably sweet.
The inward man is thus renewed day by day, and experiences
a continued restoration. The flowers of joy and devotedness
to God incessantly spring up in the heart, and it is always
spring time within.

There are many Christians who know of no other nourishment for their inward life than the moldy bread of long past
experience. But no true peace results from this. Inward
religion does not consist in a life of morbid security, arising
from the recollection of having once received the forgiveness
of sins. Where a real spiritual life exists, there is also constant

activity, unceasing striving against sin, repeated humiliation before God, and renewed experience of His favour. Were it otherwise, why should the Lord put into His children's lips the daily petition, 'Forgive us our trespasses!' He that is washed need not be again entirely washed, but only his feet, and that continually.

The inmost meaning of the scene under consideration has thus been unfolded before us. It belongs to the method of salvation, and as regards its whole extent, was certainly apprehended only in the sequel by the understandings of the disciples. That which they doubtless understood better, at the moment, was the exterior act, and the example it afforded. To this our Lord's closing explanation is limited, to which we have now in conclusion, to direct our attention.

After the Lord resumes His upper garments, and reseats Himself at the table with His disciples, He again opens His gracious mouth and says to them, 'Know ye what I have done to you?' By this question He refers once more to the profounder meaning of His action, which He had brought sufficiently near to the comprehension of His disciples by the remark, 'now are ye clean, but not all.' At these words every doubt must have vanished as to the spiritual cleansing here alluded to.

'Ye call me Master and Lord,' He continues, and adds, in majestic self-consciousness, 'Ye say well, for so I am.' He then says further, 'If I then, your Lord and Master, have washed your feet; ye also ought to wash one another's feet. For I have given you an example that ye should do as I have done to you. Verily, verily, I say unto you, the servant is not greater than his Lord, neither he that is sent, greater than he that sent him. If ye know these things, happy are ye if ye do them.'

In these words, that part of Christ's act which is intended as an example is set before us. The original word, translated in our version 'example,' includes in it the twofold idea of symbol as well as example, and therefore points out to us a deeper meaning than appears on the surface. It will be known to you that many have supposed our Lord here intended to institute an outward ordinance for His Church. But there is not the slightest foundation for such an idea; nor is the Lord to blame that the washing enjoined by Him has in some places degenerated into the mere formality of an outward, empty ceremonial.

The Lord, by this act, commanded to His disciples that brotherly love which flows from His own heart into ours, manifests itself in real self-denial, and willingly condescends to the most menial offices. We ought also to wash one another's feet, even in a literal sense, when necessity and circumstances require it. We ought not to imagine ourselves too high and lofty for any kind of assistance, however apparently degrading, since Christ has left us such a brilliant example in this respect. Acts of love never degrade, however menial they may be. They did not degrade the Lord of Glory; how, then, should they degrade us His unworthy servants?

But it is chiefly in a spiritual sense that we ought to follow the example of our Lord. We are naturally much inclined to accuse each other of faults, and we judge and grieve each other by our severity. But the Lord recommends a washing of the feet, which arises from the charitable intention of cleansing and divesting our brother of some besetting sin. This can not indeed be done without mentioning the particular offence; but there is a great difference between humility, which never judges others without first judging itself, and self-righteous faultfinding, which holds up to the poor sinner the catalogue of his transgressions. He who washes a brother's feet in the sense intended by our Lord, places himself on the same footing with him as a sinner; enters compassionately into his fault; reveals it to him with forbearance and undissembled frankness; melts his heart by gently reminding him of the riches of divine goodness, which he has repaid with ingratitude; and after having thus washed his feet, while inciting him to repentance, he does not forget to wipe them also, by unveiling the throne of grace, depicting to his view the cross of Calvary, announcing to him the mercy of Him who has received gifts, even for the rebellious, and by dropping into his wounds the balm of the gospel.

Certainly we never wash each other's feet in this manner until we know what the Lord has done for us in particular. The mystery of His cross must first have been revealed to us in the light of the Holy Spirit ere we are able thus to wash one another's feet. We must first have experienced that in the substantial antitype, which Simon Peter experienced in the type. Christ Himself must first wash us before we can wash the feet of any in the manner intended by Him. Let the words, then, ever sound in our ears: 'If I wash thee not, thou hast no part with me.' May they expel all false security from our souls; give us no rest day or night until they cast us down at His footstool, and if He has not yet cleansed us, call forth from our bosoms the words of Peter: 'Lord, not my feet only, but also my hands and my head!'

Chapter 5

The Passover

The passover is being celebrated – the most important, glorious, and joyful of the festivals of Israel; the birthday-feast of the chosen people – that festival which has been kept for fifteen hundred years, and annually greeted with fresh delight; upholding, by its mere occurrence, the historical truth of the wonderful deliverance of Abraham's seed from the sword of the destroying angel, by the sprinkled blood of lambs. As the festive memorial of this great event, it continually called for renewed thanksgiving and humiliation before the Father of mercies. With the necessity for spiritual deliverance, it equally revived the hope of redemption by the blood of the promised Prince of Peace, of which the deliverance experienced in Egypt was a type.

Let us then cast a transient look at the typical feast itself. The angel of divine justice had been sent from the throne of the eternal Majesty to smite all the first-born in Egypt, and to sweep them away from the face of the earth. To the seed of Abraham, however, a means of deliverance was given. Each head of a family was ordered to take a male lamb out of his flock, kill it, sprinkle its blood on his doorposts, and then quietly and confidently remain in his dwelling. 'And the blood,' said the Lord, 'shall be to you for a token upon the houses where you are; and when I see the blood, I will pass over you, and the plague shall not be upon you to destroy you, when I smite the land of Egypt' (*Exod.* 12:13).

Who does not perceive in this divine ordinance the symbolic announcement of the eternal redemption projected for sinners in the counsels of God? Who still doubts that the Lamb, on which the deliverance depended, signified Christ, the only Saviour – that the slaying of the lamb had reference to Christ's atoning sufferings and death for sinners – that the sprinkling of the doorposts with the blood of the victims foreshadowed to the believing sinner, the divine imputation of the merits of the great Surety to all who should humbly submit to His method of salvation, by repentance and faith in the atoning blood of the Lamb of God?

This great symbolical announcement of salvation was handed down through successive ages; and the wondrous deliverance in Egypt was annually brought to the recollection of the people by the Feast of the Passover. They then beheld the lambs – those significant types of the expected Lamb of God – led to the slaughter, and at the sight of their streaming blood, the thanksgivings of the people were renewed for the deliverance wrought for their forefathers in Egypt, as well as the joyful hope of that spiritual deliverance for which they waited. In this hope they encouraged themselves, and exclaimed, with increasing confidence, 'He who shall bear our sins, will come without fail, for we have here the seal and pledge of the faithful and true God.' And while consuming the paschal lamb in the family circle, after the observance of the sacrificial rites, they rejoiced to find another divine idea in this un-pretending outward act, namely, that a faithful appropriation and reception of that which God would impart to sinners in the blood of Christ should form the only condition attached to a participation in eternal salvation.

We have now arrived at the moment in which Christ connected the institution of His sacred Supper with the

Passover. The word 'connected,' however, does not sufficiently convey our meaning. We designate the matter more correctly when we say that Christ has exalted the Mosaic festival of the Passover by changing it into His sacrament. It is erroneous to suppose that the Old Testament is abrogated or put aside by the New. For in reality, not the minutest part of the Mosaic rites and ceremonies is abrogated; on the contrary, the whole is exalted from the state of type and shadow to that which is real and substantial. This is the meaning of that saying of Christ, 'Think not that I am come to destroy the law, or the prophets; I am not come to destroy, but to fulfil. For verily I say unto you, till heaven and earth pass, one jot or one tittle shall in no wise pass from the law till all be fulfilled' (*Matt.* 5:17, 18).

Even as the blossom on the tree is not annihilated, but, fading, passes over into the fruit, and experiences in the latter a more substantial life, so all the types and shadows of the Old Testament were divinely ordained to be realized in the New. The Old Testament figure of the priesthood, for instance, received its fulfilment in Christ, as well as the atoning sacrifices of the tabernacle and temple, which were types of His sufferings and death; while the whole of the Levitical ritual, with reference to purging, washing, and purifying, formed its substantial antitype in the spiritual purification by the word, blood, and Spirit of Christ.

This is a remarkable fact, and ought greatly to strengthen our faith. The whole of Christ's work of redemption thus appears in all its parts as the vital fulfilment and realization of a cycle of types and figures, presented for upward of a thousand years, to the eyes of the people of Israel and of the whole world. Can this be mere chance, or only the contrivance of human forethought and calculation? Impossible! Here we see the over-ruling hand of the living and true God. Here is His plan, His work, His performance. He that doubts this, doubts the existence of the sun at noonday. It is only in nature that we meet with God under a veil, while in His revelation, all veils and coverings are removed. Only seclude yourselves for a time, for the purpose of biblical study, and send up repeated and heartfelt aspirations for divine enlightenment, and you will unceasingly observe infallible traces of Jehovah, and there will be no end to the discoveries you will make of all that is wonderful and glorious.

Now, as the deliverance in Egypt found in Christ's atoning sacrifice its fulfilled and substantial antitype, so likewise did the divinely-ordained Passover in the Lord's Supper. Come, therefore, and see! The table at Jerusalem is prepared; and all that the feast requires is served up. The mysterious act of the washing of the disciples' feet has just been concluded; the bread may now be broken and the food enjoyed. The disciples are deeply affected. The Master, who was made like unto His brethren in all things, sin excepted, and in whose bosom beat a human heart which deeply sympathized with the poor children of Adam, sees before Him the paschal lamb, and in it the type of Himself. He is 'the Lamb of God that taketh away the sin of the world,' even as He had caused Himself to be announced by His forerunner, John, at the commencement of His course. As a fresh testimony that He was so, He had made His entry into the Holy City on the same day on which the paschal lambs were wont to be brought in for the slaughter.

After they had again sat down, Jesus begins, in tones of heartfelt tenderness, to say to His disciples, 'With desire have I desired to eat this passover with you before I suffer.' O, observe what a glimpse He here gives us into the sanctuary of His inmost soul! He has heartily desired to keep this feast with them. But for what reason? It doubtless appeared sweet and pleasant to Him to pass the last hours of a life devoted to the service of others, in the peaceful circle of those who harmonized with Him, and who were the germinating seed of His Church, away from the discordant sounds of unbelief and the noise of an opposing world. It must also have been consolatory to Him to celebrate the close of His career in the bosom of affection, and in the society of His confidential followers, and then take His leave of them in an undisturbed and peaceful manner.

But do not suppose that, in what has preceded, you have exhausted the causes of His desire. Beware, especially, of ascribing to the Lord any thing of that sickly nature, which is usually termed sentimentality. As in Him all was sound, and full of pith and energy, so He was also a perfect stranger to our morbid sensibility, our selfish pleasure in effeminate and visionary sensations. That which caused Him to long so ardently for this Passover was, doubtless, love; not, however, a love that seeks enjoyment, but which burns to do good, to beatify, and bless.

Our Saviour's desire to partake of this last Passover doubtless arose chiefly from His heartfelt longing for the coming of that hour in which He should be able to make an end of our state of condemnation, and nail to the cross the handwriting that was against us. He also cordially rejoiced in anticipation of this peaceful evening, as the point of time when He should be permitted, in His intended and mysterious institution, to make His will, so to speak, in favour of His beloved followers, and with the consent of His heavenly Father, to bequeath to them the fruits of His atoning sufferings and death. In a word, it was for the sake of the sacrament to be then instituted, that He longed so ardently and earnestly for the approach of this His last Passover feast. Long had this institution of His love presented itself as an attractive memorial, to His mind. Hence you may judge of the importance which ought to be attached to this sacred ordinance. An act which had simply reference to the establishment of a friendly festive memorial, would never have been to the Son of God the object of such a profound, ardent, and long-cherished desire.

The words, 'With desire have I desired,' are of themselves sufficient to refute the rationalistic view of the Lord's Supper. They impress upon the sacred feast the stamp of a divine mystery of a sacrament. O, my Lord and Saviour, thus ardently did Thy heart long for the moment when Thou couldst bequeath this legacy of Thy loving-kindness to us sinners! Even the horrifying night of death, which was so soon to close around Thee, did not hinder Thee from thoughts of such compassion! O, how hast Thou loved us to the end! And yet who loves Thee in return, and thanks Thee as he ought for the rich inheritance bestowed upon us, or duly estimates this gift of Thy grace!

With the expression of heartfelt desire our Lord connects one of a prophetic nature, and soon after adds another of a similar character: 'For I tell you,' says He, 'that I will not any more eat thereof, until it be fulfilled in the kingdom of God.' As if He had said, 'We are about to part; our connection with each other will be henceforth of a different kind. But we shall see each other again, and once more sit at meat together.' We ask inquisitively and anxiously, When? and, further, inquire what it is that now presents itself to the mind of our Lord, and elevates Him above the pain of parting? The eye of His spirit looks into the distant future. He says, 'I will not any more eat thereof until it be fulfilled in the kingdom of God.' The Lord knows what He is saying, and rejoicing in spirit, sees what He refers to clearly and distinctly before Him. We only perceive something of it in the dawning distance; but even this is sufficient to cast a reflection of the Saviour's joy into our hearts.

The Lord's Supper has not yet experienced its final fulfilment. It points prophetically to something further, and even greater and more glorious. A feast of the reconciled and redeemed is yet forthcoming, with which our present communion stands in proportion only like the copy of the original or like the foretaste to the full enjoyment. When this feast shall be celebrated, faith will have become sight, that which is in part have become that which is perfect, and strife and conflict have terminated in enduring triumph. This high festival, which shall nevermore be interrupted, will be held at the moment when the kingdom of God shall be accomplished and completed. Something new will then take the place of our present communion. Ask me not wherein it will consist. It is certain, however, that our Lord, in the words, 'I will not any more eat this passover with you, until it be fulfilled,' does not merely intend to say, 'till we shall rejoice together in the perfect glory of My kingdom, and with all the redeemed.' We are not entitled thus generally to explain His language. The expression He makes use of does not refer merely to something indefinitely spiritual; the addition, which the Lord afterward makes, is quite at variance with such a view.

It belonged to the ritual of the Passover that four cups should be handed round, having reference to the four promises in the divine announcement of the miraculous deliverance in Egypt, viz.: '1, Jehovah, will bring you out, deliver, redeem, and take you to be my people, and will be your God.' After presenting one of these cups, during the social meal at Jerusalem, probably the first of the four, which must not be confounded with the cup *after* supper, mentioned in Luke 22: 20, the Lord thus expresses Himself, 'I say unto you, I will not drink of the fruit of the vine, until the day when I shall drink it new with you in my Father's kingdom.'

What does this mysterious sentence mean? Does He only mean to say, 'I will drink no more passover wine, but will eventually enjoy that heavenly felicity with you which is signified by the wine, in full measure, in the Church triumphant?'

The Lord could not possibly have intended that we should thus generalize the meaning of His very striking language, so solemnly introduced with the words, 'I say unto you.' But in Christ's perfected kingdom on earth there will be something similar to our communion prepared for us, at which, perhaps as from the tree of life in Paradise, we shall again eat, and where we shall again drink as from the fountains of Eden! Our Lord really seems to hint at something of this nature, although the kind of eating and drinking, for which the glorified creation will furnish the elements, may, for the present, remain a mystery to us.

Suffice it to say that the Saviour here undoubtedly points out the Passover of the New Covenant – in which He elevates and transforms that which was typical in the Old – as the prelude of a great and festal jubilee, which awaits His believing followers in the future of the kingdom of God. That which exalts the sacrament of the Lord's Supper to such a prelude will appear in the sequel of our meditations. O that it may be manifested as such to the experience of all who approach it, and cause them to exclaim with delight 'This is none other than the house of God, this is the gate of heaven!' This would assuredly be the case, if they only came duly hungering, thirsting, and believing. A single participation of the sacred ordinance would then teach them more of its true nature and object than a hundred theological discourses. They would then leave the holy place inwardly rejoicing in the language of the Psalmist, 'Thou preparest a table before me in the presence of mine enemies. Thou anointest my head with oil, my cup runneth over!'

Chapter 6

The Institution of the Lord's Supper

The Passover had been kept, the paschal lamb had been consumed by the guests with feelings of deep emotion, and the festive cup had been several times sent round as was customary. The moment had now arrived when after singing the great 'Hallel,' or psalm of praise, the meal should be concluded, and the signal given to the guests to rise up and depart. Instead of this, what occurs? The Master, to whom all eyes were directed, rises from His seat – not, as is soon perceived, to leave the room, but – to commence a new and still more solemn act than that of eating the Passover. In the capacity of the head of the family, He again takes the bread, breaks it, and after giving thanks, distributes it to His disciples. He then likewise reaches them the cup, and commands them all to drink of it.

Let us cast a look at the actions with which our Lord accompanied the words of institution of the Supper. We read, first, that 'the Lord ... took bread' (*1 Cor.* 11:23). Observe, He took bread, and not the flesh of the paschal lamb. This He did that He might not countenance, in any way, such rude and gross ideas of the sacrament as those expressed by the Jews at Capernaum (*John* 6:52), and that He might, beforehand, meet the error, as if there were still room in the New Testament for the sacrifices of the Old. The bread which He took was the unleavened passover cake, which, however, was not subsequently used; for the first Christians, with the apostles at their head, at their communion, which they were wont almost daily to celebrate at the close of their love-feasts, evidently made use of the customary bread; that is, such as was used at table, and therefore leavened.

'The Lord took bread' – this most indispensable of all the means of nourishment and sustenance, the product of the most valuable of earth's fruits, which presents, at the same time, such an extremely striking image of Him without whom we have no spiritual life. But you ask, 'Is the bread only an emblem, a figure?' I inquire, in reply, whether you wish to dispute the position, that we must regard the elements of the sacred ordinance, in the first instance, as signs, symbols, and figures? If so, you must overlook the Lord's words in John 6:51, 'I am the living bread, which came down from heaven, and give life unto the world;' as well as many other of His expressions of a similar kind. The divine 'corn of wheat,' which, that it might not remain alone, but bring forth much fruit, fell into the ground, and, by the heat of Gethsemane, and the fire of the Cross, was prepared to become the spiritual food of poor sinners, is reflected, like the sun in the dewdrop, in the sacramental bread, and by the latter is exhibited to our view.

After the Lord had taken bread, He lifted up His eyes toward heaven, and 'gave thanks' – that is, He poured out His heart in praise and thanksgiving to His heavenly Father. For what did He render thanks? O my friends, for what else than for the decision of divine mercy, to save such poor sinners as we, which He saw in spirit, as already accomplished in His blood, and for the deliverance of the children of Adam from the curse of the law, the power of Satan, and the gulf of perdition. It was they who lay continually upon His heart; to whose restoration all His cares and anxieties were directed, and whose exaltation and beatification was the object of His highest interest and sweetest hope. He gave thanks. O, with what adoring delight will the holy angels have caught this costly incense in their golden censers, and have borne it up to God! He gave thanks. We ought also to give thanks. But it is well for us, that in this, as in everything else, He intercedes for us, and covers our guilt with His obedience, and our deficiencies with His fullness.

However, He did not merely give thanks, but, according to Matthew's expression, He also blessed. The Saviour pronounced His benediction, not only upon the cup, but also upon the bread. And wherefore? Was it in order to separate the elements from a common and profane use to one that was higher, spiritual, and holy? Doubtless, He had this also in view. But where Jesus, the High Priest, blesses, we ought to think of something more substantial than a mere designation and setting apart of the kind above mentioned. We ought to expect that influence is then exerted, and reality produced. And O, what superabundant richness and fullness of blessing have rested on the bread and wine of the communion from the benediction, which our Lord pronounced upon them! Since that festal evening, how many thousands have received heavenly refreshment, invigoration, and encouragement by their means! How many a wounded heart, in the course of eighteen centuries, has been healed, how many fainting spirits revived, and the passage through the dark and mortal vale illumined, alleviated, and sweetened! and how innumerable are those who, till the end of time, will joyfully experience all this! Such is the blessing of the Prince of Peace, which extends even to the bliss of the eternal hills.

After our Lord had given thanks and blessed, He 'broke' the bread. Nor is this without a deeper meaning, as He

Himself declares immediately afterward, in the words, 'This is my body, which is broken for you.' Hence the whole of the apostolic statements of the institution of this sacred ordinance do not fail to record this breaking of the bread. Jesus broke it as symbolic of that which should soon occur to His own body, by which He should become our atoning sacrifice and the Bread of life. In the breaking of the bread He depicted His own death to the eyes of the disciples; and the sublime and admirable tranquility with which He did so, again testifies of the infinite love to sinners which pervaded His heart.

Our Lord presented the bread, thus broken, to His disciples; and it is here that we see Him in His proper office, and favourite vocation. Giving, presenting, and communicating are His delight. As then, so now, His hand is stretched out in His feast of love. We, His servants, retire, as regards ourselves, entirely into the background, while administering the communion. We are then nothing but His instruments. He Himself is always the dispenser and giver.

At the consecration of the cup, the same formula was repeated as at the consecration of the bread. After renewed thanksgiving and blessing, our Lord presented it to His disciples, and invited them all to drink of it. He calls the cup His blood, even as He designated the bread His body; and, both elements united, indicate and represent the whole Christ, inasmuch as He gave His life, which is 'in the blood,' unto death, as an atoning sacrifice for us.

That the Lord did not select water but the fruit of the vine, for the symbol of His shed blood, was done from the wisest motives, and only enlarges and diversifies the meaning of the selected symbol. Christ is the real vine, and we possess divine life, only in so far as we, like the branches, grow through Him, and are pervaded by His influence. Besides, the cup reminds us of the wine press of torture and agony, in which the Son of God was to become our Saviour and Mediator, while the bread represents His body, offered for the deliverance and blessedness of His believing people.

What an incomparable legacy, therefore, has the Lord left us in His sacred Supper! What a fullness of heavenly blessings and mercies has He showered down upon us in this unpretending institution! Let us therefore highly estimate this precious bestowment. Let us often avail ourselves of it by repeated and devout approaches to the sacred table for the sanctification and glorification of our inner man. Only let us be careful to appear in true communion attire – in child-like simplicity and godly poverty of spirit; and on our return from the holy place, we shall feel ourselves constrained to render heartfelt and joyful thanks unto Him, who has bought us with His blood, and be more than ever resolved to live and die to His praise.

Chapter 7

'Lord, Is It I?'

We return to the chamber in which our Lord and His disciples had assembled to eat the Passover, previous to the institution of the sacred ordinance of which we have been treating. We find the disciples in a state of great excitement, in consequence of the unexpected announcement, which had fallen from the lips of their beloved Master, that one of them should betray Him.

The Lord had revealed to them a painfully affecting secret. He had told them that among them was an unhappy mortal, who would have no part in the kingdom of God, and would never see life. The blood of the Lamb would not cleanse him from sin, nor the righteousness of the Mediator cover him; on the contrary, he would continue what he was, a child of the devil, with regard to whom it would have been better had he never been born. This reprobate would spurn from him the only ground of salvation, betray the Lord of Glory, and thus become irrecoverably the subject of death and the curse, and plunge himself into eternal perdition. It was this which Jesus revealed to them; and how do they receive it? Do they say, 'Talk as you please, the consequences will not be so fatal. Eternal perdition? there is no one who need apprehend any thing of the kind, since God is love.' No, they do not think thus. The idea which pervades their inmost souls and retains the upper hand is this: 'He, who at one glance surveys heaven and earth, the present and the future, and in whose mouth no guile was ever found, affirms it;' and hence it is that this expression causes them such anxiety and alarm.

The Lord has also revealed something of a similar kind to us. We likewise hear from His lips, that in all ages, though many are called, yet only few are chosen and find the path to life; while, on the contrary, many, who had likewise better never have been born, walk the road that leads to destruction. There is no want of such pitiable characters in the present day; for He asserts it who can not lie.

The peace of the disciples is at an end, after this appalling disclosure. They can not leave the matter thus; they must ascertain who is intended; and they do not seek the culprit at a distance, but among themselves.

Observe here, that it is no infallible sign that we are not ourselves the sons of perdition, because people regard us as the children of God, and because our external deportment seems to justify their opinion. For among those who are respected, and reputed as blameless characters, among churchmen and those who are apparently devout, nay, even among those who frequent the Lord's Table, may be found such as are rushing onward to destruction. In congregations where the gospel is preached, Satan entraps individuals in the snare of religious self-deception, as well as in the pits of infidelity and ungodliness. Among those to whom the dreadful words will be addressed, 'I never knew you,' not a few will be found, who, with good reason, are able to say, 'Lord, have we not eaten and drunk in thy presence? have we not prophesied in thy name? and in thy name done many wonderful works?' The disciples were aware of this; and hence, on the Lord's informing them that there was one among them who was accursed, they were by no means satisfied with being merely in their Master's immediate vicinity. Let us follow their example in this respect, and not seek at a distance those who shall eventually perish. Let us commence the inquiry within our own walls, and not exclude ourselves from those whom we regard as being possibly the deplorable people in question. On the contrary, let each first examine himself. It is not only those who openly revolt, and swear allegiance to the enemies of God and His Anointed, who are hastening to perdition, but there are also others, with the Bible in their hands, and the name of Jesus on their lips, who finally perish.

In order that their investigation may not prove fruitless, the disciples resort to the Light – the brightest and most pen-etrating in the world – which never deceives nor shines with a delusive radiance. It is to Jesus they refer – to Him who tries the heart and the reins, and fathoms every depth. 'Lord,' they ask, one after the other, deeply concerned and grieved, 'Is it I? Is it I?' And O, how affecting is this trait, how pleasing and worthy of imitation!

David drew near to this Light when he prayed, 'Search me, O God, and know my heart; try me, and know my thoughts, and see if there be any wicked way in me.' Those who try themselves by any other light, only deceive themselves like the Pharisees of old, who trusted in themselves that they were righteous, and despised others.

Let us inquire into the result of the investigation, and in so doing, we arrive at the most important and pleasing part of the subject. The son of perdition is discovered. Each of them brings him bound to the Lord, and delivers him up to His judgment. 'Each of them?' you ask with surprise. Yes: with one exception, all of them have found the sinner in their own persons. Hear the anxious inquiry which they address to their Master, 'Lord, is it I?' and observe the downcast look and tearful eye with which they accompany it. What do they mean by this? They each intend to say, 'Lord, I feel my heart so corrupt that I am capable of committing any evil, and when the wind of temptation blows in that direction, it were even possible for me to betray Thee as Thou hast said; unguarded, and left to myself, I can not depend upon myself in any respect. Alas, I feel that I am sold under sin, and with my best resolutions, I find I am only like a reed, shaken by the wind.'

Such, we may suppose, were the feelings of the disciples. But while they thus judge and condemn themselves, a gracious look from their beloved Master assures them of their mistake; and this is immediately confirmed to them, still more intelligibly, by His declaration that it was not one of the eleven, but that he who dipped his hand with Him in the dish, was the man that should betray Him.

Let us attend to the important lesson to be derived from this striking scene. They who really perish in the world – the children of wrath – are those who either do not acknowledge themselves to be sinners in the sight of God, or who, when conscious that they have sin within them, neither judge themselves, nor deliver themselves over to the Lord for judgment.

All those, however, who have discovered in themselves the sinner, who is capable of all evil, and in holy indignation bring him bound before the Holy One of God, and honoured the sentence of condemnation pronounced upon him by the Supreme judge as just and righteous, and imploringly entreat that he may be destroyed by the Holy Spirit, and a new man, a man of God, may be produced within them in his stead – such characters we pronounce blessed; for from the moment of this self-condemnation, they are marked out as individuals against whom the judicial sentence of the supreme tribunal is withdrawn, and who have no need to tremble at any accusation of Moses or Satan. 'If we judge ourselves,' says the Word of God, 'we shall not be judged;' and in another place, 'They that humble themselves shall be exalted.'

Let us, then, listen to the exhortation of the Prophet Jeremiah, and 'let us search and try our ways, and turn again to the Lord.' God grant that 'in his light we may see light.'

Chapter 8

Judas Iscariot

About the same time that the Word became flesh in Bethlehem, and the angels of God sang their seraphic anthem at His appearance, there was joy also in the cottage of Simon of Carioth, in the tribe of Judah, for there likewise had a son, though only a mortal, seen the light of this world. His parents, thankful and hopeful, called the boy 'Judas,' that is, the praise of God, or the confessor; and thus recognized the Almighty who had graciously given him to them.

The little boy was well-formed, and of pleasing appearance; for it was not yet written on his forehead what he should eventually become, and what should befall him in the course of his earthly pilgrimage. Ah! we now regard that domestic event with other eyes, and look upon the unhappy parents with poignant grief, for we know that prophetic passages had reference to him: 'Yea, mine own familiar friend, in whom I trusted, which did eat of my bread, hath lifted up his heel against me' (*Psa.* 41:9). 'As he loved cursing, so let it come unto him; as he delighted not in blessing, so let it be far from him' (*Psa.* 109:17). 'Let his days be few, and let another take his office' (*Psa.* 109:8).

We are without any tradition respecting Judas' earlier life; but we certainly do not mistake if we take it for granted that his gradual development was such as to justify uncommon hopes. He soon showed himself possessed of superior abilities, acute understanding, and energetic will, and therefore seemed, as he was probably soon conscious himself, to be capable of deeds of a superior kind than the limited current of quiet, civil life affords opportunity for performing. It was to be foreseen that he would eventually render himself conspicuous on the stage of public life in some way or other. Accordingly, as with the abundance of his talents, he fell under heavenly or adverse influence, he would necessarily develop himself, either as a chosen instrument of God or as an apostle and standard-bearer of Satan. Alas! he took the left-hand road, and we exclaim respecting him, with deeper and more well-founded grief than Isaiah concerning the king of Babylon, 'How art thou fallen from heaven, O Lucifer, son of the morning!'

The heathen world has no Judas, and could not produce such a character. Such a monster matures only in the radiant sphere of Christianity. He entered into too close contact with the Saviour not to become either entirely His or wholly Satan's. There was a time when, with reference to Judas, 'the candle of God shone upon his head, and when the secret of God was upon his tabernacle.' Once he was not wanting in susceptibility for impressions of the most devotional kind, and his soul was capable of every noble elevation of feeling. The appearing of the 'fairest of the children of men' in the glory of His marvellous deeds, attracted him, in His character of Saviour and the Friend of sinners. He swore fealty to the banner of Jesus with youthful enthusiasm, though with an unbroken will; and the Searcher of Hearts, perceiving the promising talents of the young man – who was really zealous for the cause of God in a certain degree – confidingly admitted him into the circle of His nearest and most intimate disciples.

This favour would never have been granted to Judas if he had attached himself to the Saviour simply from interested motives. At the moment when he offered his services, he was no hypocrite, at least not consciously so. And when he afterward prayed, studied the Word of God, and even preached it with the other disciples, it was doubtless done for a time with a degree of inward truthfulness: it was only in the sequel that he resorted to intentional deception and dissimulation.

The Lord appointed him to the office of receiver and almoner in His little circle; and assuredly did so for no other reason than that He perceived he was the fittest for that vocation. Many have profanely supposed that the Lord committed the purse to him in order to tempt him; but such a thought is wholly to be rejected. On the contrary, that circumstance affords us an additional confirmation of the fact that Judas, at the commencement of his discipleship, possessed the full confidence of his Master, although it could not have been hidden from the latter that the disciple was still deficient in a thorough knowledge of Himself, and especially in contrition of heart, to which a participation in the salvation of God is inseparably attached.

Amid pious sentiment, an evil root remained within, which was the love of the world, and especially of its gold and empty honour. And, in fact, Judas deceived himself when on attaching himself to the cause of the great Nazarene, he supposed he was following the attraction of a high and noble purpose; his fellow-disciples believed it no less of him. The latent wound did not escape the Saviour's eyes, but the mischief was not incurable, and Christ had appeared in order that, as the divine Physician, He might heal the sick, and bind up the wounded.

The compassionate love of Jesus left no means untried to accomplish the cure; but alas! the result did not correspond with His tender and unwearied solicitude. It only too soon appeared that the pleasing enthusiasm which had borne Judas on its wings so near the Prince of Peace, was, in its inmost centre, any thing but pure fire from heaven. For the more his delusive ideas concerning the real nature of Christ's kingdom were dispelled by the Lord's manner of life, as well as by His expressions and discourses, the fainter burned the torch of his specious zeal, and what remained of it in his heart was the impure fire of a selfish, earthly expectation and desire.

O do not let us deceive ourselves! even the most magnanimous characters, as long as they are not sanctified by Christ, are capable, according to circumstances, of acting not only meanly, but even basely and vulgarly. The natural man, in his most intellectual form, does not lose his centaur-like nature; the consequence of which is, that after having been engaged in possibly the most elevated pursuits, he is found the next moment creeping, like the serpent in Eden, upon his belly, and eating of the dust of the earth.

The period arrived in which Judas actually laid his thievish hand, for the first time, upon the charitable fund intrusted to him; and after he had once broken through the barriers of his moral consciousness, the next and every subsequent embezzlement became easier and less objectionable. But the condemning voice of conscience was now awakened by the sight of his sacred Master. The Light of the world was to him a burning fire; the Saviour of sinners, even by His mute appearance, an inquisitor before whom he must either expose himself as a guilty criminal, or envelop himself in the veil of hypocritical deceit; and he chose the latter.

For a considerable time he thought himself safe in the disguise of his conscious hypocrisy, until the scene occurred in the house of Simon the Leper at Bethany. Mary's devotedness to the Saviour induced her to pour the costly ointment upon Him. Judas, destitute of feeling for the tenderness and deep significancy of the act, endeavoured to depreciate it by the sanctimonious, and yet rude remark, that the ointment had better have been sold, and the product given to the poor. But the Lord, immediately interfering for the aggrieved woman, praised her work as 'good,' and as an act which should never be forgotten; at the same time reproving the ill-timed censure of the heartless hypocrite with the serious words, which must have penetrated into His inmost soul, 'The poor ye have always with you, but me ye have not always.' From those words, and still more from the painfully compassionate look which accompanied them, the hypocritical disciple became fully aware that the Lord saw through him, and knew of his crime.

This was a decisive moment for Judas – a moment in which blessing and cursing were once more offered to his choice, and one which must necessarily exercise a definite influence for good or evil on the further development of his inward life. The erring disciple must now either cast himself down at Jesus' feet, with streams of penitential tears, and seek, by a frank confession of his lost condition, deliverance and mercy at the throne of grace; or his mortified pride must gain the victory, and by urging him to the opposite course of a willful hardening, afford Satan the opportunity of imparting the infernal spark of secret bitterness against Him.

You know which of these two courses Judas took. Immediately after his Master uttered these words, which were only a mild reproof, and intended to heal, Judas hastened away from the company at Bethany. He now felt himself more at home, and more in his element among the adversaries of Jesus than in the sphere of his previous confederates. The bargain of the thirty pieces of silver was concluded – more from a secret thirst of revenge, than from avarice and the love of money. Judas met the remonstrance of his conscience with the excuse that it would be an easy thing for the wonder-working Rabbi if He chose, to save Himself from the hands of His enemies. However, he knew only half of what he was doing. He had

plunged himself into a vortex against which he was unable
to struggle. He no longer guided himself; another dragged
him away behind him. He had reached the horrible state of
those whose 'feet stumble upon the dark mountains.'

It might have been supposed that Judas would have been
no longer able to bear the company of Jesus. We nevertheless
soon see him again in his old place among the twelve. I know
not whether that which drew him thither was the tormenting
uneasiness he felt, and the inward curse, or whether it was
the apprehension of drawing down suspicion upon him if he
were absent; or perhaps he even calculated on the possibility
of the Saviour's establishing a kingdom, according to his
views of it, and was desirous of reserving the part he had to
play in such a case. Probably all these motives co-operated
to induce him to present himself among them. Suffice it to
say that we meet the son of perdition in the last social evening
circle at Jerusalem; and we see the Lord again trying every
thing to save the soul thus sick unto death. From a delicate
wish to spare his feelings, He does not require him to give up
the custody of the money, but leaves him still in the office
assigned him.

It was necessary, however, that the Lord should give him
to understand the danger in which He knew the poor man's
soul to be placed; and hence, while sitting at table, the
Saviour begins, with deep emotion and affectionate grief, to
say to His disciples, 'Verily, verily I say unto you, that one of
you shall betray me!' The eleven are struck with inexpressible
amazement. They look at each other with alarm and grief,
and break out in turn into the anxious inquiry, 'Lord, is it I?'
The son of perdition does not discover himself. Ah, only a
few minutes now remain of his day of grace! A voice from
within, as though it were his good angel, says to him, 'Reveal
thyself, Judas; throw down the mask, and escape from eternal
perdition, before the door of mercy is closed.' But Judas

resists, and envelopes himself still more deeply in his disguise; for another voice still more powerfully pervades his soul, and drowns every better feeling within him. The Lord then defines His meaning more particularly, and says, 'One of the twelve that dippeth his hand with me in the dish, the same shall betray me,' and then solemnly pronounces the woe upon the man who should commit this heinous crime, and reveals to him his fate.

The hearts of the eleven tremble. Simon Peter beckons to the disciple who leaned on Jesus' bosom to inquire who it is of whom their Master is speaking. John then ventures, though timidly, to ask, 'Lord, who is it?' The latter now tears away the last shred of the mask from the traitor's face, and says, 'He it is to whom I shall give a sop, when I have dipped it. And when he had dipped the sop, he gave it to Judas Iscariot, the son of Simon.' The disciples shudder, and Judas stands, pale as a corpse, trembling, his eyes wandering, and completely unmanned. 'O Judas, there is still time! The sounds that have hitherto smote thy ear were all intended to call thee to repentance. Bethink thee; cast away thy disguise; confess, and cry for mercy!' 'But shall I confess?' – thinks Judas to himself. 'Shall I give honour to Him who has so mercilessly exposed me? – condemn myself, in the presence of my comrades, to eternal disgrace, and show myself before all the world as a miserable coward? No, I'll be a man and act accordingly.'

Such was probably the language of his soul, and with a mixture of boldness and profound perturbation, while swallowing the sop, in hypocritical indifference, notwithstanding the unmistakable words of the Master, he still ventures to stammer out the question, 'Master, is it I?' The Lord now giving up the son of perdition, with infinite grief of heart replies, 'Thou sayest it.' That moment, the evil will of Judas overcame the last and most powerful attraction of mercy, and the sin against the Holy Ghost was perpetrated. The day of salvation closed; the hour of the visitation of divine mercy expired; the angels of peace sorrowfully removed from his side, and Satan triumphantly entered into him. The saying of the Saviour, 'One of you is a devil,' was now verified. The most terrible specimen of humanity which had hitherto trod the earth, now appeared upon the stage.

Then said Jesus unto him in conclusion, 'That thou doest, do quickly!' thereby giving him to understand that He was fully aware of his intention. He intimated to him at the same time that He henceforth regarded him as the instrument by which His heavenly Father would deliver Him up to the sufferings to which He was on the point of submitting from voluntary love to sinners. The eleven knew not how to explain the words, 'That thou doest, do quickly.' Some of them thought, in their simplicity, that because Judas carried the bag, the Lord had said to him, 'Buy those things we have need of against the feast,' while others imagined their Master had given Judas a hint to distribute something to the poor – so far were they from having any idea of the crime which one of their number was about to commit. The latter, however, understood the Lord Jesus better. But let us not overlook the circumstance, that Jesus while saying, 'That thou doest, do quickly!' dismissed the traitor from the circle of His confidential followers, and from the chamber in which they were assembled. And probably those expositors are right who, on the testimony of the beloved disciple, consider that Judas was no longer present when the sacrament was instituted.

Scarcely had the son of perdition left the room and the Lord Jesus saw Himself alone with His eleven faithful disciples, when the burden was removed from His heart. The Saviour breathes more freely, and then begins with sublime elevation of soul to say, 'Now is the Son of man glorified, and God is glorified in him. If God be glorified in him, God shall also glorify him in himself, and shall straightway glorify him.'

Judas went out. With awful significance, the narrative adds, 'And it was night.' Yes, night externally and internally. We see the deplorable being now entirely sold under the influence of the powers of darkness, and fitted for committing the most horrible crime. Although he is confused and half unconscious of what he is doing, the gloomy power to which he has submitted himself hurries him away in its whirl, and he is no longer able to direct his steps as he pleases.

O Judas, Judas! happy would it have been wert thou the only one of thy kind! But the name of thy brethren, even in the present day, is legion.

From the camp of the world comes the infernal war-cry, 'Away with Jesus and the doctrine of His cross!' Phenomena such as those which meet us in the present day, were never before seen in the world in such anti-christian atrocity and massiveness. The traitor, Judas, is again visible on the stage, full of deadly hatred to God, in a thousand colossal antitypes: and if there is one doctrine of the Holy Scriptures which finds in the present day its tangible confirmation, it is that of the existence of a Ruler of Darkness, and of a kingdom of infernal powers. The prophetic expression in the Revelation is fulfilled, 'The devil is come down unto you, having great wrath, because he knoweth that he hath but a short time.' The pentecost of hell is being accomplished, and it pours out its spirit over mankind like a shower of fire and brimstone, and its shield-bearers and apostles shoot up from the earth, like the fungus, in a night.

Let every one beware of being baptized with such a baptism! He that does not decide for the Lord today, may tomorrow be found opposed to Him, and carrying the banner of Satan. Neutrality is a forlorn position. He that enters but half-way into the prevailing tendency of the present day, finishes his course before he is aware that he is in the snare of the devil.

Let us therefore hasten to the Lord Jesus, and devote ourselves, with body and soul, unto Him as an entire offering, which is but our reasonable service. Recourse to His wounds is still open today, but may perhaps not be so tomorrow. Rise up therefore, and secure your souls; and pray that you may be preserved from the snares of Satan, and from the hour of temptation which shall come upon all the inhabitants of the world, to try them that dwell upon the earth.

Chapter 9

The Woe Denounced

Were any one to ask me what passage in the whole Bible I regarded as the most awful and appalling, I should not require to reflect long before giving him an answer. I should neither refer to the words in Deuteronomy 27:26, 'Cursed be he that confirmeth not all the words of this law to do them;' nor to the assertion in John 3:36, 'He that believeth not the Son shall not see life, but the wrath of God abideth on him.' Nor should I call to mind the overwhelming words of the Apostle Paul to Bar-Jesus, Acts 13:10, 'O full of all subtlety and all mischief, thou child of the devil!' nor the denunciations of our Lord Himself against the scribes and Pharisees, Matthew 23. On the contrary, I would refer the inquirer to the dreadful woe pronounced upon Judas, and feel assured that he would confess that nothing more appalling and awful can be found in the sacred volume, than is contained in the woe which Jesus uttered upon His betrayer. Many a one who has passed unscathed by Sinai, has been compelled by it to cry for mercy with a broken heart.

Listen: 'Woe unto that man by whom the Son of man is betrayed; it had been good for that man that he had never been born!' Who is it that utters these dreadful words? Consider this at the outset, and the words will then begin to unfold their horrors. Oh, that another had uttered them, and not He from whose lips they emanated! Oh, that they had come forth from the mouth of one like ourselves, a mortal, a human prophet, a poor sinner! But it is Jesus from whose lips the denunciation proceeds; it is the King of truth, the Friend of sinners, who utters it; and it is impossible to state what an enormous weight and dreadful emphasis this circumstance alone attaches to the words. For in them we hear not the voice of passion, but the voice of Him who could justly say of Himself, 'I am meek and lowly of heart.' It is the considerate testimony of One whose own heart bleeds at being obliged to pronounce such a sentence on the man who had been His confidant.

'But,' say you, 'since the Lord knew that it would have been good for that man had he never been born, why did He not prevent his birth? Why did He not hinder the marriage of his parents? Why did He not smite the mother of Judas with barrenness, as He formerly smote Michal? Or why did He not take the babe to Himself while in the cradle? Why did He give him time and space to ripen for such a state of reprobation? Why did God do this, since He is Almighty, and love itself?'

Restrain such inquiries, my readers. Be satisfied to remain in ignorance. No human spirit fathoms the depths of God's government of the world. To us it is a sealed mystery how the all-loving God can suffer men to be born whose course of life He sees, by virtue of His omniscience, will terminate in the abyss of eternal perdition. We can only infer from hence that the unsearchable God must love in a different manner from men, who have no idea of a love which goes hand in hand with justice. Consider, besides, what would become of liberty, if God were, in a compulsory manner, to hinder any one from destroying himself and perishing? What would become of the splendour of His throne, if, in order to avoid punishing, He put aside His justice? Finally, we have no need to be anxious how the Eternal God will eventually account for every single act of His universal government, but may rest assured that on the great day of revelation, He will constrain all that have breath to join in the words of Moses, 'The Lord is a rock; his work is perfect; for all his ways are judgment; a God of truth and without iniquity; just and right is he.'

Let us now consider, a little more closely, the woe denounced by our Lord upon His betrayer, and let it unfurl its horrors to our view. The Lord commences His sentence with a 'Woe!' and when Christ pronounces a woe, no one in heaven or in earth can any longer say, 'Peace be with thee!' 'It would have been good for *that man*' – an uncommon mode of expression in the mouth of the Good Shepherd. He does not otherwise call poor sinners thus. That appellation has in it something of a repudiating nature, and a sound of separation pervades it. Jesus dismisses Judas from the circle of His disciples, and regards him henceforth as a stranger. How awful is this, and how overwhelming! What will become of the unhappy man, now that the only One who could have saved him, lets him go? God grant that the Prince of Peace may call us by another name than the strange and icy appellation, 'That man!' I can not imagine any thing more horrible than to be compelled to hear Him say, 'I know thee not: I know not whence thou art; I never knew thee, Depart from me!'

'It had been good for that man had he never been born.' The Lord could not have expressed Himself in a more appalling manner respecting the desperate condition of the traitor, than He did in these words. A mere denunciation of woe would still have left us some hope for the deeply-fallen being; or, at least, would not have excited in us such dreadful ideas of the misery to which he was hastening as this declaration forces upon us, by which the last prospect of a possible rescue of the disciple is annihilated. O the heart-rending view, which this assertion affords us into the depths of perdition! How horrible must the fate of the reprobate be, when the Lord Himself affirms that Judas had cause to curse the day of his birth! O if the fate of the rejected were partially tolerable, the King of Truth would never have spoken thus. But while giving us most plainly to understand that nothing better could be desired for the son of perdition than a return to nonentity, He thereby gives us an idea of hell, which ought to make all our bones to quake. And can we suppose that there really exists a way of escape from such a state of condemnation? If such were the case, would our Lord have made use of language such as He here employed concerning Judas? No, never! We should then have heard milder words from His lips. Then indeed, it would have been better to be born, than never to have been. In this case a man would still have reason to bless God for the hour of his birth, and none to execrate and curse it. But Jesus Himself asserts that it would have been good for Judas had he never been born; and we, therefore, know enough to banish the last hope of his recovery. It is dreadful to face this alternative; but according to our Lord's words, it is unavoidable. The eternity of hell-torments, therefore, is established. Their worm dieth not, neither is the fire quenched in those haunts of woe.

After having considered the dreadful import of these awful words, let us now inquire respecting their application and limitation. We lament over the unhappy disciple; but let us beware lest the denunciation pronounced against him be uttered respecting us; seeing that it is possible for the same reasons, as with Judas, that it were good for some had they never been born. It is, of course, not in my power to point out with certainty the individual to whom these appalling words are applicable; but I may say that he who finds within him certain characteristics, has reason to fear for his soul. For he that shares them with Judas, shares also in his condemnation. You anxiously inquire, 'What are those characteristics?' I will therefore cursorily bring them before you, that you may examine yourselves by them.

Let me, first of all, point out to you, that a degree of outward propriety affords no reason for the tranquilizing idea that you do not belong to those who had better never been born. For observe, that Judas had also outwardly forsaken the world, and had been nourished up with the milk of the divine Word; had lived, subsequently, continually among the children of God, been innocently regarded by them as a brother, had prayed and fasted with them, belonged to the personal retinue of the Prince of Peace, had been His disciple, had assisted in preaching His gospel, had suffered reproach for Christ's sake, had – like the rest – wrought miracles in the name of Jesus; and yet, notwithstanding all this, 'It had been good for him if he had never been born.' O take this to heart and beware of regarding your respectability, your devotions, your religious knowledge, your good name among believers, and the like, as a secure defence, behind which you are safe from the flames of hell!

But now turn your eyes inward, and give an account of yourselves to Him in whose name I address you. There are those in the world who envelop themselves in the mantle of religion, in order, like Judas, to conceal a devil beneath it. Secured from the judicial eye of the world, they would gladly serve the demons of lust, avarice, or pride; and on this very account they put on the mask of religion. I now ask, are you one of these?

There are those also, who, though often aroused and awakened, still refuse to give themselves to Christ, because they are held in bondage by some secret sin, which they have not the courage to condemn and renounce. Hence, they indulge in it with a gloomy composure, the result of habit; and in time, their guilt increases to such a degree that they would consent to any thing rather than it should be brought to light. Are there any of this class among my readers?

Again, there are people who, minutely examined, have only one care, which is, lest it should be discovered that they have never been converted, although they have been for years regarded as being so. Hypocrisy has become instinctive within them, and without being aware of it, they are always occupied in disguising their words, looks, gestures, and actions, in such a manner that their true character and sentiments may not be discovered. Is this the case with any of you?

There are likewise individuals, who have so often succeeded in withstanding the thunders of truth directed against their carnal security, that they are become, as it were, bomb-proof against the most appalling horrors of the eternal world, and equally unsusceptible to the sweetest allurements of divine love. Are any of my readers thus hardened?

Further, there are those who, at the cost of a little of their money, aid in building the kingdom of God, yet are displeased on hearing that this kingdom flourishes and progresses. Had they been present at Mary's evidence of tender and sacred affection in anointing the Saviour, they would also have been ready to say with Judas, 'Why this waste? The money had been better spent for worthier purposes.' Nay, such people even experience a malicious pleasure; if, for instance, the missionary cause, to which, for the sake of appearances, they may possibly have contributed, seems to retrograde, and when, generally speaking, the zeal for the cause of God appears to abate. I ask, Are there any of my readers who are the subjects of such feelings?

Finally, there are individuals, who are so far overcome by the truth of the gospel, as to feel compelled to bear witness to it in their consciences, but do so reluctantly, and against their will. Hence, as often as they hear or read any thing that encourages the idea in them that they can obtain admittance into heaven without Christ, from whose method of salvation they would gladly escape, they feel inwardly comfortable. Are there such among you? Examine your inmost motives, and know that whoever belongs to one or the other of these classes, I do not indeed say of him that it would have been good for him had he never been born; but I do say that there is the possibility of this being the case. Such a one has reason to fear that the awful inscription on the tombstone of Judas may at length be transferred to his.

Yes, you tremble; you are horrified. If it were otherwise, and you could yawn amid such startling truths, or even laugh at them in satanic defiance; there would not require much more to authorize me to tell you, in the name of God, that 'it had been good for such a one that he had never been born.' But God forbid that I should exceed the limits of my duty. I know there are those to whom the sentence upon Judas does not refer, although they fear lest it should apply to them. Let me characterize, in a few brief traits, these individuals, that no one may despair who is justified in praising God for His mercy.

I make no reference here to those who can exultingly say, with Paul, 'I know whom I have believed;' for, being firmly rooted in the life of grace, and 'sealed by the spirit of promise,' they would only smile were I to endeavour to prove to them that the sentence in question did not apply to them. But I address myself to you, ye troubled ones, who are tossed to and fro on the sea of doubts, and who are still in uncertainty whether you may bless the day of your birth, or have reason to curse it.

I understand the cause of your unhappiness. Neither the fact of your feeling yourselves destitute of faith, love, and strength to lead a holy life, nor that you daily stumble and feel defective, decides any thing. Do you desire to be able to say with the bride in the Canticles, 'My beloved is mine, and I am his?' And if, as a condition of this happiness, you were compelled to bear the cross, in its most painful form, after the Lord Jesus, would you not resolve to do so without hesitation? Would you sacrifice that which is the dearest to you, in order to be able to assure yourselves that you belong to Christ? If you reply in the affirmative to these inquiries, I will declare to you, in the name of Him who 'hears the cry of the needy, and will not despise their prayer,' that the woe pronounced upon Judas has no reference to you, and that the glad tidings that you may bless the hour in which you first saw the light of this world, are for you.

O it is good that you have been born! You are set apart for great things. You are destined to serve the Lord God as vessels of His mercy. He intends to adorn His temple with you as the mirrors of His glory. He desires to exhibit you in the sight of heaven, earth, and hell, as proofs of what the blood of the cross is able to accomplish. He has selected you to join the choir of those who chant the mighty Hallelujah to Himself and the Lamb. When you were born, angels stood around your cradle. Over your head a sublime voice whispered, 'I have loved thee from everlasting!' Your parents pressed an heir of heaven to their bosoms. You entered upon this vale of tears only to pass through it with rapid steps, and then to find your abiding home in 'the Jerusalem that is above.' God wrote your names in the book of life. The righteousness of His Son was the first robe He threw around you; and the last with which He will adorn you will be the radiant garment of heavenly glorification. It is well for you, therefore, that you have been born. It would have been grievous if you had been wanting in the rank of beings; for one voice less would then have resounded in the vast jubilee chorus at the throne of God, and one pearl less would have glittered in the diadem of the heavenly Prince of Peace. Therefore, thrice hail that you exist! In spite of all the wretchedness you may be experiencing, you have infinite reason to bless the Lord. We heartily rejoice at joining with you in praising Him.

Chapter 10

The Walk to Gethsemane

We return to our narrative at a solemn moment. The Lord Jesus has just instituted the sacred ordinance of His love – the Lord's Supper – and, according to custom at the Feast of the Passover, He commences with His disciples, in the silence of the night, the 'Hallel,' or great song of praise, which consisted of Psalms 115 to 118. It is the first time that we find our Saviour singing; for the original Greek word admits of no other interpretation. The Lord, thereby, forever consecrates vocal music in His Church. Singing – this language of the feelings, this exhalation of an exalted state of mind, this pinion of an enraptured soul – is heaven's valuable gift to earth.

Adopted into the service of the sanctuary, how beneficial and blissful is its tendency! Who has not experienced its power to raise us high above the foggy atmosphere of daily life; to transport us so wondrously, even into the precincts of heaven; to expand and melt the heart; to banish sorrow, and burst the bonds of care? And it can effect greater things than these, when the Spirit from above mingles His breath with it. A thousand times has it restored peace in the midst of strife, banished Satan, and annihilated his projects. Like a genial breeze of spring, it has blown across the stiff and frozen plain, and has caused stony hearts to melt like wax, and rendered them arable, and capable of receiving the seed of eternity.

We find the Lord of glory singing with His followers. O, if David, who wrote those psalms, could have supposed that they would experience the high honour of being sung by the gracious lips of Him who was the supreme object of his songs and the sole hope of his life, he would have let the pen drop in joyful astonishment from his hand. But what a seal does the Lord impress upon those psalms, as the real effusions of the Holy Spirit, by applying them to Himself, while thus singing them in the most solemn hour of His earthly course! Would He have sung them, especially at that moment, if they had not contained the pure words of God? The Lord's singing them, therefore, is a powerful proof of the divine inspiration of the Holy Scriptures. In fact, we are only treading in His footsteps when we resign ourselves unhesitatingly to this sacred Word. And ought not this consciousness greatly to encourage us, and to overthrow every fresh doubt that may arise?

Millions in Israel had already sung the great 'Hallel' after the Feast of the Passover, during the thousand years which had elapsed since David. But with feelings such as those with which the Lord Jesus sang it, no one had ever joined in it; for the four psalms treated of Himself, the true paschal Lamb, and of His priesthood and mediatorship. His sufferings, conflicts, and triumphs, first gave to those psalms their full reality. Psalm 115 praises the blessings of divine grace, for which a channel to our sinful world was to be opened by the Messiah's mediation. In Psalm 116 the Saviour Himself lifts the veil from the horrible abyss of suffering to which He was to be delivered up for sinners: 'The sorrows of death compassed me, and the pains of hell gat hold upon me,' is its language. But the psalm also praises the glorious deliverance which He should experience after enduring those agonies –

'Thou hast delivered my soul from death, mine eyes from tears, and my feet from falling. I will walk before the Lord in the land of the living.'

Psalm 117 calls upon the nations to glorify the riches of divine grace, which they were to derive from the atonement of the divine High Priest. Psalm 118 concentrates what had been previously testified – first, as regards the cross: 'They compassed me about like bees; they are quenched as a fire among thorns. Thou hast thrust sore at me that I might fall.' Then the Redeemer's confidence: 'The Lord is my strength and my song. The Lord is on my side, therefore will I not fear. I shall not die but live, and declare the works of the Lord.' Then the deliverance: 'I will praise thee, for thou hast heard me, and art become my salvation.' Then the redemption which resulted from the offering up of Himself: 'The voice of rejoicing and salvation is in the tabernacles of the righteous. The right hand of the Lord is exalted: the right hand of the Lord doeth valiantly. Open to me the gates of righteousness; I will go into them and praise the Lord. This gate of the Lord into which the righteous shall enter.' And, finally, the victorious and all-subduing power of the kingdom of His grace upon earth: 'The stone which the builders refused, is become the headstone of the corner. This is the Lord's doing; it is marvellous in our eyes.'

These are all features in the portrait of the future Messiah, and references to what would befall Him on earth, and to the work He would accomplish. And He, in whom all this was to be fulfilled, had now appeared, and His foot already trod the soil of this world. The Lord Jesus beheld His own image in the mirror of the words of prophecy generally, as well as in these Passover Psalms in particular; and He sang the sacred verses with the clear and full consciousness of His position as High Priest, Redeemer, and Mediator. After the singing He went out to the Mount of Olives.

He proceeds upon His path, and oh, how much is laid upon Him! The guilt of thousands of years, the world's future – the salvation of millions! He goes in order, in His own Person, to plant the seed-corn of a new heaven and a new earth. Alas! whither should we have been going had He not traversed this path for us? Our future state would have ended in unquenchable fire. He knew this. That which He undertook stood every moment, in all its magnitude, present to His soul. But the glorious result of His undertaking was equally obvious to Him. At every step He apprehended Himself as being sent by the Father to close up the chasm which sin had caused between God and the creature, between heaven and earth.

The Saviour walks onward in the silence and obscurity of the night, accompanied by His disciples, all of them deeply affected by the solemn transactions which had just taken place in the chamber at Jerusalem, and yet greatly cheered by the gracious words which had proceeded from the lips of their divine Master. The Lord then breaks the thoughtful silence, and says, to the astonishment of His disciples, 'All ye shall be offended because of me this night; for it is written, I will smite the shepherd, and the sheep of the flock shall be scattered' (*Matt.* 26:31). In these words our Lord indicates the point of view from which He contemplated His approaching sufferings. He is minutely acquainted with the anguish to be endured.

The Lord regards His passion as an unconditional necessity. Had He not viewed it as such, how easy would it have been for Him to have withdrawn Himself from it in the darkness of the night! But He voluntarily yields Himself up to it; for, while saying, 'this night,' He is on His way, with a firm step to the garden of Gethsemane, the first stage of His sufferings.

He perceives, most clearly, the end and object of His passion; 'for,' says He, 'it is written, I will smite the shepherd, and the sheep of the flock shall be scattered abroad.' These words are taken from Zechariah 13:7, 'Awake, O sword! against my shepherd; and against the man that is my fellow, saith the Lord of Hosts. Smite the shepherd, and the sheep shall be scattered, and I will turn mine hand upon the little ones.' The Lord explains this passage by His own words. Its chief import is, 'I, the Lord of Hosts, will smite, with the sword of justice, My Shepherd – the Man that is My fellow, the Messiah; and the sheep of the flock – His disciples, friends, and followers – shall be scattered.' 'Thus it is written,' says the Saviour; and that which is written in the Book of God will come to pass.

The Lord Jesus says expressly that this prophecy was about to receive its fulfilment in Him. He therefore represents Himself as smitten of God, and for what cause is sufficiently evident from other passages. He appeared in our stead as suffering and atoning for sin. In Him, as Mediator, was realized the execution of the irrevocable sentence – 'Cursed is every one that continueth not in all things that are written in the book of the law to do them,' for the honour of God, the restoration of the majesty of the law, and our own redemption.

It is thus, and no other way, that the subject must be apprehended, or the entire history of the passion becomes an obscure labyrinth. It must be thus, or hundreds of passages stand before us as inexplicable enigmas. It must, or the horrible fate of the Holy One of Israel sounds like a shrill discord through the history of mankind, and renders questionable the very existence of a divine providence and government of the world.

The Lord well knew that reason would object to this; he therefore said, 'All ye shall be offended because of me this night.' Reason mistakes, and knows nothing of divine things, until the heart obtains an insight, a living insight, into its own necessities. Only become as anxious for salvation as Zacchaeus or the thief on the cross – how different will the words then sound in thy ears, 'I will smite the Shepherd.' Thou wilt then know that the Almighty must smite.

The words, thus quoted by our Lord, clearly manifest His consciousness of the true meaning of His sufferings. We therefore easily understand His exclamation, 'I have a baptism to be baptized with, and how am I straitened until it be accomplished;' as well as His subsequent agonizing prayer, 'Father if it be possible, let this cup pass from me!' Doubtless, the love of the Father to His only-begotten Son never forsook Him for a moment. Jesus continued the object of His supreme good pleasure and tenderest affection. But the experience and feeling of His Father's love was to be for a time withdrawn from Him, and the consciousness of being forsaken of God was to take its place.

Admire here, first, the faithfulness of the Good Shepherd. He had just told them expressly, that they should all be offended because of Him that night. What tender forethought is here manifested! The offence was unable to extend too far. When the sufferings of their Master commenced, they were able to say to themselves, 'He knew what would befall Him and yet He voluntarily met His sufferings. It was, therefore, requisite for the accomplishment of His work, that He submitted to them.'

But the Lord informs them further, that the Holy Scriptures and with them the will and counsel of God, were to be fulfilled in His sufferings. What a powerful support did He thus afford them against the days of sorrow – a support which secured their faith from a total shipwreck. He told them, in conclusion, that though the sheep of the flock would be scattered, yet they would continue His sheep, and not be cast off because of their unfaithfulness. This He stated to them when informing them, that after He should come forth triumphantly from all His sufferings, and have overcome death itself, He would again gather them around Him in peace and joy. Thus did His parental care provide for them, not merely with reference to the present, but also to the future, and prepared the way to prevent evil ensuing, and to bring them every needful blessing. O how secure we are, when once we intrust ourselves to His superintendence! It may happen occasionally, that we may feel offended, nay, even depart from Him for a time, and follow our own ways; but He does not leave us long to go astray. He again seeks us out; for with respect to all His sheep, His words remain true, 'They shall never perish, neither shall any man pluck them out of my hand.'

'But after I am risen again,' says the Lord (*Matt.* 26:32). He here looks with joyful confidence across the anxious sea of His approaching sufferings, to the subsequent triumph. He doubtless called to mind the ancient prediction, 'When thou shalt make his soul an offering for sin, he shall prolong his days.' He who knows how to follow His steps, in thus laying hold of the divine promise, has discovered the secret of joy.

Let us place our feet upon the lofty and immutable rock of the Word and promises of God. How safely and pleasantly may we then abide, even when the gloom of night spreads itself around us, and the storm and tempest assail us! We are then conscious that the clouds which cause us apprehension, cover only a part of our real heaven; for the distant horizon continues bright; and that which is still more remote, promises, after every night of sorrow, a day in which the sun will no more go down.

'But after I am risen again, I will go before you into Galilee.' Galilee is therefore the rendezvous, the land of reunion and meeting. Once there, He has no further cup of agony to drink, and His followers will no more be offended in Him. He is then no longer the Man of Sorrows, but clothed in majesty and the victor's glory, He meets His beloved friends, and greets them with the salutation of peace.

'I will go before you into Galilee.' Even for us, there is something in these words, if we are able to read between the lines. 'After I am risen again.' Assuredly, that resurrection for which we wait, will not tarry – the final elevation of His kingdom from its deep reproach – the manifestation of Him, on whose head are many crowns, after His long envelopment in gloom. Perhaps the day will soon appear. When He shall have made His foes His footstool, have gathered His elect from the four winds, and bound and shut up Satan in the bottomless pit – then shall we also remove to the Galilee of peace and joy, where we shall behold Him, face to face, whom, having not seen, we love, and shall greet Him with songs of rejoicing and rapture.

But though we may see the dawn of this period upon earth, yet we know another Galilee, whither He has preceded us, and which probably lies nearer us than the former. I mean that Galilee, on the shores of which so many weary pilgrims daily cast anchor; that Galilee, where the hand of Jesus wipes away the last tears from the eyes of the favoured newcomers; that Galilee, where the song is continually sung of 'the Lamb that was slain,' and of the blood in which our robes are washed and made white. O thou Galilee above, thou land of perfect union with Him, who is the object of our love, how does the thought of thee exalt and cheer our spirits during our pilgrimage through this vale of tears! Thou Galilee beyond the clouds, how blest is he, whom Jesus has preceded, in order to prepare a place for him on thy ever verdant vales and sunny hills!

'Blest, indeed,' you respond, 'if we were only sure of landing there at last.' If you are not yet sure of it, delay not to let the Lord assure you of it. Everywhere, and at every hour, He inclines His ear to you, and especially where He spreads His sacred table for you. There, also, is a kind of Galilee, whither He has preceded you, in order to meet with and bless you. His Word informs you that you shall also see Him face to face, eventually; and He is willing now to favour you with a foretaste of this vision. Draw near, therefore, and receive grace for grace out of His fullness; be blissfully assured of His Presence, and of His willingness to take you eventually to His heavenly home, where there is fullness of joy, and where there are pleasures for evermore.

Chapter 11

The Converse by the Way

We left the Lord Jesus proceeding to the lonely garden, to which He was wont to resort, in the darkness and stillness of the night. His mind is occupied with the thought of His approaching death. His followers press more closely around Him, as is usually the case when the moment of separation is at hand, and the grief of parting overwhelms the oppressed mind. Conversation becomes brief and mono-syllabic, and long pauses of entire silence intervene. Jesus now opens His mouth. The thought of Himself and His approach-ing sufferings retires into the background. That which affects Him more deeply is His love for and care of His flock.

Addressing Himself to Peter, who appears to be the most grieved, and who clings to Him the closest, He says, 'Simon, Simon, behold, Satan hath desired to have you, that he may sift you as wheat' (*Luke* 22:31). What language is this, rendered doubly appalling by the darkness, and the circum-stances under which it is uttered! At the very moment when the disciples are to be deprived of their only help and shield, they are informed of the approach of the most dreadful of enemies. The Lord expresses Himself strangely, and in a manner calculated to excite the greatest astonishment. 'Satan,' says He, 'hath desired to have you' – that is, he has challenged you, laid claim to you, and begged to have you, that he might manifest his power in you, in order to prove that your goodness is naught, and your conversion only specious and deceptive.

The Lord occasionally permits the wicked one to try his .power to tempt the redeemed to a certain point. He does so, in order to prove to the infernal spirits the invincibility of those who confide themselves to Him, and thereby to glorify His name; and also, that He may purify His children as gold in such a furnace of temptation, and draw those, who live no longer to themselves, deeper into the fellowship of His life.

It was an ordeal of this kind to which the disciples were now to be subjected. The murderer from the beginning had wagered, so to speak, that if liberty were given him, he would cause their entire apostasy. Christ sees the infernal vulture wheeling round the heads of His followers. He dares not conceal it from them, lest the assault should take them by surprise; and He therefore says to them emphatically, fixing His eye especially upon Simon, whom the adversary had principally in view, 'Simon, Simon, behold, Satan hath desired to have you, that he may sift you as wheat.'

They are now aware of the adversary's design. O that they would take every syllable of this address to heart! Warning and comfort are here wonderfully mingled. 'Like wheat,' says He, would they be sifted – an operation which, as is well known, only scatters the chaff, while the noble grain remains. The result, therefore, is salutary. It will only be a cleansing and purifying – certainly not according to the devil's plan and design, but wholly through the intervention of divine grace. Those who are thus sifted overcome indeed, but only after being made painfully conscious of their own weakness; and hence they know more assuredly to whom their victor's crown in reality belongs.

But let us listen to the Lord Jesus further. He displays to us, still more deeply, the greatness of His affection. After

uttering the appalling warning just mentioned, He looks
kindly at His disciples, and, as if He would encourage them,
says to Simon, 'But I have prayed for thee, that thy faith fail
not.' O where is there a faithful friend and guardian to be
compared to Him? The Gospel narrative often conducts us
to the scene of His acts and miracles, and not infrequently
removes the veil from His more quiet converse with His
beloved disciples, and reveals to us the sacred spots where
He exercised His priestly office; but here it favoured us with
a look into the solitude of His closet. Scarcely was the Lord
aware of the intended assault, especially upon Peter, than He
sought retirement, and in prayer, commended the endangered
disciple to the protection and preservation of His heavenly
Father. And the object of His prayer was that Simon's faith
might not fail in the storm of temptation.

Do not, however, suppose that Simon alone was privileged
above other believers, in being the object of such affectionate
solicitude. Listen to the Saviour's intercessory prayer, in John
17, and you will be convinced of the contrary. Hear Him
exclaim, 'Holy Father, keep, through thine own name, those
whom thou hast given me, that they may be one, as we are.'
'I pray not that thou shouldst take them out of the world,
but that thou shouldst keep them from the evil.' 'I in them,
and thou in me, that they may be made perfect in one; and
that the world may know that thou hast sent me, and hast
loved them, as thou hast loved me.' Think not that these
sublime words have reference only to our Lord's immediate
disciples; for, listen further – 'Neither pray I for these alone,
but for them also which shall believe on me through their
word. That they all may be one, as thou, Father, art in me,
and I in thee.'

Thus hath the faith which the Holy Spirit produces in us,
a pledge of endurance in our Lord's intercession. It may be
assaulted, tried, and shaken, but can not be extinguished or

annihilated. Simon was given to know this, in order that he might be in possession of a sufficient weapon when assailed. But in case of his succumbing, this consciousness was to serve him as a staff by means of which he might successfully leap over the abyss of despair.

'I have prayed for thee,' says our Lord, 'that thy faith fail not.' He knows that Peter will fall. He already sees in him the faithless disciple who denied his Master; and yet He feels toward him only like a tender mother, in seeing her darling child in danger. The Saviour's chief care is lest Simon should despair after his fall; and that, at the proper time, he should take courage to return to Him. Hence, He says, with the kindest forethought, 'And when thou art converted, strengthen thy brethren.' After thy unfaithfulness, thou mayest again take comfort in thy Good Shepherd. Nay, thou shalt be still further empowered, for when thou hast returned to Him, thou shalt strengthen thy brethren; thou shalt continue His apostle, and, in future, feed His lambs.

'When thou art converted, strengthen thy brethren.' Scarcely are we able to cease listening to these words. It almost seems as if Simon would only become a real apostle after his fall. And such was really the case; for otherwise God would not have permitted it. The first and essential quality of a herald of the gospel is ever a thoroughly broken and contrite heart. For it is only after having obtained mercy as guilty criminals, that we are in a position to 'strengthen the brethren'. After having ourselves vitally experienced that without Christ we can do nothing, but every thing with Him, we then become real evangelists, able also to 'bind up the broken-hearted', and to 'strengthen the feeble knees'.

Simon does not enter into the spirit of our Lord's words. 'Lord,' he exclaims almost angrily, as if some false imputation had been cast upon him, 'though all men should be offended because of thee, yet will I never be offended. I am ready to go with thee to prison and to death.' How excellent, and yet how full of self-confidence! Nevertheless, a zeal for his Master flames forth from him, which I can only wish pervaded us likewise.

A holy earnestness dictated Peter's words: but ah! he promised too much! 'How so?' you inquire with astonishment. 'Had not Jesus prayed for him, that his faith might not fail?' Assuredly; and had Peter founded his confidence on this, he might have vowed unshaken fidelity even unto death. But Simon vaunted himself on his own strength, and meant to say, 'My love is a pledge to thee that I will not deny thee.' 'The heart of man is deceitful above all things;' and he who depends on sensations and feelings leans upon rotten supports. However spiritually rich and strong we may believe ourselves to be, let us never promise any thing in self-dependence, nor ever plant our feet upon the waters until the Lord calls to us to come, and stretches out His helping hand toward us. But he who rests on the strong arm of Immanuel, and seeks strength from Him, may say more boldly still than Simon, 'Lord, I am ready to go with thee, both to prison and to death!' The Lord will not put his faith to shame, but be a strong refuge for him in the midst of the storm.

Scarcely has Simon, in all simplicity, uttered his heroic assertion, than he receives a second warning from his Master's lips. The Lord now informs him plainly what threatens him: 'I tell thee, Peter, the cock shall not crow this day before thou shalt thrice deny that thou knowest me.'

The Lord foresaw Peter's denial; then why give him the warning? It was directed to the restoration of the fallen. After Peter had denied his Master, he could say to himself, 'He told me beforehand what would occur. He saw it coming, and warned me. Although He perceived that I rejected His warning, yet He did not reject me, but spoke kindly and graciously to me as before.' The Lord appointed the cock to incite him to repentance, and by his morning call, at the proper time, to bring the fallen man again to Himself, and cause him to shed tears of contrition. Thus the Saviour's affectionate solicitude extended far beyond the temptation and the conflict; and prepared a remedy for the wounds occasioned by the denial.

After the Lord had finished speaking to Simon, and arranged every thing for the restoration of the zealous disciple, in the season of contrition and weeping, He turned to the disciples in general. 'He said unto them, when I sent you without purse, and scrip, and shoes, lacked ye any thing?' The disciples did not call to mind that they had ever been in want, and cheerfully confessed it to their Master's honour by saying, 'Lord, never!' The Lord had acted toward them as He generally acts towards His children whom, in the time of their first love, He leads very gently, and with parental care and kindness.

It might be thought that after this declaration of His disciples our Lord would say, 'Be not careful, therefore, in future, for such will always be the case.' Instead of which, He tells them just the reverse, and that in the future they would not unfrequently find it otherwise. 'But now,' says He, with reference to the whole of their future course of life, 'he that hath a purse, let him take it, and likewise his scrip. But he that hath none, let him sell his garment and buy a sword.'

How are these words to be understood? Generally speaking, they announce to the disciples, that conflict, danger, distress, and manifold trials awaited them, for which they must prepare; but that they might then firmly confide in Him, whom they had ever found a faithful Friend in time of need. At the same time, He gives them clearly to understand that henceforth they must not rest too confidently on the same obvious and wondrous guidance which they had hitherto experienced, because their life would in future partake more of the common course of human affairs, and that the direct interposition, by means of which the hand of eternal love had hitherto sustained and provided for them, would give place to a more indirect divine aid, for which faith would be required. It would then be necessary, besides prayer and looking up to heaven, to apply the ordinary means of provision, defence, and aid. Let him who had a purse and a scrip not cast them away, but take them, and make use of them. Manly resolution, foresight, and prudent calculation are no longer to be despised, but to be practised and employed. Nay, he that had no sword ought to sell his garment and buy one.

But then, as if the Lord had intended to say, 'Be not astonished at that which I have just told you, for the disciple is not above his Master, and what is hostile to Me, will also be so to you.' He reminds them that His own path would terminate in ignominy and suffering: 'For I say unto you, that this that is written of me, must yet be accomplished in me, And he was reckoned among the transgressors; for the things concerning me have an end.' The Lord here refers to Isaiah 53, particularly to the twelfth verse of that chapter, and expressly testifies that what is written there of Jehovah's servant, – that He should bear the sin of many, make intercession for the transgressors, and by His obedience and vicarious sacrifice, justify and eternally redeem His people – is said of Himself. He thus dispels every doubt respecting the only correct interpretation of that portion of Scripture. It treats of Him, His person, work, and kingdom. He also affords His disciples a strong light upon the mysterious obscurity of His approaching passion; and, finally, points out to them that the way to the crown is by the cross and that His people ought scarcely to expect a better fate, in this evil world, than He, who would have to endure the accursed death of the cross, and to be numbered with transgressors, and accounted and rejected by the world as the off scouring of all things.

But what does our Lord mean by the words which immediately follow – 'For the things concerning me have an end?' Certainly not what He had intended to convey in the words, 'This that is written must yet be accomplished in me.' The Lord unmistakably refers to the warning previously given to His disciples; and the import of His language is threefold. He intends to say, in the first place, 'You must not arm your-selves on My account, nor in My defence; for, as the Lamb of God, slain from the foundation of the world, I must patiently resign Myself to the appointed sufferings, which are indis-pensable for your reconciliation to God.' Next, 'The measure of that agony on which your redemption depends is exhausted by My passion. You may, therefore, boldly go forward, as being by one offering forever perfected.' And, lastly, 'Whatever you may have to suffer in future has nothing to do with your reconciliation to God, since that which had to be endured to atone for sin and to extinguish guilt, is laid upon and has an end in Me. If you suffer, it is only for your purification, and while it does not become Me, it is befitting for you to defend your lives and preserve them for My service, for the brethren, and, in case of need, to protect them by all legit-imate means.'

Such was our Lord's meaning, which, however, the disciples do not comprehend, but explain it as a call upon them to protect Him by force against His enemies, as Peter actually endeavoured to do in the sequel. Under this idea, they show Him the swords, with which two of them, including Simon, were armed, as was customary with wandering Galileans, and childishly, though with the best intention, say, 'Lord, behold, here are two swords!' 'It is enough,' rejoined the Saviour, breaking off mournfully – as if He had said, 'Let us leave the matter for the present; you will better understand My meaning later.'

Part Two

THE HOLY PLACE

Chapter 12

Gethsemane – Conflict and Victory

It is night. The Lord has left Jerusalem with His eleven confidential followers, fully aware of what awaits Him. In deeply affecting converse He descends with them into the dark vale of cypresses, where once, during the reign of the kings, the fire blazed, in which the abominations of idolatry were consumed to the honour of Jehovah. Here He crosses the brook Kedron, over which His royal ancestor, King David, when fleeing from his son Absalom, passed barefoot and in sackcloth, deeply bowed down by his own guilt and that of his people. Affected by momentous recollections, and sunk in the contemplation of expressive types and shadows, the Saviour arrives at the entrance of the garden of Gethsemane (the oil-press) at the foot of the Mount of Olives, where ancient gigantic olive trees, to this day, point out to the pious pilgrim the very spot where the Lord of Glory wept over the misery of the human race, and prayed and agonized for their redemption. We know that the Lord frequently retired to the solitude of that peaceful enclosure, after the heat and burden of the day, in order, by sacred converse with His heavenly Father, to strengthen Himself anew for His great work. Luke expressly remarks that He went 'as he was wont,' to the

Mount of Olives, but with feelings such as He had never before known upon entering that silent retreat.

The song of praise, with which He had left the friendly chamber at Jerusalem with His disciples, had long been ended. The Lord's solemnity increased, and it was evident that His soul became increasingly oppressed. Every one perceived the alteration in the Master's feelings; and, there-fore, it did not seem strange to the disciples that, on arriving at the garden gate, He should say to them, with deep emotion, 'Sit ye here, while I go and pray yonder.'

The disciples, obedient to their Master's dictate, seat them-selves at the entrance of the inclosure, while He Himself, after beckoning to Peter, John, and James, His most con-fidential friends, to follow Him, goes before them deeper into the interior of the garden. It is of importance to Him, for the sake of His future Church, to have eye-witnesses of that solemn scene. He is also incited to take the three disciples with Him, by the purely human feeling of the need of affectionate and comforting fellowship in His approaching conflict. How beneficial it is, in seasons of trial, to be sur-rounded by friends who watch and pray with us! Christ was not a stranger to any purely human feeling of necessity. He was made in all things like unto us, but without sin.

The voice which resounded through the garden of Eden cried, 'Adam, where art thou?' but Adam hid himself trembling, behind the trees of the garden. The same voice, and with a similar intention, is heard in the garden of Gethsemane. The second Adam, however, does not withdraw from it but proceeds to meet the High and Lofty One, who summons Him before Him, resolutely exclaiming, 'Here am I!' Let us follow Him into the nocturnal gloom. But what awe seizes upon us! The beings we there meet are well known to us; but how is their appearance changed! All is enveloped in mysterious obscurity, and the distress of our hearts increases every moment at the sight.

It is the eternal Father Himself who here presides; but what is left for us, in His presence, except to exclaim with job, 'Behold, God is great, and we know him not, and darkness is under his feet!' His only and supremely beloved Son appears before Him in a position which might melt the flinty rock to pity; but compassion seems a stranger with Him, who yet said to Zion, 'Though a woman may forget her sucking child, yet will I not forget thee!' We are tempted to break out with David into the piteous cry, 'Hath God forgotten to be gracious, and is his mercy clean gone forever?' For look, what a scene! Again and again does the Son cast Himself on His Father's bosom, with ardent supplication; but His ear listens in vain for a favourable Amen! from on high. There is neither voice, nor response, nor attention, as if the Eternal had in wrath retracted His words, 'Call upon me in the day of trouble; I will deliver thee, thou shalt glorify me!' and had no longer a heart for Him, who lay in His bosom before the foundation of the world. The cup of horror does not pass from the trembling sufferer; on the contrary, its contents become every moment more bitter. Louder sound the cries of the agonizing Saviour; more urgent becomes His prayer; but the Lofty One is silent, and heaven seems barred as with a thousand bolts. A holy angel, indeed, at length approaches; but why an angel only, instead of the immediate and consoling vision of the Father? Does it not almost seem like irony that a creature should be sent to strengthen the Creator? And what kind of invigoration was that which was only attended with an increase of suffering? For we read, 'And being in an agony he prayed more earnestly, and his sweat was as it were great drops of blood falling to the ground.'

But now let us fix our eyes upon the suffering Saviour. Scarcely do we know Him again, so enveloped is He in an impenetrable covering of agonizing mystery and contra-diction. He is the Man beheld in spirit by Jeremiah, and described in the words, 'His heart is turned within him, and all his members quake.' He is the desolate individual, who testifies of Himself in the Psalms, 'I am a worm, and no man.' He announced Himself as the Redeemer of the world, and yet, who seems to require deliverance more than He? He bears the sublime title of 'Prince of Peace'; yet where ever was there one more destitute of peace than He? See how He applies at one time to His Father, and at another to mere human beings for comfort to His desponding soul, and does not find what He seeks, but is compelled to return disappointed. His eye is filled with tears, His lips with cries, while His heart is crushed as in a wine-press, which forces a bloody sweat from all His veins. Is this the One who was once the strength of the weak, the comfort of the sorrowful, the support of the feeble, and the shield of the combatant? Is this the Holy One of Israel, who formerly was prepared for every thing, and joyfully exclaimed, 'Lo, I come to do thy will, O my God! yea, thy law is within my heart'?

And now look also at His disciples, who fill up the measure of these incomprehensible things; while their Master is struggling with death in indescribable agony, we see even the most select of the little troop lying on the ground, overpowered with sleep. He rouses them, and almost supplicates them to watch with Him only a little while; but they slumber again, as if unconcerned about Him, and leave their Master to His sufferings. One of their number is he who said, 'Though all should be offended with thee, yet will not I, though I should die with thee!' Another is the beloved disciple, who once lay on Jesus' breast, and the third is he who formerly answered so resolutely in the affirmative to the question, 'Can ye drink of the cup of which I shall drink, and be baptized with the baptism wherewith I am baptized?' Behold here the little dependence to be placed on human fidelity!

But let us contemplate this mysterious conflict in Gethsemane a little more closely. Scarcely had Jesus, with His three disciples, penetrated a few paces into the garden, when 'he began' – therefore before their eyes, 'to be very sorrowful and very heavy.' In these words, the history gives us a hint that something unheard of before, now came over Him. At the same time, it intimates that the distress which seized Him was voluntarily endured by Him, after due preparation. Mark, according to his peculiar manner of depicting the awful scene more in detail, gives us a clearer idea of the Saviour's distress, by saying, 'He began to be sore amazed.' He makes use of a word, the original of which implies a sudden and horrifying alarm at a terrible object. The Evangelist evidently intends to intimate thereby that the cause of Jesus' trembling must be sought, not in what might be passing in His soul, but in appearances from without which forced themselves upon Him; something approached Him which threatened to rend His nerves, and the sight of it to freeze the blood in His veins.

Immediately after the first attack, Jesus returns to His three disciples, with words which cast a strong light upon His inmost state of mind. He says, 'My soul is exceeding sorrowful, even unto death.' This does not indicate merely the measure, but also the nature and kind of suffering. We read in the sequel, that 'he was in an agony,' or, as other translators have it, 'he wrestled with death.' It was in the horrors of this state that our Surety felt Himself placed – not merely in the way of beholding them, but also in that of a mysterious entering into them. Whatever men may say, without holding firmly by the idea of a Mediator, the horrors of Gethsemane can never be satisfactorily explained. A mere representation of the death of the sinner, from which Christ came to redeem mankind, could not have laid hold of the Holy One of Israel so overpoweringly. He entered into much closer contact with 'the last enemy.' He emptied the cup of its terrors.

Observe now to what a height His distress increases. With the candid confession, 'My soul is exceedingly sorrowful, even unto death,' He hastens back to His three friends, like one who, in his feebleness, welcomes even the slightest support and consolation, and speaks to them no longer like a master to his servants, but like one who is oppressed and in need of comfort, to His brethren who may possibly be able to afford Him help. 'Tarry ye here,' He says, 'watch with me.' He means, 'Do not leave me; your presence is a comfort.' It is not they, but He, who is to be pitied.

'Tarry ye here.' In what terrific vicinity must He have found Himself, that even the sight of these poor, frail disciples, seemed so desirable and beneficial to Him. 'Watch with me.' This expression points out still more minutely the distress of His soul; for, though intended to serve as a warning to His disciples to be upon their guard in this hour of temptation, yet He claims, at the same time, their sympathy for Himself, and requests their compassion, possibly even their intercession.

Scarcely had He uttered these words to His disciples, when He tore Himself from them, and proceeded about a stone's throw into the recesses of the garden. Here we see Him sinking on the ground, first upon His knees, and then on His face, and the supplicating cry now forces itself, for the first time, from His deeply agitated soul, 'Abba, Father, all things are possible unto thee; take away this cup from me; nevertheless, not what I will, but what thou wilt.' Yes, He would gladly have been spared the cup which was given Him to drink, the contents of which were so horrible; for it is a real Man, susceptible of every painful feeling, that suffers within Him. He wishes its removal, however, simply on the condition which is invariable with Him, that it should be in accordance with His Father's counsel and will. He says, 'If it be possible;' He does not, however, mean this in the general sense, for He had already said, 'All things are possible unto thee;' but He thinks only of a conditional possibility, within the limits of the object for which He had appeared in the world.

But it may be asked, 'How can Christ still inquire whether the redemption of mankind can be accomplished without the cross and the shedding of His blood?' This, however, is not His object. The Lord's question confines itself to the present horrors – the cup of Gethsemane. Let this circumstance, therefore, again remind us that the self-renunciation of the Son of God essentially consisted in His divesting Himself, to a certain point, of the use of His divine perfections generally, and of His unlimited omniscience in particular; in consequence of which He was in a position to walk in the same path of faith with us, and, according to the expression of the apostle, to 'Learn obedience by the things which he suffered.'

The prayer of the divine Sufferer knocked at the door of the divine audience-chamber with all the force of holy fervour and filial resignation, but no echo greeted His ear. Heaven maintained a profound silence. The Suppliant, then rising up with increased anguish from the ground, hastens again to His disciples, but finds them – how inconceivable! – sunk in deep sleep. He awakens them, and says to Peter, first of all – 'Simon, sleepest thou? Couldst thou not watch one hour?' An overwhelming question for the presumptuous disciple, whose mouth had just before been so full of assertions of fidelity even unto death! He then addresses this solemn warning to the whole three – 'Watch ye, and pray, lest ye enter into temptation. The spirit truly is ready, but the flesh is weak.'

That which led Him back to the disciples this time, beside the need He felt of consolation for His agitated soul, was His ardent affection for them, who, like Himself, were surrounded by dangerous and infernal powers. 'The hour of darkness,' to which He had referred in a warning manner on a previous occasion, had arrived. The prince of this world had appeared on the stage in complete armour. The mysterious stupefaction and inability of the disciples manifests the baneful influence of the atmosphere they breathe. It was, therefore, necessary that they should summon up all the powers of their mind and spirit in order not to succumb to the temptation to offence, unbelief, and apostasy. The words, 'The spirit is willing, but the flesh is weak,' must not be explained as an excuse for the slumberers, but be regarded as an additional reason for the warning He addresses to them.

The Lord again returns to the deeper shade of the garden, and prays a second time in a somewhat altered form – 'O my Father, if this cup may not pass from me, except I drink it, thy will be done!' One of the Evangelists mentions that He prayed 'more earnestly this second time.' He does not mean that He urged His suit to be spared more importunately than before; but that, on the contrary, as soon as He perceived from the silence of His heavenly Father that His petition was refused, He strove, with an increased expenditure of strength, to enter still more deeply into the obedience of faith. Meanwhile His inward horror continued to increase.

After rising up from prayer, He again sought His disciples, but found them still sleeping – 'Sleeping for sorrow,' as the narrative informs us; 'for their eyes were heavy.' And on being awakened, 'they wist not,' in their stupor, 'what to answer him.'

The Lord withdrew a third time into solitude, and prayed the same words. An angel now descends to the suppliant Saviour, and approaches Him in order to 'strengthen him.' This sudden appearance of a heavenly being must, in itself, have afforded the Lord no small comfort, after His mental imprisonment in the sphere of sinful men and lost spirits. Probably the mission of the angel was to strengthen His exhausted frame, and revive His fainting spirit, in order that in the last and most painful part of the conflict, the body, at least, might not succumb. For immediately after the return of the angel, 'Being in an agony, he prayed more earnestly, and his sweat was, as it were, great drops of blood falling down to the ground.' What a spectacle! Does it not afford a dawning apprehension of the nature and importance of Immanuel's sufferings, and shed a degree of light upon the darkest and most terrific moment of the conflict in Gethsemane?

Let us refer, once more, to that mysterious prayer at which the world is so often inclined to stumble. It has been found difficult to make it agree with the Lord's love to mankind, with His submission to His Father's will, with His omniscience, and with His previous composure and resolution in announcing the sufferings that awaited Him, that He could suddenly desire to be freed from these sufferings.

First, as regards the objection derived from our Lord's omniscience, we repeat what we have formerly stated. The self-renunciation of the Eternal Son consisted essentially in this, that during His sojourn on earth, He divested Himself of the unlimited use of all His divine attributes, and leaving that eternity, which is above time and space, He entered upon an existence circumscribed by time and space, in order that He might tread the path of the obedience of faith, like ourselves, and perfect Himself in it as our Head, High Priest, and Mediator. As 'the Servant of Jehovah,' which title is applied to Him in the Old Testament, it was His part to serve, not to command; to learn subjection, not to rule; to struggle and strive, but not to reign in proud repose above the reach of conflict. How could this have been possible for one who was God's equal, without this limitation of Himself? All His conflicts and trials would then have been only imaginary and not real. He did not for a moment cease to be really God, and in the full possession of every divine perfection: but He abstained from the exercise of them, so far as it was not permitted by His heavenly Father.

Observe, secondly, that the Lord in Gethsemane does not pray to be delivered from His impending sufferings generally but only for the removal of the horrors He was then enduring. How could He desire any thing contrary to the counsel of God, who, when His disciples had exhorted Him against thus giving Himself up to suffering, rebuked them so severely? He only asks, if it be possible for the cup to pass from Him; and means that cup alone, whose bitterness and horrors He was then tasting.

Finally, the doubt whether the urgency of Christ's prayer stands in accordance with His love to sinners, as well as with His submission to His Father's counsel, is completely destitute of foundation. He only asks His Father whether, without infringing upon the work of redemption, this cup might pass from Him. That He has only this conditional possibility in view, and does not claim the divine omnipotence in general for His rescue, He clearly shows by that which precedes His question. 'Father,' says He, 'to thee all things are possible;' by which He intends to say, 'I well know that My conflict shall end at Thy pleasure; but wilt Thou be able to will its termination without thereby frustrating the redemption of sinners? If not, then refuse My request; I will then drink the cup to the dregs.'

His obedience to His Father resembles His love to Him. The invariable language of His heart was, 'Not as I will, but as thou wilt.' As soon as He became assured, by the continued silence of His heavenly Father, that the world could not be otherwise redeemed than by His completely emptying this cup: He did not permit the wish to avoid the suffering to be heard again; but with the words, 'My Father, if this cup may not pass from me except I drink it, thy will be done!' He accomplished the great sacrifice of the willing resignation of His whole self to His heavenly Father.

The cup of horror has been emptied to the very dregs. Our Lord raises Himself up from the dust, and hastens back to His disciples. The whole manner of His behaviour, tone, and deportment is now essentially changed, and indicates encouragement and consciousness of victory. We behold Him coming forth triumphantly from the conflict, and armed and prepared for all that is to follow. 'Sleep on, now, and take your rest,' He begins to say with reproving seriousness, 'It is enough.' 'For my sake' – is His meaning – 'you need no longer watch; I require your assistance no more. My conflict is ended.'

But what means the addition, 'It is enough?' What else than 'Your slumbers will now cease of themselves?' The words that immediately follow require this explanation. 'The hour is come; behold the Son of Man is betrayed into the hands of sinners.' He intends by these words to say, 'The body is now concerned, and your liberty is at stake; who will think any longer of sleeping under such circumstances?' He knows what hour has struck. Not without a degree of apprehension, but still perfect master of His feelings, He courageously prepares for being delivered into the hands of sinners, with whom, by this expression, He evidently contrasts Himself as the Holy One.

'Rise up!' says He at the close, expressive of the valorous resolution which His language breathed. 'Let us go;' continues He, 'lo, he that betrayeth me is at hand!' What a momentous appeal is this! The Champion of Israel goes forth to attack and overcome, in our stead, death, hell, and the devil, in their strongest holds. Let us adoringly bow the knee to Him and accompany Him with hallelujahs.

Thus has the most mysterious scene the world ever witnessed passed before us in all its affecting circumstances. In no earthly martyrdom is there any thing which remotely corresponds with the conflict of Gethsemane. It is obvious, on the contrary, that in treating of it, we have to do with sufferings which are unique in their kind. Let us ascribe thanksgiving, and blessing, and praise unto Him who endured such great things for us.

Chapter 13

Gethsemane – Import and Result

I confess that whenever I am called upon to treat of the sacred mysteries of Gethsemane, I can not divest myself of a certain degree of awe. I feel as if there stood at the gate of that garden a cherub, who, if not with a flaming sword, yet with a repelling gesture refused admittance, and emphatically repeated our Lord's injunction to tarry outside, while He retires to pray. A feeling always seizes me, as if it were unbecoming to act as a spy on the Son of the living God in His most secret transactions with His heavenly Father; and that a sinful eye ventures too much in daring to look upon a scene in which the Lord appears in such a state of weakness and abandonment that places Him on the same footing with the most miserable among men.

Besides, I know that I am expected to introduce the reader into depths which make the head turn giddy to look down upon; to solve enigmas, the complete deciphering of which I must despair of on this side of eternity; to explain mysteries, for the unseating of which my own soul vainly languishes; and to draw aside veils which, as often as I attempt it, seem the more to thicken. But the Gospel brings the mysterious narrative before us for consideration, and hence it is incumbent upon us to enter into its sacred gloom, and seek to comprehend as much of it as human apprehension is capable of.

The events in the garden of Gethsemane, with their scenes of horror, have passed in review before us. If we are not entitled to regard the position in which we find the Saviour there as altogether extraordinary, superhuman, and singular, we should do better to close the gate of that enclosure, and withdraw the Holy One of Israel from the eyes of the world, if we wish to save His honour, and that of His Father. If, in Gethsemane, we have to do with Jesus only as a prophet or teacher, His office, as such, there suffered the most complete shipwreck; since we can not then avoid the conclusion that He must, Himself, have been at fault with regard to His doctrine, and have lost the courage to die for it. If He is to be regarded in Gethsemane only as the model of unconditional resignation to God, we must say that He scarcely attained even to this, since Stephen and many other martyrs have appeared greater than Jesus, with His bloody sweat and agonizing prayer that the cup might pass from Him. If we are to look upon Jesus only as a Man desirous, by his example, of sealing the truth that in the time of distress, the Lord God is near His people with His help and consolation – the question again recurs, where does such a tranquillising fact appear, since the very opposite shows itself, and the holy Sufferer languishes from being forsaken of God? If, finally, He must be viewed as a proof of that overcoming peace which never departs from the just, but accompanies him in every season of distress: we look around us in vain, even for such a testimony; for instead of peace, a horror seizes upon the Holy One of God which gives Him the appearance of one who is on the brink of despair.

We must, therefore, have to do in Gethsemane with something essentially different from what I have just mentioned, or Gethsemane becomes the grave of the Lord's glory. Heaven must fall, the order of the divine government be annihilated, and Christianity be forever destroyed, if the Holy Scriptures compel us to regard the cup which Jesus drank, as essentially the same as that of which Job, Jeremiah, Paul, and many others partook. Jesus' cup contained something far more dreadful.

Know, however, that the Combatant in Gethsemane loses nothing in our esteem by His being 'sore amazed and very heavy.' We do not stumble at seeing Him tear Himself loose from His disciples, and then, prostrate in the dust, hear Him exclaim, 'My soul is exceeding sorrowful, even unto death!' Even His thrice uttered anxious petition, 'Father, if it be possible, let this cup pass from me!' and His taking refuge with His weak disciples, as well as His requesting them to watch with Him one hour for His consolation – nay, even the bloody sweat, which flowed from His veins, and dropped from His sacred body to the ground – however much we may feel astonished, whatever sorrow it may cause our hearts, and however deeply it may horrify us – it does not make us take offence, nor cause our faith to suffer shipwreck.

In our view, brilliant stars shine over the darkness of Gethsemane. We possess the key to its mysteries and the depth of its horrors; and we find it in the sentiment, which, in every variety of form, pervades the whole Bible: 'God hath made him to be sin for us, who knew no sin, that we might be made the righteousness of God in him.' As long as Christ's position as Mediator is not acknowledged, the events in Gethsemane will continue a sealed mystery. Every attempt to explain them otherwise than by the fundamental article of His vicarious mediation, must be forever unavailing. Only through the light which it affords us, is every thing rendered clear and intelligible to us in that appalling scene. The most striking contradictions are then reconciled, and that which is the most strange and apparently incomprehensible disappears, and seems perfectly natural. The divine Sufferer in Gethsemane must be regarded in His mysterious relation to sinners. He here appears as 'the second Adam,' as the Mediator of a fallen world, as the Surety, on whom the Lord 'laid the iniquities of us all.'

Three causes lay at the basis of Jesus' mental sufferings – the one more awful than the others. His agony was caused, first, by His horror of sin, by amazement at the abominations of our misdeeds. The transgressions which were divinely imputed to Him, that He might suffer for them as the Representative of sinners, crowd into the sphere of His vision in the most glaring light. His view of them is very different from the view taken by man in his darkened state. They present themselves to His holy eyes in their naked deformity, in their unutterably abominable nature, and in their soul-destroying power. In sin, He sees apostasy from the Almighty, daring rebellion against the Eternal Majesty, and base revolt against the will and law of God; and surveys, at one view, all the horrible fruits and results of sin, in the curse, death, and endless perdition. How was it possible that the pure and holy soul of Jesus, at the sight of such horrors, should not tremble and shudder, and be seized with a nameless abhorrence, of which we, who are so deeply infected by sin, have no conception? Only imagine personified holiness placed in the midst of the pool of the world's corruption! May it not be supposed, how a sinless messenger, sent to Him from the Father, needed only to enter into such a horrible sphere of vision, in order, by his mere appearance, greatly to comfort and refresh the Saviour?

But do not let us conceal it from ourselves, that the sore amazement and heaviness which the Saviour experienced in Gethsemane, would still remain an inexplicable mystery, were we not permitted to conceive of Him as standing in a still nearer relation to our sins than that of merely beholding them. We not only may do so, but are even compelled to it by the Scriptures. The Redeemer as Mediator would have been able to suffer the punishment due to our sins only by having a consciousness of them. The personal feeling of guilt – that worm in the marrow of life – certainly renders punishment what it is, and forms its peculiar essence and focus. But if the doctrine of the satisfaction rendered by Christ is opposed on the ground that He was holy, and that, therefore, it was a contradiction and an impossibility for Him to have inwardly felt the condemning sentence of the law like a criminal – those who do so would become guilty of a very hasty and presumptuous procedure. They would then be overlooking the supernatural and mysterious union, into which the God-man and second Adam entered with us, as our Head, and by which He received into Himself – not our sinfulness, for He remained immaculate as before – but our consciousness of guilt, together with its terrors.

You ask how this was practicable? Something corresponding with it, though in a remote degree, may be met with even in our human affinities and relations. A father may take his son's faults and improprieties to heart, or a friend those of his friend, in such a manner as to be compelled to sigh, mourn, humble himself with brokenness of heart, and wrestle with God for mercy on account of them, as if they were his own. When we remember the energy of love and sympathy with which Christ regarded us in our guilty state, and the further fact that He became actually identified with our race, the doctrine that He was made intimately conscious of our guilt is not unreasonable. We comprehend how the Psalmist could exclaim concerning the Messiah: 'My iniquities have taken hold upon me, so that I am not able to look up; they are more than the hairs of my head;' nor any longer wonder at Christ's behaviour in Gethsemane. The mystery of His horror, amazement, and dismay is solved.

Besides the abominable nature of sin, the Lord experienced its curse; and in this we perceive the second explanatory cause of the terrors of Gethsemane. He feels Himself as a culprit before God. All that is implied in being separated from God, deprived of His favour, estranged from His affection, and a child of wrath, He feels as deeply, inwardly, and vitally, as if He Himself were in that situation. He descends the gradations of such feelings into the distress of the damned, and into those infernal horrors where the prophetic lamentations in Psalm 22 find their fulfilment: 'Be not far from me, for trouble is near, for there is none to help. My strength is dried up like a potsherd, my tongue cleaveth to my jaws, and thou hast brought me into the dust of death.' His soul is unconscious of God's gracious presence, and tastes only the pain and distress of abandonment. Instead of intimate nearness, He experiences only a feeling of distance on the part of God. But He was not to be spared these bitterest drops in our 'cup of trembling,' in order that the words of prophecy might be fulfilled in Him: 'He hath borne our griefs and carried our sorrows' (*Isa.* 53:4). Even the heavenly peace of His heart belonged to the things which it was necessary for Him to sacrifice as the ransom for our souls. Can we, therefore, feel surprised that when His sufferings rose to this state of inward abandonment, the inquiry as to the possibility of the removal of the cup should, with still stronger effort, be wrung from His soul?

The third cause of our Lord's bitter distress in Gethsemane is to be sought in the world of fallen spirits. It is beyond a doubt that Satan essentially contributed to the horrors of that scene. The Lord Himself intimates as much in the words, 'The prince of this world cometh,' and 'This is the hour and the power of darkness.' And His repeated call to His disciples, when overcome by gloomy slumber, to watch and pray, lest they should enter into temptation, places it beyond question in what kind of atmosphere they were at that moment. The infernal powers have been let loose upon the Divine Redeemer. They are permitted to array against Him all their cunning, might, and malice. If they are able to drive the soul of the Holy One of Israel to despair, they are at liberty to do so. It is certain that they assailed Him in the most fearful manner, and strove to induce Him to suspect the conduct of His Father toward Him, and tortured Him with insidious dissuasions from the work of human redemption. Suffice it to say that our Lord's faith, as well as His patience, fidelity, and perseverance in the work He had undertaken, were never put to a fiercer ordeal than under the fiery darts of the 'wicked one' which He endured in Gethsemane. Here the complaints of Psalm 18 were realized: 'The sorrows of death compassed me, and the floods of ungodly men made me afraid. The sorrows of hell compassed me about, the snares of death prevented me.'

Thus has the night of Gethsemane become light to us, although that light be glimmering. The connection between that scene of horrors and the garden of Eden, of which it is the awful antitype, is unmistakable. While in paradise the first Adam reposed in the lap of divine love, and, like a child at home, held peaceful converse with Jehovah and His holy angels, we see, in the garden of Gethsemane, the second Adam sinking in agony to the ground, under the oppressive burden of guilt, languishing, forsaken, and horrified in the company of dark and infernal spirits. How evident it is, from this contrast, that what was transgressed and violated in the former, was suffered and compensated for in the latter; and how loudly does the narrative itself testify to the truth, that Christ suffered in the character of a satisfying Surety, and an atoning Representative!

After having thus developed the mystery both of the causes and nature of Christ's suffering in Gethsemane, so far as we have been enabled so to do, let us now inquire into the blessed result which has accrued to us from them. For this purpose it is necessary that we should apprehend the conflict in Gethsemane, not in the abstract, but in its inseparable connection with the whole of Christ's mediatorial sufferings. We see in every single stage of our Saviour's passion, some particular part of the salvation He accomplished brought before us in a clear and obvious light.

Let us hasten to Gethsemane, therefore, when we feel oppressed in a world where selfishness reigns paramount, and what still remains of the charity of the Gospel threatens to expire in self-seeking and self-love. The loving Saviour, whom we behold struggling for us in Gethsemane, continues ours; and how faithfully, ardently, and disinterestedly is He attached to us! What a price did it cost Him to elevate such unworthy creatures as we are from our misery, and to procure eternal salvation for us!

Resort to Gethsemane when you stand uncertain which way to choose – whether to give yourselves to God or to the service of the world. Gethsemane will make it evident to you what sin is. Look at Jesus. He did no sin, but only took upon Him that of others. How did it fare with Him? 'Now is the hour and the power of darkness,' said He. He was given up to the assaults of the infernal hosts. How they fell upon Him! How they tormented His holy soul! What horrible company! what nameless terrors! But know that what tortured Him for a time, menaces you forever! Think of being eternally doomed to endure the society and the scourges of the infernal powers! Is it possible to conceive of any thing more terrible? Remember the rich man in the Gospel, who vainly besought a drop of water to cool his parched tongue. Who among you can bear to dwell with devouring fire, or abide with everlasting burnings? Be irre-solute no longer. On the left yawns the pit, on the right shines the crown! Sin begets death, but the fruit of righteousness is life and peace.

Let us repair to Gethsemane, lastly, when the storms of temptation roar around us, and Satan goes about seeking whom he may devour. The days in which our lot has fallen are dangerous, and few there are who are not carried away with the stream of impiety. Even in the circle of the believing and the pious, how much weakness of faith, decrepitude of spirit, want of peace, and discouragement do we perceive! He, therefore, who wishes to be secure, must resort to Gethsemane. There we shall not only find a Confederate in the conflict, who will point the way to victory – there we shall not only be aroused with the alarming cry, 'Watch and pray lest ye fall into temptation;' but there the conviction is renewed within us, that the prince of this world is already judged – that every rightful claim of the adversary upon us is extinguished, and that what the evil one suggests to us of an abominable nature against our wills, falls upon his own head, and not upon ours, since it has been long ago atoned for by the bloody sweat of Immanuel, in the case of penitent sinners, and can only have a purifying effect upon us according to the will of God. This faith is the victory, which has already overcome the prince of darkness.

Looking thus at Gethsemane, in its proper light, it becomes to us an 'Eden,' and is transformed, with its horrors, into a peaceful retreat. Within its circuit we are safe from the judicial inquiry, 'Adam, where art thou?' In this garden flows the never-failing river of God, which waters the new paradise. How many thousand anxious souls have gone forth out of it, from the conflicting bustle of the world, into divine Sabbatic repose! Its holy gates are open to us. Come, therefore, let us reverentially enter, and inhale its peaceful atmosphere!

Chapter 14

The Sudden Assault

After coming off victorious from His spiritual conflict in Gethsemane, the divine Sufferer prepares to enter upon the thorny path of bodily affliction. His being taken prisoner, His being brought before the bar of judgment, His condemnation by the Sanhedrin, and His passage to the cross, are only symbolical representations of infinitely more exalted events, which were behind the veil, in the relations of the Mediator to God, the supreme judge. He who is unable to regard the individual scenes of our Lord's passion from this point of view does not penetrate through them, and will never find his way in the labyrinth of the history of our Saviour's sufferings.

We imagine ourselves still enveloped in the darkness of that eventful night, in which our Lord said, in a tone of serious warning, to His disciples, and which may still be uttered to thousands in the present day, 'All of you shall be offended because of me this night.' Scarcely has the Saviour risen up from the ground when a new cause of alarm awaits Him. Before His disciples are aware, lanterns and torches are seen glistening amid the gloomy bushes of the valley, and a murderous band, armed with swords, staves, and spears, is seen approaching along the banks of Kedron. The powerful preparation made for this occasion is partly in order to serve as a mask, as if they were banded together for the purpose of seizing a dangerous conspirator and rebel; and partly in consequence of a secret fear and apprehension that they might probably meet with some unexpected opposition. It is truly an infernal host with which we have to do – the body-guard of Satan.

We first perceive the priests, the ministers of the sanctuary. What accusation have they to bring against Jesus? This – that He is undermining their proud hierarchy, stripping them of their false glory, snatching from their hands the sceptre of despotism over the consciences of the poor people, diminishing their tithes and resources, and intimating to them, that they ought to place themselves in the ranks of publicans and sinners. All this was intolerable to these proud and domineering servants of mammon, and hence their hatred of the Lord of Glory.

Near the priests we behold the Pharisees, those blind leaders of the blind, the representatives of the delusive idea of individual merit, and hence, also of repugnance to a doctrine which affords a hope of salvation only by grace, and even to the most pious leaves nothing but the freely bestowed righteousness of Another. It is easy to understand how these men were offended at a Teacher who set up regeneration as a vital condition for all: whose language was, 'The Son of Man came not to be ministered unto, but to minister,' and who testifies of Himself saying, 'I am the way, the truth, and the life, no man cometh to the Father but by me.' Let us here ask ourselves, whether, until the Spirit enlightens our darkness, we are willing to be nothing, and that grace should be every thing?

In the scribes, who appear next in the band, we see the expression of a spurious wisdom, accompanied by spiritual ambition. No wonder, therefore, that such characters are also met with among the conspirators against Jesus. They, the learned among the people, were told that they must take their places at the feet of the Rabbi of Nazareth. They, the masters in Israel – were they to submit to this? How could such an idea fail to rouse and enrage conceited men to the utmost?

There was also a latent vexation at the numerous defeats and mortifications they had sustained in the face of the people, as often as they had ventured to assail Him. How victoriously had He always driven them from the field! How had He caught them in their own craftiness! How had He taken them captive in the very snares they had laid for Him, and then openly disgraced and triumphed over them! These were the things for which they could not forgive Him.

Under the command of the ringleaders above mentioned, we observe the servants of the high priests, those blind instruments of their superiors, who, though less guilty, are any thing but guiltless; and then also, the mercenaries of the Roman temple guard. For the most part, they know not what they are doing. More reprobate than they, appears the despicable troop who, for money or favour, have voluntarily joined the band. These cowardly flatterers and men-servers carry their baseness to such a point that they dispose of their independent judgment for the most miserable price in the world. Woe to such worthless characters!

Who is it walks at their head, with a gloomy face and confused look? Who is the man, muffled up in a cloak, and bearing the impress of a forced, rather than of a natural bravery in his mien? Ah, we recognize him! It is the son of perdition, of whom it was written a thousand years before: 'He that did eat of my bread hath lifted up his heel against me.' It is the wretched man who wears the garb of discipleship only as the poisonous adder is clothed in its glistening skin; the hypocrite, who conceals himself in his apostolical office, like the murderous dagger in its golden sheath. Sin is perfected in him, and condemnation ripened to maturity. In darkness and bitterness, he now hates Jesus as the darkness hates the light.

He has got beyond the period when he might have broken with Jesus with indifference, and then have gone on his way without troubling himself any more about Him. But he has now given way to all the feeling of an infernal revolt. He is furious against Him, as though the meek and lowly Jesus were an implacable judge, by whose holiness, purity, and love, he feels himself condemned for his own treachery, hypocrisy, and malice. He had long felt painfully uneasy in the company of Jesus. How could it be otherwise? A bird of night can not bear the light of the sun. Think not that the lure of the thirty pieces of silver was a sufficient cause for his treachery. It was infernal in its nature, and must be sought much deeper. The unhappy disciple had already imbibed that furious spirit, which incessantly stings the lost in hell to curse and blaspheme Him who judged them, and of whom they are obliged to testify, that all His judgments are just.

'Rise, let us be going. Behold, he is at hand that doth betray me!' From whence resounds this courageous and resolute call? From the same lips, out of which the cry of pressure and distress had only just before ascended to heaven, 'If it be possible, let this cup pass from me!' But now, behold the glorious Conqueror! He emerges from the horrible conflict in Gethsemane, as if steeled both in body and soul. His whole bearing breathes self-possession, manliness, and sublime composure. No sooner was He aware who it was that presented the cup to Him in Gethsemane, than He willingly emptied it, and knows henceforth that the terrors and horrors which may be in reserve belong to the indispensable conditions with which the completion of His great mediatorial work is connected. This consciousness enables Him to take firm steps on the path of suffering. He clearly sees that whatever of evil awaits Him, is the result of His Father's counsel.

When the Lord says to His disciples, 'Rise, let us be going!' He does so in order to show them His altered state of mind, and because He was desirous that they should all be present at His arrest, that, as eye-witnesses, they might afterward inform the world how their Master had voluntarily delivered Himself up into the hands of His enemies, and not as one who was vanquished by them.

But see what occurs? Before the multitude that came against Him has reached the place, He proceeds several paces toward them with a firm step. In opposition to the conduct of our progenitor in paradise, who, on the inquiry, 'Adam, where art thou?' sought concealment, our Lord approaches the armed band and asks them the simple question, 'Whom seek ye?' The world was to learn that the Lord was led to the slaughter, not by mistake, but intentionally, because He was the just and Holy One of Israel; and it was for this reason also, that the Saviour asked, 'Whom seek ye?'

The answer of the armed band was clear and decisive: 'Jesus of Nazareth,' say they. After thus making known their object, the Lord, with the sublime composure of the divine Mediator, who not only knew all that should befall Him, but was also clearly conscious of the cause, results, and final consequences of it all, said to them, 'I am!' Great and significant expression! It was never uttered by the Saviour without being accompanied with the most powerful effects (*John* 8:58,59). What occurs on His making use of the words on the present occasion? On hearing them the whole band of officials start, give way, stagger backward, and fall to the ground as if struck by an invisible flash of lightning, or blown upon by the breath of Omnipotence.

That which thus powerfully affected them was, undeniably, the deep impression of the Deity of Jesus, by which they were for a time overpowered. His majestic, though simple declaration, called forth in them, in its full strength, the conviction of His superhuman glory. But this mental emotion would not alone have sufficed to stretch the whole troop bodily, as by magic, in the dust, if an act of divine omnipotence had not accompanied it. The Lord overthrew them, in order, in the most forcible manner, to force upon them the conviction of His divine superiority, as well as to leave the world an actual proof that it was not through compulsion or weakness, that He became a sacrifice for it, but in consequence of His free determination.

The murderous band lie at His feet, prostrated by a single expression from His lips. What would have hindered Him from walking triumphantly over them; and, after fixing them to the ground, departing uninjured and uninterrupted? But He only aims at displaying His supremacy and independence, and after attaining this object, He permits them to rise again from the ground. Their prostration in the dust before Him points out to unbelievers the situation in which they will one day be found. The homage which they refused to Jesus here below, He will in due time compel them to render Him. The knee that would not bow to Him in voluntary affection, will at length be constrained to do so by the horrors of despair.

After the armed band, by the Lord's permission, had again raised themselves up, He repeats the question to them, 'Whom seek ye?' accompanied this time by an overwhelming irony. As though one who had been mistaken for a vagrant and arrested as such, should suddenly display to the view of his captors the royal star on his breast, and should calmly say to them, 'Whom did ye think to catch?' So here, likewise, with our Lord's question, 'Whom seek ye?' only that here is more than an earthly king.

'Jesus answered, I have told you that I am He. If, therefore, ye seek me, let these go their way.' How sweet and full of promise are these sounds! O how well the Lord was able to preserve the most perfect self-possession in every situation, however terrible; and, with His anxiety for the completion of the work of redemption, to mingle the minute and inconsiderable with the stupendous and sublime. While girding Himself for His mysterious passage to the cross, He does not forget, in His adorable faithfulness, to rescue His disciples from the approaching storm; 'If ye seek me,' says He, 'let these go their way.' The evangelist adds, 'that the saying might be fulfilled which he spake, Of them which thou gavest me have I lost none.'

'If ye seek me, let these go their way.' An expositor has very judiciously remarked on these words, that there was a delicate propriety in Christ's not saying, 'These my followers,' or 'These my disciples,' but only indefinitely, while pointing to them, 'these.' For had He applied either of the previous appellations to them, it would have been construed by the armed band as meaning 'my partisans.'

In other respects, the simple expression, 'Let these go,' uttered with emphasis, was all that was needed for the safety of His disciples. It was not a request, but a royal command, and at the same time, a hint to the disciples as to what they had to do. It was a signal for their temporary retreat from the scenes of His suffering. It would have been well for Simon Peter had he obeyed His Master's faithful hint. At that period they were unable to cope with such a 'fight of afflictions,' and would certainly, for a time, have all of them suffered shipwreck as regards their faith, if they had followed their Master further on His path of humiliation, not to speak of the danger which would besides have threatened their liberty, and even their lives. Christ bore upon His heart the welfare and safety of His followers, and so graciously provided for their security during the approaching storm.

But do not let us overlook the rich consolation for believers in every age, which this act of our Lord's includes. For He has uttered the words, 'If ye seek me, let these go their way,' to other bands than those at Gethsemane, on our behalf. In their more profound and general sense, He spake them also to hell, earth, and the devil, for it was He whom they really sought, laid hold of, and brought low. But as regards His believing people, they have forever exhausted their power upon Him, and have left in Him their sting. And as far as these hostile powers seek in the present day any thing more than to sift or try the followers of Jesus, an insuperable barrier is placed before them by these words. They can never destroy those who are in Christ. In the words above mentioned, we have a passport which insures us a safe escort across the frontier into the heavenly Jerusalem. Let us therefore honour this document, for the seal of God rests upon it.

Chapter 15

The Traitor's Kiss

We direct our eyes, once more, to the armed multitude who had reached the garden of Gethsemane in quest of Jesus. They have just risen up from the ground on which they had been thrown by the power of the Lord's word, 'I am!' Among those who had been thus hurled to the dust was Judas. It might have been supposed that this renewed manifestation of the majesty of Jesus would have finally scared the son of perdition, like some fiery sign or signal of danger, from his traitorous path. But he had undertaken to act the part of a leader; and what a coward would he have appeared in the eyes of his patrons and superiors had he not resolutely performed his promise! Suffice it to say, he again stands before us at the head of the murderous band. His bearing indicates a hypocritical resolution; but something very different is expressed in his averted looks and convulsively contracted lips, as well as in the restless working of the muscles of his pallid countenance. But he has pledged his word and concluded his contract with Satan. The traitorous signal must follow. Hell reckons on him, and would not for the world lose the triumph of seeing the Nazarene betrayed into its hands by one of His own disciples.

We may have read and heard a thousand times of this horrible fact, and yet as often as it is repeated, we are astonished afresh, as if we had never heard it before. Can there be a more appalling or more deeply affecting scene than this treacherous betrayal of his Master? Where did every personified goodness and consummate wickedness, heaven and hell, meet in more open and awful contrast? Scarcely can we support the overpowering impressions which we here receive of the superabundance of divine love and meekness on the one hand, and the fullness of Satanic wickedness on the other! We are witnesses of a parting scene – one of the most melancholy and mysterious the world has ever beheld – Jesus and His disciple Judas, separated forever.

Before we view, in the traitor's kiss, the mature infernal fruit of his inward corruptions, let us cast a look at the prophecies respecting him and his course of life. In Psalm 41 we read, 'Mine own familiar friend in whom I trusted, which did eat of my bread, hath lifted up his heel against me.' In Psalm 109, 'Let his days be few; and let another take his office. As he loved cursing, so let it come unto him; as he delighted not in blessing, so let it be far from him. As he clothed himself with cursing like as with a garment, so let it come into his bowels like water, and like oil into his bones.' And in Psalm 69, 'Let his habitation be desolate, and let no one dwell in his tents.'

That which led Judas into fellowship with Jesus was probably the hope of acting a prominent part in the kingdom of his wonder–working Master. Finding that he had formed an erroneous idea of that kingdom, which was the reverse of what he expected, he seizes, as we have already seen, the money with which he was intrusted, to compensate him in a small degree, for his disappointment. The scene at Bethany then occurred, which convinced him that his baseness was discovered; and he then gave way to those feelings of animosity and hatred which afterward prompted him to betray his Master for thirty pieces of silver. We have seen how, after receiving the sop from the latter, the devil entered into him, and from that moment he became the entire property of Satan.

Let us now return to the scene we were contemplating. The sign of betrayal which had been agreed upon had been rendered superfluous by the voluntary approach of Jesus, and His majestic declaration concerning Himself. The armed band, however, were unwilling that Judas should forego it. Hence they hinted to him by their looks, to keep his word; and Judas, to conceal the discouraging impression which the overwhelming words of Jesus had produced upon him, as well as in the furtive hope of disarming the anger of the Holy One of Israel against him by the mark of affection which ac-companied his flattering salutation, approaches the Lord under the mask of friendly intimacy, welcomes Him with the formula of hearty well-wishing, 'Hail, Master!' and ventures, like a poisonous viper hissing forth from a rose-bush, to pollute the Son of man, amid the plaudits of hell, with his treacherous kiss!

This act is the most profligate and abominable that ever emanated from the dark region of human sinfulness and degeneracy. It grew on the soil, not of devilish, but of human nature, although not without infernal influence, and hence it may be attributed in all its infamy, to our own race. It con-demns our whole race, and at the same time places beyond question the entire necessity of an atonement, mediation, and satisfaction, in order that our souls may be saved. The kiss of Judas is the indelible brandmark on the forehead of mankind, through which their 'virtuous pride' receives the stamp of lunacy and absurdity.

Would that the traitor's kiss had remained the only act of its kind! But, in a spiritual sense, Jesus has still to endure it a thousand-fold to this hour. For, hypocritically to confess Him with the mouth, while the conduct belies Him – to exalt the virtues of His humanity to the skies, while divesting Him of His divine glory, and tearing the crown of universal majesty from His head – to sing enthusiastic hymns and oratorios to Him, while trampling His Gospel by word and deed under foot – what is all this but a Judas-kiss with which men have the audacity to pollute His face?

'Hail, Master!' exclaims the traitor. These words are like two poisonous daggers in the heart of the Holy One. He calmly accepts them, nor does He refuse even the infernal kiss itself. He knows that this grief of heart was also a drop of the cup which His Father had apportioned Him, and that at the bottom of this horrible act lay the determinate counsel of the Almighty. It is a testimony to the divine endurance of the Lord Jesus; for the traitor would not have chosen this as the signal for betraying his Master had he not been aware of the latter's boundless long-suffering. Thus, with the very kiss with which he delivered Him up to His captors, Judas was compelled to glorify Him, and enhance our ideas of the infinite condescension and love with which he had been favoured by the Saviour.

'Friend,' says the Lord Jesus, with pathetic seriousness, wherefore art thou come?' Who would have expected such mildness on the present occasion? A 'Get thee behind me, Satan!' would have been more appropriate in the eyes of many. Instead of which, we hear a sound like the voice of a parent tenderly concerned for the soul of his deeply seduced child. Certainly, an outburst of flaming passion would not have been so annihilating to the traitor as was this exhalation of compassionate charity. The word 'friend,' or, as it might be more correctly rendered, 'companion,' recalled to his mind the privileged position with which, as having been received into the circle of the Lord's most intimate associates, he had been favoured. This address reminded him also of the many manifestations of unspeakable kindness and grace with which he had been loaded for three whole years.

'Companion,' says the Lord, 'wherefore art thou come?' or, 'why standest thou here?' The dreadful question rolls like terrific thunder through the traitor's heart. His conscience awakes in a moment from its deadly sleep, and feels itself carried away, as by an Almighty hand, to the bar of divine judgment. But Judas forcibly resists his own conscience, stifles the confession on the lips of his inward monitor, and succeeds in again compelling it to silence and apathy. Hence the Lord has nothing left but to let the stroke fall upon the door of his heart, which, if it does not succeed in breaking it open, acts as the knell of eternal reprobation to the traitor.

The Lord now calls him by his name, as men hope to awake a lunatic sleep-walker, who is seen treading on the edge of a precipice, before casting himself down. 'Judas,' says the Lord, with emphasis, as if He would leave nothing unattempted for his rescue, and as if He intended by it to say, 'Does not the mention of thy name remind thee that thou art called after the noble and princely tribe of which thou art a scion, and yet dost thou come to Me in this manner?' After thus mentioning his name, our Lord plainly characterizes his deed. Yet even then we hear Him giving a turn to His speech, as if He disbelieved the possibility of the traitor's purpose. As if still questioning it, He says, 'Betrayest thou the Son of man with a kiss?'

'Betrayest thou the Son of man with a kiss?' This is, there-fore, the eternal farewell to the miserable apostate from the lips of the Saviour of sinners. Woe to the unhappy man! Hell triumphs over him, heaven forsakes him, and the hollow thunder of that question still rolls over the head of Judas.

Deeply affected, we close our meditation. Let what has been brought before us have its full effect upon us. Let no pharisaical thanking God that we are not like that man, weaken the impression. The germ of what he was, lies in each of us, and may develop itself before we are aware, unless we place ourselves betimes under the protection of divine grace. Satan has not yet ceased 'Going about as a roaring lion, seeking whom he may devour.' Let us, therefore, hasten to save our souls and guard our hearts, like a city besieged by the enemy. But our arms of defence must be sought where alone they can be found – beneath the wings of Christ. He is our rock and our fortress, our refuge and strength, and our very present help in every time of need.

Chapter 16

The Sword and the Cup

A singular occurrence interrupts the regular course of the sacred narrative of our Lord's passion, and serves as additional proof of how difficult it is for human thought to elevate itself to God's thoughts, especially as displayed in the work of redemption. In the scene we are about to contemplate, a disciple smites with the sword, an action, which, however well meant, is, nevertheless, directed against the very ground and basis of the world's salvation. Let us rejoice that eternal love pursues its even path, and does not require our help in the accomplishment of its object.

After the mild but overwhelming words addressed to the traitor, our Lord voluntarily offers Himself to His enemies. How horrible to see the Lord of Glory fallen upon and surrounded like a robber and a murderer! The disciples witness it; but the sight renders them beside themselves. If, at the traitor's kiss, their blood congealed with horror, it now begins to boil in their veins. They can not bear that it should come to such a pass. 'Lord,' say they, as with one voice, 'shall we smite with the sword?' While speaking, they themselves give the answer; and before their Master has time to say a word, Peter's sword is unsheathed, and the first blow in defence is struck.

We understand what was passing in Simon's heart. The words our Lord had uttered on the road to Gethsemane, respecting his denying his Master and his own reply, still fermented within him; and he was anxious to show that in accordance with his own assertion, he would rather die than forsake Him. Full of these ideas, and doubtless with a confused remembrance of what the Lord had said respecting the purchase of swords, he blindly attacks the troop with his blade of steel, and smites Malchus, one of the high priest's servants, on the right ear, so that it is severed.

It is undeniable that an ardent and sincere affection had its essential part in this act of Peter's; but certainly, it was not love alone which nerved his arm on this occasion; he was equally as anxious to save his own honour as the person of his Master. Had Peter been in earnest with his question, 'Lord, shall we smite with the sword?' the Lord would certainly have answered him by saying, 'Simon wilt thou pollute the glory of My submission? Is it thy intention to expose us to the suspicion that we are only a company of political demagogues? Dost thou propose affording our opponents a ground of justification for coming against us armed? And wilt thou again offer the hand to Satan for the frustration of the entire work of redemption?'

In this, or a similar manner, would the Lord have spoken; for certainly, if Simon and the rest of the disciples, who were also ready for the combat, had succeeded in their attempt, the plan of the world's salvation would have been obstructed, since the Lamb of God would then not have been led to the slaughter. The great truth that the salvation of sinners could only be accomplished by the offering up of the God-man was still a profound mystery to the disciples, and continued so until the day of Pentecost broke the seals and disclosed to them its sacred depths. And to this day it is the Spirit only that opens the understanding and solves the difficulty.

The confusion caused by Simon's thoughtless assault is indescribable. The whole scene suddenly changes. The troop, drawing their swords, now prepare also for the conflict, and the sacred soil of Gethsemane is on the point of being transformed into a battle-field. A shriller discord could not have interrupted the entire purpose of Jesus, than arose out of that inconsiderate attempt. To all appearance, Peter had for the moment drawn his Master entirely out of His path; and in what danger had the thoughtless disciple, by his foolish act, involved the Eleven, who formed the tender germ of the Lord's future Church! They would doubtless have been together overthrown and slain without mercy, had not the Lord again interfered at the right moment.

Scarcely had the blow been struck, when the Saviour stepped forward, and while turning to the armed band, rebuked the storm in some measure, by these words – 'Suffer ye thus far' – that is, 'Grant me a short time, until I have done what I intend.' It is a request for a truce, in order that the wounded man may be healed. Be astonished, here again, at the humility, calmness, and self-possession which the Lord exhibits even in the most complicated situations and confusing circumstances. Even in the reckless troops, He honours the magistracy they represent; and does not order and command, but only requests them for a moment to delay seizing His person.

By a significant silence, they gave their assent to His wish. But how they are astonished on seeing the Lord kindly inclining to Malchus, and touching his wounded ear with His healing hand, when the blood instantaneously ceases to flow, and the ear is restored uninjured to its place! We are also astonished at this miracle – the last and not the smallest, by which the Saviour manifested Himself on earth, as the God-man. And we admire in it, not merely His power, which shines forth so gloriously, but likewise His love, which did not exclude even His enemies from its beneficial operation, as well as His care of His disciples, whom, by the healing of

Malchus, He secured from the sanguinary revenge of the murderous troop. Nor must we overlook the wise forethought with which the Lord, by this charitable act, defends His kingdom for the future from all misunderstanding as to its real nature. It is not a kingdom of this world, but one in which revenge is silent, meekness heaps coals of fire on the adversary's head, and where evil is recompensed with good.

While the Lord was stretching out His healing hand to the wounded man, He opens His mouth to Peter, and utters, for the instruction of every future age, the highly important words respecting the use of the sword, His voluntary abasement for sinners, and His unconditional submission to His Father's will.

He begins by saying, 'Put up thy sword again into its place, for all they that take the sword, shall perish with the sword.' According to the views of some parties in the Christian Church, this passage altogether prohibits the use of the sword. But Scripture must be compared with Scripture, and what is termed 'the analogy of faith,' is the first principle of biblical exposition. In the words above mentioned, our Lord gives us a hint that the sword has also 'its place,' where it may justly leave the scabbard; and hence 'the powers that be' are described in Romans 13:4, as 'not bearing the sword in vain,' seeing that they are 'the ministers of God, and revengers to execute wrath upon him that doeth evil'. Now, if they commit the sword to any one – whether to the executioner, the soldier, or to a private individual for his own defence: it is then drawn in a proper manner; while in the two first-mentioned instances, the responsibility attaches solely to them; but the sword is unconditionally and in every case withdrawn from private revenge, which is essentially different from self-defence.

Least of all is the sword in its place with reference to the interests of the kingdom of God. There, on the contrary, the words are applicable, 'Not by might, nor by power; but by my

Spirit, saith the Lord! The weapons of our warfare are not carnal, but mighty, through God, to the pulling down of strongholds.' There the victory is gained by the power of the testimony, by the blood of the Lamb, and by the patience of the saints. The blood of the martyrs is the seed of the Church. Her laurel wreath is the crown of thorns, and meekness is her weapon. If reviled, she blesses; if persecuted, she suffers it; if defamed, she entreats (*1 Cor.* 4:12, 13).

In this mode of passive overcoming, by which alone the world is conquered and brought into subjection to the Prince of Peace, the latter Himself is our Forerunner and Leader. Hear what He says, 'Put up again thy sword into his place; for all they that take the sword shall perish with the sword. The cup, which my Father hath given me, shall I not drink it? Thinkest thou that I cannot now pray to my Father, and he shall presently give me more than twelve legions of angels? But how then shall the scriptures be fulfilled, that thus it must be?' (*Matt.* 26:52–54).

O what a profound and comprehensive view is here afforded us into our Lord's sublime knowledge of His divine Sonship! How the veil of His abject form is here drawn aside, and how does the whole majesty of the only-begotten Son of the Father again display itself before us like a flash of lightning in the darkness of the night! He continues the same in the obscurest depths of humiliation; and in the consciousness of His divine dignity, always rises superior to the opposite appearance in which He is enveloped. If He would, He had only to ask, and the Father would send twelve legions of angels for His protection (consequently a legion for each of the little company). How must Peter, on hearing these words from his Master, have felt ashamed for imagining that, if he did not interfere, the latter would be left helpless and forsaken. For Simon knows that his Lord is not wont to use empty phrases, and that he must, therefore, take the words concerning the celestial powers that stood at His command in their literal sense; and yet the idea could occur to him that he must deliver such a Master from a few armed mortals, as though He were defenceless!

But was it really in the Lord's power to withdraw Himself from His sufferings by angelic aid? Without the shadow of a doubt. Having voluntarily resolved upon the great undertaking, He could, at any moment, have freely and without obstruction, withdrawn from it. Every idea of compulsion from without must be banished far from the doing and suffering of our Redeemer. Hence, there is scarcely a moment in His whole life, in which His love for our fallen race is more gloriously manifested. A heavenly host, powerful enough to stretch a world of adversaries in the dust, stands behind the screen of clouds, waiting at His beck, and burning with desire to be permitted to interfere for Him and triumphantly liberate Him from the hands of the wicked while He, though ill-treated and oppressed, refuses their aid, and again repeats, more emphatically by the action than by words, 'Father, thy will, and not mine, be done!' 'Thus it must be,' says He. Carefully observe also this renewed testimony to the indispensable necessity of His passion. 'How, then, shall the Scriptures be fulfilled,' he adds. The words of Moses and the prophets are 'a lamp unto his feet, and a light unto his path.' His language still is, 'The cup which my Father hath given me, shall I not drink it?' Great and momentous words! Let us spend a few moments in meditating on them.

A cup is a vessel which has its appointed measure, and is limited by its rim. The Saviour several times refers to the cup that was appointed for Him. In Matthew 20:22, He asks His disciples, 'Are ye able to drink of the cup that I shall drink of?' By the cup, He understood the bitter draught of His passion which had been assigned Him. We heard Him ask in Gethsemane, at the commencement, if it were not possible that the cup might pass from Him; and here we find Him mentioning, with the most unmoved self-possession, 'the cup which his Father had given him.' We know what was in the cup. All its contents would have been otherwise measured out to us by divine justice on account of sin. In the cup was the entire curse of the inviolable law, all the horrors of conscious guilt, all the terrors of Satan's fiercest temptations, and all the sufferings which can befall both body and soul. It contained likewise the dreadful ingredients of abandonment by God, infernal agony, and a bloody death, to which the curse was attached – all to be endured while surrounded by the powers of darkness.

Here we learn to understand what is implied in the words, 'Who spared not his own Son, but freely gave him up for us all.' 'The Lord laid on him the iniquities of us all.' 'I will smite the Shepherd, and the sheep shall be scattered.' 'Christ hath redeemed us from the curse of the law, being made a curse for us.' 'God made him to be sin for us, who knew no sin.' All that mankind have heaped up to themselves against the day of God's holy and righteous wrath – their forgetfulness of God – their selfish conduct – their disobedience, pride, worldly-mindedness – their filthy lusts, hypocrisy, falsehood, hardheartedness, and deceit – all are united and mingled in this cup, and ferment together into a horrible potion. 'Shall I not drink this cup?' asks the Saviour. 'Yes,' we reply, 'empty it, beloved Immanuel! we will kiss Thy feet, and offer up ourselves to Thee upon Thy holy altar!' He has emptied it, and not a drop remains for His people. The satisfaction He rendered was complete, the reconciliation effected. 'There is now no condemnation to them that are in Christ Jesus.' The curse no longer falls upon them. 'The chastisement of our peace lay upon him; and by his stripes we are healed,' and nothing now remains for us but to sing Hallelujah!

Chapter 17

Offering and Sacrifice

We shall confine our present meditation to the state of resignation in which we left our great High Priest, at the close of the last chapter. He yields Himself up to His adversaries, and suffers them to do with Him just as they please.

With what feelings the holy angels must have witnessed their Lord being thus taken prisoner – they whom the Saviour's humiliation never for a moment prevented from being conscious of His real character and dignity; and who, wherever He went, perceived in Him the Lord of glory and the King of kings, before whose throne they only ventured to approach with veiled faces! Let us realize, if possible, what they must have felt at that moment, when, looking down from the clouds, they saw the High and Lofty One surrounded by the officers, as if He had been the vilest of criminals; the Prince of heaven taken captive with swords and staves; the judge of the world fettered like a murderer, and then dragged away under the escort of a crowd of ruthless men amid blasphemies and curses, to be put upon trial! May not a cry of horror have rung through heaven, and the idea have occurred to those holy beings that the measure of human wickedness was now full, and that the day of vengeance on the ungodly earth had arrived? We can so easily forget, in His appearance as a man, who it is that we have before us in the humbled individual of Nazareth; and it is only now and then that it flashes through our minds who He really is. But then our hearts become petrified with amazement, and we can only look in silent astonishment.

But however dreadful His position may be, the Saviour bears with composure these outrageous proceedings. He delivers Himself up, and to whom? – to the armed band, the officers and servants. But we are witnesses here of another yielding up of Himself, and one that is veiled and invisible; and the latter is of incomparably greater importance to us than that which is apparent to the outward senses. Christ here gives Himself up to His Father, first, as 'an offering' (*Eph.* 5:2). How shall we sufficiently appreciate the excellency of this offering? Behold Him, then, as One against whom all hell may be let loose without being able to cast the slightest blemish on His innocence; as One who endured the fiercest ordeal without the smallest trace of dross; who boldly withstood the storm of temptation; who, in a state of the most painful inward privations, preserved unshaken His love to His Father; and, although His Father's heart seemed turned away from Him, yet regarded it, as before, as His meat and drink to do the will of Him who sent Him; who, in a situation in which acute agony forced Him to sweat blood, could nevertheless pray from the bottom of His heart that not what He desired, but what the eternal Father wished and had determined respecting Him, might take place. Such is the dazzlingly pure, immutably holy, and severely tested offering which Christ in His own person presents to the Father.

Regard Him now as submitting Himself, not only to the disgrace of a public arrest, but also to the fate of a common delinquent, in obedience to His Father's will. Hear Him address His enemies. With the majesty, freedom, and sublime composure of One who marks out Himself the path on which

He is to walk, in accordance with His Father's counsel, He says to the multitude, and especially to their leaders, the chief priests, and the captains of the Jewish temple guard, and to the elders, the assessors of the Sanhedrin, 'Are ye come out as against a thief, with swords and staves to take me? I sat daily with you, teaching in the temple, and ye laid no hold on me, nor stretched forth your hands against me.'

Our Lord intends that these words shall serve as a testimony, not merely to those that heard them, but also to the whole world, that He was led guiltless to the slaughter, and that no power on earth would have been able to overcome Him, had He not, when His hour was come, voluntarily yielded up Himself in free submission to His Father's will. Until He had completed His ministerial office, no enemy dared to touch Him. Nor had they been able to discover any thing in Him which might have enabled them to prosecute Him. The invisible barrier is now removed. 'This,' continues the Saviour, to the profound confusion of His adversaries, 'this is your hour and the power of darkness.' His meaning is, 'By an act of the divine government the chain of Satan has been lengthened, that it may do with me as it pleases.' What self-possession and divine composure are in these words! With unreserved willingness does He yield Himself up to the most disgraceful treatment. His soul continues in a state of equanimity and serenity, just as if they were not jailers' assistants, who bound Him with cords, but followers and friends.

But what benefit do we derive from the fact of Christ's giving Himself up so completely and devotedly to the Father? The greatest and most beatifying of which thought is capable. Listen! Jehovah says in His law, 'Ye shall not appear before me empty.' Consider, that if we wish to inherit heaven, we cannot do without salvation. We now possess it, and the days of our grief and shame are at an end. We may now boldly appear before the Father, knowing that He loves us, and has opened the gates of His palace to us. But what have we to exhibit to Him that is meritorious, sufficient – yea, more than the angels possess? We have, indeed, nothing of our own, in the records of our lives we perceive only transgression and guilt. But God be thanked that we need nothing of our own, and are even warned against trusting and depending upon any thing of the kind. We are instructed to appeal to the righteousness of Another, and this is the living 'offering' of which we speak – Christ, with the entire fullness of His obedience in our stead. If He was accepted, so are we, since all that He did and suffered is placed to our account. For, 'as by one man's disobedience many were made sinners, so by the obedience of one shall many be made righteous.' Those who are in Christ are no longer transgressors in the sight of God, but pure, blameless, and spotless. What a blissful mystery! If you are unable to believe it, grant it at least a place in your memory. The hour may come in which you will be able to use it; for we have often had occasion to witness how it fared at the last with those who supposed themselves among the most pious and holy of mankind. Whatever of a meritorious and approved character they imagined they possessed, nothing remained when the light of eternity and approaching judgment threw its penetrating rays upon their past lives. The splendour of their virtues expired, their gold became dim, and that which they had preserved as real worth, proved only tinsel and valueless.

What is to be done in such a case? How weave together, in haste, such a righteousness as God requires, and without which no man can enter heaven? What answer are we to make to the accusers that open their mouths against us – Satan, the law, and our own consciences, which say to us, 'Thou art the man'? If we are not to give ourselves up to despair, something which is not ours must be bestowed upon

us, which we may offer unto God as the ground of our claim
to salvation. The living offering which Christ made of Himself
can then alone suffice, and that abundantly, to recommend
us to God. Possessing this, we no longer need be mute in the
presence of our accusers. In Christ, as our Surety, we fulfilled
the conditions to which the heavenly inheritance is attached.
Henceforth, who will accuse us, who will condemn us? We
rejoice with Paul, and say, 'Therefore, being justified by faith,
we have peace with God through our Lord Jesus Christ.'

The Lord Jesus appears in our narrative not only as an
'offering,' but also as a 'sacrifice.' Our sins are imputed to
Him, and in His sacred humanity He endured what they
deserved. Let us therefore consider Him in the character of
our Representative, and the sufferings He endured, and the
wrongs He sustained will then appear in their proper light.

A blissful and heart-cheering mystery is here presented
before us. If I possess saving faith, I find myself in a peculiar
relation to the Sufferer at Gethsemane. For know that the
horrors He there experienced are not His curse but mine.
The Holy and the just submits Himself, representatively, to
the fate of the guilty and the damnable; while the latter are
forever liberated, and inherit the lot of the holy Son of God.
Wonderful and incomparably blissful truth! Our only shield
and comfort in life and death!

O ye blessed, who belong to Christ, who can worthily
describe the glory of your state! We hail the wondrous
exchange which the eternal Son of God has made with you.
We glorify the Surety and the Liquidator of your debts. Never
forget the nocturnal arrest of your High Priest. Paint it, in
bright and vivid colours, on the walls of your chambers. If
you are again reminded of the curse which your sins had
brought upon you, accustom yourselves to regard it only in
this sacred picture, where you no longer behold it lying upon
you, but upon Him, in whose agonies it eternally perished.

Therefore, let not shadows any longer disturb you. There will never be a period in eternity when you will be compelled to say to your enemies and accusers, 'Now is your hour and the power of darkness.' Your Representative uttered it, once for all, for you; and henceforward only the hour of triumph and delight, which shall never end, awaits you. Peace be with you, therefore, ye who are justified by His righteousness, and forever perfected by His one offering! No longer dream of imaginary burdens, but know and never forget that your suit is gained to all eternity. Behold, Christ yonder bears your fetters; and nothing more is required of you than to love Him with all your heart, and embrace Him more and more closely who took your entire anathema upon Himself, that you might be able eternally to rejoice and exclaim, 'Jehovah Zidkenu – the Lord our Righteousness.'

Chapter 18

Christly before Annas

The armed band have executed their object with regard to Christ, and the Eleven, perceiving it, have fled to the right and left. Surrounded by a bristling forest of swords and spears, the Lord Jesus suffered His hands to be bound, like a captive robber, by a troop of rude mercenaries, in the name of public justice. Think of those hands being bound which were never extended except to heal and aid, to benefit and save, and never to injure, except it be considered as a crime to uncover to mankind their wounds, in order to heal and bind them up; to destroy the Babels of delusion, and in their place to erect the temple of truth; and to pull down the altars of false gods, in order to make room for that of the only true God.

Jesus bound! What a spectacle! How many a prophetic type of the Old Testament finds its fulfilment in this fact! If you inquire for the antitype of Isaac, when bound by his father as a lamb for a burnt offering; or for that of the ram on Mount Moriah, which was caught in the thicket because God had destined it for the sacrifice; or of the sacred ark of the covenant, when it had fallen into the hands of the Philistines, only, however, to cast down the idols of the latter; or of that of Jacob's son arrested and imprisoned in Egypt, whose path lay through the company of criminals, to regal dignity and crowns of honour; or for that of the paschal lambs, which, before being slaughtered for the sins of the people, were wont to be tied up to the threshold of the temple; or finally, for that of the captive Sampson, who came forth victoriously from the conflict with the Philistines – all these types and shadows found their entire fulfilment in Jesus, thus bound, as their embodied Original and Antitype.

Jesus bound! Can we trust our eyes? Omnipotence in fetters, the Creator bound by the creature; the Lord of the world, the captive of His mortal subjects! How much easier would it have been for Him to have burst those bonds than Manoah's son of old! However, He rends them not; but yields Himself up to them as one who is powerless and overcome. This His passive deportment must have for its basis a great and sublime intention. And such is really the case, as we have already seen.

Behold them marching off in triumph with their Captive. They conduct Him first to Annas, the previous high priest, the father-in-law of Caiaphas, a sinner a hundred years old. But why first to him? Perhaps out of compliment to the old man, who probably wished to see the fanatic of Nazareth. His being brought before him, however, seems to have been the result of a secret arrangement between him and his son-in-law; and he, the old Sadducee, was perhaps more deeply interested in the whole affair than outwardly appears to be the case. The preliminary hearing, which now commenced, was doubtless instituted by him, and not by Caiaphas. Annas was evidently residing in the high-priestly palace with his son-in-law.

Thus, the Lord stands at the bar of His first judge – one of those miserable men, of whom, alas! not a few are to be found among us, and who, 'twice dead,' estranged from the truth of God, and satisfied with the most common-place occurrences of life, treat the most sublime things only as a spectacle;

and visibly bear on their foreheads the brandmark of the curse. Certainly it was not one of the least of the sufferings of the Holy One of Israel to see Himself delivered into the hands of such a man, so destitute of every noble feeling. And only look how the hoary-headed sinner domineers over and puffs himself up against the Lord of Glory, although he is not even the actual high priest. Jesus, however, endures with resignation all the indignities to which He is subjected, and we know for what reason He does so. We are acquainted with the mysterious position He occupies, in which He not only shows us, by His own example, that His kingdom is not of this world, but also that He fills it as our Surety, whom it became to present to the Eternal Father the sublime virtues of a perfect self-denial and resignation in our stead.

Annas proceeds with the hearing of the case, and interrogates our Lord respecting His disciples and His doctrine. He hopes that the statements of Jesus may enable him to bring an accusation against the former as a politically dangerous association, and against the latter as being wicked and blasphemous heresy. In his questions, he is presumptuous enough to treat our Lord as the disguised head of a party, and a secret plotter, notwithstanding that He brought forward His cause in the most public manner, and walked every where in broad daylight.

The world still acts like Annas. It will not acknowledge that we possess the real and eternal truth of God. The world can not bear that believers should call themselves 'true Christians,' and never fails to attach some opprobrious epithet to them. However boldly we may preach our doctrine, and however completely we may prove that we confess and believe nothing else than what the whole Christian Church has believed and professed before us, and for which the noblest and most excellent of men in every age have lived and died – yet the world persists in maintaining that our faith is only the religion of narrow-minded fanatics. It strives, by these artful suspicions, to keep the truth far from it, and thus to give its ungodly and carnal proceedings at least a semblance of correctness.

The Lord answers the old priest's questions regarding His doctrine; for it was less requisite here to defend the honour of His person than that of His cause, which was, at the same time, the cause of God, and which He, therefore, felt called upon to vindicate. He also wished to make it clearly known throughout all ages that He was condemned and crucified solely because of His asserting His divine Sonship. 'I spake,' says He, 'openly to the world' – that is, 'I opened my mouth boldly.' Yes, in all that He spoke, the profound assurance and powerful conviction of being the Lord from heaven was perceptible. He spoke, knowing that he that was of the truth would hear His voice, and acknowledge His word to be the word of the living God. Nor did He deceive Himself with reference to this. To this day, when any one is delivered from the snare of the devil, he needs no other proof of the truth of the words of Jesus; since his heart hears them as if spoken direct from heaven, and discovers between the language of Jesus and the most intellectual discourses of mere mortals, a gulf so immense that it is incomprehensible to him that he did not long before perceive it.

The Lord Jesus continues: 'I ever taught in the synagogue and in the temple, whither the Jews always resort.' He had done so, and no one had ever been able to prove that He had taught any thing which was not in strict accordance with the Old Testament Scriptures, and did not most beautifully harmonize with the nature and being of a holy God. The masters in Israel were compelled, by His discourses, mutely to lay down their arms.

'In secret have I said nothing,' says the Lord Jesus further. No, not even that which was enigmatical, obscure, and mysterious, much of which was explained only in the course of centuries, while other things remain, to this hour, partially closed and sealed to us, and await their elucidation. He knew that these things would long be inexplicable to His people; but this did not hinder Him from uttering them. This is another proof that He was clearly conscious that His doctrine was divine, and would therefore continue to the end of time.

'Why askest thou me?' – says our Lord in conclusion. 'Ask them which heard me what I have said unto them; behold, they know what I have said.' How could the Lord testify more strongly to the purity and divinity of His doctrine, than by calling upon His judge to summon before him all those, either friends or foes, who had ever heard Him speak, and ask them if they were able to say any thing against Him which might furnish ground for accusation. Nor to the present day does He show any witnesses, but appeals as before, on behalf of His cause, to all who hear and receive His Word; and these unanimously, from their own conviction, confirm it, and will ever do so, that the doctrine of Jesus is of God, and that He has not spoken of Himself.

While the Lord is speaking, one of the servants of the high priest rises up and smites Him on the face, while saying, 'Answerest thou the high priest so?' From this circumstance, we may perceive what is intended with respect to Jesus. This first maltreatment gave the signal for all that followed. It did not escape the servant how completely his master was embarrassed by the simple reply of the accused; and this rude blow was the only means which presented itself of rescuing him from his painful and disgraceful dilemma. The fellow well knew that it would be allowed him – nay, that he would only rise by it in the favour of his master.

For this very crime alone, which must not be placed to the account of a single individual, but to our corrupt human nature, to the guilty race of Adam, it was fit that hell should open its mouth and swallow it up, as the pit formerly did Korah and his company. But Jesus came not to hasten our perdition, but to prevent it. We therefore do not behold the wicked man scathed by lightning from heaven, nor his hand withered, like that of Jeroboam, on his stretching it out to smite.

'Answerest thou the high priest so?' As if the Lord, who knew better than any one else what was becoming in His converse with mankind, had infringed upon reverence due to the sacerdotal dignity. But how often are we treated in a similar manner when the truth which we proclaim to the men of the world can not be assailed. We are then called bold, presumptuous, obstinate. What is left for us, in such situations, except to make use of our Master's own words, 'If I have spoken evil, bear witness of the evil; but if well, why smitest thou me?'

How overpowering was this speech to both master and servant! It was like the stroke of a hammer, driving the sting of their evil conscience still deeper into the marrow. The blow on the cheek, with its accompanying brutal language, was only a clear proof that the miserable men felt themselves unable to bring any thing of a culpable nature against the Lord. By acting thus, they only smote themselves in the face, since by their conduct they made it evident how deeply and painfully they had felt the truth.

Thus our Lord and Master came forth perfectly justified from this first examination, and the high priest and his satellites were covered with disgrace. In their fate we see reflected that of all those who dare to lift the shield against the Lord's cause, which, through the power of inward truth, victoriously repels every attack. Whatever may be planned and undertaken against it, it invariably comes forth like the sun shining in the mists of the valley, and calmly looks down on all opposition and gainsaying as upon vanquished enemies.

Chapter 19

The Judicial Procedure

Night still reigns. The city of Jerusalem lies for the most part in profound slumber, and has no presentiment of the awful events which are occurring within its walls. Occasionally, isolated footsteps are heard along the streets, in the direction of the high priest's palace, the windows of which, now glaring at an unwonted hour with the light of lamps and torches, cause events of an extraordinary nature to be inferred. Let us also repair thither.

An assembly of high rank, collected together in the spacious hall of audience, receives us. It is the council of the seventy rulers of Israel, with the high priest as its president. A venerable assembly, as regards its appointment; the most illustrious and awe-inspiring in the whole world; since, sitting in the seat of Moses, in the midst of the chosen people, its office is to administer justice according to the book of the law, and in the name of the Most High God. Next to the president we perceive the men who had previously filled the office of high priest. Behind these, we observe the representatives of the four and twenty classes of the priesthood. Then follow the elders or rulers of the synagogues, while the rest of the assembly is composed of the most eminent doctors of the law, men well versed in the Mosaic statutes and the traditions and ordinances of the Rabbis.

It was the primary duty of these men, as keepers of the sanctuary, to maintain the observance of the ordinances of Jehovah among the people; to settle the legal differences of the various tribes; to watch over the purity of doctrine and of divine service; and to examine and judge any heresies that might spring up. It certainly belonged to the privileges and even duties of the authority thus constituted, to bring before them a Man who gave Himself out for the Messiah; and to examine Him in the strictest manner. And that it did not occur to the Holy One of Israel to dispute their right to this, is clearly manifest from the reverence, which, apart from the moral qualities of its individual members, did not fail to show itself in His deportment during the whole course of the proceedings.

Before this supreme tribunal the Saviour of mankind stands bound. However, we must not limit the great judicial procedure to that which is visible, but must see beyond it the invisible world. The Lord does not stand at the bar as a Holy One, but as the Representative of sinners. Our catalogue of crimes is displayed before Him, as if they were His own. Our sins are charged upon Him, for He bears them. He is laid in the scales of justice with our transgressions, for they are imputed to Him. What may then have passed between Him and the Majesty upon the throne, is concealed from us by the veil of eternity. One thing, however, we know, that He stood there in our place. Had He not appeared, that position would have been ours; and woe unto us, had we been made responsible for our sins! Such a thought need no longer terrify us, if we belong to Christ's flock. What was due from us, He has paid. We come no more into condemnation, since He has taken our place. We know no longer any judge; for the judge is our friend. How blissful is this consciousness! Eternal praise to Him to whom we owe it all!

But we return to the hall of judgment. The council seek for witnesses against Jesus. They seek, because unsought, nothing of the kind presents itself. That which is unsought is all in His favour. But they have already decided to put Him to death. Why? Because He spoils the game of the proud men who have Him in their power, and every where comes in the way of their selfish practices. They dislike Him because He disturbs them in their sinful haunts, because He disapproves of the ways of vanity in which they walk, judges their ungodly and carnal deeds, and pronounces them deficient in that righteousness which avails before God. And because, for these reasons, they dislike Him, they seek for witnesses against Him. And what kind of witnesses do they bring? Those who not only contradict one another incessantly, but themselves every moment! while the witnesses which we bring forward in behalf of our faith, are the devout seers and prophets, the holy evangelists and apostles, the thousands of martyrs, who, in His strength, have sung their psalms to Him in the midst of the flames – yes, we appeal to the entire history of His Church, as well as to the daily experience of all believers, as a continuous testimony in favour of Him who is the object of our love, and of the truth of His cause.

The council of the Sanhedrin, who are anxious to clothe their legal murder with at least an appearance of justice, take great pains to find witnesses against Jesus. But a more fruitless undertaking was perhaps never attempted. Desperation then advises an extreme course. A number of bribed witnesses are suborned – who strive to fasten one or other false accusation on the Holy One. But what is the result? They expose themselves, with those who hired them, in the most barefaced manner, and serve only as a new foil to the innocence of the Accused. What they adduce condemns itself as an absurdity, and not even that is attained which was indispensably required by the Mosaic Law, that their testimony should correspond. They become more and more confused, refute one another against their will, and remind us of the word of the Lord by the mouth of Zechariah the prophet, 'I will smite every horse with astonishment, and his rider with madness' (*Zech.* 12:4).

The venerable assembly now finds itself in the most painful dilemma. At length, two witnesses come forward, and hope by means of an expression which the Lord had uttered a year before, to make amends for the deficiencies in their accusation. The words adduced are those in John 2:19, 'Destroy this temple, and in three days I will raise it up.' Even at the time, this expression was most maliciously misinterpreted by the Jews who were present. 'Forty and six years,' said they, 'was this temple in building, and wilt thou rear it up in three days? But he spake,' says the Evangelist, 'of the temple of his body.' The two hirelings were aware of this. It seemed to them, however, a very suitable expression to make use of for casting upon Jesus the appearance not only of an ungodly boaster, but also of a crime against the divine Majesty, by blaspheming the temple. Thus we hear them say, 'He boasted that he was able to destroy the temple of God, and to build it again in three days.'

Even the high priest is not yet base and inconsiderate enough to pronounce his judicial decision upon such miserable and suspicious evidence. His conscience was still sufficiently susceptible to make him feel the pitifulness and worthlessness of these last testimonies; and the secret apprehension that such a judicial inquiry might not satisfy the people, as well as the impressive, sublime, and commanding tranquillity which the Accused opposed to the wretched fabrication of the two witnesses, restrained him from it. Thus in the end, the whole inquisitorial proceeding of the judge, only tended to our Lord's glorification, since by it His spotless innocence was placed in the clearest light. Yes, He is the Lamb without spot, which it was necessary He should be, in order to take away our guilt.

But how does the Accused conduct Himself during the judicial procedure? His whole conduct is extremely significant and remarkable. With a judicial mien, which only partially covers his perplexity, the high priest says to Him, in an imperious tone, 'Answerest thou nothing to what these witness against thee?' 'But Jesus,' as we are told by the narrative, 'held his peace.' How eloquent was this silence! And why make many words on this occasion since His enemies, though against their will, witnessed so powerfully in His favour that He needed no further justification? He was silent. How easy would it have been for Him, by a few words, to have most painfully exposed the august assembly! But He honours in it, as before, the powers ordained of God, although they may be guilty of injustice; and viewing the matter thus, He deems it becoming Him to hold His peace. The essential meaning of His silence, however, lies still deeper. His holding His peace is the reflection of a more mysterious silence before another and higher than any human tribunal; and regarded from this point of view, it may be considered as a silence of confession and assent.

When a criminal makes no reply to the accusations brought against him before a human tribunal, it is regarded as an admission of his guilt. Thus we must also regard the silence of Jesus, who, having taken upon Him, before God, the sins of His people by a mysterious imputation, deems Himself worthy of death and the curse. By mutely listening to the accusations of His judges, without attempting to exculpate Himself, He wishes outwardly to intimate the actual offering up of Himself as a culprit in our stead. Thus He is silent, not only as a lamb, but also as the Lamb which taketh away the sin of the world. His silence enables us to speak, and gives us power and liberty to lift up our heads boldly against every accusation, while trusting to the justification wrought out for us by the Redeemer.

May the Lord instruct us all when to speak and when to be silent; the former, by enlightening the darkness of our natural state; and the latter, by an application to our hearts and consciences of the consolatory mystery of the sufferings of Jesus for us! There is only one way of escaping the horrors of future judgment, and that is the believing apprehension of all that our Surety has accomplished in our stead. May God strengthen our faith for this purpose more and more, and enable each of us from the heart to explain, in the words of the apostle, 'Thanks be to God for his unspeakable gift!'

Chapter 20

The Fall of Peter

In addition to all His other sufferings, our blessed Lord had also to endure that of being denied by one of the little company of His confidential disciples, on whose fidelity He ought to have been able to reckon under all circumstances. His heart was not to be a stranger to any grief or pain, in order that He might be to us in all things a compassionate High Priest. But how would the Scriptures have been fulfilled, had He not also experienced the fate of His living prototypes – Joseph, delivered up by his brethren, and David forsaken in the season of his calamities – or how could He have verified the prophetic language of the Psalmist, 'Lover and friend hast thou put far from me, and my acquaintance into darkness'?

Let us join ourselves in spirit to Simon Peter. If any one was ever ardently attached to the Saviour, it was he; but he was only partially conscious of what it was that he loved in Jesus. The mystery in His vicarious character, and the consequent necessity for the offering up of Himself as a sacrifice for the sins of the world, were still concealed from him. He had only a kind of general perception that his salvation in some way depended upon fellowship with Jesus, and that without Him he would infallibly perish. In Peter, as in many churches where the Gospel is not preached in all its fullness, faith and love preceded religious knowledge and discernment. More the subject of feeling than of a divinely enlightened understanding, Peter reminds us of that class of our brethren, of whom we are wont to say that though they possess the burning heart, yet they are still in want of the light of the Holy Spirit. The new life is implanted in its germ, but the development itself is still far behind, and much remains for the Holy Spirit to enlarge and complete.

Peter was like the man in the Gospel, who went to war without first sitting down and counting the cost. He might have already perceived that he was acting foolishly, when after his rash assault on the servant of the high priest and the Lord's subsequent resignation of Himself to the hands of His enemies, his zeal was instantly extinguished, so that he was cowardly enough to take to a disgraceful flight with the rest. True, he again bethought himself after a time; but that which induced him to follow his captive Lord at a distance, was, in reality, more the spur of pride, than the noble impulse of a 'love strong as death.'

He had spoken openly and loudly of never denying his Master, and even of going to death with Him; and what would be thought of him if he were now to break his vows and vanish from the field? No, he was resolved never to be regarded as a coward. Where his Master is, there he must be. He goes forward with feeble knees and inward reluctance. What would he give if some unavoidable and obvious hindrance were to block up his way and prevent his further advance! In fact, such a wished-for obstacle seems to present itself, in the gates being closed as soon as the band, with their captive, have entered into the court yard of the high priest's palace. If we mistake not, he is already preparing to depart; but before the entrance, he meets with a friend and fellow-believer, who was known to the high priest; and who, being on amicable terms with him, went freely in and out of his house. The latter addresses a few words to the door-keeper, and Peter, whether willingly or unwillingly, is admitted.

Simon passes with tottering steps over the threshold of the opened gate, and thus sets foot on the scene of his trial. O that he had now cast himself down in prayer before God! But instead of this, he still depends upon himself, and upon the chance of accidents and circumstances. Satan and the world already stand armed against him on the field. He had no need to fear them, if he had only put on the breastplate of faith.

Let us now consider the melancholy event which took place in the court yard of the high priest. At the moment when Simon is admitted, at the intercession of his friend, the damsel that keeps the door, holding up her lantern to his face, regards him with a look as if she knew him, but is not quite sure of it. Peter, seeing this, turns away his face, and hastens as quickly as possible past the woman, lest she should recognize him. In the centre of the court yard the soldiers had kindled a fire, to protect themselves against the raw, cold, morning air, and, crowding round it, pass the time in talking and joking; while inside the house the proceedings against Jesus are going on.

Peter, who feels uncomfortable enough in such an atmosphere, approaches the noisy group, and with a careless mien, as if only anxious to warm himself, takes his place among them. In fact, his denial had now commenced, for his intention was evidently to appear to the mercenaries as if he belonged to their party, and shared their sentiments with regard to the Nazarene. Not a little pleased at having thus attained a twofold object – the safety of his person, and the being able to say that he had manifested his courage in thus mingling with the adversaries, and fulfilling his promise not to forsake his Master – the pitiable hero sits there and expects that he will be able to witness the future course of events without danger to himself.

Of a sudden, a painful stop is put to these calculations. The porteress, who wished to assure herself whether or not she had mistaken the stranger whom she had admitted, steals thither unobserved, and mingling among the soldiery, discovers, by the light of the flickering flame, the lurking guest; and looking over his shoulder into his face, she asks him, with a triumphant and malicious leer, 'Wast thou not also with Jesus of Nazareth? Art thou not one of his disciples?'

Who can describe Peter's confusion at this question? At the moment when he thought himself so safe, to be so suddenly assailed! However, he recollects himself, and replies with the emphasis of one whose honour is assailed, 'Woman, I know him not. I know not what thou sayest.'

Alas! Alas! He that offered to take up the gauntlet for Jesus, even if thrown down by the king of terrors, succumbs at the first idea of danger, suggested by the question of a menial servant! Who does not perceive from his language the tempest of accusing and excusing thoughts which rages within? 'I am not; I know him not,' is first uttered with tolerable decision. But then, condemned by conscience, he seeks to bear out this denial in some measure by adding, 'I know not what thou sayest. What dost thou mean? I do not understand thee.'

While stammering out this lamentable prevarication, he rises from his seat, under the influence of alarm and inward rebuke, and retires unobserved from his dangerous position. He bends his steps toward the gate, in the hope of finding it open and being able to make his escape. The cock now crows for the first time, but the state of excitement which he is in does not suffer him this time to hear the warning sound, the more so, since the way is unexpectedly blocked by another maidservant, who, calling to the soldiers who assemble round her, says, in a more definite manner than the former, 'This fellow was also with Jesus of Nazareth!' The mercenaries are gratified by the stripping off of Peter's disguise, since it affords them the desired materials for additional joke and pastime. 'Art thou not also one of his disciples?' they ask, in a rude and threatening tone – 'Thou belongest also to the sect!'

What is the poor man to do now? After his foot has once slipped, we see him fall into a state of complete vacillation. The way to the second transgression is always rapidly traversed after the commission of the first. Peter now denies his Lord again, and this time more boldly than before, 'Man,' says he, 'I am not,' and then adds an asseveration; nay, even so far forgets himself as to speak of his Master in a contemptuous tone while saying, 'I know not the man!' They believe him, since no one would speak thus of his friend, if he were not the refuse of faithlessness and falsehood. They do not imagine Peter to be capable of such baseness, and therefore they let him go. O what a disgrace for the disciple to have convinced the troop that he could not be Jesus' friend.

Restless and fugitive, like a stricken and chased deer, the unhappy disciple wanders about the remote parts of the courtyard, but to his horror finds every outlet of escape closed against him. For a while he succeeds in withdrawing himself from the view and further molestation both of the spearmen and domestics. Then, after the lapse of about another hour, a fresh crowd surrounds him, who have at length come to the conclusion that the stranger must certainly belong to the disciples of Jesus. 'Surely,' say they, with greater confidence than before, 'thou art also one of them;' and when he again begins to defend himself, they convict him of falsehood by his own words, and exclaim, 'Thy speech bewrayeth thee; thou art a Galilean.' Another soldier, attracted by the noise, looks him full in the face, and adds his confirmation to their assertion, by saying, 'Of a truth this fellow also was with him.' Last of all, a servant of the High Priest approaches, a kinsman of him whose ear Peter had cut off at Gethsemane, and says, 'Did not 1 see thee in the garden with him?'

Peter now finds himself completely entrapped. How is he to act? Two ways are open to him, either to reveal his disgraceful denials by a candid acknowledgment, or else to act his lamentable part completely through, in which case he must carry his barefaced falsehoods to the utmost. In a state bordering on desperation he decides upon the latter. In the confusion of the moment, he is quite the old fisherman, the rough sailor again – nay, even much worse than he had ever been before, and heaps oath upon oath, and curse upon curse, to confirm his assertion that he knew not the Man. Abjuring his salvation, he exclaims, 'I know not the man of whom ye speak.' And he gives them this assurance with a gesture and in a tone as if no one under heaven was more despicable in his esteem than 'that man,' and as if a more outrageous injury could not have been inflicted upon him than by such a supposition. He is apparently beside himself at the grievous wrong which he is enduring.

But the more violently he protests and cries out, the more obvious is his Galilean dialect; and the more this is the case, the more certain at length are the mercenaries that they have not been mistaken in him. The measure of his sin is now full. The soldiers leave him to himself without giving him any further trouble, and turn their backs upon him, either out of contempt, as deeming such a renegade unworthy of being stamped as a martyr, or else because, by the opening of the doors of the judgment hall, a new spectacle attracts their attention in a higher degree.

We break off, for the present, with painful feelings. Is it, then, possible for the children of God to fall so far back into their former state? Yes, my readers, if, instead of commending themselves, in true humiliation of spirit, to the grace of God, they enter the lists in presumptuous self-confidence, and rush themselves into danger. In this case, there is no security against their experiencing similar defeats. The new man, in those who are regenerate, does not attain to such an un-limited superiority over the old, as no longer to require, on all occasions, the continuance of divine influence for the overcoming and restraining of the latter. It is true that the former will never yield to the flesh for long together, but in due time will again trample it under foot. It may, however, be the case, as it was with Peter, that the old Adam, under the pressure of seductive and darkening influences, may again burst his fetters, and, manifesting his depravity before God and man, may obtain a considerable advantage over the new man. Hence the Lord's pointed admonition to His disciples to watch and pray lest they fall into temptation. Simon Peter vowed and promised, certainly with the purest intentions, but neglected to watch and pray. What was the consequence? The first blast of temptation miserably overthrew him, and all his vows and promises were scattered to the winds.

'Let him therefore that thinketh he standeth, take heed lest he fall.' In the kingdom of God, indeed, a defeat may bring more blessings than a victory. But woe unto him whom this truth would render reckless! Such a one would be in danger of being never raised up from his fall by the hand of divine grace. And though he might rise again, yet no one can calculate how far a relapse into sin might affect at least the present life, by its destructive consequences. Therefore, let us ever bear in mind the apostolic exhortation, 'Put on the whole armour of God, that ye may be able to stand against the wiles of the devil;' as well as those other words of the same apostle, 'Endure hardness, as a good soldier of Jesus Christ.'

Chapter 21

The Great Confession

We return to the judgment hall of the Sanhedrin at a moment when profound and gloomy silence reigns. But even this pause has its import. The Spirit of Truth does His office in the assembly. Shame and embarrassment take possession of every mind. The false witnesses have acted their part most wretchedly, and stand unmasked. Their contradictory evidence only tends to their own disgrace. The sublime bearing of the Accused, expressive only of innocence, completely paralyses His adversaries.

Every eye is now fixed on the presiding head of Israel. Every look seems to ask with amazement, 'What art thou about, thou priest of the Most High? Where is thy wisdom; what is become of thy dignity?' He, meanwhile, finds himself in the most painful situation in the world. Anxiety, both for the preservation of his official dignity, and for the result of the whole affair, torments his soul. There the proud hierarch sits, and his thoughts take tumultuous counsel how the difficulty may be overcome, and how he may escape from the pressure.

Such is the end of the judicial procedure against the Holy One of Israel. I ask, who has lost the cause? – Jesus or His judges? Be assured that the world's great process against Christ will eventually end in a similar manner. It will terminate in the utter confusion and despair of all who oppose Him.

Therefore let not His adversaries imagine that they have brought the case against Him to a close.

The perplexity of the high priest is great. How can he conceal his embarrassment? He must give the affair another turn. But of what kind? His ideas whirl round like a fiery wheel. All at once a thought occurs to him, which he deems fortunate. But it is not by mere accident that it presents itself to him. A greater than he overrules and controls the scene. The hierarch convulsively snatches up his falling dignity from the dust, and, with visible effort, while enveloping himself in the gravity of his office, he solemnly steps forward a few paces, and makes known his intention to cite the Accused before the throne of the Almighty, and to call upon Him to testify on oath, and under invocation of the name of the Most High God, who He is; whether He is really the person whom He is regarded as being and lets Himself be taken for by His followers, or whether He is a false prophet and a deceiver. We rejoice at this measure, though evidently more the result of desperation than of calm consideration. The affair will now be decided. Think of a testimony on oath by Jesus respecting Himself! There was nothing else wanting to satisfy our utmost wishes.

Now, give heed. The greatest and most solemn moment of the whole process has arrived. The high priest, re-assuming all his dignity, opens his mouth to utter the sublimest of all questions. 'I adjure thee,' says he, 'by the living God that thou tell us whether thou be the Christ, the Son of the Blessed.' He makes use of the legal form of adjuration which was customary in Israel. It was in this form that the oath was administered and taken. The person sworn answered without repeating the form itself, with a single 'Yes' or 'No;' being conscious at the same time, that the answer he gave, if it deviated from the truth, would be punished by the High and Lofty One, who had been invoked as a witness, with His righteous displeasure and the loss of eternal salvation. The high priest thus solemnly calls upon Jesus, as it were, for His credentials, while making the basis of the entire Christian religion the object of his inquiry, and in so doing, he is perfectly justified by his official position.

What is it, therefore, to which Jesus is to swear? Let us above all things be clear upon this point. He is, in the first place, to testify whether He is the Christ – that is, the Messiah. Caiaphas, the steward of the divine mysteries, indicates by that name the Object of prophecy, who, as Prophet, is to bring down the light of eternity to the earth; as High Priest, to give His own life as an atonement for the sins of the world; and as King, to establish an everlasting kingdom of grace and peace. This dignified Being is called the 'Lord's Anointed,' or 'Christ.' But Caiaphas knows that this 'Christ' will be a Man, and yet at the same time 'the Lord Most High:' such as David and Daniel saw in vision; and Micah, as one 'whose goings forth have been of old, from everlasting.' He knows that the Messiah will be the Son of God, in a manner such as no one else in heaven or on earth is entitled to be called. He will not only be like Jehovah, but Jehovah's equal, and thus really God. From this sublime point of view, Caiaphas asks, 'Art thou he?' and believes that in the event of Jesus affirming it, he would be perfectly justified in pronouncing Him a blasphemer, and as such, in condemning Him to death.

What greater or more momentous question was ever put than this? What would have been the consequences, had an answer in the negative ensued? What mercy would then have been the portion of the sinful race of man? Jesus might then have been whatever He pleased – the wisest philosopher, the chief of the prophets, the most perfect model of virtue – nay, an angel and seraph of the first rank – all would not have availed us, and hell would have been the termination of our pilgrimage.

If a negative had followed upon the high priest's question, it would have extinguished all our hopes; it would have fallen like a lighted torch into the citadel of our consolation; the whole edifice of our salvation would have been overthrown, and we should have been hurled into the open jaws of despair. For think of what is included in this one question. 'Art thou Christ, the Son of the Blessed?' In it Caiaphas inquires if the hour of our redemption has arrived; if there is a possibility of a sinner being saved; if an atoning power can be ascribed to the obedience of Jesus; and if the Suretyship of Christ can in reality be of any avail to transgressors. All these questions and many more are answered in the negative, if a simple negation had issued from the lips of Jesus to the interrogatory, 'Art thou the Son of God?' But if it be answered in the affirmative then they are affirmed to all eternity. And who is there that is not anxious for the reply? Well, then, give me your attention, and open your hearts to the truth.

The all-important question is propounded. Deep silence reigns in the assembly. Every heart beats audibly, and every eye is fixed on the Accused. Nor do our hearts remain unmoved. We also stand, trembling with expectation, before the high-priestly tribunal. We are aware of the astonishing miracles by which Jesus has magnified Himself. We were witnesses how He displayed His superhuman glory at the bier of the young man of Nain and at the grave of Lazarus. We have seen Him in the endangered vessel, when the rage of the elements ceased at His beck, and on the stormy lake, where the wild waves became firm beneath His feet, and spread a crystal carpet for the King of nature.

But all these might have been the acts of a prophet sent from God, and the marvellous performances of a human possessor of divine power. Such a person, however, could not have coped with our misery. We heard Him say, 'He that hath seen me, hath seen the Father also,' for 'I and the Father are one,' and 'before Abraham was, I am,' with other expressions of a similar kind. But still, with reference to these expressions, the tempter might suggest to us that they must not be apprehended literally, but are only to be understood of the moral glory of Jesus.

And thus an assertion was still requisite, which should put to shame all the arts of infernal perverters of language; a testimony was still desirable concerning the person of Jesus, the undoubted nature of which would be able to annihilate all the objections of skepticism; and how could this be done in a more satisfactory manner than by a solemn declaration on oath? It is this which is about to take place. Jesus is asked if He is the true God and eternal life? – for this is all comprised in the appellation, 'Christ, the Son of the Blessed,' in the mouth of a believing Israelite. He therefore that hath ears, let him hear what the Person at the bar of Caiaphas testifies of Himself, before the face of the Almighty, the Man in whose mouth, even according to the confession of His murderers, was found no guile.

There He stands in the presence of the council of the nation, to all appearance 'a worm and no man.' Greatness and dignity appear to rest only on those who surround Him. In Himself you perceive nothing but lowliness and poverty. There He stands, with His head bowed down, His hands bound, and surrounded by armed men like a robber. He stands there, ready to sink with weariness from the sufferings He has already endured, forsaken of His friends, inveighed against by His enemies, apparently the offscouring of the earth, and incomparably wretched. To this deeply abased and sorely stricken Man, the question is solemnly put by the first and principal person in the nation, whether He will swear by the living God that He is the Son of the Blessed?

He is therefore now constrained to lay aside all disguise; and for our sakes He gladly lifts the veil. As long as the investigation was confined to wretched accusations, Jesus was silent; but after the affair had taken such a different and much more serious turn, it was requisite to bear testimony to the truth, and declare Himself definitely with regard to His Person. He knows that His answer will cause His death, but He dares no longer refrain.

He is constrained to speak by the reverence which fills His heart for the sacred Name by which He is adjured. He is constrained to it by the submission which He owes to the dignity of him who calls upon Him to answer on oath. He is constrained to it by His love and holy zeal for the truth, and especially by His tender solicitude for us, poor sinners, on whose behalf He appears at the bar of judgment. It is not the Sanhedrin alone, before which He feels Himself placed; He sees, in spirit, His whole Church assembled around Him; He sees a whole world in breathless excitement, and all the kindreds of the earth, grouped around Him, full of expectation. The ear of His whole Church to the end of time hangs upon His lips; and He knows that the moment has arrived when He must place a firm and immutable support beneath its faith, for thousands of years to come. He therefore opens His mouth, and testifies before the throne of the living God, with clear consciousness, considerately, formally, and solemnly, 'Thou hast said it. I am.'

Here you have the great confession. What an affirmation is this! It lifts us up above all doubt and apprehension. It places our faith on an everlasting foundation. It establishes and seals our entire redemption, and is the grave of every scruple. But that no shadow of obscurity might rest on the real meaning of His testimony, He makes an addition to His affirmation. He unveils the future, and says, 'Hereafter shall ye see the Son of man sitting on the right hand of power, and coming in the clouds of heaven.'

It was impossible that it could be more clearly testified who Jesus was than was now done. If His testimony is true, it is then also true that all are lost who will not believe on Him, and that nothing remains for those who refuse to bend the knee to Him, but 'a fearful looking for of judgment and of fiery indignation, which shall devour the adversaries'. It is true that whoever is not born of water and of the Spirit, can not enter into the kingdom of God, and that he that believeth not the Son shall not see life, but the wrath of God abideth on him. For this likewise is testified by Him, who answered, 'I am,' before the council; and if the latter be true, so is also the former. Hasten, therefore, to commit yourselves to the hands of Him, beside whom there is none to help you, either in heaven or on earth; nor be such enemies to yourselves as to choose death and the curse, now that life and immortality are brought to light, and offered to you freely in the Gospel. In reliance on the sacred oath of the Saviour, turn your backs upon the world, and cast yourselves into the arms and upon the heart of the only Mediator.

'I am!' – answered Jesus; and if He had not been, at the same time, the sacrificial Lamb destined to suffer for the human race, millions of voices would have sealed His testimony with their 'Amen!' The seraphim with their golden harps would have hovered over Him and have exclaimed, 'Jesus, thou art He!' From the foundations of the earth, which were laid by Him, would have resounded the same testimony; and the Eternal Father, with that voice which causes the mountains to tremble, would have called down from heaven, 'This is my beloved Son, in whom I am well pleased.' But silence reigns above, below, and around Him. The Priest of God is in the sanctuary, engaged in offering up His sacrifice. There all is silent. His enemies are permitted only to rage.

When Caiaphas hears the unequivocal confession, in order to manifest his hypocritical indignation at this supposed piece of impiety, he rends his clothes, by which act he uncon-sciously intimates symbolically the approaching dissolution of the typical priesthood, now that in the person of Christ, the true Priest had appeared. In a few hours the temple will close; the offering up of lambs and of goats will have reached its termination in the sight of God. The Lord of heaven and earth will then retire forever from the Holy of Holies, made with hands, in order in future to take up His abode in those who are of a humble and contrite heart.

The high priest rends his clothes and says, 'What further need have we of witnesses?' The man is in the right. Had Jesus unwarrantably presumed to declare Himself to be the Son of God and the judge of the world, He could not have been guilty of a more heinous blasphemy than by so doing. But why, ye judges of Israel, must that necessarily be false which He had just testified of Himself? Why should it be utterly inconceivable that He was the promised Lord from heaven? Was there any thing in His life to contradict the assertion? In spite of all your efforts, what did you find that was disreputable in it? You can accuse Him of nothing, except that, in the declaration just made, He had unduly exalted Himself – which you must first prove – and in an unauthorized manner had appropriated divine honour to Himself. You were compelled to confess that He came forth from your examination pure as the light of heaven.

And tell me is the testimony to His Sonship which He has just given, wholly isolated and unsupported? On the contrary is not His entire manifestation on earth a confirmation of it? Was it not established by voices from on high? Did not numbers of unheard-of signs and wonders surround it, like so many proofs of its truth? And has it not, as powerful witnesses in its favour, the whole choir of prophetic announcements which were most literally fulfilled in Him?

Such are the questions we might put to you, ye judges of Jerusalem. But you would not that this Man should reign over you; and, therefore, you refused to acknowledge Him as that which He declared Himself on oath to be. Woe unto you, ye models of all judicial injustice! What will become of you when the day draws nigh in which you will be brought up for judgment, and when every thing shall be brought to light that was hidden in obscurity!

'What think ye?' asks the high priest. The whole assembly, then, as with one voice, taking the word from his lips, exclaim aloud, 'He is guilty of death.' Just so, as standing in our room and stead, it is really the case. Other and more exalted voices than those of the council mingle in the verdict. But what kind of death is it of which He is declared to be guilty? The death to which Jesus was condemned, He endured as the Representative of our guilty race. By His death He took from ours its sting, which is sin. All fear of death in the children of God is henceforth needless and groundless; and His saying remains forever true, that 'Whosoever believeth on him shall never see death.'

We close our present meditation. You see the alternative which is placed before you – either forever to break with Jesus, and approve of the bloodthirsty sentence of the Sanhedrin, or to cry 'Hosanna' to the lowly Nazarene, and fall in humble adoration at His feet, as God manifest in the flesh. There is here no middle path. How, therefore, do you decide? Even sound reason advises you to take part with us. In Jesus' affirmation on oath before the high priest, behold the immutable Rock which bears and sustains our belief in Him! Build the house of your hopes for eternity thereon, and you shall never be confounded; for the mouth of the Lord hath spoken it!

Chapter 22

Peter's Tears

Our present meditation will console us for the grief we experienced when considering the depth of Peter's fall. We here witness the shedding of tears, which, next to those that flowed from our Lord Himself at the grave of Lazarus, over ungodly Jerusalem, and in Gethsemane, may be regarded as the most remarkable that were ever shed upon earth. They have dropped, like soothing balm, into many a wounded heart. May they not fail to produce a blessed effect on many others!

We again meet with Peter at the moment when, completing his denial of Jesus, he formally abjures his discipleship with heavy curses. Observe, this is done by the very individual from whose lips the great confession had previously proceeded, 'We have known and believed that thou art the Christ, the Son of the living God;' and the ardent and sincere declaration, 'Though all men should forsake thee, yet will not I.' But what are even the best of men when left for a moment to themselves? And what would become of the most faithful of Christ's followers, if the Lord were only for a short time to remove the restraints of His grace? Oh, the folly of trusting to the finest feelings, seeing that we are not sure of them for a single second!

Peter has first to learn, in the school of experience, like us all, that we presume too much if we rely upon ourselves, even in the most trifling temptation. The love of Christ constrains us to venture every thing for Him; but it is only the belief in Christ's love for us, and the trusting to His gracious power and strength, that enables us to overcome. He who trembles at himself, as being capable of denying his Master, will gain greater victories than he who deems himself sufficiently strong to be able to say, 'Though all men forsake thee, yet will not I.' 'Thou standest by faith,' writes Paul in Romans. 'Be not high-minded, but fear.' 'Therefore,' says the same apostle, 'I will rather glory in my infirmities, that the power of Christ may rest upon me.'

Peter is vanquished. Hell triumphs. Nevertheless, hell begins to cry 'victory' too soon. Listen to what is passing in the judgment hall of the palace. The appalling sentence has just been uttered in the midst of a tumultuous uproar. 'What further need have we of witnesses! He has blasphemed God, and is guilty of death.' 'Who?' we ask, astonished. 'Simon Peter?' No, another – a Holy One; even He who once exclaimed, 'I lay down my life for the sheep.' He is now ready to do so, and Peter belongs also to His flock from whom the curse is transferred to Him, the Surety, and with respect to whom the words are henceforth applicable, 'They shall never perish, neither shall any man pluck them out of my hand.' Yet a little while, and there is One who will be able to give such a turn to the whole affair that it must tend rather to the advancement than the injury of the Gospel.

Just as Peter has filled up the measure of his sin by a formal repudiation of his Master, the cock crows. What is the result? A return to sober-mindedness, repentance, and tears. God only knows with what clamour Satan deafened the disciple's ears so that the first cry of the feathered watchman did not penetrate into them.

An awakener of some kind or other is appointed to every one. Wherever we may be, there are voices which call us to repentance. Nature, as well as our whole life, is full of them, only our ears are heavy and will not hear. There is an awakening call in the rolling thunder, which is a herald of infinite majesty – in the lightning, which darts down before thee, carrying with it destruction – in the stars, which look down upon thee – in the flower of the field, which, in its transient blooming and fading, depicts thy own brief existence upon earth.

Nay, where are we not surrounded by awakening voices? They sit upon the tombstones of our church-yards, and their language is, 'It is appointed unto men once to die, and after that the judgment.' Their warning voice resounds from every funeral car that rolls past thee. It may be heard on every birthday which thou celebratest; in every fit of illness by which thou art attacked; in every danger that threatens thy life; as well as in that secret uneasiness which incessantly steals through thy soul.

And besides these general calls to repentance, do we not find something similar in every family circle and in each individual? One misfortune after another has lately crossed thy threshold. Oh, how many alarming voices have been contained in these strokes of the Almighty's rod! You feel your strength decaying, and that the sun of your life is declining. Do you not hear in this fact the crowing of the cock? On every side we may be conscious of it – in visions of the night, in the events of the day, in serious thoughts, which we are unable to prevent, in sermons and admonitions which are addressed to us.

The cock in the court-yard of the high priest crows a second time, and this call enters and finds a response. Day begins to dawn upon Peter, awakened by the remembrance of his Master's warning, and while reflecting on the abyss into which he has plunged himself.

Let us, however, return for a few moments, to see what occurred in the council hall just before this second warning.

Something of importance has just taken place. The Accused
has declared upon oath that He is the Son of the living God.
The high priest, in dissembled indignation, rends his clothes.
Amid wild uproar sentence of death is pronounced upon the
Holy One of Israel, and the minions of justice seize Him to
lead Him away into the court-yard, and there vent upon Him
their unlicensed fury. The divine Sufferer has just passed
through the doorway into the court-yard when the crowing
of the cock reaches His ear. 'And the Lord turned himself;'
we know toward whom. That sound announced to Him His
disciple's fall, and His eye and His compassionate heart go in
search of him. Such is Jesus the Saviour. He embraces His
followers with more than maternal tenderness, and their want
of fidelity does not prevent His being faithful. What waves
of sorrow beat over His head, and yet He can forget every
thing in His anxiety for His fallen disciple! Sooner than one
of them should be forgotten, He would forget the government
of the world; and would suffer the nations to take their
course, rather than lose sight of one of His little ones. And
happy are ye who are the weak of the flock, the poor and
needy above others! It would seem that you lie the nearest
to His heart.

Deeply was Peter immersed in the mire of sin, yet the Lord
turned toward him. Who among us would have troubled
himself further about such a faithless deserter from the ranks?
If such characters were referred to us, it would go ill with
them. How ready we are to stamp and reject such stumbling
brethren as hyprocrites! Instead of moving a finger to restore
them, we not infrequently plunge them deeper into the mire,
and persecute them worse than the world does.

The Lord, on the contrary, whose right alone it is to judge
in such cases, is not ashamed to deign to act the part of the
woman in the Gospel, who having lost one of her pieces of
silver, strikes a light, seizes the broom, and ceases not to stir

up the dust till it is discovered; and when found, she calls her neighbours together, and says, 'Rejoice with me, for I have found the piece of silver which I had lost.'

His children are dearer to Him than the brethren often are to us. Tell me, you that are parents, do your erring sons and disobedient daughters cease to be your children because of their aberrations? Do you not rather still more deeply feel that they are bone of your bone, and flesh of your flesh? Does not your love to them increase with the danger to which you see them exposed? And are you not more fully conscious, when compelled to weep over them, that your life is bound up with theirs, than when they merely caused you joy? If ye then, being evil, can not reject your own seed, how should He be able to forget those who are of His flesh and blood, who said, 'As my Father loveth me, so have I loved you;' and by the mouth of His prophet, 'Can a woman forget her sucking child that she should not have compassion on the son of her womb? Yea, she may forget, yet will I not forget thee. Lo, I have graven thee on the palms of my hands.'

Peter, though fallen, still belonged to Him. Though he had acted wickedly, yet his Master's love for him remains unchanged. See how carefully He looks round after him! Certainly, had it not been the Lord's will that we should believe that the covenant of grace, on His side, stood inviolably fast, He would have hesitated to have set before us such examples as those of David and Peter. 'And Jesus turned and looked upon him.' Yes, 'though we believe not, yet he abideth faithful; he can not deny himself;' for 'the foundation of God standeth sure; having this seal, the Lord knoweth them that are his.'

The Lord turned Himself. The conversion of every sinner begins with that for which David prays, 'Look upon me!' By nature we are like dry bones in a huge church-yard, and can not come to Him. But as soon as the Lord begins to look upon us, we enter into closer connection with Him, and feel that He is near us. We are conscious of being deeply and wondrously affected by things, which, otherwise, we scarcely noticed. The idea occurs to us, in a variety of circumstances, that God intends by them to call us to repentance, and we are often inclined to say with Jacob, 'Surely the Lord was in this place.' The Almighty is then no longer distant from us on some far-off height, but pervades our chamber, and meets us in the daily occurrences of life. Not a day passes without something happening which compels us to say, 'It is the Lord!' Yet this state of things may continue long without our attaining to real conversion of heart. But when the faithful Shepherd begins to follow after us, He does not leave us without accomplishing His purpose.

It was not simply the crowing of the cock that raised the disciple from his fall. Nor did the turning of the Lord toward him produce the desired effect. A third and more powerful means was added. What was it? A word, a call, an exhortation? No; a look which the eye of the Keeper of Israel cast upon His disciple, who was staggering on the brink of destruction. This look did wonders. 'The Lord turned, and looked upon Peter.' What a look must that have been! What divine sorrow and love must it have expressed! and how accompanied by the effulgence of the Spirit and the radiance of divine grace! It acted both as a sword to wound, and as a balm to heal. It struck like destroying lightning, and at the same time expanded itself like refreshing dew.

Oh, there is inexpressible power in the look of the Lord! With a look of majesty He beholds the earth, and it trembles. With a judicial look He overtakes the sinner, who exclaims, 'I perish at His presence.' His dying look on the cross melts stony hearts, and transforms lions into lambs. With a look of forgiving mercy, He makes a contrite soul forget heaven and earth in its happiness; and by means of a grieved and loving look, He restores lambs to His fold, which had long gone astray in the wilderness. To this day His people feel that His eyes are upon them, and according to what they read in them, their peace or joy rises or falls.

The Lord's look does not fail of its effect upon Peter. No sooner do the disciple's eyes meet His, than the magic band which held him is dissolved, the infernal intoxication dispelled, his ear opened, and reflection returns – nay, sin is acknowledged – his heart is melted – the snare is broken, and the bird has escaped. 'Gracious God,' is now his language, 'how deeply have I fallen! Wretch that I am, was not all this foretold me? Said He not on the way, 'Before the cock crows twice, thou shalt deny me thrice?' Woe is me, that in foolish presumption I repelled the warning, and only remember it now, when it is too late! I vowed to go with Him to prison and to death; and yet I am the first to deny and abjure Him! How is it that the earth still bears me, and that heaven's lightnings do not blast me! Instead of which, He who so kindly forewarned me, and whom I nevertheless abjured and ignored, deigns me still a look of pity and compassion!'

Such may have been the language of Peter's soul, when, as the narrative informs us, 'he remembered the word of the Lord, which he had spoken to him.' He would have infallibly become a prey to despair, had not the Saviour's loving-kindness made every arrangement for preventing Satan from sifting the poor disciple too severely. His Master's prayer, that his faith might not fail, had surrounded the abyss, as it were, with a balustrade, and by His injunction, that after his conversion, he should strengthen his brethren, had made preparation for wiping away his tears long before they fell. O how did the soothing influence of all the words which the gracious Friend of sinners had spoken to him, shed itself upon his heart, when to them was added that look so full of mercy and compassion!

Peter, by the look of his Master, is wholly dissolved in grief and humiliation. As if he were unworthy to appear before God or man, he begins to 'weep bitterly.' O how much is reflected in these tears! What thorough contrition before God, what holy indignation against sin, what an ardent thirst for grace, and what fullness of fervent love to the Lord beam forth from their pure light! 'Cast me not away from thy presence! Whom have I in heaven but thee?' are the aspirations which issue from his heart. All his desire and longing centre in this, that he may again rejoice in the favour of the Lord. Though he were to become an outcast from the world all the days of his life, yet he would gladly submit, if he might only again hope for mercy. His tears announce the birth of a new man. The old, presumptuous, self-seeking, self-trusting Adam is dead, and a man of humility, filial resignation to God, and sincere desire that the name of the Lord may alone be glorified, rises, phoenix-like, from his ashes.

It is said that a tear glistened in Peter's eye as long as he lived. If this is any thing but a legend, it was not a tear of sorrow only, but of joy at the mercy experienced. The remembrance of his fall never left him for a moment; and in the degree in which it kept him low, it sharpened his spiritual vision for the mystery of the cross and of salvation by grace. This is abundantly evident, especially in his first epistle. He there comforts believers with the cheering assurance that they are 'kept by the power of God through faith unto salvation.' He calls upon them to 'hope to the end for the grace that shall be revealed.' He impressively reminds them of the weakness and evanescent nature of every thing human, while calling to their recollection the words of the prophet: 'All flesh is grass, and all the glory of man as the flower of grass. The grass withereth, and the flower thereof falleth away.' He speaks of 'the precious blood of Christ as of a Lamb without spot,' with a fervour which immediately indicates him as one who had deeply experienced its healing power. It is he who addresses the warning to us, 'Be sober, be vigilant; for your adversary the devil goeth about as a roaring lion, seeking whom he may devour.' And when he quotes the psalm in which it is said, 'The eyes of the Lord are upon the righteous; and his ears are open to their cry; but the face of the Lord is against them that do evil' – does it not seem as if he intentionally referred to that look from his Master which had once so overwhelmed him and cast him to the ground?

O how much of the guilt of denying Christ, either in a gross or subtle manner, rests upon us all! How much reason have we to be alarmed at the words, 'He that denieth me, him will I also deny before my Father in heaven.' Let us therefore cover our heads with our mantles, and with Peter, go out and weep bitterly; that a day of grace may also dawn upon us, and that the words of the apostle may be also applicable to us, 'Such were some of you, but ye are washed, ye are sanctified, ye are justified in the name of the Lord Jesus, and by the Spirit of our God.'

Chapter 23

'Prophesy unto Us, Thou Christ!'

The sentence is passed upon Jesus. Its import is nothing less than death to the Accused. The judicial assembly, after its first sitting, which began during the night, has been adjourned for a short time, amid wild and triumphant uproar. Meanwhile the divine Sufferer is given up to the reckless band of officers and spearmen, who shamefully ill-treat Him, and they do so the more boldly, because it is done with the assent of their superiors.

Jesus is now in their power, and He must dearly pay the penalty of His conduct. 'But why must He suffer? What has He ever done to offend them?' O how much, notwithstanding His best intentions! Did He not, in His own sacred Person hold up to them a mirror, which presented to them the dark image of their own ungodliness? – and such treatment did not please them. Was not an evident proof afforded, by His brilliant example, that they were going the wrong road? – and convictions of this kind cut them to the heart. By His calling upon them to be reconciled unto God, had He not plainly told them to their face that they had hitherto lived estranged from God? Did He not repeatedly tell them that a new birth was an indispensable condition attached to the

entering into the kingdom of heaven? – and what else were
they to understand from this than that in their present state
they were in danger of perishing? – but who likes to hear of
such things?

It was thus that a mass of rage and vexation had by degrees
accumulated within them. A horrible state, it is true, but one
which only testifies for Jesus. Believe me, the adversaries of
the Lord and His Word among us are, for the most part, like
a wounded stag flying from the hunters. They feel that the
teachings of Christ destroy their false peace, condemn their
carnality, and demand the sacrifice of their idols; and hence
they are averse to and incensed against Him even to blasphemy. They joyfully greet every attempt which tends to
degrade Jesus to a mere human Rabbi; for all their efforts are
directed solely to escape from the obligations they lie under
to Him. Almost in every case where enmity against Christ is
manifested, it may be traced to these corrupt motives. The
Christian religion disturbs and awakens the conscience;
hence their hatred and animosity to it.

Before we approach the revolting scene in the courtyard
of the high priest's palace, let us again call to mind who it is
we have before us in the individual thus ill-treated. We are
about to witness unheard-of outrages, at which the rocks
might rend with horror. If the Person to whom our eyes are
directed had been only an earthly dignitary, even then the
contrast of his dreadful fate with his exalted position would
greatly horrify us, and we should be unable to refrain from
calling out, 'You go too far; cease your ill-treatment; men
whom the Lord places in such high positions ought not to be
treated in so disgraceful a manner!'

But here, as you know, is a greater than any human poten-
tate. It is upon the King of kings and Lord of lords, in whom
dwelleth all the fullness of the Godhead bodily, that the
recreants trample with their dirty feet. It is in the face of

Eternal Love that they spit. It is the Source of Life whom they smite with their fists, and it is He whom the heavens adore that they insult with their venomous tongues, which are set on fire of hell. Yes, it was upon Him that all this was inflicted, who had just before affirmed on oath, in the full consciousness of His divine dignity, that He was the Christ, the Son of the living God and who had afterward added, 'I say unto you that hereafter ye shall see the Son of Man sitting on the right hand of power, and coming in the clouds of heaven.'

It is, therefore, a monstrous spectacle which is presented to our view. The world never afterward beheld any thing similar. Every one must be conscious that Christ freely and voluntarily gave Himself up to the horrible treatment He experienced; and the idea of One who was overcome and yielded to superior power, must be wholly excluded. He who was thus covered with insult was neither weaker nor less powerful than at the moment when, with a single word, He overthrew the whole company of His adversaries. Though He may seem to be nothing but a broken reed and a worm trodden under foot, yet the sword of Omnipotence is not the less girded upon Him, nor the bow of His strength broken. What but a single word from Him was requisite, and the murderous band would have lain annihilated at His feet? But He did not make use of His power. He suffered voluntarily. It is with His own consent that He is plunged into these depths of horror. Imagine, therefore, the magnitude of the purposes which lie at the basis of this resignation of the Holy One of Israel. The sufferings of Jesus as such, compel us to admit their atoning signification.

Let us come nearer to the scene. The Holy One appears in this sinful world. Scarcely does He show Himself than mankind act toward Him as if they were hyaenas and devils. To such a degree is heavenly purity become odious to them, and that which is divinely reverent, abominable! Alas! what is done to Thee, Thou who art fairer than the children of men! How is Thy benignant countenance disfigured! One would gladly close one's eyes to such a spectacle. Hast Thou merited this at our hands, O Eternal Love? Is this the due reward for Thy loving-kindness? And yet, however much Thou art insulted, Thou will not forsake us, till Thou has rescued us from the curse, even though it should cost Thee Thy life. O what is left for us but to sink down in the dust, to cover our faces, and to melt into glowing tears of penitence and thankfulness!

Look what occurs! When sentence is pronounced upon a malefactor, and the judicial decision is read, a solemn silence usually pervades the auditory, and a feeling of solemnity takes possession of them. Every one feels the majesty of the law, which, whenever transgressed, justly demands satisfaction. In the condemnation of Jesus, however, no feelings of this nature appear to have been excited in the reprobate host of His adversaries. Scarcely has the word 'Guilty' been uttered, when they fall upon Him; and, O, what revolting scenes are now unfolded to our view! Alas! what will become of our Lord and Master!

They have now got Him among them, and they load Him, first of all, with the vilest execrations and insults. But they are not satisfied with thus heaping obloquy upon Him. They smite Him with their hands. But even this does not satisfy their thirst for revenge. He must feel more painfully still how utterly He is despised. They open their mouths against Him, and, horrible to relate! they spit upon His sacred face. Nor is their rage yet cooled, nor their satanic inventions exhausted. The reprobates seek for some new outrage, and it soon occurs to them. They have heard how the object of their ill-usage had just before solemnly asserted in the council-chamber, that He was Christ, the Son of the living God, and for this

He must now be especially punished. The arrows of their bitterest ridicule are therefore directed against His Messiah-ship, and particularly against His prophetical office. They bind the eyes of the patient Sufferer with a cloth, then smite Him with their fists, and exclaim, amid peals of sneering laughter, 'Prophesy to us, thou Christ, who it is that smiteth thee!'

But I will let the curtain drop. Who can longer contemplate such a scene? It is too appalling! What infernal wickedness meets our view! And from whence does it proceed? From the human heart. But how could a race that is capable of such things be received into the favour of God, without an atonement and a Mediator? What would have become of the glory of His justice and holiness, if He had suffered such degenerate beings to be spared without a Satisfaction? Nor ought you to regard the perpetrators of the outrages we have been describing, as depraved above all others. According to its inmost being, every natural human heart is alike. Even those who refuse to hear of redemption and atonement, do not fail, unconsciously and involuntarily, to condemn human nature, every moment, in the most grievous manner. Hear their language, 'Friendship lasts only during prosperity.' 'Every man has his price.' 'In the misfortunes of our best friends we find something that does not displease us.' Such are the expressions which are constantly flowing from the lips of the men of the world. How completely do they thereby pro-nounce the human heart to be depraved and corrupt!

But to return to the question – 'Prophesy unto us, thou Christ, who it was that smote thee?' From the lips by which these words were uttered, they were only blasphemous ridicule and a burst of depravity. But in themselves, and apart from the feeling which accompanied them, they appear in the form of a question of the first importance; and he that has found the right answer to it, is acquainted with the groundwork of our salvation and entire redemption.

Many have impiously repeated the inquiry of the reprobate troop, and have thought within themselves, 'How does
He know whether we honour Him, or trample upon Him?
Where is He to be found? Eighteen centuries ago, He went
the way of all flesh, and the dead rest in their graves.' By
acting thus, they have, as far as they are concerned, again
bound His eyes, and sneeringly said to Him, 'Prophesy, if
thou art still alive, and hearest, and seest, who it is that
smote thee!' And how many of those who now say, 'Who is
Jesus, that I should be afraid of Him, or even humble myself
before Him?' when once He replies to them, will call upon
the rocks to fall upon them, and the hills to cover them,
that they may be hidden from the face of Him that sitteth
upon the throne, and from the wrath of the Lamb! O let
no one suppose that the judge of the world will suffer
Himself to be mocked with impunity. Rather let them 'kiss
the Son, lest he be angry, and they perish from the way,
when his wrath is kindled but a little.'

'Prophesy to us, thou Christ, who it is that smote thee!'
The mockers received no reply to this question. Jesus was
silent. But we may give a different turn to the inquiry, and
the answer will prove consolatory. Let those who are earnestly
seeking salvation, and the contrite in heart, humbly inquire,
'Who it was that smote the Lord?' and they will receive a
satisfactory reply. At first, indeed, it will alarm them; for it
will be, 'not those miscreants; but it is thou who hast made
Me to suffer with thy sins, and wearied Me with thy iniquities.
For thy transgressions was I smitten.' And when He Himself
prophesies this to you by His Spirit – how evident it will then
become to you; how will you humble yourselves in the dust
before Him; how the wish will then depart to lay the blame
upon Caiaphas, Annas, and the spearmen; how vitally are
you persuaded that they were only your representatives, and
how will you hang down your heads, and learn to smite upon

your breasts with the publican! How will you tremble for your souls, and earnestly seek for salvation and a Mediator!

But know that this is only half the answer to your question. Continue to ask, and it will not be long before a gracious message will be delivered you. This will be its import: 'The hand that smote Me would have crushed you. The curse fell upon Me which was destined for you. I drank the cup of wrath which your sins had filled. I drank it, that it might be replenished for you with everlasting mercy.' And when this conviction pervades you, do not doubt that it is really from Him. 'God made him to be sin for us;' 'Christ hath redeemed us from the curse of the law, having been made a curse for us.'

You now know who it is that smote the Saviour, and that it was the sin of each of us. Does not this clearly appear from the circumstances of our Lord's passion themselves? Does it not seem strange to you that Jesus acted so patiently, meekly, and resignedly under such barbarous treatment? Is it not wonderful that His tormentors were suffered to go unpunished? Korah and his company had no sooner rebelliously attacked Aaron's priestly dignity, than the Lord rent the ground beneath their feet, and sent them down quick into the pit. Uzzah was guilty of a seemingly slight irreverence toward the ark, and the anger of the Lord was kindled against him, and smote him, so that he fell dead on the ground. But how much more is there here than the ark and Aaron the priest! Here they trample the Son of God in the mire, and the judge of quick and dead is mute. Rightly understood, it is God Himself who smites the Sufferer, on whom the chastisement of our peace was laid; and what He endures are the strokes of that sword, to which Jehovah said, 'Awake, against my Shepherd and the man that is my fellow.' They fall upon Him, that we sinners might be forever exonerated.

Such is the solution of this great mystery, and the complete answer to the question, 'Who smote thee, thou Christ?' No sooner does the light of a Propitiation shine upon the obscurity of the events of the passion than all is cleared up, and the deepest mysteries are unsealed.

Chapter 24

Christic before the Sanhedrin

The morning breaks, and announces the dawn of the most important and momentous of all earthly days. It is Good Friday, that most dreadful accuser of the sinful world, but at the same time, the birthday of its salvation and the dawn of its eternal redemption. It is the day typified by the deliverance of the chosen race out of Egypt, and annually announced to the believing Israelites for upward of a thousand years in the great day of atonement, which was the chief object of their hopes and desires. All the radiations of grace which had ever beamed upon them were only preliminary emanations of this day, which still slept in the lap of a far distant future; and whenever God favourably regarded a sinner, it was solely on the ground of the propitiation by the blood of Christ, which was actually made upon this day.

Notwithstanding the very early hour, the members of the council at Jerusalem are up and in full activity. They are preparing a second examination of Jesus, 'that they might put him to death.' But have they not already established His guilt, and pronounced sentence against Him? Certainly they have. But yet they are not satisfied, and would gladly find out other and more decisive proofs against Him, than those on which their judgment was founded.

They now meet in their hall of session, which was in one of the buildings of the Temple, in the character of a regular plenary assembly, because their first meeting in the high priest's palace – apart from the absence of several of its members – bore the aspect of being accidental and tumultuous. The council or Sanhedrin, was the supreme court of judicature of the later Jews, and consisted of seventy-one members, including the chief priests, elders, and doctors of the law, or scribes, under the presidency of the high priest, which, formed on the model of the seventy elders whom Moses joined with him for the administration of justice during the journey of the Israelites through the wilderness, had to judge and decide in all national Jewish, and particularly in ecclesiastical affairs.

Christ, according to Matthew 23:2, regarded this authority as being divinely sanctioned, and submitted without objection to its citation. Before this tribunal Peter subsequently stood as a pretended wonder-worker, and again in company with John, as a deceiver of the people; further, Stephen, as a blasphemer, and Paul, accused of being a false prophet.

We now see our Lord brought a second time before this court. He is conducted up the hill on which the Temple stands by an armed escort. It is His last passage along that road, and by a remarkable coincidence, it occurs at the same time with the paschal lambs, which are on that day brought to the priests for sacrifice. What may have been His feelings on this occasion! He certainly thought of the typical journey of Abraham to Mount Moriah, which was now so visibly fulfilled in Him. For Christ, as the antitype of Isaac, is now proceeding to the altar of God upon the same path which once His human type, led by his father, had trodden for the

same purpose. Christ, indeed, does not say like Abraham's
son, 'My father, behold the fire and the wood, but where is
the lamb for a burnt-offering?' He knows who the Lamb is
whom God has provided, and willingly bows to the divine
decree. He has to recognize His type not only in Isaac, but
also in the ram whose horns were caught in the thicket, and
which Abraham, at Jehovah's command, took, in order to
slay it in the place of his son.

The sitting of the Sanhedrin commences. The accused
stands at the bar. He is again asked by the judge, 'Art thou
the Christ? tell us!' as if He had not already plainly told them
that He was. But it would seem as if they hesitated to deliver
Him up to death, as a deceiver and a blasphemer, on this
account, without any thing further – nay, as if they involuntarily sought to prolong the affair, because a slight echo of
the voice of conscience told them – not, indeed, that He
really was what He gave Himself out to be – but that it
possibly might be the case. The Lord opens His mouth; and
now mark how the tables are turned, and the accused
becomes judge, and His judges the delinquents. 'If I tell you,'
says He, 'ye will not believe; and if I also ask you (that is, if I
were to attempt to convince you by proofs), ye will not answer
me, nor let me go.'

Oh, how many there are in the present day, to whom these
words are applicable! I do not now refer to people who are
entirely indifferent to religion. I mean such as are continually
inquiring who Christ is, and would seem to have no rest until
they were convinced. But although He is brought before
them, first in one form and then in another, still they do not
believe.

The Church tells them, but they say, 'The Church may
err. What do the contemporaries of Jesus say?' The apostles
tell them, as with one voice, 'He is the Word that was with
God from the beginning, and was God; the brightness of the

Father's glory, in whom dwelt all the fullness of the Godhead bodily.' But to this they reply, 'Love is blind, and enthusiasm is visionary.' They will only receive what Jesus says of Himself. And Jesus comes forward and announces Himself, not only as the light of the world, the truth and the life, but as greater than all this – as one with the Father, as being before Abraham, and to whom all power in heaven and earth is given. Do they now believe? They start; but before we are aware, they again slip out by means of a variety of questions, such as, 'Did the historians rightly understand Jesus? Are His expressions to be taken literally? Is it possible for Deity to become incarnate?'

They will not believe. This is the solution of the problem. They are horrified at the thought of being obliged to crucify the idols of their own wisdom and righteousness, as well as the honours and pleasures of the world for the sake of Christ. They see an abyss open between them and the Lord, which threatens to swallow up nothing less than their entire glory and self-sufficiency, and they start back from such a death. They are still too conscientious to part with Him decidedly, like the Gadarenes, and to say, 'What have we to do with thee?' but not conscientious enough to give admission to the truth. They rather let the matter rest and come to no decision.

The Lord renews His declaration. The constituted authorities demand it, and He obeys. Besides, it is of importance to Him that the world should know, with certainty, who He was, and whom they crucified. From the summit of the eminence on which the Temple stood, He surveys in spirit the human race and the ages to come. He once more raises the veil from His humble guise, and baring the regal star upon His breast, He says, 'Hereafter shall the Son of man sit on the right hand of the power of God.' A sublime expression, evidently having reference to the remarkable passage in

Daniel 7:13: 'One like the Son of man came with the clouds of heaven.'

The priests and scribes could not for a moment doubt that by this He declared Himself to be the Messiah promised by the inspired seer, and thus claim divine nature and essentiality. His prediction concerning His approaching sitting at the right hand of power, or of the Divine Majesty, is nothing less than a decided declaration that He would divide the throne of glory with His heavenly Father, and with Him rule the world in equal perfection of power. The Sanhedrin, conversant with the language of the prophets, understood the words in this sense. 'Art thou then the Son of God?' cried they all, as with one voice. 'Ye say that which I am,' replied He, with majestic firmness and composure.

The Lord has repeated His great confession. The whole assembly rise in indignation and astonishment. One exclaims louder than the other, 'What need we any further witness; for we ourselves have heard it from his own lips?' True, they have heard it from His own mouth. This their confession has been recorded in heaven and will, without fail, be brought against them at the day of judgment. Wherewith, then, will they justify their refusing to pay homage to the Lord, seeing that in reality they needed no further witness? On account of this testimony they condemned Jesus to death, and by so doing, for the confirmation of our faith, only established the fact of the testimony having proceeded from His own lips.

After sentence of death on the divine sufferer has thus been confirmed, the officers approach, in order again to put on His fetters, which had been for the time removed. He willingly offers His hand, that the words of Isaiah might be fulfilled, 'He was oppressed, and he was afflicted, yet he opened not his mouth. He is brought as a lamb to the slaughter, and as a sheep before her shearers is dumb, so he opened not his mouth. He who had just before solemnly asserted His equality with God, with the consent of the whole heavenly world, appears now in fetters like a rebel. How monstrous the contrast, how great the contradiction! But how obvious it is that it is a voluntary act on the Lord's part; and how dearly do we again read in the soul of the holy Sufferer the words, 'Then I restored that which I took not away!'

His fetters have contributed to procure our redemption; for Satan would have held us eternally captive had Jesus preferred liberty to bonds. Heart-affecting it is to see that those hands which were only employed in offices of mercy are bound with cords like the hands of a felon, by the very world to which they were extended only in blessing. But God be thanked that He restrained the lightning of His wrath from destroying the rebels when they thus laid hands upon His Holy One! For in those cords which bound the limbs of Jesus, were hidden the fetters which would have forever bound sinners in hell.

The officers have done their task. The whole assembly then breaks up, in order, contrary to custom and etiquette, personally to bring the accused before the governor, and by their appearing in a body, to force from him the confirmation of their sentence of death. Herein was fulfilled the Saviour's prediction, that He should be delivered unto the Gentiles. This feature in the proceedings belonged to that which was symbolical in the history of His passion. The whole world was to have occasion, in its representatives, to manifest its real position with reference to the Holy One of Israel, and its participation in the guilt and the need of redemption. As regards sin and the curse, we have all fellowship with Israel; as well as in the vocation of grace.

He whom we have seen proceeding bound to the second court of justice, sits now, having long since accomplished His work, at the right hand of the Majesty on high, as keeper of the heavenly blessings which He purchased for us. Let us bow in humble adoration before Him and not let Him go till He has granted us all the blessed results of His passion.

Chapter 25

The End of the Traitor

How much depended upon our High Priest accomplishing the work of atonement in the robes of purity! If a blemish was found in the lamb, it was deemed unfit for sacrifice. 'Such a High Priest became us,' saith the Scripture, 'who is holy, harmless, undefiled, and separate from sinners.' And such a one do we possess. God has spared nothing in order to dispel every doubt on this subject. To this end He gave up the Surety to the scrutiny of the acutest investigators in the world. But to their no small vexation, they tried in vain to find a single spot in Him and are compelled, either in plain words or by their conduct, to testify concerning Him, 'We find no fault in this man.'

It was of great importance that the Argus eyes of the scribes and Pharisees discovered nothing culpable in Him. But it adds much to the weight of this fact, that nothing of the kind could be traced in the Lord Jesus by the man whom we shall now see descending into the pit. It was of much greater importance to him than to them, to be able to convict the Lord of a single sin. Could Judas have been able to say to himself, even with a shadow of truth, 'He whom I am betraying deserves being delivered into the hands of justice,' what would he not have given? He was compelled ardently to wish, for the sake of his peace of mind and his present and eternal salvation, that he might discover Jesus to be in some respects a transgressor. A single sin found in Jesus would have been a great comfort and a sweet solace to him in the torment which he felt within. But however diligently he sought not one dark point could he discover, nor did the slightest spot meet his scrutinizing eye.

Judas finds himself in a dreadful condition. Consoling himself with the wonder-working power of Jesus, the delusive idea that his Master needed only to exert His will in order to escape from the hands of His enemies; when he saw his Master actually condemned, and dragged bound and escorted by the whole Sanhedrin to the residence of the governor, the last anchor breaks which had hitherto held the man secure against the storm of despair. The incorruptible judge in his breast has now free scope for his accusations, and thunders in his ears, 'Thy villainy has succeeded – thy Master is going the way to death, and thou art the means of it. On thy head rests the entire guilt of the bloody end of this Just One. Thou, who didst eat of His bread, art the viper which has given Him the deadly bite. Woe, woe unto thee, traitor, murderer, and accursed!' O the fearful agony which takes possession of his breast at these arrows of conscience, the boundless distress which falls upon him! It seems to him as if he saw the flaming abyss of hell yawning at his feet. The darkness of despair weighs heavily on his soul. O how the accursed blood-money sears his conscience! It seems to him as if it were the pay of Satan and the wages of hell that he carries about with him; nay, as if he had bartered for it the salvation of his soul. And this was what he had really done.

See him hurrying along, urged forward by the raven wings of mental agony. God has forsaken him. The pitiable wretch rushes to the Temple. He must rid himself of the accursed wages of sin. He seeks for the chief priests and elders and having found them, he approaches them, pale as a corpse, and filled with rage and hatred against these instruments of his fall, and confesses boldly and openly saying, 'I have sinned, in that I have betrayed innocent blood.'

Hear these words, they are of great importance. Why? Has Judas become Jesus' friend? By no means; his heart was still embittered against Him. Was his testimony to the innocence of Jesus of advantage to him? On the contrary, by it he only drew down on him the displeasure of his superiors, and increased the dreadful nature of his crime. How strongly and triumphantly must the heavenly radiance of Jesus' innocence have been reflected, even by the darkened mirror of his treacherous soul, that he could not refrain from honouring Jesus by such a confession! Truly, scarcely ever has a more powerful hymn of praise to the holiness of the Lamb of God been heard, than sounds in our ears in the despairing outcry of His betrayer; and where has the innocence of Jesus been more powerfully attested than by the testimony which the unhappy murderer is compelled by conscience to give against himself? Thus, the Lord Jesus celebrated a brilliant triumph in the midst of the deepest gloom of His humiliation. He triumphs as One whom no one could convince of sin – as the Lamb without spot – as the Holy One of Israel.

The Lord celebrates His second triumph in the event we are about to contemplate as the only salvation which is prepared for sinners. Singularly enough He is glorified by His betrayer even in this quality. Judas here performs apostolic service – not intentionally on his part, although on God's part. He serves as a fearful example, how a man may undertake every thing, in order to free himself from sin and its attendant curse, and yet not succeed, as long as the Lord Jesus is not his, and as long as he does not belong to the Lord Jesus.

Behold the miserable man! The horrible deed is done, and he already acknowledges it as a crime. In him we have not to do with an entirely hardened villian. He feels the greatness of his guilt, confesses it, and bitterly repents of it. What would he give, could he undo the wicked deed! He hastily returns to the men in whose service he had sinned, brings them back the accursed bribe; prefers enduring shame, disgrace, and much more besides, rather than let the blood-money remain in his hands; confesses freely and openly the impious act he has committed; does not seek to alleviate it, but directly says, 'I have sinned, in that I have betrayed the innocent blood!' and shows that the abhorrence he displays at the crime he has committed is earnest and sincere.

When the priests refuse to take back their pieces of silver, and haughtily turn their backs upon him with the cold and cutting words, 'What is that to us? See thou to that!' he casts the money down in the Temple, and thereby gives them to understand that he destines it for the poor, or other sacred purposes. In this scene, we perceive something dreadfully retributive, when we call to mind the hypocritical words, 'Why was not this ointment sold, and the money given to the poor?' with which the unhappy disciple once presumed to deprecate Mary's laudable work of love. He is now compelled although with other money to verify in an awful manner what he then uttered in dissimulation.

But what more could be desired than what the sinner did here? Here was self-condemnation, resolutions of amendment, and even earnest endeavours to repair the evil he had done. And yet of what use was it all? Sin remained and Satan's chain was unbroken. The trembling of the wretched man is in vain, as well as his repentance, confession, and his moral resolutions and vows. All this was insufficient to purge him from his sin. All these laudable acts do not procure him mercy.

Judas perishes horribly. Why? Is it because his sins exceeded the measure of divine forgiveness? O, not so! Is it because he

was a thief and a cheat? Such was the thief on the cross in a
much higher degree, yet he found the way to paradise. Is it
because he betrayed the Holy One of Israel? Thousands did
the same and yet were saved. Was it because he laid hands
on himself? I tell you, that even if he had not done this, but
had lived for years together, and spent them in serious
attempts at amendment, he would still have perished for this
one single reason – that Jesus was not his; he was not under
Jesus' blood. Thus the perdition of Judas must serve, like no
other event, to show in striking colours, how impossible it is
to do without Jesus; and the latter triumphs in this, as in
almost nothing else, as the only and exclusive Saviour of
sinners.

Jesus alone enables us to obtain mercy and to reach
heaven. If He be not gracious to thee, it is in vain for thee to
rise early and to sit up late, in order by such means to work
out thy salvation. Thou labourest and accomplishest nothing;
thou gatherest and puttest it into a bag with holes, thou
weavest spider's webs, which are unfit for clothing. But if Jesus
is thine, thou hast already gained thy cause; fruits of peace
fall into thy lap from a tree, which is not of thy planting;
thou canst boast of thy Saviour's righteousness, while thou
art still striving against sin; and art reconciled unto God
without an atonement being required at thy hand. Why then
dost thou delay to embrace Him, and make Him thy all in
all? Say with the apostle, 'The life which I now live in the
flesh, I live by the faith of the Son of God, who loved me,
and gave himself for me;' and when these words are verified
in thee, thou art safe to all eternity.

Judas is exhibited to us in the history of the Passion in order
that sin, with all its horrors, may appear in the full blaze of
day, and that redemption may appear in all its splendour, and
Jesus be visibly glorified, not only as the Holy One, and the
only way of salvation, but also as the Saviour of mankind.

If ever the dreadful nature of sin was manifested in any one, it was so in the traitor. Here, it first of all, presents to us its entire hatefulness and darkness, which appears only the more striking when contrasted with the heavenly light, which beams forth from the person of Christ. Here it makes itself known as the great deceiver, which promises its servants mountains of gold, but rewards them with horror and terror. Besides, it is here manifestly shown how it scoffs at every human attempt to extract its sting; how no penitence can banish it, no tears wash it away, and no good resolutions annihilate it; but it obstinately remains in defiance of all this; hands over its subjects to Satan, and after embittering their life on this side of the grave, transfers them finally to an eternal night of death, and gives them up to endless perdition.

Look at the traitor in his stage of despair, and behold how sin sits upon his shoulders, like a hideous spectre! Observe how he hurries along, restless and fugitive, but the spectre accompanies him and becomes increasingly frightful as he proceeds. He expects to get rid of his horrible burden by returning the thirty pieces of silver; but in vain are the attempts to settle accounts with sin at such a rate. Judas has recourse to the chief priests and elders, but they know of no remedy against sin. Driven at length to desperation, he casts himself into the arms of death; but even the latter does not relieve the soul from the fiend.

Judas may divest himself of his body, but he does not thereby lay aside his guilt. He may part with his life; but sin does not, on this account, depart from him. He can leave the world, but his impious act follows him across the bound- aries. He may strangle himself, but his iniquity is not de- stroyed by so doing: on the contrary, greater scope is thus afforded it to unfold its whole power and dominion. It does not prevent his body from bursting asunder, but carries away the soul with it to everlasting fire. Approach the grave of

Judas. No angels are watching there, nor does the guardian eye of God stand open over it. No rose of hope blooms on its grassy mound. Night-shade and thistle alone vegetate there. And what is the inscription on his tombstone? It is short and horrifying – 'And Judas went to his place' – and indicates in an awful manner how far the desolating, destructive, and fatal power of sin extends.

Who was there that was able to cope with this monster? He who is being dragged yonder in chains before the judgment-seat of a heathen, and at the sight of whom Judas despairs, instead of breaking out into exclamations of joy – He it is who enters the lists against it. Christ, by imputation, was the Lamb which took upon Himself the sin of the world, so that by the representative endurance of the curse due to it, He might deprive it of its sting, in behalf of all those who should believe on Him. Christ is glorified here as the Saviour, since every one must feel convinced that the son of perdition suffers shipwreck solely because he disdains to cast himself patiently and believingly into the arms of Him whom he has betrayed. Had he done so Christ would have infallibly brought him safely into the haven of eternal peace. But why did Judas not do so? Partly because he was still too proud to honour Him, by suing for His mercy, who had torn away his hypocritical mask, and against whom his soul was still deeply embittered. Partly, also, because he had given way to despair; for Satan did not cease to suggest to him that there was no longer any hope for him.

Could Judas have summoned up sufficient humility and courage to turn his tearful eye to Jesus as did afterward the dying thief, he would have met only the look of forgiving mercy; and O what different sounds would have saluted his ear, than the horrifying language of the chief priests and elders, who said to him, 'What is that to us? See thou to that.' There was no want of grace, even for a man in his desperate condition; and although his sin was 'red like crimson,' yet the blood of atonement would have sufficed to wash it white as snow. But the devil carried him away in the whirlwind, like the vulture the lamb it has seized upon; nor did he rest till he had completed his triumph over him, and had gotten secure possession of the soul of him who had thus become his booty.

The world has never beheld a more tragic spectacle than this. One who was ordained and fitted to become a distinguished vessel of salvation and blessing to mankind gives himself up to despair in the presence of the world's Deliverer and plunges into the gulf of eternal perdition, instead of laying hold of the hand extended for his rescue. It would seem as if even death and hell disowned this son of perdition, just as the world had previously done in the person of the chief priests and elders. The rope with which the miserable man had hung himself snaps asunder. The tree which he had selected as the instrument of his death, shakes him off again with horror. The strangled wretch falls down, burst asunder, and his bowels gushing out, lie scattered on the ground.

While these horrible things are enacting, the chief priests and elders are consulting together, what should be done with the thirty pieces of silver, which Judas, in his state of desperation, had thrown back again. 'It is not lawful,' say the hypocrites, unconsciously stigmatizing themselves, 'to put them into the treasury, for it is the price of blood.' They say right; for according to Deuteronomy 23:18, the treasury of the Lord was not to be defiled by blood-money or the price of a dog. Were not these men equally guilty of the heinous crime with the traitor himself, to whom they had paid the thirty pieces of silver? And though they were in equal condemnation with him, yet they assume to themselves not only the place of his judges, but with a haughty mien, contrast themselves with him as keepers of the law and the holy places.

Who does not feel almost more sympathy with the despairing disciple than with these proficients in falsehood and dissimulation? Who can say that it may not be more tolerable in the day of judgment for the former, than for these arrogant and heartless hypocrites!

They agree together to purchase, with the wages of iniquity, the potter's field – a piece of ground belonging to a potter; and destine it for the burial place of those pilgrims who might die in Jerusalem without having any tomb or place of sepulture of their own. Thus, even the money, for which our Lord was bartered, must be productive of good. And is there not in this transaction a distinct hint that Christ yielded up Himself that we, poor pilgrims in the vale of death, might rest in peace? The purchased field was thenceforward known by the semi-Syrian name of 'Aceldama,' or 'the field of blood'. A monument was thus erected to the lost disciple and his crime; which still speaks to the traveller and says, 'There is no more offering for sin unto him, who treads under foot the blood of the Son of God.'

The evangelist, after narrating the purchase, observes, 'Then was fulfilled, that which was spoken by Jeremy the prophet, saying, And they took the thirty pieces of silver, the price of him that was valued, whom they of the children of Israel did value, and gave them for the potter's field, as the Lord appointed me.' Matthew combines here, as respects their chief import, two prophetic passages; the first of which belongs to Jeremiah, but the other to Zechariah, whose name is not mentioned. We read the words of Jeremiah, in chapter 19:11–13 as follows: 'Thus saith the Lord of Hosts, even so will I break this people and this city, as one breaketh a potter's vessel, that can not be made whole again, and they shall bury them in Tophet, till there shall be no place to bury.' The words of Zechariah we find in the eleventh chapter of his prophecies, where we read in verse 13, 'And the Lord said unto me, Cast it unto the potter; a goodly price that I was prized at of them. And I took the thirty pieces of silver and cast them to the potter, in the house of the Lord.'

Tophet, where once the image of Moloch stood, was at the same time, the piece of ground where the potters of Jerusalem procured the clay for their handicraft. This Tophet was the potter's field which was bought by the elders for thirty pieces of silver. But when Matthew says, 'Then was fulfilled that which was spoken by Jeremy the prophet,' the meaning of the Holy Spirit who guided the evangelist's pen is this – 'God so ordered it that the elders of Israel purchase the field on which the curse of Jeremiah rested, thus making it the property of the Jewish State. By so doing they transferred that curse to themselves and the people.' It was not therefore the purchase of the field itself, but rather the symbolic appropriation by it of the divine curse upon Tophet, which received its final accomplishment in the destruction of Jerusalem by the Romans, that is here described as the fulfilment of Jeremiah's prophecy.

The hour of the threatened judgment was at hand, when He who was the perfection of God's pastoral faithfulness, was valued on the part of Israel, at the trifling price of thirty pieces of silver. For this small sum, Judas, as representing his nation, disposed of his part in the Saviour, and the children of Israel by their rulers bargained for the Holy One to slay him. But by the fact of the traitor, in despair, hurling the murderer's reward from him, and casting it down in the Temple, the blood-money (a bad omen) was returned to the congregation of Israel. This act, which was not without divine intervention, called fearfully and significantly to mind the thirty pieces of silver mentioned by Zechariah, and could only be explained to mean that the Almighty now renewed, more impressively than before, the threatening He had pronounced against Jerusalem and its sanctuary, in the symbolical act of His prophet. And the circumstance that the Jewish rulers hit upon the idea of purchasing the accursed spot completely impresses the seal of truth on that explanation.

Hence it is evident that the spirit of prophecy uttered the words of Zechariah and Jeremiah with a conscious reference to the event which occurred in Jerusalem after the lapse of centuries; and that God permitted the transaction between Judas and the rulers of Israel to assume, in so striking a manner, a form corresponding with those ancient prophetic sayings, only because He would give the ungrateful flock of His people a new and tangible sign that the time of maturity for destruction, and the long announced and terrible judgments of His hand had now arrived. Matthew therefore says with perfect justice, 'Then was fulfilled that which was spoken by Jeremy the prophet.' Actual predictions found their final accomplishment. Even as the Holy Spirit had distinctly pointed, in Zechariah to the thirty pieces of silver – so in Jeremiah, He had pointed to the purchase of the potter's field by the priests and elders.

Let him who gives himself to Christ do so without reserve; and whoever is desirous of holding communion with Him, let him always walk before Him without disguise. Let him who is overtaken by a fault seek the throne of grace without delay; and he that is conscious of being under the dominion of a single sin, let him not cease to watch and pray, until its power is broken by the mercy of Him who bruised the serpent's head. The germ from which a Judas may spring when fructified by hell, lies concealed in all of us. Let us therefore make room for the Holy Spirit in our hearts, that He may destroy it and make all within us new!

Chapter 26

Christle before Pilate

The day has just dawned – the most momentous, decisive, and eventful in the world. It greets our Lord with dreadful insignia. It approaches in a blood-stained robe, a crown of thorns to encircle His brow, in the one hand, and in the other, the scourge, the fatal cup, and the accursed tree; while it rises upon us with the olive-branch of peace, the divine acquittal, and the crown of life. O sacred Friday, day of divine compassion, birthday of our eternal redemption, we bless thee, we greet thee on our knees!

We find the holy city in unwonted commotion. Masses of men move along the streets. A spectacle like that which now presents itself, had never before been witnessed. The whole Sanhedrin has risen up to conduct a delinquent whom they have condemned to death, in solemn procession to the Roman authorities, in order to wrest from the latter the confirmation of their sentence. And who is it they are dragging thither? The very man who was recently received, in the same city, by the same crowd of people, with loud hosannas, and was exalted and celebrated as no one had been before. It is Jesus of Nazareth, respecting whom they cried exultingly, 'Blessed is he that cometh in the name of the Lord!' and of whom, even His enemies could not refrain from testifying that a great prophet had arisen among men. He now meets us as the offscouring and refuse of the same people, who shortly before strewed palms and wreathed chaplets for Him!

Were we able to look into the hearts of the Jews, and especially into those of their chief priests and rulers during their procession to the Roman praetorium, we should see in them a glowing furnace of rage and vexation. It was dreadful to them to see themselves compelled to this open exhibition of their subjugation to a foreign yoke. But the bloodthirstiness under which they languished for the extirpation of the hated Nazarene outweighed their boundless ambition and national pride. Foaming with indignation they proceed forward with their victim, and are compelled, by this procession, to testify against their will, that the sceptre has departed from Judah, and that the time so definitely pointed out by the dying Jacob for the appearance of the Shiloh, to whom the gathering of the people should be, had now arrived.

It will doubtless be, in some measure, the conviction of every one that God must necessarily have pronounced an eternal curse on such ruthless reprobates as the characters just described, if no mediating Surety interposed to take their curse upon Himself, and render satisfaction to divine justice in their stead. To suppose that the Most High could pardon such sons of Belial, without anything further, would be to demand the overthrow of the whole moral government of the world, and to require nothing less than that God should act in opposition to Himself and cease to be God.

Reason cannot believe in the possibility of salvation for a race like that of Adam irrespective of an atonement; and scarcely anything in the world appears more rational than the scriptural doctrine of the redemption of sinners by the mediating intervention of the Son of God. I confess that all that is within me would rise up in the greatest excitement and astonishment, were I to behold the thrice holy God embracing without such an intervention, the worthless assemblage at Jerusalem in the arms of His love. But when I see in the midst of those transgressors the Lamb which taketh away the sin of the world, I then see that God could open the gates of paradise even to the most degraded of that generation of vipers.

Behold the adorable Prince of Peace bound like a criminal, and covered with ignominy! Since we are aware of His Surety-ship, although we may feel deeply affected at His infinite humiliation, we are not struck and astonished. We can even bear to be told that the visible sufferings He endured were only the faint reflection of the incomparably more horrible torments which He secretly suffered; and that the host which surrounds Him with swords and spears forms only a part of the escort which accompanies Him, since another part, which is invisible and behind the curtain, is commanded by Satan himself. For when Christ experienced what was due to us, we know that it included all these horrors. Nothing more nor less befell Him than what was destined to be endured by us on account of our sins. What an unspeakable gift do we therefore possess in the bleeding Lamb! Would too much honour be done Him if our whole lives were one continued adoration of His Name?

They bring the Lord Jesus to Pilate, the Roman governor. The Almighty permits circumstances so to connect themselves together that the whole world, in its representatives, must participate in the condensation of the Just One. Hence His death becomes the common crime of our race, and every mouth is stopped before the judgment seat of God. They conduct the Lord to Pilate; and thus what the Saviour had before so distinctly predicted when announcing His passion, was literally fulfilled: 'Behold,' said He, 'we go up to Jerusalem; and the Son of man shall be delivered unto the chief priests and unto the scribes, and they shall condemn him to death, and deliver him up to the Gentiles.'

We now see the accomplishment of this prediction. By so doing Israel filled up the measure of its guilt. For the second time they hand over their brother Joseph to the uncircumcised and to strangers. By this transfer they typified, at the same time, their own fate. The world's salvation, intended for them in the first instance, was by them most ungratefully given up to the Gentiles; while they themselves were thenceforward left to languish in darkness and the shadow of death.

The procession arrives at the governor's palace. They lay hold of their prisoner, and rudely push Him into the open portal of the house. Why do they act thus? The narrative informs us, that 'they themselves went not into the judgment hall lest they should be defiled, but that they might eat the passover.' Their idea was not in accordance with a right understanding of the divine law; but they obeyed the arbitrarily invented ordinance of their rabbis, which stated that they exposed themselves to defilement by entering a house, and especially a Gentile one in which leaven might be found. But they had no objection that their captive should be thus defiled. They even purposely push Him into the house they deemed unclean, and thus tangibly and symbolically expel Him, as a publican and a sinner from the commonwealth of Israel. But all this was to happen thus, in order that Christ's character as the sinner's Surety might become increasingly apparent, and everyone perceive in Him the Man who, by virtue of a mysterious transfer, had taken upon Himself every thing that was condemnatory in us.

There is no feature in the history of the passion which is devoid of significance. Throughout there is a manifestation of superior arrangement and divine depth of purpose. This forcible urging of the Holy One of Israel into the house of a heathen is typical. We could weep to see Him who was love itself pushed forward by the rude hands of the brutish multitude. But we will not weep over Him, but over ourselves and our race, which is capable of such depravity and devilishness. Let us not overlook, however, the evangelical emblem that meets our view even in this detail of the narrative. Christ entered for us alone where real and serious danger menaced us, even into the horrible abyss of the curse of the law, the prison of death, and the regions of darkness, in order to exhaust upon His own sacred person the force of the terrors which were prepared for us, and leave us nothing but peace, salvation, freedom, and blessing.

But what shall we say to the conduct of the Jews who, full of the leaven of all ungodliness, while making no conscience of laying their murderous hands on the Holy One of God, act as if they were too conscientious to enter the house of an impure heathen, lest they should come in contact with the leaven which could not defile them? What a striking example do these 'whited sepulchres' prove of the truth of our Lord's words in Matthew 23:27, and what a complete commentary do they yield us on the words that follow: 'Ye blind guides which strain at a gnat, and swallow a camel!' Would to God these wretched people were the only ones of their kind! But they meet us in every form and colour, even among those who call themselves Christians. Who is not acquainted with individuals who scrupulously abstain from worldly amusements, and carefully avoid coming into social contact with the worldly-minded, and yet vie with the world in all the arts of dissimulation, uncharitable judgment of others, and hateful scandal and even go beyond it?

Who does not know those who believe that they would be committing a great crime if they performed the slightest labour on Sunday, or if they were not the first at every performance of divine service; while it never occurs to them to regard as sin the secret service of mammon to which they are devoted – who on no account would suffer themselves to be seen at a theatre or a ball – in which they do well – but forgive themselves without hesitation, for compensating themselves for that privation by taking part in imagination in all the enjoyment and pleasures of the world, not less than the most frivolous characters of the age – who never fail to appear at the institution of beneficent establishments and associations, and head the list of the contributors while they make no scruple of secretly practising deceit and imposition in their trade and business, or of acting unjustly or severely toward those who are under them, or of their avarice and greediness for transitory honour?

One of the crafty devices by which men pass by the moral claims which God makes on our conduct is that instead of bowing to the divine yoke, they form and impose another more pleasing to the flesh; thus trying to make it appear as if they performed more than God's commands enjoined upon them. But he is mistaken who supposes that by such counterfeit holiness he shall be able to settle accounts with the Most High; and he dishonours and insults Him who hopes to bribe Him with 'cups and platters,' outwardly clean, but inwardly full of 'ravening wickedness.' 'The eyes of the Lord,' said the prophet Hanani to Asa the king, 'run to and fro throughout the whole earth, to show himself strong in the behalf of them whose heart is perfect toward him.' He desires the whole man and not mere fractional parts. He that cannot resolve to devote himself to His service without reserve loses nothing by withdrawing himself entirely, and placing himself at the disposal of the world and his own lusts. There is no medium betwixt belief and unbelief. True conversion is a new birth, and not a patching up of the old garment. The life of godliness is a harmonious organization, and not a sticking together of single acts of piety.

Pilate soon begins to suspect why the Jews pushed their culprit toward him through the gate, but feels so little offended at this that he pretends ignorance, and magnanimously steps out to them to ascertain the object of their coming. He considers that he has only to do with contracted and narrow-minded Jews, and deems that it comports both with his refinement and his dignity to tolerate their prejudices.

Pilate then went out unto the people, and said, 'What accusation bring ye against this man?' He assumes the appearance of unbelief and indifference, but he was able to take a more unprejudiced view of the matter than the Jews, and cannot think, after all he has hitherto heard of the Nazarene, that they would be able to bring any serious charge against Him.

To the governor's question of what Jesus is accused, the haughty and insane reply is returned by His accusers, 'If he were not a malefactor, we would not have delivered him up unto thee.' In this impudent speech, their entire refractoriness toward the hated Romans is made apparent. It is the rebelliousness of fettered slaves, the fury of caged wolves. Here again we perceive also the furious pharisaism of the priests and the people; for though they are endeavouring to murder innocence and do the devil's work, yet because *they* do it, it must be right and blameless. Can pride go beyond this? Do not let us overlook the circumstance, however, that by their arrogant language they hope to disguise the embarrassment in which, in spite of all appearance to the contrary, they have involved themselves. They know of nothing from which they can form a well-guarded charge against their delinquent, and think that the bold front they put on the affair will compensate for what is deficient in proof and testimony against Jesus.

Alas! they do not entirely fail in their object. Pilate suffers himself to be overawed by their determined appearance, and places the first foot on that slippery path on which we shall afterward see him carried forward, from one crime to another, against his will, and finally ending in the abyss of perdition.

'Then said Pilate unto them, Take ye him, and judge him according to your law.' What worthless behaviour in a judge who ought to administer law and justice in the land! We already see how little he cares whether Jesus lives or dies, only he would not willingly have the blood of a Man upon his soul whom his conscience absolves as innocent.

'Take ye him, and judge him according to your law.' The heathen governor would gladly have escaped from sharing the guilt of murdering the Righteous One whom the Jews had delivered up to him. But he will not succeed in his object on the path he is now pursuing. He must either decide for or against Jesus. He is compelled either to take the part of the Holy One, to the setting aside of all private considerations, or to afford his sanction to the most cruel and bloody deed the world ever witnessed. But the case is similar with us. There is just as little room left us for a neutral position as was left him. The Holy One of Israel comes into too close a contact with us to be quietly passed by. If we refuse to do Him homage, we are compelled to aid in crucifying Him. We cannot escape the alternative of rejecting Him, if we will not decidedly devote ourselves to Him. He testifies too loudly to our consciences that He is the Lord, to suffer us quietly to part with Him with a mere passing compliment. If we wish to separate ourselves from Him, nothing is left for us but to say, in positive opposition, 'We will not have thee to reign over us!' God grant that this may not be the case with any of us, but may He enable us to exclaim with the apostle Thomas, 'My Lord and my God!'

The Jews close the outlet before Pilate's face by which he hoped to escape from any participation in the dreadful crime of the murder of Jesus, by giving him a reply which ought to have made him feel deeply ashamed, 'It is not lawful for us, ' say they, 'to put any man to death.' Pilate knew this, and what confusion of ideas and increasing perplexity does the man betray, who, though he was the supreme judge, could recommend to the Jews themselves the execution of an act of justice to which they had no right according to the existing laws.

Or was Pilate induced to express himself thus foolishly from having no idea that the accusers of Jesus were bent upon His death? This is also conceivable. But his miserable attempt at an escape is wholly frustrated, as it deserved. There is something really tragic in the fact that circumstances should so concur and be interwoven with each other that it would seem as if Pilate was to be drawn into the blood guiltiness of the Jews. And this will assuredly be the case if he cannot resolve to give his heart and pay homage to Jesus, even as every one who obstinately resists the call to conversion must increasingly fill up the measure of his sins and accelerate his ripeness for destruction.

'It is not lawful for us to put any one to death.' They were not permitted to do so. When on one occasion they tumultuously stoned a supposed heretic to death, the Roman authorities probably leniently overlooked it. But in order to a formal accusation, and death by crucifixion in particular, they could not act without superior consent. Hence they openly, though with stifled rage, confess their dependence on the Roman tribunal. Their thirst for revenge upon the Nazarene, however, this time outweighs their national pride. The Man they hate is doomed to be crucified and to perish ignominiously. Such are their thoughts. But the Lord in heaven also exercises an influence in the affair. The Evangelist remarks, 'That the saying of Jesus might be fulfilled which he spake, signifying what death he should die.' John has reference here to the words recorded in chapter 12:32, of his Gospel, 'And I, if I be lifted up from the earth, will draw all men unto me,' adding the explanatory remark, 'This he said, signifying what death he should die.'

In the tumultuous assemblage before the governor's palace at Jerusalem we are therefore unexpectedly aware of a divine intimation respecting the Saviour. The counsel of the Eternal Father displays itself, and in its depths a cross is described for His only-begotten Son. For the sake of the symbolical meaning included in it, the accursed tree was selected in the counsels of eternity as the instrument of the Saviour's death. The brazen serpent in the wilderness, as well as the wave-offering of the Tabernacle, early shadowed it forth to the people of God. It now stands erected in history, in the ministry of the gospel, and in the minds of men, and manifests its wonder-working and attractive influence.

We conclude our meditation strengthened afresh, as I hope, in the twofold conviction that our forgiveness uncon-ditionally demanded a vicarious sacrifice, and that the whole of our Lord's passion can only be properly understood when regarded from such a point of view. We are astonished at the wisdom of the Almighty who has so wonderfully solved the greatest of all problems – that of the restoration of a race which had fallen under the curse to the divine right of sonship without thereby denying His holiness. This solution is found in the Saviour's obedience and death. Let us adoringly bow the knee to Him, and join with thankful hearts in the song of the Church triumphant, 'Worthy is the Lamb that was slain, and hath redeemed us to God by his blood, out of every kindred and tongue, and people, and nation!'

Chapter 27

The Accusations

After the Jews had gained their first victory over the governor, for as such they might account it, in having succeeded by their imposing attitude in wresting from him the reply, 'Take ye him and judge him according to your law,' they proceed with increasing courage and bring forward accusations against their prisoner, by which they hope completely to influence the Roman and induce him to favour their murderous project. They are acquainted with his weak side – his pride of office, his ambition, and in particular, his dependence on the favour of his imperial master; and toward this point they direct their assault. They abstain from repeating before a heathen tribunal, accusations against Jesus which they could successfully bring forward against Him in their Jewish Sanhedrin. Instead of an ecclesiastical, they make before Pilate a political charge. They accuse the Lord of a threefold crime, which, because it is imputed to Him in a certain sense by His opponents and the enemies of His kingdom, even in the present day is worthy of particular investigation.

'We have found this fellow perverting the nation.' This is the first of the three charges brought against Him. They intend by it to say, 'This Man seeks to lessen the respect due to the constituted authorities.' But to bring forward against Jesus a charge like this, some shadow of truth was requisite, and this they found in the position which the Lord had taken with reference to the priests and scribes. For as regards the priests, our Lord certainly did not instruct His disciples to place their trust in them as their real mediators with God, or to seek in their sacrifices the cause of their justification in His sight. If by this, He detracted from the authority of the sons of Aaron, He did nothing more than reduce this authority to the correct measure intended by God. But where had He denied to the priesthood of Israel the authority of a divine institution and refused it the reverence and submission which belonged to it as such?

As long as Jesus had not fulfilled the entire requirements of His high-priestly calling, and as long as the great atoning sacrifice had not been offered on the cross, He gave all honour to the Levitical priesthood, for the sake of their divine appointment. Not only did He visit the temple as the house of God and celebrate the festivals of Israel as sanctified by Him, but he obediently submitted also to all the Levitical statutes enjoined by Moses, from the circumcision and presentation in the Temple, to the eating of the paschal lamb.

Not only so, but He did not fail to enjoin upon others the punctual fulfilment of their ecclesiastical duties; so that He did not absolve the leper whom He had healed from presenting himself to the priests and offering the sacrifices appointed by Moses in such a case.

The Lord acted toward the elders of the people, whether they were Pharisees or Sadducees, as He did toward the priests. It is true that as the Master of all, He reproved their errors and sins, as appears from Mark 7:13, and refused in any manner to justify their human invented ordinances and traditions by which the Word of God was only weakened and rendered void. He nevertheless unhesitatingly recognized their divine appointment, as you will remember is evident from Matthew 23:2, 3, where he says, 'The scribes and

Pharisees sit in Moses' seat. All therefore, whatsoever they bid you observe, that observe and do; but do not ye after their works, for they say and do not.' Could this be called weakening the respect due to the constituted authorities, or was it not rather the contrary?

He turned the people aside only from those authorities which did not deserve the name, not being divinely instituted and appointed. But this does not exclude the fact that He most expressly, though in the spirit of Christian liberty, today claims the submission of believers to the official ordinances of the Church, which He has Himself instituted and sanctified. The pastoral office, with its various spheres of operation, is established by Him. He says to those who preach His Word, 'He that despiseth you, despiseth me.' He points them out to us as stewards of the divine mysteries and says to the members of the churches by the mouth of His apostle, 'Let the elders that rule well be counted worthy of double honour.' 'Obey them that have the rule over you and submit yourselves; for they watch for your souls.' It is thus the Lord supports the authorities of the Church which rest on divine institution and only properly rejects with all earnestness and emphasis, those unjustifiable assumptions which are contrary to the Word of God.

The second accusation which is brought against the Lord Jesus by the Jews, is that of 'forbidding to give tribute to Caesar.' Truly, a more unjust accusation than this they could not have invented against Him. It is devoid of the slightest foundation; and we are compelled to believe that it occurred to them only because they were still smarting under the disgrace of the defeat they had experienced at His hands when they endeavoured to draw from him a disloyal expression.

Luke mentions this affair in the twentieth chapter of his Gospel. The chief priests and scribes sought, even at that time, how they might lay hands upon Him; but their evil conscience made them afraid of the people, in whose esteem they had already begun to sink considerably. That which they did not venture to execute by force, they sought to attain by craftiness and under the assumed appearance of what was just and right. For this purpose they induced some worthless individuals to attempt to take hold of His words, so that they might have an ostensible ground for delivering Him up to the civil power. The bribed emissaries approach the Saviour in the garb of reverential submission and ask, with the innocent mien of those who seek instruction, 'Master, we know that thou sayest and teachest rightly, neither acceptest thou the person of any, but teachest the way of God truly. Is it lawful for us to give tribute to Caesar, or no?' The net was cunningly spread, but in such a manner that they were caught in it themselves. The Lord immediately saw through the snare and tore away the hypocritical mask from them by the simple question, 'Why tempt ye me? He then asked them to show him a penny, which being done, He takes the coin, holds it up to them and asks, 'Whose image and superscription hath it?' They answer, 'Caesar's.' And He said unto them, 'Render therefore unto Caesar the things which be Caesar's, and unto God the things which be God's.' The narrative informs us that they could not take hold of His words before the people, and they marvelled at His answer and held their peace.

This single expression of our Lord's perfectly suffices to show us what was His political principle, if I may so call it. A heathen emperor then reigned over Judea, an enemy to God and His cause. But still he ruled, and wielded the sceptre. The coin which bore his image testified of this. The Lord commanded that it should be returned to him to whom it belonged. What else did he intimate by so doing, than that which was subsequently enjoined upon us by His apostle in His name, in Romans 13:1–3, 'Let every soul be subject unto the higher powers. For there is no power but of God: the powers that be are ordained of God. Whosoever therefore resisteth the power, resisteth the ordinance of God; and they that resist shall receive to themselves condemnation. For rulers are not a terror to good works, but to the evil. Wilt thou, then, not be afraid of the power? Do that which is good, and thou shalt have praise of the same.'

Christ is so far from favouring revolt, that He threatens with judgment all resistance to the existing authorities, whatever they may be, as though it were a rebellion against the majesty of God Himself. He enjoins us in His Word, to be 'subject to our masters with all fear, not only to the good and gentle, but also to the froward.' If a tyrant rule over us, there is no question as to what is our duty, according to our magna charta, the Holy Scriptures. In the autocrat and the despot we have to recognize a chastening rod raised against us by the hand of God, and quietly endure it while calling to mind our sins.

The third and last accusation brought against Jesus is that He had said of Himself that He was Christ, a king. They wish Pilate to understand this in a political sense. But how far the Lord was from causing or fostering such an idea of the object of His coming into the world, we well know. The Jews attempted by force to make Him act the part of a king; and would have borne Him on their hands and loaded Him with homage and crowns of honour. But as often as He perceived any movement of the kind, He escaped from the multitude and hid Himself. And when His own disciples expressed similar sentiments respecting the kingdom He came to establish, He never failed to reprove them severely, to rectify their mistakes, and to impress upon them the fact that His kingdom came not with outward observation but was within them.

The Jews also were well aware how far it had always been from His intention to found a kingdom according to their views; and this was the very thing which irritated them above every thing else and kindled their animosity against Him. Nevertheless their effrontery extends so far that they now impute to Him as His desire and aim, what they had fruitlessly laboured to induce Him to attempt.

But as certainly as Christ did not come to establish an earthly kingdom; so surely will His dominion eventually swallow up all the kingdoms of the world and become itself an earthly empire. The potentates of this world will deposit their crowns and sceptres in homage at Jesus' feet, in order to receive them back consecrated and as a fief from the hand of the King of kings. The people, enlightened and returned to the Shepherd and Bishop of their souls, will submit with delight and affection to a government in which the gentle guidance of their Prince of Peace is alone perceptible. The legislation will have, as its basis, the word of the living God, and the economy of the state will rest upon the foundation of the gospel. The offerings which the common weal may require, will be tendered by the impulse of voluntary affection, and the 'swords will be turned into plowshares and the spears into pruning hooks.'

Daniel looked forward to this jubilee-period of the kingdom of Christ when he exclaimed, 'But the kingdom and dominion, and the greatness of the kingdom under the whole heaven shall be given to the people of the saints of the Most High, whose kingdom is an everlasting kingdom, and all dominions shall serve and obey him.' In the same manner, Zechariah refers to this subjugation of all worldly empire to Christ, when he significantly predicts that 'In that day, shall there be upon the bells of the horses, holiness unto the Lord, and the pots in the Lord's house shall be like the bowls before the altar.' The song of praise for this period of triumph and fulfilment lies already in the archives of divine revelation, 'The kingdoms of this world are become the kingdoms of our

God and of his Christ!' and our Lord comforts us with the anticipation of this period while teaching us daily to pray in blissful hope, 'Thy kingdom come!'

We have now been convinced that nothing could be more groundless than were the accusations brought against our Lord before Pilate. Every investigation which took place terminated only in His greater glorification. We rejoice at this result; for you know how much we are personally interested in His coming forth justified from every tribunal. 'Just and right is he.' No guile was ever found in His mouth, and He was the personification of every moral virtue, and in this respect, He has left us an example, that we should follow His steps.

Chapter 28

Christel a King

Let us now return to the Mighty Captive. He suffers Himself to be judged in order that He may subsequently interfere, both legally and effectually on our behalf, who had become amenable to divine justice. In every step of His path of suffering, He proves Himself to be the Man who 'restored what he took not away.' But He would not have been such a Mediator if, even in His form of humiliation, He had not been at the same time 'higher than the heavens.' Thus His super-human glory breaks forth victoriously on every occasion through the obscurity of His lowliness like the sun through the veil of clouds. Nor can He so entirely restrain it as to prevent at least a few glimmerings of it from constantly shining forth.

We find in Pilate a degree of humanity and of susceptibility for something better. He is not the cold, shallow, wornout man of the world, to which many would degrade him. God, indeed, will judge him, but not with the lukewarm, who disgust Him, and whom, like the Laodiceans, He will spue out of his mouth.

The governor, after listening to the accusations of the priests and rulers, returns thoughtfully into his palace, and commands Jesus to be again brought before him. The sacred sufferer appears in silence in the chamber of His judge. It is evident that the Roman can not avoid feeling a degree of veneration for the wonderful Man; and who is there can do otherwise? Even the rudest scoffers feel in their consciences, the sting of their attacks upon the Lord Jesus, and endeavour by means of ridicule, to drown the reproving voice within them for their enmity to Him.

Pilate begins his examination by asking, 'Art thou the king of the Jews?' This he seems to have uttered in a mollified tone, in the full expectation of His saying in reply, 'God forbid that I should seek after such high things!' Much would he have given to have heard such a declaration from His lips, partly, that he might have a legal ground for officially rejecting the accusation of the malignant Jews, and partly in order, in an easy manner, to get rid of the Nazarene, of whose innocence he is fully persuaded.

Jesus, however, does not give the desired answer in the negative; but, on the contrary He affirms it, after rectifying the false views of His kingdom with which the governor was imbued. He begins His reply to Pilate's question by asking in return, 'Sayest thou this thing of thyself, or did others tell it thee of me?' These words were calculated to remind the judge of his duty, not to enter further upon things merely of a suspicious nature, which like the charge brought forward by the Jews, bore the stamp of falsehood upon its front. 'Of thyself,' the Saviour intended to say, 'thou dost not surely speak thus, since, being in possession of intelligence respecting My conduct, thou art doubtless sufficiently convinced of the absurdity of the Jewish accusation. But how does it consist with the dignity of thy office, that thou condescendest to treat such a groundless charge in such a serious manner?'

There is also a profounder meaning in our Lord's words, which may be expressed as follows: 'Is it of importance to thee – and such it ought to be – to inquire, whether, and in what sense I am a king; or was the impulse to thy question given thee by the language of others?' Had Pilate been able to answer the first in the affirmative, that hour would have been to him a time of eternal salvation. But his answer was not of a kind to induce the Saviour to initiate him more deeply into the mysteries of His kingdom.

Our Lord's question is still put in a certain sense to all. It is of the highest importance whether as inquirers we approach the kingdom of truth by impulse from without or from a feeling of inward necessity. Those who approach the Lord and His Word from an inward impulse, and for the sake of their soul's welfare, will behold 'the King in his Beauty,' and find unsealed the mystery of godliness.

The governor has not wholly misunderstood the Lord's words, even in their profounder meaning, and clearly perceives that Jesus seeks to make an impression upon him, and to incite him to be serious with regard to the question concerning His kingdom. But scarcely does he perceive our Lord's intention than he adroitly evades it, and says, 'Am I a Jew? Thine own nation and the chief priests have delivered thee unto me. What hast thou done?' We see how purposely he tries to liberate himself from Him, as though he feared lest the awe-inspiring influence which the deportment of Jesus exercised over him might become stronger, and in the end overpowering. 'Am I a Jew?' he asks, and thereby means to say, 'Canst Thou expect me to have any regard to the question whether Thou art really the promised Messiah or not? What have we citizens of Rome to do with the hopes of the Jews?'

Observe here how Pilate is the inventor of the oft-repeated artifice of infidels – that of regarding both the Old and New Testament only as Oriental literature. They are anxious to excuse their estrangement from Christianity on the ground which Pilate takes, of not being a Jew. It is a current saying with such people, 'Every nation has its own sphere of religious ideas; and hence what responds to the peculiarity of one nation, is not, on that account, for all.' The prophets – nay, even the Lord Himself and His apostles, are treated just like the sages of Grecian antiquity, or the Saphis of Persia, and the Brahmins of India. There, as here, men investigate under the pretence of retaining what is good. But the idea of belonging to any particular religion, like that of Palestine, as if it were the universal religion, they reject. What blindness! Is the sun of no use to the north, because it rises in the east?

Our Lord easily perceives how little inclined the governor is to lend his ear to deeper explanations, and therefore, He confines Himself to the placing the charge made by the Jews in its proper light. 'My kingdom,' says He, 'is not of this world. If my kingdom were of this world, then would my servants fight, that I should not be delivered to the Jews; but now is my kingdom not from hence.'

Do not leave unobserved how carefully He selects His words, while thus defending Himself, lest He should infringe upon the truth even by a mere omission. He does not deny that He came to establish a kingdom and expressly calls it *His* kingdom; He only repels the groundless suspicion of His having intended to overturn the existing authorities and to establish a new political state. Had this been His intention, says He, 'then would my servants fight, that I should not be delivered to the Jews.' He does not, however, say that His kingdom makes no claim eventually to the government of the whole world, or He would have denied more than was consistent with truth. He only asserts that His kingdom was not of *this* world, and clearly intimates, by laying the emphasis on the word 'this,' that another aeon than the present would certainly see His delegates seated on thrones, and His Word and gospel the magna charta of all nations. It is particularly to be observed that in the sentence, 'Now is my kingdom not from hence', the word 'now' evidently refers to a period in which His kingdom should occupy a very different position from that which it occupied at that time.

Pilate listens with astonishment and with a degree of uneasiness to our Lord's speech and then affected by a reverential impression respecting the Person of the accused, he says, 'Art thou a king then?' One might have thought he would have said, 'I clearly see that thou art not a king.' But it would appear that the idea became increasingly strong in him that this Jesus was really a king, although in a different sense from what the Jews declared He pretended to be. But the case is similar with regard to many in the present day. These people are conscious of a superior nature in Jesus, but they continue in their unbelief, and are never clear in their own minds about the person of Christ. In the bottom of their soul the question of Pilate again is heard, 'Art thou a king then?' And when, notwithstanding, they try to defend the bulwark of their unbelief, nothing is left them but by constraint to belie the voice of truth within them, which thousands, alas! do, because a recognition of Christ as a king would cost them the delight they experience in the service of the world and sin.

What answer does the Lord Jesus make to Pilate's question? 'Thou sayest it, I am a king. To this end was I born, and for this cause came I into the world, that I should bear witness unto the truth. Every one that is of the truth heareth my voice.' He is, therefore, a king. He boldly asserts it Himself. Not for a moment did the shame and suffering He was enduring succeed in obscuring in Him the consciousness of His superhuman dignity and majesty.

May you who are our brethren in the Lord, in the midst of the weakness of the flesh, and the various afflictions through which you have to pass, never wholly lose the divine consciousness of your adoption. Christ is a king; you are, therefore, not in error who wear His uniform and have trusted your life and destiny to His hands. You are perfectly justified, not only in speaking of Christ's kingdom, but also in bidding adieu to the last doubt of its final victory and eventual sway over the world, although His kingdom is not of this world, or, as He majestically expresses Himself, like one looking down from the heights of heaven upon the earth, 'Now is my kingdom not from hence' – that is, hath no earthly origin.

Christ is a king. 'To this end,' says He, 'was I born, and for this cause came I into the world, that I should bear witness of the truth.' Two objects are mentioned here; the first has reference to His royalty, by which He asserts that He was no adventurer but was born a king, such as the wise men from the east correctly honoured when they hailed Him as the new-born king of the Jews. The second has reference to His bearing witness. In the words, 'I was born,' He indicates His incarnation. But, lest Pilate, or any one else, should erroneously suppose that Jesus included His whole origin in these words, He adds, 'I came into the world;' thereby intimating His heavenly descent, and His existence before He appeared in the flesh – yea, before the world was.

We ought highly to esteem such testimonies of His eternal and divine nature from His own lips. Their value is increased in an age like the present which is so full of scepticism, and which so boldly dares to stamp the Lord Christ as a mere man. Had this really been the case, nothing would be left us but to close our churches and bury all our hopes, because the latter rest wholly on the divinity of Jesus Christ. Let us therefore cleave firmly to this doctrine, seeing that it is clearly and fully asserted in the sacred Scriptures, especially at a time when, to use the language of the apostle Peter, there are many 'false teachers who privily bring in damnable heresies, even denying the Lord that bought them, and bring upon themselves swift destruction.'

It is pleasing to observe how the Lord, out of consideration for the governor, imperceptibly leads him from His kingly office to the circumstance of His bearing witness, and to the truth as its object. He hopes by so doing to touch the string which would be the first to reverberate at the sound of the gospel. The perverted Roman was also an inquirer after truth, for this question belonged to the Grecian subjects of study which the Romans had also taken up, and a seeking after truth belongs to human nature. Some one well observes here, that 'Jesus lays hold of Pilate by the only topic by which He could make an impression on him.' Thus carefully does the Lord proceed in the exercise of His pastoral office, while taking into account the particular inward state of every individual whom He strives to save.

Christ, however, did not come into the world to join Himself to the seekers after truth as their confederate, but rather to lead them on to the aim they were in search of, and thus bring them to the Sabbath of repose. He did not come, as some think, to bring down truth from heaven to earth, but as He Himself says, 'to bear witness of the truth.' Truth already existed, interwoven in the history of Israel, and clothed in the inspired language of Moses and the Prophets. Christ only bore witness to it, and confirmed it in the most comprehensive manner, accomplishing prophecy in Himself, and presenting in His own person, the realization of the law's fulfilment. In His whole conduct He exhibits to the world the divine origin of the law, and in the events of His life, that of prophecy. He bore witness of the truth, inasmuch as in His own person, while casting down all that is false, He was able to display it in all its splendour in the face of heaven, earth, and hell.

But how was it that the Lord, who never abruptly passed from one idea to another, connected His witnessing for the truth with His kingdom and dominion? Did He mean to say that His kingdom was only a sphere of tuition, and He in so far only a king, as He was able to reign over the minds of men by His teaching? By no means. He does not bear such witness as a king, but as a prophet; and points out the way in which He will establish His kingdom, which He intimates in the words, 'He that is of the truth heareth my voice.' Yes, those who hear His voice are the citizens of His kingdom.

The expression, 'every one that is of the truth,' betokens an inward preparation for conversion, which no one experiences without the operation of grace. No one is by nature of the truth; but all men are liars, since they love darkness rather than light, because the light reproves them for their sins and disturbs their repose; and because they press error to their bosoms and shut themselves up against the entrance of truth which menaces their sensual pleasures with danger and urges them to a life of self-denial. But as soon as the Spirit gains room, the love of delusion gives way to the ardent desire to be freed from it. By the operation of the Spirit of God we become joined to those who are of the truth. Then, if the divine Teacher utters His voice, how does our inmost soul echo to the sound of His light and life-giving words. If He then says, 'Come unto me, ye that are weary and heavy laden,' how gladly do we accept the gracious invitation! If He then unveils His glory and beauty, how do our longing souls rush into His arms rejoicing!

Therefore, let us not cease to call upon the King of Truth to help us, and not leave us till He has attuned the chords of our soul in such a manner that His Word may find a full and abiding echo in us. Let us entreat, above all things, the hearing ear, the understanding, believing, child-like, and simple heart, and plead His gracious promise to guide the meek in judgment, and to teach the humble His way.

Chapter 29

'What Is Truth?'

'He that is of the truth', said our Lord, 'heareth my voice.' Pilate then said unto Him, 'What is truth?' Some have found in these words a gentle sneer; others the expression of a complete indifference to religion. But neither of these explanations fully accord with the man's character. The words are more profound and important. They shed light upon an entire age, and upon the inmost state of mind of thousands of its children.

Pilate lived in days which might be designated as those of the mature education of mankind, so far as we understand by that expression, intellectual and moral culture, to which the children of Adam, left to themselves, and by the exercise of their own natural powers and abilities, are able to attain. Not only had art reached its highest perfection, but philosophy was also at the summit of its boldest investigations; and even to the present day we admire the systems which, by the effort of highly gifted reasoning powers, they called into existence. But still there was no satisfactory basis for them to rest upon. Although the human mind had brought to light much that was probable, yet any thing certain and infallible was sought for in vain. Even the greatest of all the sages of antiquity confessed that only if a God were to descend from heaven would it be possible for men to attain to that which was sure. Nay, the saying became commonplace, that only one thing was certain, which was that we could know nothing of things above the reach of the senses, and even this was not entirely certain.

Pilate stands before us as the true representative of the social culture of his age. Though we must not take it for granted that he ever deeply studied the various systems of philosophy, yet, like others of his own rank, he was doubtless acquainted with the essential results of philosophical investigation, while to the literature of his age he was doubtless no stranger. This man's path through life brought him into contact with the Lord from heaven, and thus placed him in a spiritual atmosphere, in which feelings and presentiments again awoke in him which seemed to have been long stifled by the breath of the frivolous culture of the age which he had imbibed.

Christ, whose very appearance produced a strange effect upon this heathen, speaks to him of another world, of a heavenly kingdom, and finally of a truth which had appeared, and which, therefore, might be really found and known. Pilate then breaks out into the remarkable words, 'What is truth?' The polished heathen of that age, and one of the better of them, displays to us by the question his inward state. 'What is truth?' was at that time the language of thousands: 'That which we see with our eyes, and feel with our hands, is the only thing that is certain under heaven. No mortal eye sees beyond the limits of the region of the senses; and though the plea of a poetic imagination may be able to satisfy those upon one stage of life and culture, it can not satisfy all.'

In Pilate's question, we may further perceive the sceptical philosopher of rank, who is not only aware that the researches of human thought lead to the most diversified and opposite results; but who also cherishes the idea that he has himself reflected and ruminated upon the labours of the wise of this world, and that by his own reasoning upon them, he has arrived at the conviction that nothing can be known or ascertained of things which lie beyond the bounds of visibility. 'What is truth?' he exclaims – 'One man calls this truth, another that, which is perhaps even something quite the opposite. Systems rise and fall. The man who seeks for truth sails upon a sea without a haven or a landing-place.'

In Pilate's question is also apparent the boundless pride of the Roman citizen, who as respects enlightenment and culture, thinks himself far above all the other nations of the earth, and the Jews in particular. Pilate utters his inquiry with a degree of inward, though transient excitement, as if he would say, 'Thou, a Hebrew rabbi, wilt surely not think that I, a Roman patrician, am going to seek instruction from thee?' The pervading tone of Pilate's question is, however, of a better kind, and is only slightly tinged with the discords hitherto mentioned. It breathes of melancholy, dejection, and even the silent despair of a heart which, with the belief in the existence of a world above the stars, cannot throw away the wish and the feeling of necessity for such a world. The soul of Pilate finds itself unhappy and desolate in the dreary waste of absolute unbelief into which it is banished.

Were we to elucidate the governor's question, and explain it as proceeding from the inmost recesses of his soul, it would probably imply what follows: 'Thou speakest of truth, alas! Truth was never given to a poor mortal to be the companion of his steps. We inquire after it, but echo, as if in ridicule of our anxious desire, only returns our question back to us. Not a single truth has rewarded the many thousand years' research of philosophic thought, and yet thou, Man of Nazareth, speakest of truth as of a resident on the gloomy earth! Death has been silent from the first; the grave below is silent, as well as the stars above; and dost thou wish to be regarded as having loosed their tongues and unsealed their mysteries?'

In Pilate there was doubtless something of the proud philosopher, something of worn-out indifference, something of the professed sceptic, something of the frivolous free-thinker and scoffer, and something of the hasty, jealous, and haughty blusterer, who, with his inquiry, 'What is truth?' also meant to say, 'How could you venture to trouble me with your Jewish matters of faith, who have things of greater importance to think of?' But still there is something beside this – something better and nobler – an unperverted inquiring mind – a longing for deliverance, but bound down, alas! by the impure and gloomy elements, which enthrall him so that he can not act at liberty.

As often as this question of Pilate's occurs to me, it appears to me as if it had not been asked eighteen centuries ago, but as if uttered in the present day – nay, it even seems to sound in my ears as proceeding from my immediate vicinity. It strikingly indicates many philosophers of our own times, and the so-called 'height' which modern intellectual refinement has reached; only that the question, in the mouths of our contemporaries, sounds infinitely more culpable than from the lips of the Roman, whose eyes had not seen what we have; for at that time Jesus was not glorified, nor His Spirit poured out from on high, nor the wondrous edifice of the Church of Christ established. But after all this has taken place, for a man to step back again to the position of Pilate, a mere heathen, is something no longer human but devilish. An infernal spark now burns in scepticism; and the dubiousness of the Roman, compared with the unbelief of our baptized heathen, is almost like an innocent lamb contrasted with a wily serpent. Unbelief is now the light-shunning offspring of a wicked and rebellious will. We feel a degree of pity and compassion for Pilate, but for infidels of the present day, nothing is left them but 'the blackness of darkness forever.'

'What is truth?' It is soon found, when earnestly sought. There are many, who inquire respecting certain truths, but studiously turn their backs upon the truth of the gospel, wherever it meets them. They would be glad to see solved a number of problems in nature and in human life; but all their research is a mere effort of the imagination, and the interest they take in it only vain curiosity. They take part in discussions respecting the creation of the world, existence after death, and the kind of life beyond the grave. But they shun the truth as it is in Jesus, and seek in a variety of ways to avoid and evade it. Eighteen hundred years ago, a Man appeared upon earth, whom no one could convict of any other crime than that of calling Himself 'the Truth,' and of having announced Himself as the Messiah, who should eventually subdue the whole world to His spiritual sceptre. Truth likewise appeared in the nomadic tents of the patriarchs of Israel, as well as in the encampments of the people of God, when wandering in the wilderness. It speaks to men in a voice of thunder from Mount Sinai, and in gentler tones from the hills and valleys of Canaan. We hear her voice on Bethlehem's plains, in the harmonious psalms of the 'sweet singer of Israel;' and it greets us in the halls of the Temple, in significant types and mysterious hieroglyphics. We approach Jehovah's seers, and our astonished eye looks up to a brilliant starry firmament. They are thoughts of truth, which shine with such supernatural radiance. Led by the hand of these holy seers, we go forward, and are greeted at length by the Truth in person. 'I am the Truth,' says One, everything about whom points Him out as more than human; and all who long for the light, are heard exclaiming, 'Thou art He!'

Then let the question of Pilate, 'What is truth?' no longer be heard upon earth. It can now only be asked by imbecility or obstinate self-deception and diabolical hatred of the light. Truth has made its entry into the world, and dwells confidingly among us, accessible to all who sincerely seek it. A philosophy that acts as if it must first bring up truth from the deep, or fetch it down from heaven, will be punished for its base ingratitude toward the God of grace by being left to grope eternally in the dark and never to reach the end of its fruitless investigations.

The true object of philosophy now would be to fathom and exhaust the inmost consciousness of the human spirit, and free from prejudice, to try the effect upon its indelible necessities of the truth which has appeared in Christ. If this were done, it would soon moor its bark, after its long aberrations, on the shores of Mount Zion, and joyfully exclaim, 'I have found what I sought, I have reached my goal.' All who seriously and sincerely inquire for truth will inevitably land at last in the haven of the gospel. Hence the Saviour was able, with the greatest confidence to say, 'He that is of the truth heareth my voice.'

Let us thank and praise the all-sufficient God for the unspeakable gift He has bestowed upon us. 'Behold, the night is far spent, and the day is at hand.' The prophetic call to 'Arise and shine for thy light is come,' has long been fulfilled. May the admonition which that call includes be responded to by us, and its promise be experienced! Let us cheerfully make room in our hearts and minds for the Truth which stands at our door, and let us walk as children of the light. He is the Truth, who is at the same time the Way and the Life. Let us cast the viperous brood of doubts beneath His feet, that He may trample upon them, and make Him our all in all, for life, death, and eternity.

Chapter 30

The Lamb of God

After his first conversation with Jesus, Pilate again comes forward into the open court before the people, bringing the accused with him. The governor's inward state is no longer unknown to us. We are acquainted with him as a man in whom all susceptibility for true greatness of soul was by no means extinguished. A silent admiration of the extraordinary Personage who stood before him prevaded the whole of the procedure respecting Him. The words He uttered, the silence He observed, His look, and His whole bearing, His humility and then again His sublime composure, His lamb-like patience, and undisturbed self-possession – all this made a powerful impression upon Pilate; and if he had given vent to that which passed fleetingly through his mind, he would, at least momentarily, have expressed something similar to the testimony given by the apostle John, 'We beheld his glory, the glory as of the only-begotten Son of God, full of grace and truth.'

The dignity of Immanuel shone too powerfully into the soul of the Roman to leave him at liberty to act toward Him as he pleased. To a certain extent, he had been inwardly overcome by Him. He is compelled to absolve Him from all criminality. He can not avoid feeling a secret reverence for Him, and is even constrained to act as the intercessor and advocate of the just One. What majesty must have shone around the Lamb of God even while suffering and ignominy rolled over His head and with what wondrous radiance must the Sun of Righteousness have broken through the clouds of deep humiliation, as to be able to constrain even a worldly-minded epicurean to such a feeling of respect!

As was the case with Pilate, so would it be with many of like sentiments in the present day, if they were to come into similar contact with Jesus. I have those in view who have long forsaken the Word and the Church of God, and intoxicated with the inebriating draught of the spirit of the age, have given up Christianity as no longer tenable, and have renounced Christ Himself without previous examination, as though He were merely a Jewish rabbi, fallible like all other mortals. O, if they could only once resolve to approach nearer to Him by an impartial study of the Gospel history, I am persuaded that they would soon find it impossible to continue indifferent to Him in future, nay, that before they were aware, they would feel constrained either to do homage to Jesus, and to give themselves up to Him with all their hearts, or else that they would hate Him, as One whose claim to rule over us we can not gainsay, but to whose sceptre we refuse to bow.

Pilate frankly says to the chief priests and all the people, 'I find no fault in this man;' thereby confirming the words of the apostle Peter, 'a Lamb without blemish and without spot.' It certainly manifests great shallowness of thought and deficiency of judgment to say only that he finds no fault in Jesus. When the latter testified that He was the Son of the living God, and the King of the kingdom of heaven, He was guilty of a great crime, if His assertions were false, and these lofty titles only assumed. But if He was correct in uttering such exalted things respecting Himself, how was it that the governor had nothing better to say for Him than the meagre testimony that he acknowledged Him only to be guiltless? But even this assurance we gladly receive, and regard with emotion the man who is so favourably inclined toward the Accused, and so powerfully affected by His innocence and moral unblamableness. Doubtless, after this testimony in His favour, Pilate would gladly have liberated Him; but the Jews, the emperor, his position, and many other causes prevent him from doing so.

When it is only the conviction of the understanding, in place of a heart burdened with the guilt of sin, which connects a man with Jesus, he will never find in Him an advocate or intercessor. Such a one does not count all things loss for Christ. Worldly honour, human favour, domestic and social peace, and the like, exercise over him a much more potent and overpowering influence. Far be it from me to act the part of a judge; but I am seriously afraid that among the number of believers in the present day, many may be found whose faith is only like that of Pilate.

Pilate having uttered his inmost conviction of the innocence of Jesus, the chief priests, not a little enraged at their defeat, foam out fresh accusations against the Righteous One. 'They were the more fierce,' says the narrative. They pour out a flood of rage and fury upon Him, and now the saying of the prophet Isaiah was fulfilled. He was oppressed, and he was afflicted, yet, like a lamb, he opened not his mouth.

The most significant and remarkable type introduced into the divine ordinances, as well as into Israel's history and ritual, was the lamb. It even meets us at the threshold of paradise in the sacrifice of Abel, as an object peculiarly acceptable in the sight of God. Later on, the lamb with its blood consecrates the commencement of the history of the Israelites. The sprinkling of the door-posts with the blood of lambs was the means of Israel's preservation in Egypt from the sword of the destroying angel and the departure of the people from Pharaoh's house of bondage.

From that time, the lamb continued to be the most prominent figure by which God typified the future Messiah to the
children of Abraham. Thenceforward it acquired an abiding
footing in Israel's sacrificial rights in general and in the yearly
Passover in particular. In the latter each household was
enjoined by the Mosaic law to bring a male lamb without
blemish or infirmity to the sanctuary, there solemnly confess
their transgressions over it, then bring it, typically burdened
with their sins, to the court of the temple to be slain; and
after it was roasted, consume it entirely, in festive communion
with joy and thanksgiving to Jehovah.

That which was prophetically typical in this ceremony
was so apparent that even the most simple mind could not
mistake it. Every one who was only partially susceptible of
that which was divinely symbolical, felt immediately
impressed with the idea that this divine ordinance could
have no other aim than to keep alive in Israel, along with
the remembrance of the promised Deliverer, the confidence
and hope in Him.

John the Baptist appears in the wilderness; and the first
greeting with which he welcomes Jesus, which was renewed
whenever he saw Him, is, 'Behold the Lamb of God, which
taketh away the sin of the world!' thereby directing the
attention of the whole world to Jesus, as if there were thenceforward nothing else worth seeing in heaven or on earth than
this Lamb of God; and by so doing, he certainly directs us to
the greatest and most beatifying of all mysteries, and to the
pith and marrow of the entire gospel. For if Christ had been
only the 'Lion of the tribe of Judah,' and not at the same
time 'the Lamb,' what would it have availed us? As 'the
Lamb,' He is the desire of all nations, the Star of hope to the
exiles from Eden, the Sun of righteousness in the night of
sorrow to those whom the law condemns, and the heavenly
Lamp to the wanderer in the gloomy vale of death.

He is all this as 'the Lamb that taketh away the sin of the world.' But this expression implies, not only that the sin of the world grieves His sacred heart, or that He endured the contradiction of sinners against Himself, and that He patiently bore the pain inflicted on Him by their sins, and by His life and doctrine aimed at removing sin. The words have a meaning which can not be properly fathomed. Christ bore the sin of the world in a much more peculiar and literal sense than that just mentioned. He bore it by letting it be imputed to Him by His Father, in a manner incomprehensible to us, so that it became no longer ours but His. 'God was in Christ, reconciling the world unto himself, not imputing their trespasses unto them' (2 Cor. 5:19). What can this mean, but that God did not leave the world to suffer for its trespasses, nor even for its sins. And if it be asked, 'Who then did suffer if the world escaped?' We find the answer in the verse where it is said, 'He hath made him to be sin for us who knew no sin, that we might be made the righteousness of God in him.'

Here we must not pass unnoticed the wonderful union and amalgamation into which Christ entered with the human race, the mysterious depths of which we shall never fathom here below. Eventually, we shall be astonished in what a profound and comprehensive sense Christ became our Head; and how literally the title belonged to Him of the Representative of our race. But then we shall also learn to know and comprehend how, without infringing upon the moral order of the world, the guilt of others could be transferred to Him, and how He could thus become 'the Lamb that taketh away the sin of the world.'

Keeping this position of our Lord in view as Mediator and Surety, the accusations which were heaped upon Christ by the Jews acquire a deep symbolical signification. Although in the abstract, as far as they have reference to our Lord in His moral capacity, they were the most abominable slanders and falsehoods; yet in another respect, they have much of truth at their basis. The world, according to God's counsel and will, discharges on its Representative, Jesus Christ, the transgressions of which itself is guilty; and the groundless accusations of the Jews serve only to place in the brightest and most brilliant light, the Lamb-like character of our great Redeemer.

Still more clearly does 'the Lamb of God' manifest itself in Christ, in the conduct which He observes, amid the furious accusations of His adversaries. Jesus is silent, as if actually guilty of all that they charge upon Him. Pilate, unable to cope with the storm which roars around him from the crowd below, almost entreats the Lord to say something in His own defence. But Jesus is silent. Pilate, occupied solely with Him, says, 'Answerest thou nothing? Behold how many things they witness against Thee! Hearest Thou not?' 'But Jesus,' as the narrative informs us, 'answered nothing, not even a word, insomuch that the governor marvelled greatly.'

How could he do otherwise, seeing that he only measured the Lord's conduct by a human standard? Every one else, at a moment when life was at stake, would have hastily brought together every thing that could have overthrown the charges brought against him, especially if so much had stood at his command as in the case of Jesus; but He is silent. Every one else would at least have demanded proofs of the truth of the shameless denunciations of His opponents; but not a syllable proceeds from Jesus' lips. Every one else in His situation would have appealed from the mendacious priesthood to the consciences of the people, and have roused the feeling of what is just and right in those who were not entirely hardened, but Jesus appealed to no one, either in heaven or on earth. Ah! had Pilate known who He was that stood thus meekly before him, how would he have marvelled! It was He before whose judgment seat all the millions that have ever

breathed upon earth will be summoned, that He may pronounce upon them their final and eternal sentence. It was
He before whom the sons of Belial, who now heap their lying
accusations upon Him, will at length appear bound in the
fetters of His curse, and who, under the thunder of His
sentence, will call upon the rocks to fall upon them, and the
hills to cover them, and hide them from the face of Him that
sitteth upon the throne, and from the wrath of the Lamb.
And He now stands before their bar, and is mute, like one
who thinks He must give up all hope of gaining His cause.

But the Lord also observes silence with regard to those who
blaspheme Him in the present day. It is a silence of forbearance, but also partly of contempt; for they likewise
blaspheme Him against light and knowledge. Eventually He
will speak to them, and then they will be constrained
tremblingly to acknowledge that they would not have Him
to reign over them. Christ is silent when His people murmur
against Him and complain of His ways and guidance. He is
mute in this case also, from the profoundest feeling of
innocence, well knowing that while supplicating His
forgiveness, they will kiss His hands for having led them just
so and not otherwise.

In other respects Christ is not silent upon earth. He that
has an ear for His voice, hears it in a variety of ways in every
place. Witnessing for Himself and His cause, He speaks at
one time in obvious judgments which He inflicts upon His
foes; and at another in tangible blessings and answers to
prayer with which He favours His friends. He speaks by the
surprising confirmations which science in its progress is often
involuntarily obliged to afford His Word; as well as by the
manifold signs of the times which manifest nothing but a
literal fulfilment of His prophecies. Hence what we read in
Psalm 19 literally becomes true: 'There is no speech nor
language where their voice is not heard. Their sound is gone

forth through all the earth, and their words unto the end of the world.'

But the chief cause of Jesus' silence amid the stormy accusations of His adversaries, has not yet been touched upon. It lies in His mediatorial position. Our Lord, the Lamb of God, the High Priest, the heavenly Surety, is silent for He takes upon Himself before the face of God all that of which He is accused, because He is willing to suffer and repay, as the mediating and universal debtor, all that we have incurred.

Beholding the Lamb of God harmoniously dissolves all our inward discords, restrains every passion, makes the commandment which is otherwise a heavy chain into a gentle yoke beneath which, led by the paternal hand of Deity, we joyfully pursue our way. In this looking to the Lamb consists 'the victory that overcometh the world.' But when our eyes open in the heavenly world, we shall behold the Lamb without a veil. No cloud will then conceal Him from us any more. We sink low at His feet in humble adoration, and join with the hosts of the just made perfect, in the never-ending hymn, 'Worthy is the Lamb that was slain to receive honour, and glory, and blessing, forever and ever.' Amen.

Chapter 31

Christ before Herod

Pilate's clear and decided testimony that he found no fault in Jesus, did not fail of its effect on His accusers. They stand aghast, and perceive the danger which threatens the result of their whole proceedings. Had Pilate manfully maintained throughout the tone of judicial decision with which he commenced, it would doubtless have burst the fetters imposed on the better feelings of a great part of the assembled multitude, and Christ have been set at liberty and even saluted with new hosannas; while the tumult thus occasioned might have been attended with serious consequences to the chief priests and rulers. They were therefore compelled to oppose such a change in the state of things by every means in their power. They consequently again raise their voices with fresh complaints. Their accusations, though uttered more noisily than before, bear evident marks of their failing courage. Instead of denouncing the Lord, as before, as a rebel and a traitor, they bring their accusation down to the unimportant assertion, that he 'stirred up the people' by his teachings, which he began in Galilee, and continued throughout all Jewry.

How easy would it have been for Pilate, by a rapid and prudent use of this favourable moment, to have triumphantly rescued his prisoner and with Him, himself and his own conscience! In order entirely to confuse and disarm his more than half subdued foes, he only needed, in a few energetic words, to have pointed out the baseness of their conduct. But fear had taken possession of the poor man. In the uproar, which only showed the weakness of the adverse party, he imagines he hears some new storm rolling over his head and how does he rejoice when the mention of Galilee seems to him to open a new way of escape. He hastily inquires 'whether the man were a Galilean?' and on being answered in the affirmative, he exclaims with delight, 'He belongs, then, to Herod's jurisdiction!' and immediately gives orders for Jesus to be conducted bound to the latter, who happened fortunately to be at that time in Jerusalem; and he feels as if a mountain were removed from his breast on seeing the troublesome captive withdraw under the escort of the chief priest, soldiers, and the crowd that followed.

We already know something of Herod Antipas, the Tetrarch of Galilee. He is the same wretched libertine who caused John the Baptist to be beheaded in prison. For this crime his conscience severely smote him; and when he heard of Jesus and His doings, he could not be persuaded but that the wonder-worker was John whom he had murdered but who had risen from the dead. A Sadducee according to his mental bias, more a heathen than an Israelite, and entirely devoted to licentiousness, he was, nevertheless, as is often the case of such characters, not disinclined to base acts of violence and capable of the most refined cruelties. Luke states respecting him that he had done much evil.

To this degraded libertine therefore, in whom every better feeling had been gradually extinguished our Lord is brought, in order that He may not be spared from any thing that is ignominious and repulsive, and that there might be no judicial tribunal before which He did not stand. The envenomed hosts of priests and Pharisees with wild uproar arrive with their prey before the residence of the Galilean king, who, on hearing what was the cause of the appearing of the unwonted crowd, orders the heads of the people with their delinquent to be brought before him. Jesus silently and gravely approaches His sovereign. The latter, as the narrative informs us, 'when he saw Jesus, was exceeding glad; for he was desirous to see him of a long season, because he had heard many things of him, and he hoped to have seen some miracles done by him.'

It may seem strange that Herod had never before seen the face of Jesus, although He so often abode in Galilee. But the Lord had never honoured Tiberias where Herod resided, with a visit, although He had frequently been near it; and for Herod to take a single step in order to make the acquaintance of the Nazarene who was so much spoken of, naturally never crossed the mind of one so destitute of all religious interest and at the same time, so proud and overbearing as his Galilean majesty. It afforded him no little pleasure so conveniently and without risk, to see his long-cherished wish fulfilled. 'At all events,' thought he within himself, 'it will afford an interesting pastime, an amusing spectacle. And if He will let Himself be induced to unveil somewhat of the future to us or perform a miracle, what a delightful hour might be spent!'

The king promised himself a recreation from the presence of Jesus such as is expected from that of a juggler or a charlatan. In this respect, he represents those frivolous people who, according to the apostolic expression, 'have not the Spirit,' and to whom even the most sublime things are only a comedy. Persons of this description venture to intrude even into the sanctuary and are apparently desirous of seeing Christ, at least as set forth in sermons, books, figures, or history, but only because of the aesthetic feeling thereby excited. Suffice it to say, that to such characters even the church becomes a theatre, the sermon a pastime, the gospel a romance, and the history of conversions a novel. O how dangerous is the position of those in whom all seriousness degenerates into empty jocularity, and every thing that ought deeply to affect them, into jest and amusement! They trifle with eternal verities.

Herod regards our Lord on His approach with an inquisitive look, and after eyeing Him from head to foot presumes to put a number of foolish questions at Him. Our Lord deigns him no answer but observes complete silence. The king continues to question Him but the Saviour is mute. Herod even suggests that He ought to perform some miracle. Jesus cannot comply with his wish and gives him to know this by His continued silence more impressively than could have been done by words. The chief priests and scribes, indignant at His passive behaviour, again begin their blasphemies and accuse Him vehemently. He regards them as unworthy of a reply and continues to observe silence.

The Lord having refused to do the will of Herod and his satellites, the miserable men infer from His behaviour that He is unable to do any thing and begin to despise Him, and even to mock Him. Painful are the mortifications that Jesus has here to endure. Even the hurrying Him about hither and thither – Pilate's sending him to Herod, to show the latter a piece of civility – Herod's returning the compliment by sending Him back to the Roman governor, that the latter may have the honour of pronouncing the final sentence upon Him – what degradation is inflicted on the Lord of glory in all this! But this is only the beginning of disgrace and humiliation. How much has He to endure in the presence of Herod and his courtiers who treat him as a juggler and a conjurer! He is urged to amuse the company by a display of His art. His ear is offended by impertinent questions; and on His making no reply to them all, the measure of insult and mockery overflows.

And tell me how the Most Holy One, who inhabits eternity, could quietly have borne to see such degradation of the Son of His good pleasure without casting forth the light-nings of his wrath upon the perpetrators of such indignities, if the Lord Jesus had endured this scandalous treatment only for His own Person, and not at the same time as standing in an extraordinary position, and exercising a mysterious mediation? But you know that He stood there in our stead and as the second Adam, laden with our guilt. 'The Lord laid upon him the iniquities of us all.' 'The chastisement of our peace was upon him.'

Thank God that such was the case; for I should never have been able to make room for the conviction that my sins would not be imputed to me, had I not at the same time, been told what had become of the sins thus taken from me, since I know nothing more surely than this, that my blood-red sins cannot be arbitrarily pardoned and overlooked or even pass unnoticed as trifles of no account. Were this the case, how would it be possible for me to believe any longer in a just and holy God? But the gospel now comes in and tells me most clearly the history of my misdeeds, how they were transferred to Him who appeared in my place; and in His intervention, I now sensibly grasp the legal ground of my absolution. The Lord stands before Herod, as he did before Annas, Caiaphas, and Pilate, not merely to be judged by men, but by God at the same time; and it is my sin for which He atones and my debt which He liquidates.

No wonder, therefore, that He resigns himself to the poisoned arrows which here pierce His heart in its most vulnerable part – that without gainsaying He listens to the most wicked imputations, and with lamb-like patience lets Himself be branded both as a blasphemer and a fanatic, a rebel and a conspirator – that He even bears with equanimity the circumstance that Herod's expectations respecting Him are gradually changed into contempt for His person – that the Lord of Glory suffers Himself to be degraded so low as to become the butt of the miserable jokes of a contemptible and adulterous court. What He endures is dreadful to think of; and yet it lay in His power with a wave of His hand, to dash the reckless company to the ground. But He does not move a finger and remains silent, for He knows that here is God's altar and the fire and the wood; and that He was the Lamb for the burnt-offering.

But however deep the humiliation in which we behold the Son of God, it is nevertheless interwoven throughout with traits which are glorifying to Him and tend to establish our faith.

Even in the childish joy which Pilate evinces at the prospect of transferring the process against Jesus to another, his deep conviction of the innocence and unblamableness of the accused is more clearly reflected than in all his oral assertions. His soul exults at the accidental information given him that Jesus belongs to the Galilean tetrarchate, which teaches us how fortunate the Roman esteemed his being thus able to escape from sharing in the guilt of condemning the Righteous One.

Of Herod it was said that he was 'exceeding glad when he saw Jesus.' This uncommon joy of the Galilean prince, that at last an opportunity was afforded him of seeing Jesus face to face, is not less important in an apologetic point of view and tends no less to the Lord's glorification than the joy of Pilate in being happily rid of Him. The Saviour must have excited a great sensation in the country and not have displayed His marvellous powers in remote corners but in places of public resort, that Herod thus burned with desire to make His personal acquaintance. And how uncommon and unique must the Lord's acts have been, that a man so totally dead to every better feeling, as that adulterer in a royal crown, should have such a desire!

Herod hoped besides that he would have seen some miracle performed by the Saviour. This expectation is again a proof that Jesus had really sealed His divine mission by miraculous acts, and that the wonders He performed were universally acknowledged to be such. Herod does not intend first to try whether Jesus can work miracles but takes His power and ability to do so for granted. But what a depth of inward corruption is betrayed in the fact that this man, in spite of his conviction of the Saviour's ability to perform divine acts, not only refuses Him belief and homage but even degrades Him to the state of an object of his scorn!

The tetrarch asks the Lord a variety of questions surpassing the bounds of human knowledge. He had therefore heard of the wisdom with which the Lord knew how to reply to questions of this kind and to solve every difficulty. Hence he involuntarily does honour to Christ's prophetical office. And even in the circumstance that Herod did not venture to go further in his ridicule than clothing Jesus in a white toga, when the latter observed a profound silence to his questions – he manifests a secret reverence for Him, and thus proves anew that Christ must have actually spoken in an ambiguous manner of His kingdom and of a dominion which He came to establish.

Finally, that the deep-rooted disagreement which had so long prevailed between Pilate and Herod, was suddenly terminated and changed into a friendly feeling by the civility shown to the latter in transferring over to him the accused Rabbi, serves again as a proof how highly these men in power thought of the delinquent brought before them. The transfer of a common criminal, or even of a notorious fanatic and swindler, would probably have been attended by no such effect. But that Jesus of Nazareth was selected to mediate the renewed approximation of the two potentates works favourably and puts an end to all former ill-will and mistrust.

Who does not perceive that this circumstance, however revolting in itself, again tends to glorify Christ in a high degree?

Something similar to that which occurred between Pilate and Herod happens not seldom, even in the present day. Parties who most violently oppose each other in other fields of research become reconciled and even confederates and friends, if only for a while, as soon as they join in the contest against Christ and His adorers. But what else do they evince thereby than that Christ stands in their way as an imposing power? An inconsiderable personage, whose claims on their submission they knew not to be well-founded, would never exercise such an influence over them; and finally, an individual whom they regarded as merely mythological, they would certainly put aside, as unworthy of their attention.

Whatever may be planned or executed against Jesus, He comes forth more than justified from it all. Hatred must glorify Him as well as love. Persecution crowns Him as well as devotedness to His cause. But if mutual opposition to Him is able to transmute bitter enemies into friends, what bonds ought the mutual homage of the glorified Redeemer to cement! 'I believe in the communion of saints', is a part of our creed. I not merely believe it, but thank God! I also see it. May the Lord awaken in the hearts of His children sentiments of real brotherly affection toward each other!

Chapter 32

Pilate Our Advocate

Pilate again finds himself in a great dilemma. By transferring the proceedings to Herod, he hoped to have escaped from his painful situation. But contrary to his expectation, the Galilean prince sends the accused back to him again, leaving it to him to terminate the affair he had once begun. The governor, not a little disturbed at this mistake in his calculations, turns again to the accusers of the Saviour and renews his attempt to rescue Jesus, and with Him his own peace of mind. He makes a speech to the priests, rulers, and the assembled populace, which, though it contains nothing but what we have already heard him state, is nevertheless worthy of our serious consideration, because in it, Pilate unconsciously and involuntarily appears as our advocate.

However strangely it may sound, Pilate becomes our advocate. He takes Christ our Head under his protection and us with Him. He legally absolves Him from all criminality and in Him His followers also. He begins his address by saying, 'Ye have brought this man unto me, as one that perverteth the people.' In a certain sense, something of this kind may be asserted of the Saviour with truth. For even as He testifies to His believing followers that they are not of the world; so He also enjoins upon them not to be conformed to the world.

He calls upon His people to 'come out from among them; for the friendship of the world is enmity with God.'

In some degree, Christians will always be separatists. God has so organized them that a union of fire with water is sooner to be thought of than of them with the multitude. Their convictions, principles, tastes, opinions, and views of things in the world, as well as their wishes, hopes, and desires, all are directly opposed to the world's mode of thinking and acting. They are by nature and kind separated from the unregenerate world.

When the rulers of Israel charged Jesus with perverting the people, they wished it to be understood in a political sense. They declared Him to be the ringleader of a band of conspirators who strove to stir up the people against the emperor and the authorities and was therefore guilty of high treason. Nor was our Lord either the first or the last of God's servants on whom such suspicions have been cast. Even Elijah was obliged to hear from Ahab the angry salutation, 'Thou art he that troubleth Israel;' to which he calmly replied, 'I have not troubled Israel, but thou and thy father's house in that ye have forsaken the commandments of the Lord and thou hast followed Baalim.' In the same manner it was said to the king concerning Jeremiah, 'We beseech thee, let this man be put to death, for he weakeneth the hands of the men of war and seeketh not the welfare of this people but their hurt.' Later on we find Paul accused before Felix, much in the same manner: 'We have found this man a pestilent fellow, and a mover of sedition among all the Jews throughout the world, and a ringleader of the sect of the Nazarenes.' And all the subsequent persecutions of the Christians under the Roman emperors took place under the pretext that the followers of Jesus were dangerous to the State, their views being directed to the weakening of allegiance and even to the subversion of the existing government.

This false accusation has been handed down from age to age, although even Pilate most earnestly took us under his protection against such calumnies. We hear him loudly declare before the assembled multitude, that neither the throne nor the state had anything to fear from Jesus and His disciples. 'Behold,' says he, 'I have examined him before you, and find no fault in this man touching those things whereof ye accuse him; no, nor yet Herod; for I sent you to him, and lo! nothing worthy of death is done unto him.' Indeed, how was it possible to convict *Him* of a tendency to revolt who established the universal principle 'Render unto Caesar the things that are Caesar's;' who seriously reproved Peter for assaulting in his defence, one of the meanest officers of the civil authorities, by saying to him, 'Put up again thy sword into its place, for all they that take the sword, shall perish with the sword;' and who enjoins upon us to 'be subject to the higher powers, since there is no power but of God.'

The Lord Jesus has passed through every examination; He has been put to one test after another, weighed in every scale, measured by every standard, and narrowly inspected by the light of a threefold law – the Levitical, civil, and moral. The veil has now to be removed from the result of the proceedings against him. The judge who has called the chief priests and rulers to be present at the solemn act, stands surrounded by a vast multitude; and when all are silent with expectation, he opens his mouth to pronounce the final sentence. He declares aloud to the assembled crowd, 'Ye have brought this man unto me, as one that perverteth the people, and behold' – this is said to the world at large – 'I, having examined him before you, have found no fault in this man, touching the things whereof ye accuse him; no, nor yet Herod, for I sent you to him, and lo! nothing worthy of death is done to him.' He concludes, and all are silent because they feel that Pilate has spoken the truth.

Now, although He who was free from sin, was in no wise guilty of death, either judicial or natural, which latter is called the 'wages of sin,' yet still He dies. He dies, who according to justice as well as the promise of God, ought not to die, but live; and dies a death which bears scarcely the remotest resemblance to martyrdom. If, by His death, He had only designed to confirm the truth of His doctrine, He would have failed in His object; since we cannot possibly think highly of a doctrine whose teacher at the .gates of eternity is compelled to make the dreadful confession that God has forsaken Him.

But tell us now, why did Jesus die? 'It is appointed unto sinners once to die, and after that the judgment;' but He was not a sinner. Even the redeemed have no other way to the heavenly world than through death, because their flesh is corrupted by sin. But in Christ's corporeality this is not the case; and yet He dies, and that in such a dreadful manner! Explain how this is. Take time to reflect. But however long and deeply you may study the subject, we tell you decidedly beforehand that you will not bring forward any rational, convincing, and satisfactory solution of this mystery.

Hear, therefore, how we view the subject, and consider whether there is room for any other. The monstrous fact that the just and spotless Jesus, notwithstanding His holiness was condemned to death, would compel us to the conclusion that the doctrine of a righteous God, who rules over all, is a delusion – that the will of man or chance alone govern the world – that there exists no divine retribution upon earth, and that it will not fare the worse with the impious than with the just – I say we should be necessarily compelled to inferences of this kind, if we were not permitted to assume that the immaculate Son of God suffered death in our stead. This view of the subject furnishes the only key to the mystery of the ignominious end of the just and holy Jesus.

But if we presuppose an atonement made by Christ for sin – and we not only may do so, but are constrained to it by the clear evidence of Holy Writ – then all is plain; all is solved and deciphered, and a sublime meaning and a glorious connection pervades the whole. God threatened Adam in paradise, saying, 'In the day that thou eatest of the fruit of this tree, thou shalt surely die.' We did eat of that fruit and incurred the penalty. But the eternal Son now appears, removes the penalty from us to Himself, and we live.

On Sinai it was said, 'Cursed be every one who continueth not in all things that are written in the book of the law to do them.' We did not continue in them, and our fate was decided. But our Surety presents Himself, endures the curse for us, and we are justly delivered and absolved. God has resolved to save sinners, notwithstanding He has said, 'I will blot the name of him that sinneth out of my book.' We believe in our salvation, for He inflicted upon Christ the punishment due to us. God promised the crown of life only to the obedient; but after Christ as our representative obeyed in our name, God can bestow the crown on sinners and yet continue holy.

Thus all becomes clear, and the most striking opposites harmoniously agree. And yet men dare to call our doctrine of the atonement made by Christ irrational, and even absurd. Look how Pilate unconsciously stands in the breach for us, by testifying to the truth that Jesus was not guilty of death. Attempt in a satisfactory and rational manner, if you can, to explain it otherwise than by the atonement made by Christ, how it was that even the holy and immaculate Son of God paid the wages of sin.

Pilate takes our part once more. He clears us of a new cause of reproach. He does not, indeed, do this directly, but he gives occasion for our being freed from it. We are accused of dispensing Scripture consolation too lavishly. We are reproved for extending the grace purchased for us by Christ to the greatest sinners and most depraved criminals. We are told that we are not justified in so doing, and that such conduct is dangerous and injurious to morality. But there is something intimated in that part of the narrative under consideration which fully repels the narrow-minded reproof, and justifies our procedure as being quite evangelical.

After Pilate has solemnly declared that no guilt attaches to the accused, he continues, 'I will therefore' – release him? not so, but 'chastise him (that is with rods) and let him go.' Only think, what injustice! We are ready to say, 'O Pilate, how is it possible that thou shouldst have recourse to such an expedient! Wilt thou scourge Him as a malefactor who said to thee with the clearest expression of truth, 'I am a King and to this end was I born, that I should bear witness of the truth,' and from the whole of whose deportment shone the radiance, not only of spotless holiness, but also of supernatural descent? O to what length does the miserable fear of man mislead thee and the pitiful anxiety for a little worldly honour and temporal comfort!'

But let us be silent. Pilate's speech, 'I will chastise him and then release him,' is still the language of numbers of this world's children. He is chastised when men tear the crown of deity from His brow, and when they silently brand Him as a deceiver and blasphemer; but then begin to commend His excellences and virtues, and thus release Him after having maltreated him. They deny that He is the only way to heaven, although He Himself has said so, and in this way He is chastised; but then again, they applaud Him as the most eminent of teachers; and thus He is let go.

Men chastise Him by insulting His members upon earth, and vilifying those who boast of His meritorious sufferings as the sole ground of their salvation; but again release Him by making an outward obeisance at His communion-table, or by confessing that He was more than Socrates or Solon. Alas! we all carry about with us by nature a secret scourge for the Lord Jesus and never omit to use it in one way or other. But if our conscience asks, after such a chastising, why we are so averse and opposed to this Just One, who never injured us, we are wont instead of feeling penitent, to hide our own naughtiness behind the traitorous kisses we bestow upon Him, and again release the ill-treated Saviour by dubious marks of respect.

But to return. It was customary in Israel to chastise those with rods who after trial were convicted only of slight transgressions and then to release them. Pilate was anxious to treat Jesus as a delinquent of this kind. One might have expected after all that had passed, by which the innocence of Jesus was placed in so clear a light, that his mediating proposition would have been responded to. But no; God had determined otherwise. It was intended that Christ should suffer as a criminal of the worst description, and that the lot of a murderer and an outcast of the human race should be His, and that not till then should the hour of redemption arrive. But why was this? For what other reason than that, according to God's counsel and will, sinners and criminals like Manasses and Rahab might have reason to believe that the great Surety suffered for them also. Jesus was obliged to descend into the regions of darkness, into the being abandoned by God, and into the extreme of ignominy and suffering, that the vilest transgressors might not despair of mercy.

If this doctrine is dangerous, why do the apostles proclaim it as from the housetops? If it is contrary to God, why has he confirmed it in the case of David, Saul, Mary Magdalen, and even in that of greater sinners than these? If it is pernicious why do those who in themselves experience the truth of it exceed all others in their hatred to sin, and their zeal for God and his glory? Does it make them negligent and unfruitful in good works? The very reverse; for he that participates in the merits of Christ becomes also by Christ's Spirit a noble tree in the garden of God, which brings forth its fruit in its season. O it is well for us that the case is as we have described it! If Christ had not endured the fate of the chief of sinners, who even among the enlightened could glory in Christ, since the Holy Spirit teaches all such to testify with Paul, 'Christ came into the world to save sinners, of whom I am chief!'

Pilate has done us a good office. Not only has he cleared us from a grievous accusation, but by the testimony he bore to the innocence of Jesus, he has also justified our view of the Lord's death and its import; and by his fruitless attempts to treat the Redeemer as a petty offender, he gave occasion to the judge on the throne of majesty to frustrate his project, and by so doing, to make it known that Christ was to bear the curse even of the greatest sinner, according to the will and counsel of the Almighty. We feel ourselves deeply indebted to the Roman for the two last pieces of service which he has rendered us, for we confess that, with the atonement and satisfaction made by Immanuel, our peace as well as our hope stands or falls.

Chapter 33

Jesus or Barabbas

We resume our place amid the wild and tumultuous assemblage before Gabbatha, the open court, where justice was wont to be administered. Pilate, who, the more he has to do with the dignified Man of Nazareth, is the more convinced of His perfect innocence continues his attempts to give the affair a favourable turn, both for the accused and himself. His very soul revolts at the idea of such a person dying the death of a criminal.

Not a few of our contemporaries resemble him in this respect. They are those who, like Pilate, speak of the moral glory of Christ with a degree of enthusiasm, but the more they regard Him from this point of view, the more they are offended at His cross. They feel a repugnance to the doctrine of the atonement made by Him for our sins, simply because they wish sin to be regarded as an inconsiderable and trifling object, which they would be constrained to view as something important and horrible if they were compelled to believe that it could only be forgiven through the condemnation of the Son of God and atoned for by His blood. Those who are unable to absolve themselves as entirely free from sin, would then be forced either to take refuge with us in the wounds of Jesus and to sue for pardon with the vilest malefactors, or carry about with them a smitten and uneasy conscience.

Hence it is altogether their interest to oppose the doctrine that the sufferings and death of Christ must be apprehended as vicarious.

Nay, I do not hesitate to affirm that all the doctrinal systems which seek to neutralize or evade the view of Christ's sufferings as an atonement proceed from a conscious or unconscious effort to weaken and lessen the enormity of sin. Those who are still satisfied with such systems are not aware of the exceeding sinfulness of sin. But those who have become acquainted with its abominable nature in the sight of God, see the necessity of Christ's sufferings and being justified by faith, have peace with God through the atonement made for us by His Son.

The governor is lost in thought; his forehead burns; his mind is distressed. What would he not give for wise counsel in this painful emergency? All at once the horizon of his soul clears up. He has hit upon a happy expedient, the idea of which did not occur to him without superior intervention. Pilate calls to mind a custom which, though it was not founded on any divine ordinance, the Lord indulgently overlooked and bore with, from being willing to make use of it as the symbol of something of a superior nature.

According to this custom it was permitted the people – as a figurative realization of the deliverance of their forefathers out of Egypt, and to increase the general joy at the festival – to ask for the liberation of some grievous offender from prison. Pilate grasps at this custom like a shipwrecked mariner the floating plank, as the only means of deliverance which is left him. He hastily passes through his mind the various receptacles of crime, in order to discover in them some malefactor whom he may confidently hope the people will never prefer to the Nazarene. He soon thinks he has found such a one, or rather God found him for him; for this was the very sinner whom the Lord deemed fit for the spectacle which was then to be presented to the world. The man thus selected is Barabbas, a vile miscreant, a rebel and a murderer. Who, thinks the governor, would grant life and liberty to such an outcast of mankind, in preference to the just Man of Nazareth?

Already secretly triumphing in the expected success of his plan, Pilate proceeds to the Proscenium and in a tone of the fullest assurance of success, calls out to the crowd, 'Whom will ye that I release unto you? Jesus Barabbas (for such was the man's whole name, according to an ancient tradition) or Jesus the King of the Jews which is called Christ? For,' adds the gospel narrative, 'he knew that the chief priests had delivered him from envy.' And such was actually the case; for that which vexed them the most was that the people followed Him.

But how foolishly did the governor act, though otherwise so prudent, in reminding the proud men by calling Him 'The King of the Jews,' how His way had but recently been strewn with palm-branches and garments, amid the hosannas of the people; and how did he thus ruin Him without intending it! But his speculation would have been a failure without that; for 'God taketh the wise in their own craftiness' who, disdaining the restraint of His Word and will, seek success by their own inventions.

The Saviour's fate is now no longer in Pilate's hands. The majority of the multitude decides, and he is obliged to abide by its decision. Had he been bold enough to follow the dictate of his own conscience and to have said with calm discrimination, 'Justice shall be done, even though the world should perish; the guiltless Nazarene is free, and those cohorts here will know how to give effect to my decision;' his opponents inwardly rebuked, would doubtless have shrunk back thunderstruck, and the people, roused from their delusion, would have loudly applauded the energetic judge. But Pilate now stands forever as a warning example of the consequence of endeavouring to satisfy both God, who speaks within us, and the world.

'Whom will ye that I release unto you?' exclaims Pilate, seating himself on the marble judgment-seat to await the decision of the people. The latter waver and hesitate, which is no sooner perceived by the priests and elders than they rush into the crowd and exert all their eloquence to stifle the germ of right feeling which begins to awake in their minds, and to blow into a flame the dying spark of animosity to Jesus.

Meanwhile, a remarkable episode takes place. A messenger, out of breath, appears before the governor, sent by his wife, who is commissioned to say to him, 'Have thou nothing to do with that just man, for I have suffered many things this night in a dream because of him.' What a remarkable circumstance! The brightness of the purity and glory of the fairest of the children of men was such as to penetrate into the heathen woman's world of dreams. We thus see how the life and actions of Jesus must have affected the hearts of those who were indifferent and even opposed to Him, and compelled them to respect Him.

Yes, by night, when the bustle of the day is silent and deep sleep falls upon men, the Spirit of Truth visits their tabernacles and approaches the couches even of those who, careless about higher objects, revel in the intoxication of worldly delusions. With the arrows of His judicial decision, He pierces by night into chambers where all that has reference to things of a higher nature otherwise finds no response. By night, ill-treated conscience assumes its right and makes itself again heard, even in the breasts of the most ungodly; and many are obliged to confess with the Psalmist, 'Thou searchest my heart, and visitest me in the night season.' God had also evidently His hand in the distressing night-vision of

Pilate's consort, and often exercises control over the world of dreams, and when He pleases makes the imagination of the unfettered spirit subservient to His purpose.

But though Pilate received a fresh divine warning by the message from his wife, yet the man had already laid down his arms and was no longer his own master. His wife's communication affected him deeply. His excited conscience whispered to him, 'Pilate, listen to the voice from another world, which warns thee against the crime of a legal murder.' He hears it, indeed, and is dreadfully disturbed, but hopes the people will act justly. The people? Poor man! Is this thy last despicable hope?

Pilate impatiently rises from his seat, and again calls out to the crowd with the mien of a suppliant, 'Which of the twain will ye that I release unto you?' We may easily infer that he added in his own mind, 'You will surely decide for Jesus.' But it is in vain to come with requests where we have not the courage in God's name to order and command. The priests and elders have succeeded in instigating the people to side with them, and the unfortunate governor hears a thousand voices unanimously and daringly reply, 'Not this man, but Barabbas.'

Such are the two individuals presented to the people to choose from at their Easter festival. The man in chains and the Prince of Life; the former a vile wretch, who in a sanguinary revolt had been seized in the act of committing murder. But Barabbas does not stand before us merely as an individual. He represents, at the same time the human race in its present condition – as fallen from God – in a state of rebellion against the divine Majesty – bound in the fetters of the curse of the law till the day of judgment; but nevertheless dignifying itself with pompous titles, without any real nobility of soul, and boasting of honourable distinctions without internal worth.

Before Barabbas was presented with Jesus to the people's choice, every prospect of his escape from the fate that awaited him had been cut off: and such is also our case. There was no idea of a ransom, nor of any liberation from the well-guarded dungeon, much less of a merciful sentence, which every one else might have anticipated sooner than this murderer. And believe me, that our case was not less critical than his. For what had we to give to redeem our souls? how escape the vigilance of those eyes which 'run to and fro through all the earth?' and how could a judge acquit us un-conditionally, of whom it is said, 'Justice and judgment are the habitation of his throne?' Barabbas' situation was des-perate, and ours no less. But what occurs? Without his own co-operation, and against all his calculation, a dawn of escape suddenly flashes through his prison. From Gabbatha resounds the governor's question to the people, 'Whom will ye that I release unto you? Barabbas, or Jesus, which is called Christ.'

How important the moment! How mysterious the change in the state of things! Barabbas thought that he should certainly be put to death. It is now Barabbas or Jesus. The deliverance of the former has at least become possible; and by what means? Solely because the rebel and the murderer is offered to the choice of the people equally with Jesus, the Lord from heaven. The lot must fall on one or the other. One will be released; the other sent to the place of execution. There is nothing to justify a demand for the liberation of both. Which of the two will be chosen – which rejected? If Jesus of Nazareth is set at liberty, Barabbas is inevitably lost. If the former is rejected, then hail to thee, Barabbas, thou art saved! His ruin is thy redemption; from His death springs thy life.

What say you to this state of things? Viewed solely in a historical light, it is certainly of minor importance, except that it serves as a renewed proof that the Son of God was spared no disgrace nor humiliation – not even that of being placed on the same footing with a murderer like Barabbas. But regarded in a superior light, that historical fact becomes of great importance. In the position in which Barabbas stood to Jesus, we all of us stood to Him. With respect to us, it might also have been said 'Who shall die – the transgressor or the Just One?' It was impossible that both should be spared. The sword of divine justice must strike either to the right or the left. The curse which we had incurred must be inflicted. The sentence of condemnation pronounced upon us impatiently waited its execution, that God might continue holy, just, and true. Here was the great alternative: these guilty creatures, or the Son of God in their stead, for He alone was able to atone for our sins. Thus we were quite in Barabbas' position. If Jesus was sent to execution, the hour of our redemption had arrived; but if He was spared we were irrevocably lost.

You already know the result. The affair takes the most favourable turn for Barabbas, and in him for us. To Pilate's utter amazement, the voice of the multitude decides in favour of the rebel. 'Release Barabbas!' cried the uproarious crowd, 'And crucify Jesus.' However wicked this decision may appear, compared with that of Pilate, who was anxious that Jesus should live, and not be put to death; still it was more in accordance with God's plan and the method of salvation that it should be so. For if the people had effectually demanded Jesus to be liberated, and Barabbas to be executed as Pilate wished, that demand would have been the funeral-knell of the human race, and the signal for our eternal perdition. But God so ordered it that the affair took a different turn; for the outcry of the people to crucify Jesus was the trumpet-sound announcing the day of our redemption.

Observe now the result of the decision. Barabbas and Jesus change places. The murderer's bonds, curse, disgrace, and mortal agony are transferred to the righteous Jesus; while the liberty, innocence, safety, and well-being of the immaculate Nazarene become the lot of the murderer. Jesus Barabbas is installed in all the rights and privileges of Jesus Christ; while the latter enters upon all the infamy and horror of the rebel's position. Both mutually inherit each other's situation and what they possess: the delinquent's guilt and cross become the lot of the Just One, and all the civil rights and immunities of the latter are the property of the delinquent.

You now understand the amazing scene we have been contemplating. We find the key to it in the words, 'God made him to be sin for us, who knew no sin, that we might be made the righteousness of God in him.' It places before us in a strong light, the mystery of our justification before God, through the mediation of Christ. In Barabbas' deliverance, we see our own. Left to ourselves, we should have been eternally lost. When Christ exchanged positions with us, our redemption was decided.

Truly he must be blind who does not perceive that in this Barabbas scene a light was divinely enkindled which should illumine the whole of the passion of God's only-begotten Son. This light would alone suffice to dispel every objection to the scriptural nature of our view of the doctrine of the atonement, if this were not also done by a whole series of striking passages from the apostolic writings.

Let us then rejoice that such is the case, and indelibly impress upon our memories the striking features of the scene we have been contemplating. Let those who are humbled under a sense of their sin and guilt behold their image in Barabbas; and one consolatory idea after another will occur to you from the sight. How comfortable the reflection that the man is wholly freed at the expense of Jesus; that however heinous his crimes, not one of them attaches to him any longer; that henceforward, no judicial procedure can be instituted against him for what he has done; and that nothing now prevents him from boldly appearing in the presence of his judge.

You also possess all these privileges in Christ, only in a more glorious form and a more abundant fullness. Since He became the criminal in your stead, you are accounted as righteous for His sake; since He was rejected in your stead, you are admitted into favour with God; since He bore your curse, you are the heirs of His blessing; since He suffered your punishment, you are destined to share His happiness. Such being the case, how ought you by faith, to rise into the blissful position assigned you and to learn in the school of the Holy Spirit boldly to say with the apostle, 'Who shall lay anything to the charge of God's elect, seeing that it is God that justifieth? Who is he that condemneth, since Christ hath died – yea rather is risen again, who is even at the right hand of God, who also maketh intercession for us?'

Chapter 34

Barabbas

The most momentous cry that was ever heard under heaven has been uttered. To the governor's question 'Whom will ye that I release unto you, Jesus or Barabbas?' the dreadful answer has been returned by the tumultuous crowd, 'Away with this man, and release unto us Barabbas!' More than an echo of this cry resounds through the world to this day; for all who reject Christ as the Saviour of sinners and are eager on the contrary for the upholding of the honour, independence and liberty of their 'old man,' likewise say in fact, 'Away with this man, and release unto us Barabbas!' But is not this the language we have inherited from our corrupt nature as such? Undoubtedly it is. Yet even from the lips of faith we hear the same.

The people, instigated by their rulers, have boldly and plainly expressed their will. They desire the pardon of the murderer and the death of the righteous Jesus. From that moment, it is pitiable to see how the judge, entirely thrown out of his course, sinks deeper at every step. Scarcely aware any longer of what he was saying, he cries out, 'What shall I do then with Jesus, which is called Christ?'

Only think of his asking the raging multitude what he must do with Jesus, who, before he put the question to them, had already answered him in the most convincing manner. His

conscience, his inward feeling of justice, the letter of the law
by which he is bound, and even the warning voice contained
in the dream of his wife – all tell him, clearly and definitely,
what he ought to do with Jesus. He ought to pronounce Him
free, and then with all the power that stood at his command,
take him under his protection against the uproarious
multitude. But where is he to find courage for this? 'What
shall I do then with Jesus?' Truly these words are an eternal
shame and disgrace to him.

But how many of our contemporaries share this disgrace
with him, since they make what they ought to do with Jesus
depend on the popular voice, the prevailing tone of society,
and what is called public opinion! I have even often thought
I heard preachers in their pulpits imitate Pilate in asking,
'What am I to do with Jesus?' and I cannot tell you how dis-
cordantly the question sounded in my ears. They did not
appear to know whether they ought to pray to Jesus or not –
whether to confess Him before the congregation to be God,
or only man – whether to recommend Him to them as redeemer or teacher; and nothing seemed more disagreeable
to them than to be compelled officially to have to do with
Jesus. But woe unto him who can still ask, 'What shall I do
with Jesus?' Such a one's mind is beclouded and he is still
very far from salvation. What has the blind man to do with
his guide who offers him his arm? the sick man with the
medicine presented to him? the drowning man with the rope
that is thrown to him? – if we know how to answer these
questions, how is it that we can be perplexed at replying to
the other?

Pilate asks, 'What shall I do with Jesus?' The people will
not leave him long in suspense. The more they see their rulers
timidly give way and enter upon the path of concessions, the
stronger grows their audacity. 'Crucify Him!' they cry, briefly
and decisively. The governor, beside himself with amazement

at seeing the fabric of his calculations so suddenly overthrown, comes again before them with the unavailing question, 'Why, what evil hath he done?' But the people, scarcely deigning an answer to the miserable judge, repeat with still greater insolence, 'Crucify Him! Crucify Him!' The increasing weakness and irresolution of the governor necessarily made the crowd believe that he himself did not regard it as any monstrous crime that Christ should be crucified.

Pilate appears as if he wished to say something more; but the people have now the upper hand, and they refuse to hear him. Wild uproar drowns his voice. In spite of every effort, he can no longer make himself heard. The heartless succumbing man has then recourse to a symbolical act. He calls for a vessel with water; and on its being presented to him, washes his hands before all the people and cries out as loudly as he can to the tumultuous mob, 'I am innocent of the blood of this just person; see ye to it!'

This renewed judicial testimony to the innocence of our great High Priest is to us very satisfactory. Pilate's urgent desire and earnest endeavour to rid himself of the crime of condemning the righteous Jesus can only aid in strengthening our faith. But we are deeply affected at the sight of the poor depressed man – how he writhes under the scourge of his own conscience and ineffectually strives to wash away from his hands the bloody spots, however much he may object to acknowledge them.

'I am innocent!' he exclaims. But what avails such an assertion? The monitor in his bosom does not confirm it; the minutes of the proceedings are referred to a higher tribunal where the decision will sound very differently. He washes his hands. O why this ceremony? Where is the fountain which yields water able to cleanse from spots like those that adhere to him? There is indeed a stream which would have produced the desired effect, but Pilate is ignorant of it.

If, in lieu of his innocence he had professed his guilt, and instead of the unavailing washing, had resorted to the blood of atonement – then he would have been safe for time and eternity, and his name have secured a place in the list of the citizens of Christ's kingdom. But Pilate, under the influence of beggarly pride will not acknowledge himself as overcome, although hell and the world never set their feet triumphantly on the neck of a more discomfited man than he. But man is by nature so constituted that he would rather give himself up to Satan in the snare of the most idiotic self-delusion than do honour to the truth, which humbles him for his good.

'See ye to it!' exclaims Pilate, hurling the entire impious act on the heads of the Jews; thereby returning upon the priests and scribes – not without God's permission 'to whom vengeance belongeth' – the very words with which they, with cruel and unpitying coldness, repelled the despairing Judas. They feel indeed the sting of those words, but know how to conceal their embarrassment and shame behind a horrible outburst of impiety. 'His blood be upon us and our children!' they cry in satanic defiance, and all the people join with them.

Dreadful indeed! As long as the world stands, a more horrifying, self-anathematizing speech has never been heard. But listen! Does it not seem to you as if a voice of thunder sounded down from the throne of Deity, crying out, 'Be it unto you according to your wish! Let his blood come upon you as you desire!' And oh! only cast a glance at the history of Israel from the moment when that unhappy demand was made to the present hour, and it will prove that you heard correctly.

How did the blood of that Righteous One come upon His murderers when the proud city of Jerusalem was laid in ashes by the torches of the Romans, and scarcely so much wood could be produced as sufficed to prepare crosses for the children of Abraham! How did it come upon them, when having slain the Prince of Peace, they were driven out like useless chaff, to the four winds of heaven, and condemned thenceforward to roam about in inhospitable regions, without a home, the scorn of all the world! How did it come upon them, when as the offscouring of all nations, and as if they were unworthy to tread the ground, they yielded up their lives by thousands and tens of thousands under heathen, Mohammedan, and even professing Christian swords and daggers!

And when we now look at them, as being still a proscribed people, according to Hosea's prophecy, 'Without a king and without a prince, and without sacrifice, and without an image, without an Ephod, and without Teraphim' – is it not as if we read the cause of their miserable banishment on their foreheads, in the words, 'His blood be upon us and upon our children'? But the mercy of God is great. He has still thoughts of peace toward His ancient people, who are not yet given up. In due time He will cause the horrible language of the curse they invoked upon themselves to have the validity of a prayer in His sight and the blood of His Son, as already experienced by individuals of that race, to come upon all Israel as an atonement. The prophet Hosea adds the joyful promise to the threatening so dreadfully verified: 'Afterward, they shall return and seek the Lord their God, and David their king.' And Zechariah opens to us the prospect of a time 'when ten men shall take hold, out of all languages of the nations, of the skirt of him that is a Jew, saying, We will go with you, for we have heard that God is with you.' The Lord Himself says, in the most significant manner, referring to the termination of their wretchedness, 'Ye shall not see me henceforth, till ye shall say, Blessed is he that cometh in the name of the Lord!' And what is the language of the Apostle Paul, with reference to them. 'God,' says he, 'is able to graft in again the branches which were broken off. For the gifts and calling of God are without repentance.'

The people, with diabolical determination, have declared their will and sealed their fate with an imprecation, than which a more impious one has scarcely ever been heard in the world. The governor is no longer able to cope with this manifestation of firmness on the part of the people. He sees himself robbed of the last particle of his moral armour, and compelled to lay down his arms, and surrender in the most disgraceful manner. How do we read? 'And so Pilate, willing to content the people, gave sentence that it should be as they required, and released unto them Barabbas, who for sedition and murder was cast into prison, whom they had desired, but he delivered Jesus to their will that he should be scourged.'

This is therefore the result of all the serious and powerful warnings which had been given to Pilate. He had received such decided impressions of Jesus' moral purity and innocence, and had even been admonished by a voice from the other world, as well as by his own conscience; and yet this disgraceful defeat – this cowardly retreat – this shameful yielding to the will of the crowd! O what is man with all his propriety of feeling and will, so long as he stands in his own strength, and has not yielded himself up with his whole confidence to God and His grace! The Lord says, 'My strength is perfected in weakness;' and hence we find Paul saying, 'I can do all things through Christ which strengtheneth me.'

Barabbas is free, although still ignorant of the decision made in his favour outside his prison, and of the fortunate lot which is fallen to him. Dejected, and even despairing of deliverance, he continues lying in his gloomy dungeon; and in every noise that reaches him from a distance, he imagines he hears the tread of the executioner coming to lead him away to the scaffold. At length he plainly hears the massive bolts of his prison door drawn back, and the rusty hinges creak on its being thrown open – but – dare he trust his own eyes? What a sight! Instead of the executioner, a messenger from the civil authorities rushes in with a smiling countenance, and brings him the amazing and almost incredible intelligence that he is free, that his life is saved. Barabbas now learns that the sentence of death has been removed from him forever, and that he has no longer to do with courts of justice, judges, or jailors; that no accusation will be listened to against him; that he is restored to the full possession of the rights and privileges of citizenship, and so situated as if he had never committed a crime; but that the sole cause of this happy change in his circumstances lies in the fact that One who was perfectly guiltless had taken his place, and trodden the path to the cross in his stead. The people at their Easter election had decided on the death of this righteous Man, and for his liberation.

All this is told to Barabbas. In the herald who informs him of it, we see the image of a true evangelist. Yes, know ye spiritually poor – ye who are bending under the weight of your transgressions, and are crying for mercy – that we have to bring you a similar message to that which Barabbas received, only of a far greater, more glorious, and incomparably more blissful nature than his. Nor are we permitted to withhold or diminish it in any degree. After Christ has made the mysterious exchange with you, we are commissioned of God to inform you in plain terms, that from the moment in which the holy Jesus took your place, you assumed His, and are installed into all the rights and immunities of the citizens of His kingdom.

You are now justified in the sight of God, and accepted of Him. No condemnation any longer attaches to you. No sin will any more be laid to your charge, no accusation given ear to against you. This we can tell you, yet not we, but the infallible Word of God in plain terms; and we call upon you in God's name to believe this Word, and to rejoice in it to the honour of Christ.

How does Barabbas act after receiving the glad tidings? The Bible does not tell us; but we may easily imagine it. If he had said to himself, 'It is impossible that this can have reference to such a criminal as I;' and had resisted when his chains were being removed, how should we designate such conduct? You would call it senseless and be justified in doing so. But I fear that this reproach may attach to some believers. Suppose Barabbas had rejected the message with a protest and had replied to the herald, 'What thou sayest is absurd and can not be founded on truth.' What would have been the consequence? By so doing, he would have insulted the herald and the authorities that sent him, and have branded them as liars.

But such is precisely your case, my friend, who in your legality resist the grace of God in Christ. You unceasingly offend not merely a human messenger, but the Holy Spirit, who speaks to you in the Scriptures; the apostles of the Lord, who so plainly testify to you of divine mercy; and Christ Himself, who assures you that whosoever believeth shall be saved. Yes, you infringe upon the glory of God, as if He only offered You a partial deliverance, and had not wholly and completely provided it.

Suppose that Barabbas had replied to the announcement of his liberty, 'No, for the present at least I will not leave my prison, but will first become another man and prove that I have amended myself.' What do you suppose the authorities would have answered? 'Dost thou imagine,' they would have said, 'that thou are liberated for thy own sake? Thou wouldst never have been free on that ground. Though thou mightest have become ten times better, thou wouldst never be able to remove the guilt thou hast contracted. In the eye of the law, thou wouldst continue a murderer as before; and if thou dost not make a free use of the pardon offered thee, know that thou wilt vainly calculate upon ever being liberated.'

Take to heart this official announcement, for it is of high importance and points out the way in which you ought to walk. Suppose Barabbas had said, 'I will remain a prisoner, until after being injurious to society, I have shown myself a useful member of it.' This might have sounded nobly; but strictly examined, would it not also be absurd? Doubtless you would have replied to him and said, 'What folly! before thou canst become useful to society, thou must become free. For, of what service or benefit canst thou be to others, as long as thou art fettered and in prison?' Take this lesson also to heart, my friends. It is applicable to so many, who foolishly seek to become holy before they make room for the comfort of pardoning mercy.

Probably, however, not one of all these ideas occurred to Barabbas. I doubt not, that on receiving the joyful message, he gladly accepted it and gave himself up to a transport of delight. He immediately shook off his chains, left his dark dungeon, exchanged his convict dress for the attire of a citizen, and made every use of the liberty offered him. He returned to his family, joying and rejoicing, and never forgot how much he was indebted to the mysterious man of Nazareth for life, freedom, and all that he possessed, who was condemned in his stead, and by His death, saved his life.

And you who like Barabbas may be still languishing in the gloomy dungeon of inward anxiety, care, and sorrow, go and do likewise. Believe the gospel message, that for Christ's sake, you are eternally liberated from curse and condemnation. Listen no longer to the accusations of Satan, the world, or your own conscience. Enjoy the fruit of the suretyship of your great Representative. Live in peace and rejoice in hope of the glory of God.

Chapter 35

The Scourging

The path of the holy one of Israel becomes increasingly dark and obscure. The night-piece of His passion carries us from the region of the tragical into that of the appalling. His sufferings increase to torture, His disgrace to infamy; and the words of Isaiah, 'He was despised and rejected; and we hid as it were our faces from him,' are completely realized.

After the momentous decision has been made at Gabbatha, and the lot of the murderer has fallen upon the just, the latter is for a while removed from the view of the people, having been given up to the armed band of executioners' assistants and led away by them, amid wild uproar, like a sheep for the slaughter, into the inner court-yard of the palace. Thither let us follow Him, although we do so with reluctance; but we must be witnesses of the scene, since it is the will of God that we should be aware of what our restoration and redemption cost our great Surety.

What now takes place? A deed respecting which a feeling comes over us as if it were improper and even sinful to behold it with the naked eye. Look at yonder pillar, black with the blood of murderers and rebels. The iron collar which is attached to it, as well as the ropes which hang down from its iron rings, sufficiently point out its cruel object. Look at the rude and barbarous beings, who busily surround their victim.

Observe the brutal vulgarity of their countenances and the instruments of torture in their hands. They are scourges, made of hundreds of leathern thongs, each armed at the point with an angular bony hook or a sharp-sided cube. Such are the instruments of torture prepared for Him, who was dear to God as the apple of His eye. We naturally think He could not and ought not to descend to such a point of degradation, but that all heaven must interfere to prevent it or that the world must perish under it. But it takes place; and neither does heaven protest against it, nor the world sink into ruin.

See, see – the execution of the sentence begins! The executioners fall upon the Holy One like a host of devils. They tear off His clothes; bind those hands which were ever stretched out to do good, tie them together upon His back, press His gracious visage firmly against the shameful pillar, and after having bound Him with ropes in such a manner that He can not move or stir, they begin their cruel task. O do not imagine that I am able to depict to you what now occurs. The scene is too horrible. My whole soul trembles and quakes. Neither wish that I should count to you the number of strokes which are now poured upon the sacred body of Immanuel, or describe the torments, which, increasing with every stroke, sufficed in other cases of this kind to cause the death of the unhappy culprit before the formal execution which this scourging usually preceded. It is enough for us to know that it lasted full a quarter of an hour; streams of blood flow from His sacred form. The scourging continues without mercy. The arms of the barbarous men begin to grow weary. New tormentors release those that are fatigued. The scourges cut ever deeper into the wounds already made. His whole back appears an enormous wound.

After the horrible act is finished, another instantly follows which almost exceeds it in cruelty. The agonized sufferer is unbound from the bloody pillar, but only to be tortured afresh. The material rods have done their duty, and mental ones of the bitterest and most poignant mockery are now employed against Him. Their ridicule is directed against His kingly dignity, even as it was on a former occasion, against His prophetic office.

A worn-out purple robe, once the garment of the leader of a Roman cohort, is produced. This is thrown over His back still bleeding from every pore, while the barbarians exult aloud at this supposed witty and appropriate idea. They then break off twigs from a long-spiked thorn-bush, and twist them into a circle, which is afterwards pressed upon His sacred head as a crown. But in order to complete the image of a mock king, they put into His hands a reed instead of a sceptre, and after having thus arrayed Him, they pay mock homage to Him with shouts of derisive laughter. The miscreants bow with pretended reverence to the object of their scorn, bend the knee before Him, and to make the mockery complete, cry out again and again, 'Hail, King of the Jews!' It is not long, however, before they are weary of this abominable sport and turn it into fearful seriousness. With satanic insolence, they place themselves before their ill-treated captive, make the most horrible grimaces at Him, even spit in His face, and in order to fill up the measure of their cruelty, they snatch the reed out of His hands, and repeatedly smite Him with it on the head, so that the thorns pierce deeply while streams of blood flow down the face of the gracious Friend of sinners.

How can we reconcile such revolting occurrences with the government of a just and holy God! A great mystery must lie at the bottom of them, or our belief in a supreme moral government of the world loses its last support. And is not this really the case? What befalls Christ befalls us in Him, who is our representative. The sufferings He endures fall upon our corrupt nature. In Him we receive the due reward of our misdeeds. With the shudder at the sight of the martyred Lamb of God ought to be joined a thorough condemnation of ourselves, a profound adoration of the unsearchable wisdom and mercy of God and the glorious accomplishment of the counsel of grace. Our hell is extinguished in Jesus' wounds; our curse is consumed in Jesus' soul; our guilt is purged away in Jesus' blood. The sword of the wrath of a holy God was necessarily unsheathed against us; and if the Bible is not a falsehood, and the threatenings of the law a mere delusion, and God's justice an idle fancy, not a single individual would have escaped the sword, if the Son of God had not endured the stroke and taken upon Himself the payment of our debts.

This He undertook. Then it thundered upon Him from the clouds; the raging billows of a sea of trouble roared against Him; hell poured upon Him all its tortures and torments, and heaven remained unmoved. What was all this but the fate which awaited guilty sinners? But since Christ endured it, the crosses which were erected for us have been thrown down; the stake which waited for us has been removed; and from the royal residence of the Lord of Hosts, the white flag of peace is held out to us poor dwellers upon earth.

The case has been well stated by an ancient writer in the following words: 'Adam was a king, gloriously arrayed, and ordained to reign. But sin cast him down from his lofty throne, and caused him the loss of his purple robe, his diadem and sceptre. But after his eyes were opened to perceive how much he had lost, and when his looks were anxiously directed to the earth in search of it, he saw thorns and thistles spring up on the spot where the crown fell from his head; the sceptre changed, as if to mock the fallen monarch, into a fragile reed; and instead of the purple robe, his deceived hand took up a robe of mockery from the dust. The poor disappointed being hung down his head with grief, when a voice exclaimed, 'Look up!' He did so, and lo! what an astonishing vision presented itself to his eye! Before him stood a dignified and mysterious Man, who had gathered up the piercing thorns from the ground, and wound them round His head for a crown; he had wrapped himself in the robe of mockery, and taken the reed, the emblem of weakness into his own hand. 'Who art thou, wondrous Being?' inquired the progenitor of the human race, astonished; and received the heart-cheering reply, 'I am the King of kings, who, acting as thy representative, am restoring to thee the jewels thou hast lost.' Our delighted first father then bowed himself gratefully and reverentially in the dust; and after being clothed with the skin of the sacrificed animal, fathomed the depths of the words of Jehovah, 'Adam is become like one of Us."

What I have now related to you is a parable, but one which rests on an historical basis. For in fact, the great exchange which Christ made with us, as regards the reversion and the right, has placed us in the full possession of glory, seeing that we are 'begotten again to a lively hope, and to an inheritance incorruptible, undefiled, and that fadeth not away, reserved in heaven for us, who are kept by the power of God, through faith unto eternal salvation.'

Chapter 36

'Ecce Homo!'

We stand before Gabbatha. The judgment-seat is still empty. The scene, as we are aware, has been transferred for a time into the inner court-yard. We know the things which have there occurred. The evangelists describe them with a trembling hand. They mention the scourging only briefly. We think we see them covering their faces with their hands at this terrific scene; but they cannot conceal from us the tears which silently steal down their cheeks.

Impatience begins to seize upon the multitude outside; when suddenly, the gate of the praetorium again opens. Pilate approaches, visibly affected, followed by One who is surrounded by a troop of jeering barbarians. Oh, what an appearance does He present! – You shudder and cover your faces. Do so and permit me, meanwhile, to relate a brief narrative to you.

Heaven's pearly gates were once thrown open and a Holy One descended into the world – such a One as the sons of men had never seen since the Fall. He was glorious beyond compare, and came to verify the dream of Jacob's ladder which connected earth with heaven. Love was His banner, compassion the beating of His heart. He sojourned three years among mortals, shedding light on those who were stumbling in darkness, filling the cottages of the wretched with temporal and spiritual blessings, inviting the weary and heavy laden to come to Him, in order to give them rest, and irradiating the darkness of the vale of death with promises upon promises, as with so many golden lights from heaven.

'I am not come,' said He, 'to be ministered unto, but to minister, and to give my life a ransom for many.' He testified that He came to redeem His people from their sins; that He would not leave them comfortless but would bring them to the Father, and elevate them to be fellow-heirs with Him in His glory. And how did He fulfil His promises, whenever any ventured to take heart and confide in Him!

Oh, what blessings must such a Guest have brought with Him to a world lying under the curse! Even the angels around the throne might have envied the pilgrims in this vale of death by reason of this visit. And as regards the children of men, 'Doubtless,' you say, 'they received Him with exultation, melted into tears of rapture, conducted Him in triumph, and knew not what they should do to manifest their gratitude to their heavenly Friend and Deliverer.'

Truly, one might have supposed that such would have been the case. 'What, and was it not so?' My friends, lift up your eyes and look toward Gabbatha. You exclaim, 'Who is yonder sufferer?' Oh, my friends, whom do you take Him to be? Look Him narrowly in the face, and say if wickedness could have vented itself worse than it has done on this Person? Alas! they have made of Him a carnival king; and as if He were unworthy of being dealt with seriously, they have impressed upon Him the stamp of derision. Look at the mock robe about His shoulders, the theatrical sceptre in His hands, and on His head, which is covered with wounds and blood, the dreadful crown of thorns.

But who is this Man thus horribly disfigured? I think you will no longer seriously inquire. The lamb-like patience, and

the superhuman resignation with which He stands before
you, point Him out sufficiently clearly. No less does the
majesty betray Him, which, in spite of all the abasement He
experiences, still shows itself in His whole deportment, as well
as the divinely forgiving love which even now beams from
His eye. Who would be found acting thus in a similar
situation? Yes, it is the Holy One from on high who stands
before you, the picture of agony. 'Behold the man!' exclaims
the heathen judge, deeply affected and faintly impressed with
an idea of some superior Being. Ah, had Pilate clearly known
what he only obscurely felt, he would at least have said, 'You
have here before you the moral pattern of our race, the flower
of humanity, and holiness personified.'

'Behold the man!' The hope is once more excited in the
governor that he would still be able to accomplish the
liberation of Jesus. 'Now,' he thinks, 'the blood-thirstiness of
the raging multitude will certainly be satisfied. In the presence
of One so full of dignity and meekness, the fury of the most
cruel must subside and right feeling return, even to the most
hardened.' Let us see what occurs. The people are about to
reply to the governor's appeal – the people, that thousand-
headed giant, of whom so much is said in commendation and
whose appearance is so imposing; whose united voice is supposed to be always correct, and even proverbially esteemed
equal to the voice of God. But what is the echo which
resounds from the breast of the powerful monster in reply to
the governor's exclamation, 'Behold the man!' 'Crucify him!
Crucify him!' rends the air, as if proceeding from a single
tongue.

'But are these impious men aware of what they are doing?'
Certainly not, in all its extent. In the person of Christ, they
would gladly dash to pieces the mirror which mutely renders
them conscious of their own deformity. In the Nazarene they
would gladly extinguish the Light of the world, which they

hate because they feel more at ease in the darkness of deception than in the broad daylight of unvarnished truth. They neither desire an external conscience, nor the exhibition of a model of virtue, nor an awakener from their deadly sleep, nor, generally speaking, any moral authority over them. On all these accounts, they are exasperated against the Holy One of Israel, and have nothing left for Him but the implacable cry of 'Crucify him! Crucify him!'

Thus they are judged. In the manifestation of Him who was 'fairer than the children of men,' our fallen nature has made it evident that its corruption is radical, its disease desperate, and its inmost tendency nothing else than enmity against the Most High God. Our race, in the murder of the Lord from heaven, has pronounced sentence upon itself, and filled up the measure of its guilt. The mute sufferer in the purple robe and crown of thorns sits in judgment upon it, and silently testifies that without mediation and an atonement, the seed of Adam in its whole extent, is exposed to the curse.

That which manifests itself at Gabbatha is only the mature fruit of a seed which grows openly or secretly in us all. Do not call this assertion unjust. As long as we have not experienced the second birth by the Word and the Spirit, we do not act with regard to Jesus, in a manner essentially different from the wretched men at Gabbatha. Like them, we are offended at the holiness of Jesus. Like them, we spit upon Him in spirit with our scorn, when He gives us to understand that we ought to bow the knee of homage to Him as our ruler. Tell me, does not Christ still wear in a hundred different forms, the purple robe and crown of thorns in the world? Is He not exposed to public ridicule, and treated as a liar and an enthusiast, because He bears witness to His superhuman dignity? Is not His name, even to this day, proscribed by thousands like scarcely any other? Does not an ironical smile dart across the lips of many, when it is mentioned with reverence and fervour?

Truly, the sins which were committed on the bleeding form of Jesus are so little to be regarded as the sins and impious acts of a few, that the accumulated guilt of the whole human race is thereby made apparent. The cruel scene at Gabbatha is not yet at an end. It is daily renewed, although in a somewhat less striking manner. The words, 'Behold the Man!' point not only to what is past, they have also a condemning reference to the present. Alas, the world became a Gabbatha! The thorn-crowned martyred form exhibited there mutely condemns us all without distinction.

But the presence of the divine sufferer acts not merely judicially and condemnatory. It also exercises an influence commanding homage and reverence. However deeply abased the Saviour may appear, He is still a King. Even in His blood-stained attire, He accomplishes a truly regal work, and in so doing, ascends a throne on which no eye had previously seen Him. It is not the throne of government over all created things; for to this the Father had long before elevated Him. Do not mistake, while contemplating the man thus covered with disgrace. If He sways even the feeble reed in his hand, legions of angels would hasten down for His defence, and lay His foes beneath His feet. Just as little is the throne He here ascends that of an avenger and a judge. This also He had previously occupied. Let no one deceive himself; beneath His robe of mockery, He still conceals the thunder and the lightning; and consuming fire, if He permitted it, would issue from His thorny crown and devour His adversaries.

'But if He possessed the power to do this, why did He not make use of it?' I answer, because beneath the robe of mockery He wears another and a different one, the purple of a compassionating love, which longs for the salvation of the lost. The new throne, which He ascends on Gabbatha, is that of a King of poor sinners and of a 'Prince of Peace.' It is the throne of grace, from whence forgiveness flows down instead of retribution. To this throne no other way is open to Him, but that on which we have seen Him walk. Before the curse could give way to blessing, the obligations of sinners must be fulfilled, their debts liquidated, and thus divine justice satis-fied. This is the great work in which we see the Redeemer now engaged. Through suffering, He acquires fresh power; immersed in ignominy, He clothes Himself with new glory.

'Behold the man!' In the mock robe in which He stands before you, He gains victories and triumphs which He never could have won in the sumptuous robe of His divine majesty. In it He overcomes eternal justice, while compelling it to change its sentence of death upon the sinner to a sentence of grace. In it, He overcomes the irrevocable law, by rendering it possible for it to withdraw the curse pronounced upon us without infringing its authority and dignity. He overcomes sin, from which He rends its destructive power; Satan, whom He deprives of his last claim to us in the way of right; and death, from which He takes away the sting. To the Man, so disfigured as scarcely to be recognized, belongs henceforth the earth, as the price of payment for His blood. From its pillars He removes the insignia and armorial bearings of all usurping authority, and replaces them with the cross, the mark of His peaceful sway. And no one dare to interfere and say to Him, What dost thou? He is complete and unassailable in His own right. The world is His, that He may let His love rule over it, and not His wrath; and if He henceforth treats penitent sinners as if they were replete with holiness and virtue, who will be bold enough to contest His right to do so?

'Behold the man!' Yes, it is a strange ornament that decks His head; but know that in this wreath He possesses and uses a power of which he could not boast while only adorned with the crown of Deity, which He inherited from all eternity. In the latter, he could only say to the dying thief, 'Be thou accursed!' In the former, He is able to say to him, 'This day shalt thou be with me in paradise!' In the heavenly crown, he could say nothing else to a Magdalene, a publican, or a paralytic, than 'Depart from me!' and give them over to perdition.

But in His crown of thorns, it is in His power to say to these guilty souls, 'Go in peace, your sins are forgiven you!'

'Behold the man!' A feeble reed is His rod of office; but with the sceptre of Omnipotence, which He wielded from the beginning, He did not perform the wonders which He works with this mark of abasement and weakness. The sceptre of His majesty did not menace the kingdom of darkness in its claim on fallen man, since retributive justice, the basis of God's throne, bounded His power with impassable limits. With the sceptre of His lowliness, on the contrary, He overturns the seat of the prince of darkness, and hell itself dares not object to, nor call it in question.

It is not in the form of 'the Master in Israel', nor in that of the glorious Son of the Eternal Father, but in the form of the divine sufferer, that He inclines the hearts of those toward Him whom He has purchased with His blood. No sooner does He display before them His suffering form, than they begin to be astonished, and feel attracted, as by a wondrous and magnetic power; and when they hear, as from His bleeding lips, that all He endured was for their sakes, it is His purple robe they first lay hold of, His crown of thorns to which they first pay homage, and His reed-sceptre to which, in joyful obedience, they bow their necks, as to that of their rightful Lord. Yes, the sight of the suffering Saviour is still the mighty power which silently changes lions into lambs, breaks and melts the stony heart, and prepares the way for His most glorious achievements.

'Behold the man!' Yes, keep your eyes fixed upon Him. Even as he is the judge and Conqueror, so He is also the Benefactor of the world. We know that He no longer stands on Gabbatha. He has long ago ascended the throne of glory, in a different robe and a different diadem from that in which we there beheld Him. But He left us His thorn-crowned image in the gospel; and oh, the wonders it has wrought in the world, and continues to perform, whenever the Holy Spirit illumines it! He appears in this form to those who are grievously afflicted, and scarcely do they behold Him than they breathe more freely, and exultingly. In this form He approaches His children when rejected and despised by the world, and when they see Him they feel already fresh courage. In this form He restores those to His flock who had let themselves be seduced from Him by the allurements of the world. A compassionate and warning look from His eye from under the crown of thorns causes them to melt in contrition at His feet. In this form He appears to His children when the shades of death begin to fall around them, and their feet tread the dark valley; and when their half-dosed eyes behold Him, they feel that heavenly peace flows down to them from His crown of thorns.

O may He thus appear to us, likewise, when our day declines, and the darkness of night surrounds us! May He then unveil His suffering form before us, when the gloomy path presents itself to our view, which we must tread alone! When the consolation of human affection no longer reaches the heart, O may He then accompany us in our solitary path, in His purple robe and crown of thorns, and all that is dark around us will be changed into heavenly light and glory! For it is in this form above every other, that the great truth is expressed, that the sentence of death, and the curse are removed from our heads to His, in order that free access to the throne of grace may be granted us, when clothed in the robe of His righteousness.

Let, then, the sound of 'Ecce Homo!' ever vibrate in our hearts, and nothing in the world ever cause His suffering form to fade from our mental view. The wisdom of the just consists, as Paul expresses it, in knowing nothing among men save Christ and Him crucified. Dying daily to ourselves and the world in fellowship with the dying Redeemer, in order daily to rise with Him to the new life in God, is our vocation. Let us be satisfied, remembering that 'we have here no abiding city.'

How long may it be before we hear the sound of another 'Ecce Homo!' But if we then lift up our eyes, a different form will present itself to our view than that which we saw on Gabbatha. The King of Glory will then have exchanged the robe of mockery for the starry mantle of divine Majesty, the wreath of thorns for a crown of glory, and the reed for the sceptre of universal dominion. He inclines the latter to us graciously as the symbol of His especial favour, saying, 'Come, and inherit the kingdom prepared for you from the foundation of the world!' And while from the interior of the heavenly city of God the never-ending hallelujahs of the blessed above greet our ears, our full hearts respond to the ecstatic acclamation, 'Worthy is the Lamb that was slain, to receive power, and riches, and wisdom, and strength, and honour, and glory, and blessing!'

Chapter 37

The Close of the Proceedings

The judicial procedure against the Lord of Glory hastens to its close. Events crowd upon and even overthrow each other. The great and decisive moment is at hand and the occurrences which take place claim our sympathy in an increasing degree.

'Crucify him!' was the people's answer to the pathetic appeal of the more than half-vanquished governor that the life of the Lord Jesus might be spared. This response completely dispossessed Pilate of his last and imaginary safe position. Behold him, now a mere object of compassion and pity, helpless, and wholly at a loss, inwardly torn and tortured by the scourge of his better-self. He again affirms the innocence of the accused, but instead of terminating the proceedings by the liberation of Jesus, as he ought to have done, he demeans himself so far as to give the cowardly advice to the Jews to take Him and crucify Him without his authority. Our compassion for the weak-minded and unprincipled man begins greatly to diminish, and we are tempted to soften our reprobation of the people thus misled and strengthened in their delusion by Pilate's weakness, and to transfer it entirely to him. Can we feel surprised that the people become more bold, the more they see the judge vacillate and give way? 'We have a law,' they cry out very determinedly, 'and by our law He ought to die, because He made himself the Son of God.'

The new accusation here brought by the Jews against Jesus, that He made Himself the Son of God, is very deserving of notice. By this they in fact assert that Jesus, in the proceedings against Him, had assumed this high and honourable title. They therefore consider Him guilty of a capital crime. It was quite clear to them that by the title of Son of God, Jesus intended to place Himself high above every creature, and even on an equality with the all-sufficient God Himself. And if our Lord had intended less than this, it was His sacred duty, on this occasion, to reject the assertion of His accusers as false, or to rectify it as a great mistake. However, He neither does the one nor the other, but observes silence, and by it, openly confirms the accusation brought against Him as well-founded.

'We have a law, and by our law He ought to die because He made Himself the Son of God.' Very true, presupposing that He had spoken falsely in the great things He asserted of Himself. The charge of a treasonable blasphemy would then have lain upon Him. Such, however, was not the case, for He was really what He gave himself out to be. But let us remember that He was now appearing in our stead; and in this position the people's sentence proves correct.

He died, the just for the unjust, and thus He became the end of the law to all them that believe. We died with Him, without personally feeling the suffering of death. In Him we emptied the bitter cup which was destined for us on account of our sins. Henceforward the law no longer stands in our way but only ministers to us in offices of love. Henceforth it may say to us, 'Behold the righteousness reflected in my demands, and know that it is now yours in Christ Jesus. As personally holy as I require men to be, you shall eventually be presented before God.'

The law is also appointed to us, who delight in the law of God after the inward man, to live so as entirely to please Him who hath bought us with his blood; to unfold to us, in every case, what is pleasing to the Lord, and wherewith we may infallibly serve Him. It is to such performances that the law is now enjoined. It is our friend, though occasionally dis-guised under a gloomy mask, and makes again the sound of its lifted rod to be heard by us. This it does, only to drive us back to the wounds of Jesus, or still deeper into them.

But having again reached this city of refuge, it greets us in its true and wholly reconciled form. It has forever forsaken its hostile and menacing position with regard to us. 'Christ is the end of the law;' and whoever is conscious of being a sinner in the sight of God, let him read these words to his complete satisfaction. In them lies the spring of my peace, as well as the dying song with which I hope, at length, gently and blissfully to fall asleep.

'He made Himself the Son of God,' cried the assembled crowd. 'When Pilate heard that saying,' we are informed, 'he was the more afraid.' We will understand the reason. The words were in unison with his deepest presentiment. Jesus had therefore declared Himself to be the Son of God. This seemed to the governor to be something highly remarkable and significant. All that he had seen of the Man with his own eyes seemed only to confirm this assertion respecting Him. 'The Son of God!' Pilate, had he been willing to have given vent to the feeling which in single moments over-powered him, would have almost called Him so; and what was there in the wondrous Man to render it incredible that He should be of other descent and superior in nature to other men? Pilate is deeply affected. His mind feels a degree of mysterious apprehension of which it had never before been the subject. He is anxious to inquire more particularly who the Nazarene is, and for this purpose retires with Him again into the interior of the palace.

Here a memorable conversation takes place between them. Pilate begins it with an inquiry which includes within it nothing less than the vital question of the whole of the Christian religion. 'Whence art thou?' says he. You perceive that we have rightly judged of what had occurred within him. His inquiry does not refer to the city or town, but rather to the world from whence Jesus proceeded. He wishes to know whether He is a son of earth, or has come from some other sphere of the universe. This of itself has become a problem to Pilate. How clearly, therefore, must the stamp of eternity have shone upon our Lord's forehead, even in His menial form!

'Whence art thou?' We perceive from the emphasis laid upon this question that if the Lord had replied, 'I am from heaven,' the governor would not have started back amazed, but would only have said, 'Then my presentiment has not deceived me, for it has already seemed to me as if Thou wert only a stranger and a pilgrim upon earth.' But the Lord gives him no such answer, and even thinks fit to leave him without any information.

We must not regard this as strange; for what benefit would Pilate have derived, if the great mystery had then been revealed to him, that 'In the beginning was the Word, and the Word was with God, and the Word was God, and the Word became flesh'? The heart of the heathen governor was not prepared for it, and his inquiry concerning the descent of Jesus, strictly regarded, must have proceeded more from vain curiosity than from desire for salvation and a need of help. Besides this, such a disclosure respecting Christ's true person and nature could only have increased Pilate's responsibility and have aggravated his condemnation at the last day, and hence it proceeded both from compassion and sparing mercy, that Jesus maintained a profound silence at his question.

How little Pilate would have felt inclined to bow to the sceptre of the Son of God had he recognized Him as such, is sufficiently evidenced from the conduct which he observed immediately after the question. For on Jesus not at once replying to him, he feels offended, and addresses the Lord in a tone of extreme excitement with the arrogant and haughty words, 'Speakest thou not unto me? Knowest thou not that I have power to crucify thee, and have power to release thee?' Hear him! How evident he makes it appear what spirit he is of! Ah, the finest feelings and presentiments of the natural man are only like a rapid vernal vegetation upon a moral morass, which just as rapidly decays. The man must be born again, or else he continues sold under sin as from the first; and his life, however moral and pious it may appear, will only be an uninterrupted chain of relapses.

'Speakest thou not unto me?' Does not the man act as if the Lord committed high treason by not immediately giving him the desired information? What presumption! what pride! 'Knowest thou not,' continues he, 'that I have power to crucify thee, and have power to release thee?' Oh, what delusion, what ridiculous and beggarly pride in one who had just before in the presence of his subjects manifested a weakness which should not have allowed him to use any longer the word 'power' without blushing, especially with reference to crucifying and releasing!

But let us listen to what the Lord says. With the majestic composure of His regal self-consciousness, he replies to the judge who so boldly boasted of his authority. 'Thou couldst have no power at all against me, except it were given thee from above; therefore he that delivered me unto thee hath the greater sin.' Admirable words, perfectly worthy of the

Lord from heaven and the Son of God! According to them, Pilate appears, although acting in his own estimation as self-existent and independent, as an unconscious instrument in the hands of the living God for a sublime purpose, only moving within limits appointed and marked out by an invisible hand. He is unable to do any thing but that which God enables him to do. Notwithstanding his cowardice and want of principle, he would not have delivered Jesus over to his murderers if it had not been pre-determined in heaven. He walks, indeed, in his own way but in leading-strings of which he is unconscious. He bears, indeed, his guilt; but, while acting thus culpably, he promotes a great and sacred object, of which he is ignorant.

The Lord immediately follows up what He has said, to humble and put the governor to shame, with something different and more consolatory. 'Therefore,' says he, 'he that delivered me unto thee hath the greater sin.' He means, 'Because thou art ignorant of Me, and knowest not why I am come into the world, thy guilt is less than that of him who delivered Me into thy hands.' The latter was primarily the high priest Caiaphas, this son of Abraham, this master in Israel, who had grown up in the light of Moses and the prophets, and, therefore, knew what the title 'Son of God' signified, and was in a position to recognize this Son of God in Christ. He, nevertheless, pronounced the sentence of death upon our Lord as a blasphemer.

This sin was the greater because committed in the daylight of scriptural illumination and against superior light and knowledge. It was not committed from weakness, but purposely; not from being taken by surprise, but considerately; not from cowardice, but from wickedness.

Observe how the Lord here again appears great. How He shows Himself afresh as the King over all, yea, as the judge of the world. With the certainty of an infallible searcher of hearts He weighs sin and guilt in the balances of the sanctuary, appoints the measure of future punishment, opens, at the same time, to the unhappy governor a prospect of mercy and possible forgiveness, and manifests the compassion of His heart, which thirsted for the salvation of sinners.

The Lord's words have not entirely failed of their effect on the mind of the governor. He clearly feels in them the sublime as well as the benevolent and charitable motive which dictated them; and hence he is induced to return to the open court, and with fresh zeal to repeat the attempt to liberate Jesus. But he then hears from the crowd below the words which break the mast and rudder of the bark of his goodwill, even on venturing out of the harbour. 'If thou let this man go, thou art not Caesar's friend; for whosoever maketh himself a king (like him for whom thou art pleading) speaketh against Caesar.'

This outcry hit the governor's weakest and most vulnerable side. He knew his master the Emperor Tiberius too well not to foresee that an accusation like that which had just been raised against him, would find only too strong a response in his suspicious mind and would cost him, the governor, his office and who knows what beside. He therefore felt assured that the emperor would pronounce the severest sentence upon him so soon as he should be informed that his viceroy had set a man at liberty who had attempted to claim the title of king over Israel. The emperor's favour was every thing to Pilate, for with it stood or fell his official dignity. Nay, the emperor's anger would have endangered his liberty and life, and it was a grave question with Pilate whether he ought to sacrifice these blessings to justice and peace of conscience.

No sooner does Pilate hear the unfortunate words, 'Thou art not Caesar's friend,' than his little remaining ability to resist gives way. He does not indeed entirely give up his efforts to set Jesus at liberty; but what he undertakes for that purpose is with the despairing consciousness that a successful result is no longer to be expected. He steps forward from the praetorium once more, again brings the accused with him upon the stage, ascends the judgment-seat, and then again begins to harangue the people. But all he now says seems only to be calculated fully to frustrate his purpose.

'Behold your king' cries he, pointing to the suffering Saviour, torn with stripes and covered with ignominy. Who does not feel from this exclamation that it was prompted by a mixture of compassion for the Man of Sorrows, and of bitter scorn toward the hated Jews? He wishes at one and the same time to gain them over to favour Jesus and to give them a very painful blow. The people naturally felt only the poisoned sting of his speech and not its moving power, and that which Pilate might have foreseen occurs. The insulted multitude rise up, like an irritated viper, and cry out more resolutely, angrily, and furiously than before, 'Away with Him, away with Him, crucify Him!'

Pilate now loses all self-possession. His passion even removes the object of his efforts from his view; like a madman destroying his furniture, so Pilate destroys the last hope of Jesus' rescue, while pouring oil into the flame of the people's rage already brightly burning. He calls out maliciously and with bitter sarcasm to the raging crowd, 'Shall I crucify your king?' He no longer knows what he is saying. Inward discomfiture and despair, accompanied by a powerless thirst for revenge render him beside himself.

The chief priests, on the contrary, know better how to preserve their coolness. To the ironical question, 'Shall I crucify your king?' they have immediately an answer at hand, which, though it casts an evil light upon themselves, could not have been more ably chosen to give the governor a moral death-blow. With pretended loyalty and devotedness toward the Roman sovereignty, they cried briefly and forcibly, 'We have no king but Caesar,' and thus give themselves, as regards Pilate, the menacing aspect as if it were they and not he who defended the endangered authority and sovereignty of the emperor.

The supposition that the matter might be regarded in the same manner by Tiberius, quite overpowered the governor. He now gives Jesus up to the people to do with him as they list. They have gained a complete victory; but woe, woe to the poor unhappy beings! While vociferating, 'We have no king but Caesar!' in which they rejected the true Messiah, as well as their hopes in Him, they verified Jotham's parable of the trees, who chose for their king a fiery bramble-bush, and unconsciously pronounced sentence and predicted a curse upon themselves for thousands of years. To this hour the Jews have no king but live without a home as tolerated aliens under foreign dominion.

We take our leave of Pilate and bid him farewell, not without sorrow. He was fitted for something better than that which we saw him display. But he wished to serve two masters – God, who spoke in his bosom, and the world at the same time; and hence his fall and his ruin. He was desirous of doing what was right, but not wholly. The seed of all the sanctifying impressions he received fell under the thorns of his unbroken pride and worldly-mindedness, and these sprang up and overpowered and choked it. Pilate fell a sacrifice to his want of decision and weakness of character, even as numberless others, though often the subject of fine feelings and res-olutions incessantly become a prey to the power of Satan.

We have very scanty intelligence respecting the governor's subsequent fate. We merely know that his inward state became gradually more gloomy and his severity increased; from whence we infer that his peace was at an end, because his conscience condemned him on account of the crying injustice committed upon the Holy One of Israel. In consequence of heavily oppressing the people he was removed by the Syrian Proconsul in the last year of the reign of Tiberius and banished to France.

It is a question whether, in his exile, he came to himself and learned to know the King of the Jews in the glory of His mediatorship. The curse which hovered over Pilate's head was written clearly enough to induce us to hope that its contents would bring him to reflection, and kindle in him a desire for mercy and forgiveness. The primitive fathers speak of documents which Pilate sent to Tiberius respecting his judicial proceedings against Jesus and his death, by which the latter was induced to cause Christ to be received among the gods. We have no reason to doubt the truth of this ancient tradition; and for the sake of those who cannot believe in the superhuman majesty of Christ, sincerely regret that these documents are lost.

But to me, the whole conduct which Pilate, though a heathen, observed toward Jesus seems sufficiently glorifying to Him. Pilate occupies his place in the Apostles' Creed as a witness for the holiness and superhuman dignity of the Lord from heaven, as well as that Christ was delivered up and crucified, not merely according to human will and design, but in accordance with the divine plan of redemption and mercy.

Chapter 38

The Way to the Cross

'Then delivered he him therefore unto them.' Alas for Pilate! Had he but known who it was, and all that he gave up in thus delivering Him! We have tasted only a little of His heavenly manna, but we would not give Him up for all the world. 'Lord, to whom else shall we go? Thou hast the words of eternal life.' We confess, indeed, with deep humiliation, that we are frequently guilty of denying His name, and whenever this is the case, we go out, weeping bitterly, with Peter, and after having been comforted by Him afresh, we again say, with stronger emphasis than before, 'We will never again deliver Him up.' We renounce the friendship, favour, and honour, of His adversaries. If the whole world were offered to us, Jesus is not to be had in exchange. Our union with Him bears the stamp and signature of eternity.

'Then delivered he him unto them.' Oh, if Pilate had had any idea whose instrument he was at that moment! But he is unacquainted with the precious words, 'God so loved the world that he gave his only-begotten Son,' and those of the apostle, 'He who spared not his own Son, but freely gave him up for us all: how shall he not with him also freely give us all things?' These testimonies, however, are known to us; we also know their mysterious depth; we hang down our heads at the words, 'Then delivered he him unto them,' and adore Him.

'Then.' He was now ready and prepared for the last great sacrificial act. He had fulfilled the law, had victoriously endured every trial of faith, and had proved Himself in every ordeal to be pure and unalloyed gold. He was 'the Lamb without spot,' obedient beyond compare, and it was just such a sacrifice as this that the God of holiness required. He must first be found worthy of a crown before He could bear the curse. All is now in readiness.

'Then delivered he him.' Now close the temple, ye sons of Aaron; the types and shadows with which ye had to do have done their duty, now that the substance has appeared. Lay aside the band from your foreheads, and the breastplate, ye ministers of the sanctuary; for know that Another now justly adorns Himself with both, and your priesthood has reached its termination.

The act of delivering over the accused has taken place; Jesus is now in the hands of His enemies, like a lamb amid wolves, or a dove in the claws of the vulture. How was David in the right when he said, 'I will rather fall into the hand of the Lord, than into the hands of man.' Look how they treat the Holy One, now that they have Him among them. They again assail Him with the bitterest mockery, cruelly and rudely tear the purple robe from His bleeding body and put on Him His own clothes again, not from compassion, but because it seems to them that the awful death to which they are now preparing to conduct Him, is no longer to be treated as a jest or a scoff, but requires a certain solemn seriousness.

The change of garments which took place in the court of the praetorium reminds us of an act in our own life. In the days of our blindness we had also divested the Lord Jesus of the glory of His inherent splendour, while presuming to deny one or other particular concerning Him, so as to leave Him little more than the title of a Jewish Rabbi, or the Sage of Nazareth. But how did we afterward alter our course, when the Lord stripped us of the garments of our imaginary righteousness, and in the mirror of His law exhibited to us our real form!

How hastily did we then put upon Immanuel His own raiment! We first gave Thee back Thy Messias-crown, and then Thy sacrificial and priestly robes, and, finally, Thy diadem as the King of Glory; for the awakened necessities of our hearts had rectified our vision and sharpened it for Thy beauty. Amid many tears of repentance and delight, we again clothed Thee in Thy original attire. Thou now standest before us in Thy full and complete array, and we will never cease to bow the knee before Thee, and to rejoice, and say with Jacob, 'Judah, thou art he whom thy brethren shall praise!'

After the soldiers had made their preparations, the awful cross appears which has since become the standard of the kingdom of Christ and the token of our salvation. During the space of three thousand years it had been constantly symbolized to the view of the believing Israelites. It is even reflected in the peculiar manner in which the dying patriarch Jacob, with crossed hands, blessed his grandsons Ephraim and Manasseh. It glimmered no less in the wave-offerings of the tabernacle and temple, which, as is well known, were wont to be waved so as to make the form of a cross appear. In the wilderness the sign was elevated to support the brazen serpent, and the spirit of prophecy interwove it in the figurative language of David's Psalms when placing in the mouth of the future Messiah the words, 'They pierced my hands and my feet.'

Look, yonder they bring it! According to the Roman custom, all who were condemned to the punishment of the cross were compelled to carry that instrument of their death to the place of execution, and even the divine sufferer is not spared this disgrace and toil. Without mercy they lay on His wounded back the instrument of torture; and, after having given Him for His escort two grievous criminals, similarly burdened and condemned to the same death, they open the gate of the courtyard toward the street in order at length to satisfy the people who had been impatiently awaiting the cruel spectacle. A low murmur of malicious joy and profound excitement pervades the mass when the three cross-bearers make their appearance. The procession sets itself in motion. In the van an armed troop on foot and on horseback; then the three victims with their crosses, surrounded by their executioners; behind these the civil and ecclesiastical authorities of the nation; and, finally, the crowding, gaping, innumerable multitude.

We silently join them in spirit. Oh, what a path is that which we now tread! Only think, it is thus the unhappy world repels the Man who entered upon it heralded by angels and in the midst of heavenly songs of praise. It is thus she rewards Him for the unwearied love with which He poured upon her the abundance of all conceivable benefits and mercies! Oh, who that is still inclined to doubt whether mankind was worthy of eternal perdition without the intervention of a Mediator, let him cast a look at this path of suffering and convince himself of the contrary!

Yonder they conduct the Man of Sorrows! One can not reflect who it is that is thus laden with the accursed tree, without feeling surprise and astonishment. But it is well for us that He traversed this path. Only observe how the form of the Lamb which taketh away the sins of the world is so clearly expressed in Him. Behold Him, and say if you do not feel as if you heard the ancient words proceed from His silent lips, 'Sacrifice and offering thou didst not desire, a body hast thou prepared for me. Lo! I come, I delight to do thy will, O my God! yea, thy law is within my heart.'

Had He shrunk back from this fatal path, His road to suffering would have represented to us that on which, when dying, we should have quitted the world. Instead of soldiers, the emissaries of Satan would have escorted us; instead of the accursed tree, the curse of the law itself; instead of fetters, the bands of eternal wrath would have encircled us and despair have lashed us with its fiery scourge. Now, on the contrary, angels of peace sent by Eternal Love will at length bear us on a path of light, illumined by heavenly promises, to Abraham's bosom. To whom are we indebted for this? Solely to the Man who totters yonder under the most awful of all burdens; and who carries away with Him everything which stood opposed to us and threatened us with destruction.

Certainly it may still be the case that during our earthly pilgrimage we are led on similar paths to that on which we see Jesus, our Head, proceeding. For the world hates His members like Himself; and Satan ceases not to desire to have His redeemed, that he may sift them as wheat. But heaven is no longer closed over our path of suffering and disgrace, nor does the black cloud of rejection and the curse obscure it. The sword of God has returned to its scabbard, and peace and hope are the gracious companions who walk by our side. Christ has deprived our fearful path of its horrors, our burdens of their overpowering weight, our disgrace and need of their deadly stings, and placed us in a situation to say with the royal Psalmist, 'Yea, though I walk through the valley of the shadow of death, I will fear no evil; for thou art with me; thy rod and thy staff they comfort me.'

Blessed therefore be the path of our Prince of Peace to the cross! Let us not cease to accompany Him daily thereon in the spirit. It will unspeakably sweeten our own painful path; for why does He take this horrible road, but to enable us to traverse ours with heads erect, because we are freed from curse and care. Upon His path He not only carries all our sins to the grave, and breaks a passage through all the obstacles which blocked up our access to the Father, but He makes, at the same time, all the bitter waters of the desert sweet, and neither leaves nor forsakes us, till He brings us safe to our heavenly home. Blessed be His holy name!

Chapter 39

Simon of Cyrene

Pilate, driven from the field by the determined opposition of the enemies of Jesus, has delivered the Holy One of Israel into the hands of His murderers, who hasten to carry the execution into effect as quickly as possible. No appeal was permitted to a rebel after being sentenced; on the contrary, a Roman law commanded that such should be led away to execution immediately after sentence had been pronounced. This was believed applicable to Him, whom the people thought they could not remove soon enough from human society, as being a rebel against God, against Moses, and against the emperor.

We left the Saviour at the close of our last meditation on the road to the fatal hill. The procession moves slowly forward enveloped in clouds of dust. What a running together from every side! What a tumultuous noise and horrible din! Spears, helmets, and drawn swords glitter in the sunshine. Soldiers on foot and horseback, priests and scribes, high and low, shrieking women and crying children, Jews and heathen, all mingled together in the crowd. At the head of the procession surrounded by guards, the three delinquents, panting slowly forward under the weight of their instruments of death. Two of them robbers and murderers, and between them, He to whom, on closer observation, the whole of this hideous exhibition has reference. Behold that bleeding Man, who according to appearance, is the most guilty of the three! But we know Him. He also bears His cross, and thus claims our sympathy in the highest degree.

Crosses were often seen, under the dominion of the Romans. A rebellious slave was very frequently condemned to this most shameful and painful of all punishments. But there is something very particular and peculiar about the cross which we see the Holy One of Israel bearing to Calvary. If we refer to the roll of the divine Law, 'If a man have committed a sin worthy of death, and he be to be put to death, and thou hang him on a tree, his body shall not remain all night upon the tree, but thou shalt in any wise bury him that day (for he that is hanged is accursed of God), that thy land be not defiled, which the Lord thy God giveth thee for an inheritance' (*Deut.* 21:22).

This remarkable ordinance of God was punctually observed in Israel. As often as a criminal was nailed to the tree of shame, he was regarded, according to the words of the law, as an object of profound abhorrence to the Almighty, and the people were conscious that God could look upon the land only with anger and disgust so long as the dead body of the criminal was not removed out of His sight. But such of them as were enlightened well knew that all this included in it a typical meaning, and had a prophetic reference to One who should hang upon a tree, on whom heaven's wrath would be poured out, but in whose atoning sufferings the curse and condemnation of a sinful world would reach its termination. But who would dare to say that in Christ the ordinance in the wilderness had found its fulfilment, if the Word of God itself had not justified such a conclusion? Turn to Galatians 3: 13, 14, where the apostle states frankly and without circumlocution, 'Christ hath redeemed us from the curse of the law, being made a curse for us, as it is written, Cursed is every one that hangeth on a tree, that the blessing of Abraham might come on the Gentiles through Jesus Christ.'

In the type of the brazen serpent, as well as in the divine ordinances respecting one that was hanged on a tree, the clearest light is thrown on the cross which the Son of God is carrying to Calvary. It is the scaffold where, according to Romans 3:25, God resolved to declare His righteousness for the remission of sins that are past, through the forbearance of God. It is the Moriah where for the benefit of a sinful world the curse pronounced in paradise is endured in the sacred humanity of the great Surety. It is the altar of burnt-offering on which the Lamb of God submitted to the sum total of that punishment which ought in justice to have fallen upon me; and the dying bed, where death is permitted to seize upon and slay another, in order that he might forever lose his claim upon me. Such is the mysterious cross which you see borne toward Calvary. It is the sepulchre of a world; for the innumerable host of those that are saved died, in the eye of God, with Christ upon it. It is the tree of life, 'the leaves of which are for the healing of the nations.'

Jesus carries His cross. When did He ever show so plainly in His outward circumstances that He bore the curse, as now? If the voice of God had sounded directly down from heaven, and said, 'This Just One is now enduring the sentence pronounced upon you,' it could not have afforded us more certainty than by this living figure of bearing the cross. Its language is powerful, and points out even to a child wherein we ought to seek the final cause of Christ's passion.

We find the Holy Sufferer, as you know, outside the gates of Jerusalem. The Scriptures attach great importance to the fact that he was led away out of the holy city. Thus we read in Hebrews 13:11, 12, 'The bodies of those beasts, whose blood is brought into the sanctuary by the high priest for sin, are burned without the camp. Wherefore, Jesus also, that he might sanctify the people with his own blood, suffered without the gate.' Here Christ is represented as the true anti-type of the Old Testament sin offerings. But since we know the nature of these, and how, by this devotional act, the sins of the transgressors were imputed to the animals to be sacrificed; and that the sinner after such sacrificial act, was absolved and declared blameless; so it clearly appears that Christ, on His being led out of the gates, was in fact burdened with our sins, and bore our curse. Thus it is we that tread the path to the place of execution; for He does so in our stead. That such is really the case, and that He does not proceed upon that road as the holy Jesus, but as the Representative of our sinful race, becomes more apparent at every step. Hence it is comprehensible how the Eternal Father could give Him up to such nameless ignominy and torment. It is on this account that no angel from above hastens to His aid; no fire falls from heaven to consume His murderers. All the circum-stances in which we see the Saviour are truly dreadful and appalling; but all exclaim, with the most powerful emphasis, 'Behold the Lord Jesus, laden with the sinner's curse!'

We have been contemplating Jesus with the sinner's cross. The scene now changes, and a new figure presents itself to our view – the sinner with the cross of Jesus.

The Holy One had proceeded forward some distance with His heavy burden, when His blood-thirsty attendants begin to fear lest He should break down under His load, and entirely succumb from exhaustion before the execution. To prevent this, they look about for some one on whom they may lay the cross of Jesus for the remainder of the way; and their eyes soon light upon a stranger, just coming from the field, whom they the sooner select for this purpose from thinking they see in his looks a secret sympathy with the Nazarene. This was Simon, born at Cyrene in Africa. He was stopped and compelled to bear the Lord's cross.

With reference to this circumstance, the words of Jesus are wont to be applied – 'Whoso will be my disciple, let him take up his cross and follow me;' and occasion is then taken from the history of this part of the passion to treat of the reproach we have to bear for Christ's sake. But this seems to me not entirely correct, since Simon does not bear his own cross, but that on which Jesus died. Something very different is, therefore, reflected in the symbolical form of the cross-bearer. It presents to our view the inward position of faith with respect to the cross of Christ, that is, to the sacrifice and act of redemption accomplished upon it. We ought to be cross-bearers in the same sense in which Simon was, only spiritually so. We are such, when the cross of Christ becomes ours in the way of self-accusation, believing appropriation, and continual dying with Christ.

We are compelled to pronounce sentence upon ourselves. But what threatens transgressors, such as we? 'Tribulation and anguish upon every soul that doeth evil.' 'The wrath of God is revealed from heaven against all ungodliness.' We read and tremble, 'Woe is me,' we exclaim, 'Miserable man that I am! I am already condemned, and accursed, and lost!' A thousand reminiscences of past transgressions crowd around us like avenging spirits exclaiming, 'Thou shalt surely die!' and the dreadful words haunt us even in our dreams. We imagine we read them in the stars, and that they are written on each of our days. Thus we are at length compelled to acknowledge that the sentence is just. Christ's cross is laid upon us, that is, we find ourselves guilty of the cross, since we feel that we are ourselves exposed to the curse which Christ endured upon it.

When, in this sense, we have taken the cross of Christ upon us, God who has humbled us, is wont, in due time, to comfort us. We again arise from the darkness and horrors of self-condemnation into the crimson-coloured sunshine of the

atonement. In the cross of Christ, we recognize the mysterious tree on which the sentence which menaced us with
eternal destruction has long ago been endured. We apprehend the mystery of the cross in its consolatory depth, and
enter into a new relation with it, embrace it as our only
refuge, and believingly appropriate the merits of Him who
suffered upon it. We now take it in a different manner upon
us than before; certainly more from necessity at first than
desire. Proud human nature resists the idea of being saved
by grace. Finally, however, we become reconciled to the
wondrous burden, and finally bear it with delight.

In a spiritual sense, we become like Simon of Cyrene. We
enter into the most vital, fervent, and blissful fellowship with
the cross of Christ. We are every where and continually
occupied with this cross, and it becomes the sign by which
we are known. If listened to in our chamber, we are heard
praying beneath the cross. If we say, 'Abba, Father,' it is the
cross which encourages us to do so. If we hope for a
favourable answer to our requests, the cross emboldens us to
expect it. If our conversation is in heaven, the cross is the
heavenly ladder on the steps of which we rise above the
world, death, and hell. The cross forms the focus of all our
heartfelt melody. If a gleam of joy rests upon our foreheads,
the cross is the sun from whence it proceeds. If we are
courageous, it is in the shadow of the cross. If we overcome
the temptations of the wicked one, the cross of Christ is the
banner under which we conquer.

We do not indeed always embrace the cross with equal
warmth and fervour. Occasionally, we bear it with indifference, unwillingly, and even as a burden. This is the case either
when the root of our life again sinks imperceptibly deeper
into the soil of this world; or when the Lord causes our
mountain to stand strong, and we take fresh occasion to
please ourselves with our own doings. But God, who is as

faithful in humbling as in comforting us, knows how to render the cross sweet to us by giving up our old man to a renewed crucifixion, and by reviving and refreshing in us the consciousness of our wretchedness in the midst of distress, disgrace, and pressure.

Generally speaking, the experience of all who in faith take upon them the cross of Christ, agrees in this, that they are ever longer drawn into the death of Him who hung upon the tree. They decrease. They consciously become personally poorer, more worthless and helpless – nay, in time, nothing remains in them of which they might boast as a ground of justification.

The more completely they suffer shipwreck as to every thing of their own, the more valuable does the cross of Calvary become to them, as the only plank of rescue from the surge. How fervently is it then again embraced, how highly and loudly praised, and how bedewed with warm tears of grateful thanksgiving, until at length the whole inward life moves round the cross, in ever closer drawn circles, like the revolving planets round their several suns.

May the Lord be pleased to impress the form of Simon the cross bearer ever more dearly upon our inner man; and in order that this figure may be the more fully produced in us, may He the more and more comprehensively unveil to us the corruption which adheres to us by nature! It is only thus that we learn to bear the cross of Christ with a holy joy. Only thus does it become to us a tree of life, from which we may pluck heavenly fruit. Only thus does it serve as a wondrous weapon by means of which we overcome the world, death, and Satan.

Chapter 40

The Daughters of Jerusalem

The road from Jerusalem to Mount Calvary is crowded with people. O that it were so now in a spiritual and ecclesiastical sense, for no other leads to life and salvation! Certainly, those whom we meet with there are not such as sympathize with Jesus in His sufferings; on the contrary, the number of such is probably very small. But let us rather meet with decided opponents on the way to the cross, than that the road to it should remain solitary and waste.

Alas! in the present day, it lies very desolate. Crowds are seen on the way to the idol temples of the world, and the pavilions of the lust of the eye and the flesh. But how few there are whose hearts are wont to beat louder when it is said to them, 'The passion-week has returned, and we are again preparing for our pilgrimage to Calvary, where the foundations of our eternal redemption are laid.'

Numbers, I fear, continue to fall a prey to spiritual death. Few of them succumb under acute diseases; the majority die of the chlorosis of complete indifference. With them it has gradually come to such a pass that even that which is the most sublime under heaven fatigues them, and the words, 'Church, divine service, and sermon,' make them yawn.

Unhappy mortals! They know not that in these characteristic features they already bear the brandmarks of impending judgment, and the signs, if not of rejection, yet of the capability of it. Satan even does not seem to think these people worthy of an energetic attack. Like dead trees, they fall to him of themselves, and he finds them in his net before he spreads it.

You do not belong to this pitiable race. We still meet you in spirit on the way to Calvary. It is true this is the way to heaven, but beware! it has also its fissures and pits which terminate in endless deserts. We read in Luke 23:27 that a great multitude of people followed Jesus. These were by no means all of them adversaries and bad characters. Many of them only wished to see what would become of Him, and therefore took at least a historical interest in His person and His cause. Know, however, that this does not suffice to save you. Take it to heart that your situation may be the same as that of these people.

We meet also, in the present day, with not a few, and their number is increasing, who have directed their attention to religion, the Church, and the affairs of the kingdom of God, as others do to politics, the arts, or any other subject. What progress Christianity is making in the world – what may be done to promote public worship – what this or that sect believes and teaches – nay, even in what sense this or that doctrine is to be apprehended, and the best mode of expressing it – these are the objects for which they interest themselves. All this is beautiful and praiseworthy; but it may be the case that in the midst of the Holy Land in which their attention is engaged, they may be ripening for perdition.

There is a natural feeling for divine things which may even become very active, by which the 'old man' is not in the least injured, nor the game of the prince of darkness spoiled. How this feeling may even extend to the scenes of our Saviour's passion may be easily conceived. But such a sympathy is not essentially different from any other, and has nothing in common with the life of faith, on which alone the eye of God is fixed.

Of a somewhat nobler nature is the interest felt by those whose sympathy with the history and cause of Christ is excited by their veneration for Him as the Holy One of Israel. Some of these characters were also among the crowd that followed; and we do not unfrequently meet, in our own circles, with such as are thus of a more refined nature. Christ presents Himself to their admiring gaze as the perfect model of all moral human greatness. Nor does any thing hinder them from celebrating with lively emotion, the Lord's passion, while magnanimously irritated against the reckless race that could crucify the only immaculate One that ever trod the earth.

But do they also pray with us, and say, 'O Lamb of God that takest away the sins of the world, have mercy upon us?' O no! This never occurs to them. Hence these worthy people go with us, indeed, on the path of the Church, and, in a certain sense, even the way to Calvary; and yet it is beyond a doubt that they are entirely deficient in the first and most essential requirements of true inward religion – a contrite heart, and a living faith in Christ as the Mediator, and equal with God.

Exasperated against the murderers of Jesus, they unconsciously join in signing the sentence of death against Him. For since they refuse to rise above His human nature, they stamp Him, who declared on oath that He was essentially one with the Father, as a blasphemer who was worthy of death. While reproaching the Pharisees, they are in reality of the same mind with them; for they are as unwilling to know any thing of a Jesus who treats them as sinners, and calls upon them to let themselves be redeemed by Him.

The women whom we see following the divine Sufferer with weeping and lamentation present to us a third kind of relation to Christ, and particularly to Christ as suffering. Here we seem to meet with the true kind of devotion for the solemn occasion. For we perceive heartfelt sympathy with the Man of Sorrows, fervent emotion at the sight of His cross, nay, even tears wept in the presence of the reviling adversaries by whom He is surrounded; and in all this a decided confession that an innocent Man is being conducted to the place of execution, who is worthy of supreme love and esteem, instead of scorn and hatred. What do we require more than we see here?

Nor does the Lord omit to deign attention to these sympathizing witnesses of His sufferings. He turns to them. For what purpose? To praise and console them, and to cheer and strengthen Himself at the sight of them? By no means. The Lord Jesus rejects the grief of the mourners as mistaken, and judges their tears to be useless and unprofitable. He who, every where, and even in the deepest sufferings, was able to preserve the most perfect serenity and presence of mind, and never for a moment lost sight of pastoral solicitude for the lost sheep of the house of Israel with which He was intrusted, says to the weeping women who followed Him, 'Daughters of Jerusalem, weep not for Me, but weep for yourselves, and your children.'

These serious words deserve to be taken to heart also by many among us. They reprove all those whose devotion for the cross likewise consists in a mere natural emotion, excited by the tragical end of the righteous Jesus, and who have nothing else but tears of pity and sentimentality for the Saviour. How much pleasing emotion, occasioned by a lively representation of the Redeemer's passion in musical oratorios, ecclesiastical solemnities, or liturgical devotions, is here rejected! It is scarcely to be conceived what a fullness of impenitence and self-righteousness may be concealed beneath such outbursts of feeling.

There are some who ascribe the tears of sympathy, which the sufferings of Christ draw forth, as a species of righteousness, and exalt them as testimonials of goodness of heart, thus making them a ground of consolation and hope. O lamentable mistake! 'Weep not for me,' says our Lord. Do you hear it? He forbids the lamenting and condoling with Him. He is not some unfortunate person of a common kind. He does not succumb to any superior power, either human, or the force of oppressive circumstances. If He pleased, He could in a moment stand before us in a crown, instead of with a cross.

He freely gave Himself up to His sufferings, in order to accomplish that which His Father had given Him to do; and the idea of 'a tragical end,' in its usual acceptation, is by no means applicable to the passion of our Lord. Tears of sentimentality and pity are nowhere so much out of place as on Calvary. While resigning ourselves to such emotions, we mistake the Lord Jesus – nay, even degrade Him, and as regards ourselves, miss the way of salvation marked out for us by God. Hence the Saviour exclaims, once for all, 'Weep not for me!' thus placing Himself entirely out of the ranks of the wretched and unfortunate of this world.

'Do tears, therefore, not belong to our devotions on this solemn occasion?' Doubtless they do; but their object must be a different one from the Person of the Lord. Hear Him say Himself, 'Weep not for me, but for yourselves and your children!' 'Ourselves!' you exclaim. Yes. In the immolation of Christ, the measure of the world's iniquities was full. It was sinful from Paradise downward. That this was the case was strikingly evident in the days of Noah, Nimrod, the judges, and kings of Israel. But 'The transgression of the Amorites was not yet full.' That even the last pretence for excuse and leniency might disappear, and the hatred of holiness, the base ingratitude and abominable self-seeking of the children of Adam might be manifested still more evidently, opportunity was afforded the human race to exhibit its real and inmost nature, when holiness in person was placed in contrast with it, and the Lord God poured upon it the fullness of His compassion.

Both these took place in the mission of Christ, the only-begotten Son, the good Shepherd. And how did the world act? It loved darkness rather than light; was filled with animosity against Him who came to redeem it from sin; and rejected Him who hurt its pride by the call to regeneration and conversion. It nailed to the cross the herald and bearer of the grace of God.

'The world?' you ask. Yes, the world. Only look a little more closely and you will find yourself amid the crowd which yonder conducts the Lord of Glory to the slaughter. In one or other of those individuals you will see your own likeness. If not in Judas, yet in Annas; if not in Annas, in the hypocritical Caiaphas, or the world-minded Pilate, or else in one of the unprincipled senators, or some other individual, you will somewhere meet with the mirror which reflects your own moral form.

Look around and say if the scenes on Gabbatha and Calvary are not incessantly renewed? If, even at present, a certain degree of courage is not required openly to confess the name of Jesus? If those who love Christ are not still reviled as pietists and hypocrites; and if those who wish to recommend the Prince of Peace to others are not every where angrily repulsed? Nay, feel in your own bosom and say if by nature you would gladly have to do with Jesus?

What feelings are excited in you when He places you among publicans and malefactors, or calls upon you to offer up to Him your mammon, or some other idol? Or when He meets you, with a reproving gesture, on the path of sensual enjoyment and requires that you should live to God and not to the world and walk in God's ways and not in your own; what are you then wont to feel. Does it ever occur to you to melt in gratitude at the Saviour's feet, when you hear it announced that 'God so loved the world that He gave His only-begotten Son, that whosoever believeth on Him should not perish, but have everlasting life'? O my friends, to this hour Christ appears to stand among us, only that by His presence our corruption and depravity may be the more conspicuous! How is it, then, that you do not understand the words, 'Weep not for me, but weep for yourselves?' Truly all appropriate devotion at this sacred season begins with lamenting over *ourselves* and judging, condemning, and acknowledging ourselves worthy of eternal death.

The daughters of Jerusalem hear terrible things said to them, but not that they may sink into hopeless despair. On the contrary, it is here the love that seeketh that which is lost, which speaks to them, and would gladly lead them, at the proper time, to repentance. 'Weep for yourselves and your children.' This is an unmistakable allusion to the dreadful malediction which the infatuated crowd at Gabbatha called down upon themselves, and with it, the indication of that sin which was principally to be lamented as Israel's chief crime, and consequently as the chief source of all their subsequent misery.

The Lord Jesus says in continuation, 'For behold the days are coming, in which they shall say, Blessed are the barren, and the wombs that never bare, and the paps which never gave suck.' What an announcement! That which was previously mourned over in Israel as a great misfortune and an equally great disgrace – the being barren and childless – will then be commanded as an enviable privilege.

'Then,' continues our Lord, obviously referring, both here and previously, to passages in the prophecies of Isaiah and

Hosea, for He lived in His Father's Word, as in the proper element of His holy soul – 'Then shall they begin to say to the mountains, Fall on us, and to the hills, Cover us.' The Saviour's sphere of vision evidently extends itself here beyond the terrible days of the destruction of Jerusalem. His words manifestly generalize themselves and point to the judgment of the last day. Those who will then be found rejecting through obstinate unbelief and persevering impenitence, their truest Friend and only Saviour will find themselves in a position in which they will prefer annihilation to a continuance of existence. They will call upon the hills to crush them and bury them forever beneath their mass of ruins. But the mountains stand and fall at God's command, and He, who will then be their enemy, has decreed for them another fate than that of annihilation. They will then implore the rocks to hide them from the face of the angry judge; but no outlet of escape will be found on the whole earth or under it, which will remove them from the searching look of Him 'whose eyes are as a flame of fire.'

What a prospect! And only consider, that He who thus lifts the veil is not some wild zealot, to whose threats no great importance need be attached; but it is He who is at the same time the truth and loving-kindness itself. How does this strengthen the emphasis of that address by which we are called to repentance in a more powerful and impressive manner than was ever before heard upon earth.

Our Lord concludes His speech to the daughters of Jerusalem with the words, 'For if they do these things in the green tree, what shall be done in the dry?' We can not misunderstand these words. In them the great Cross-Bearer represents Himself as a mirror of the wrath of God. Since He is the Just One and the Life, He calls Himself 'the Green Tree.' Glory and happiness became Him individually, and not suffering; yet He endured unparalleled disgrace and torture.

But that which He experiences must be of the same nature and description with that which is threatened, and which awaits the ungodly. Had it been otherwise, the inference which the Lord bids us draw from His sufferings, with regard to the future fate of the impenitent sinner would not be true, and the comparison He makes inappropriate. If they were only merciful sufferings which befell the Saviour, how could they serve as a criterion for the future lot of those with whom divine grace had nothing more to do?

But Christ's sufferings were vicariously endured punishments; and His words have now a meaning, which is this: 'I, the Green Tree, bear imputatively only the sins of others; and the thrice holy God is not angry with Me personally. Yet how horrible is the cup which is given Me to drink! Judge from this what will eventually be the fate of those, who, as dry wood and unfruitful trees, will have to suffer for their own iniquities, and at whose judicial visitation, the wrath of a holy God will by no means conflict with His love and tenderness.'

Therefore let us not overlook the danger in which we are, so long as we are found carnally-minded, estranged from God, and unthankful despisers of the delivering grace of Him, whom the Almighty tore from His paternal bosom, in order that by Him He might deliver us unworthy creatures from destruction, and bring us back to Himself. Let us be conscious of our enormous guilt, and no longer delay, with the holy grief of a publican or a Magdalen, sincerely and heartily to weep over ourselves.

It is thus, I repeat it, that our devotion should begin, when commencing the solemnities of the passion week. But should they begin with it only, and not end in the same manner? Look at the Saviour. Why does He travel the path of suffering? Because He intends to pay our debt, and blot out our iniquities. Let us follow Him in spirit; for how much are we interested in this His passage to Calvary! He goes to nail the handwriting that was against us to His cross. The Green Tree gives itself up to the flames which ought to consume the dry. The path He treads is a sacrificial one, a path of satisfaction and mediation. Had He not trodden it, we should have been the heirs of eternal death, or else the throne of God must have sunk into ruin and the justice of God would have degenerated into injustice. But He did pass through it, and now deliverance is secured, however heinous our guilt. Let us approach His cross in spite of Satan and the world, open before Him the tear-bedewed pages of our book of transgressions, implore mercy upon our knees, lay hold of the great forgiveness in the blood of the Lamb, and resign ourselves entirely and unconditionally to the thorn-crowned King, that, along with the bands of the curse, He may also loose us from those of the world and the flesh. After this has been done, we may say with propriety that we have celebrated the passion of our Lord.

May He grant us all such a celebration! We implore it the more fervently now that we are about to enter the Most Holy Place of the history of our great High Priest's sufferings. Let us prepare ourselves for this solemn approach by calling to mind the infinite blessings which Christ has purchased for His people by His death on the cross, and by loving Him, who thus loved us, and gave Himself for us!

Part Three

THE MOST HOLY
PLACE

Chapter 41

The Crucifixion

'The Lord is in his holy temple; let all the earth keep silence before him.' Let these words of the prophet Habakkuk be the language of our hearts on entering into the Most Holy Place of the Gospel history.

The most solemn of all days in Israel was, as we well know, the great day of atonement, the only day in the year on which the high priest entered into the most holy place in the Temple. Before he approached that mysterious sanctuary, the law enjoined that he should divest himself of his costly garments, and clothe himself from head to foot in a plain white linen dress. He then took the vessel with the sacrificial blood in his hand, and, thrilling with sacred awe, drew back the veil, in order, humbly and devoutly, to approach the throne of grace, and sprinkle the atoning blood. He remained no longer in the sacred place than sufficed to perform his priestly office. He then came out again to the people, and, in Jehovah's name, announced grace and forgiveness to every penitent soul.

We shall now see this symbolical and highly significant act realized in its full and actual accomplishment. The immaculate Jesus, of whom the whole Old Testament priesthood, according to the divine intention, was only a typical shadow, conceals Himself behind the thick veil of an increasing humiliation and agony; that bearing in His hands His own blood, He may mediate for us with God His Father. He realizes and accomplishes all that Moses included in the figurative service of the tabernacle. The precise manner in which this was accomplished we shall never entirely fathom with our intellectual powers; but it is certain that He then finally procured our eternal redemption.

Once more we return to the road to the cross, and in spirit mingle with the crowd proceeding to the place of execution. They are just passing the rocky sepulchres of the kings of Israel. The ancient monarchs sleep in their cells, but a dawning resurrection gleams upon their withered remains when the Prince of life passes by. The procession then enters the vale of Gehenna which once reeked with the blood of the sacrifices to Moloch. But there is another still more dreadful Gehenna; and who among us would have escaped it, had not the Lamb of God submitted to the sufferings, which we now see Him enduring?

We are arrived at the foot of the awful hill, but before ascending it, let us cast a look on the crowd behind us, and see if, amid all the hatred and rancour that rages there like an infernal flame, we can discover any traces of sympathy and heartfelt veneration for the divine Sufferer. And lo! an estimable little group meets our eye, like a benignant constellation in the darkness of the night. O we know them already, these deeply distressed mourners! We first perceive the pious Salome, the blessed mother of the two 'sons of thunder.' She desires to set her children an example of faithfulness unto death, and we know that both James and John afterward showed themselves perfectly worthy of such a mother. Near Salome walks Mary, the near relative of the blessed virgin. She had also the great privilege of seeing her two sons, James the Less and Joses, received into the immediate fellowship of the great Master. But alas! when the sword came upon the Shepherd, they were also scattered with the rest of the flock; while it seemed to their excellent mother a paramount duty to appear, instead of her children, and by her own fidelity, to cover their flight. And lo! yonder walks Mary Magdalene, sobbing aloud, who had experienced, above others, the delivering power of Him who came to destroy the works of the devil. O how she appears dissolved in grief and sorrow!

But who is she with tottering step, leaning on the disciple whom Jesus loved, dejected more than all the rest, who covers her grief-worn face? It is the sorely tried mother of our Lord, in whom Simeon's prophecy is now fulfilled, 'A sword shall pierce through thine own soul also.' But she had scarcely the smallest presentiment that it would be accomplished in such a manner. But look up, Mary! Cast thyself with all thy grief, into the arms of the eternal Father. Dost thou see thy Son going to be crucified? He also sees His. He who is crowned with thorns is His Son as well as thine. O look at the dear disciple, who though inconsolable himself, tries to support the deeply grieved mother of his Lord. What a scene! But how gratifying is it to perceive that love for the Man of Sorrows has not wholly become extinct upon earth! Nor shall it ever expire. Be not concerned on that account. In that mourning group you see only the first divinely quickened germs of the future kingdom of the divine Sufferer. From a few, a multitude that no man can number will ere long proceed.

After this cursory retrospect of the Saviour's attendants, let us again put ourselves in motion with the crowd. Only a few steps upward, and we reach the end of the dreadful pilgrimage. Where are we now? We are standing on the summit of Mount Calvary – Golgotha – horrifying name – the appellation of the most momentous and awful spot upon the whole earth. Behold a naked and barren eminence, enriched only by the blood of criminals, and covered with the bones of executed rebels, incendiaries, poisoners, and other offscourings of the human race. An accursed spot, where love never rules, but where naked justice alone sits enthroned, with scales and sword, and from which every passer-by turns with abhorrence, a nocturnal rendezvous of jackals and hyenas.

Only think, this place, so full of horrors, becomes transformed into 'the hill from whence cometh our help,' whose mysteries many kings and prophets have desired to see, and did not see them. Yes, upon this awful hill our roses shall blossom, and our springs of peace and salvation burst forth. The pillar of our refuge towers upon this height. The Bethany of our repose and eternal refreshment here displays itself to our view. Truly the ancients were in so far correct in their assertion, that Mount Calvary formed the centre of the whole earth; for it is the meeting-place where the redeemed, though separated in body by land and sea, daily assemble in spirit, and greet each other with the kiss of love.

Not less correct were they in the legend that father Adam was buried beneath Mount Calvary – this hill being really Adam's grave, when by the latter we understand the fallen sinful man, whom we all carry about in us, and who was crucified with Christ on Golgotha. It is strange that to this day the learned dispute the position of this hill, and that there is scarcely a prospect of ascertaining the place with certainty. But it was the divine intention that the material mount should be exalted into the region of that which is spiritual; and such is actually the case. It finds its abiding-place in the believing view of the world.

On that awful mount ends the earthly career of the Lord of Glory. Behold Him, then, the only green, sound, and fruitful tree upon earth, and at the root of this tree the axe is laid. What a testimony against the world, and what an annihilating contradiction to everything that bears the name of God and divine Providence, if the latter did not find its solution in the mystery of the representative atonement! Behold Him, then, covered with wounds and ignominy, and scarcely distinguishable from the malefactors among whom He is reckoned. But have patience. In a few years, Jerusalem that rejected Him glorifies Him in the form of a smoking heap of ruins, as the beloved Son of the Most High, whom no one can assail with impunity; and surrounded by the lights of the sanctuary, living monuments arise, in three quarters of the globe, bearing the inscription, 'To Christ, the Redeemer of the world.' But before these things take place, a horrible catastrophe must occur. The life of the world only springs forth from the death of the Just One. The hour of His baptism with blood has arrived.

Alas! alas! what is it that now takes place on that bloody hill? O heart of stone in our breasts, why dost thou not break? Why, thou cold and obdurate rock, dost thou not dissolve in tears of blood? Four barbarous men, inured to the most dreadful of all employments, approach the Holy One of Israel, and offer Him, first of all, a stupifying potion composed of wine and myrrh, as usual at executions. The Lord disdains the draught, because He desires to submit to the will of His heavenly Father with full consciousness, and to drink the last drop of the accursed cup. The executioners then take the Lamb of God between them, and begin their horrid occupation by tearing, with rude hands, the clothes from off His body. There He stands, whose garment once was the light, and the stars of heaven the fringe of His robe, covered only with the crimson of His blood, and divested of all that adorned Him, not only before men, but also in His character as Surety, before God – reminding us of Adam in paradise, only that instead of hiding Himself behind the trees at the voice of God, He cheerfully goes toward it; reminding us also of the Old Testament high priest, His mysterious type, who, before he entered into the most holy place to make atonement, exchanged his rich attire for a simple white robe.

After having unclothed the Lord, and left Him, by divine direction, only His crown of thorns, they lay Him down on the wood on which He is to bleed; and thus, without being aware of it, bring about the moment predicted in Psalm 22, where we hear the Messiah saying, 'Be not far from me, for trouble is near; for there is none to help. Many bulls have compassed me about; strong bulls of Bashan have beset me round.' O what a dying bed for the King of kings! My friends, as often as we repose on the downy cushions of divine peace, or blissfully assemble in social brotherly circles, singing hymns of hope, let us not forget that the cause of the happiness we enjoy is solely to be found in the fact that the Lord of Glory once extended Himself on the fatal tree for us.

Oh, see Him lie! His holy arms forcibly stretched out upon the cross-beam; His feet laid upon each other and bound with cords. Thus Isaac once lay on the wood on Mount Moriah. But the voice that then called out of heaven, saying, 'Lay not thine hand upon the lad!' is silent on Calvary. The executioners seize the hammer and nails. But who can bear to look upon what further occurs! The horrible nails from the forge of hell, yet foreseen in the sanctuary of eternity, are placed on the hands and feet of the righteous Jesus, and the heavy strokes of the hammer fall. Dost thou hear the sound? They thunder on thy heart, testifying in horrible language of thy sin, and at the same time of the wrath of Almighty God. Oh, how many sleepers have awakened from their sleep of death under the echo of those strokes, and have escaped from Satan's snare! Awake also thou that art asleep in sin, and rouse thyself likewise, thou who art lulling thyself in carnal security! How many a proud and haughty heart has been broken into salutary repentance by those strokes! Oh, why does not thy heart also break? For know that thou didst aid in swinging those hammers; and that the most crying and impious act which the world ever committed is charged to thy account.

See, the nails have penetrated through, and from both hands and feet gushes forth the blood of the Holy One. O these nails have rent the rock of salvation for us, that it may pour forth the water of life; have torn the heavenly bush of balm that it may send forth its perfume. Yes, they have pierced the handwriting that was against us, and have nailed it to the tree; and by wounding the Just One, have penetrated through the head of the old serpent. O let no one be deceived with respect to Him who was thus nailed to the cross! Those pierced hands bless more powerfully than while they moved freely and unfettered. They are the hands of a wonderful Architect who is building the frame of an eternal Church – yea, they are the hands of a Hero, which take from the strong man all his spoil. And believe me, there is no help or salvation, save in these hands; and these bleeding feet tread more powerfully than when no fetters restrained their steps. Nothing springs or blooms in the world, except beneath the prints of these feet. The most dreadful deed is done, and the prophetic words of the Psalm, 'They pierced my hands and my feet,' have received their fulfilment. The foot of the cross is then brought near to the hole dug for it; powerful men seize the rope attached to the top of it, and begin to draw, and the cross, with its victim, elevates itself and rises to its height. Thus the earth rejects the Prince of Life from its surface, and, as it seems, heaven also refuses Him. But we will let the curtain drop over these horrors. Thank God! in that scene of suffering the Sun of Grace rises over a sinful world, and the Lion of Judah ascends into the region of the spirits that have the power of the air in order, in a mysterious conflict, eternally to disarm them on our behalf.

Look what a spectacle now presents itself! The moment the cross is elevated to its height, a crimson stream falls from the wounds of the crucified Jesus. This is His legacy to His Church. We render Him thanks for such a bequest. It falls upon spiritual deserts, and they blossom as the rose. We sprinkle it upon the door-posts of our hearts, and are secure against destroyers and avenging angels. Where this rain falls, the gardens of God spring up, lilies bloom, and what was black becomes white in the purifying stream, and what was polluted becomes pure as the light of the sun. There is no possibility of flourishing without it, no growth nor verdure, but every where desolation, barrenness, and death.

There stands the mysterious cross – a rock against which the very waves of the curse break. He who so mercifully engaged to direct this judgment against Himself hangs yonder in profound darkness. Still He remains the Morning Star, announcing an eternal Sabbath to the world. Though rejected by heaven and earth, yet He forms the connecting link between them both, and the Mediator of their eternal and renewed amity. Ah see! His bleeding arms are extended wide; He stretches them out to every sinner. His hands point to the east and west; for He shall gather His children from the ends of the earth. The top of the cross is directed toward the sky; far above the world will its effects extend. Its foot is fixed in the earth; the cross becomes a wondrous tree, from which we reap the fruit of an eternal reconciliation. O, nothing more is requisite, than that God should grant us penitential tears, and then, by means of the Holy Spirit, show us the Saviour suffering on the cross. We then escape from all earthly care and sorrow, and rejoice in hope of the glory of God. For our justification in His sight, nothing more is requisite than that, in the consciousness of our utter helplessness, we lay hold on the horns of that altar which is sprinkled with the blood that 'speaketh better things than that of Abel.' And the Man of Sorrows displays to us the fullness of His treasures, and bestows upon us, in a superabundant degree, the blessing of the patriarch Jacob on his son Joseph: – 'The blessings of thy father have prevailed above the blessings of my progenitors unto the utmost bound of the everlasting hills.'

There stands erected the standard of the new covenant, which, when it is understood, spreads terror around it no less than delight, and produces lamentation no less than joy and rejoicing. It stands to this day, and will stand forever. And wherever it is displayed, it is surrounded by powerful manifestations and miraculous effects. Look how the missionary fields become verdant, and a spring-time of the Spirit extends itself over the heathen deserts! Hark how the harps of peace resound from the isles of the sea; and behold how, between the icebergs of the north, the hearts begin to glow with the fire of divine love! From whence these changes? these resurrection-wonders? From whence this shaking in the valley of dry bones? The cross is carried through the land, and beneath its shade the soil becomes verdant and the dead revive.

'I am crucified with Christ,' exclaims the apostle, and by these words points out the entire fruit which the cross bears for all believers. His meaning is, 'They are not His sins, for which the curse is there endured, but mine; for He who thus expires on the cross, dies for me. Christ pays and suffers in my stead.' But that of which Paul boasts is the property of us all, if by the living bond of faith and love we are become one with the crucified Jesus. We are likewise exalted to fellowship with the cross of Christ in the sense also that our corrupt nature is condemned to death, our old man, with his affections and lusts. We see the cross of Calvary unfold its full and peace-bestowing radiance. It arches itself, like a rainbow, over our darkness, and precedes us on our path of sorrow like a pillar of fire. O that its serene light might always shine upon our path through this vale of tears, and as the tree of liberty and of life, strike deep its roots into our souls! Apprehended by faith, may it shed its heavenly fruit into our lap, and warm and expand our hearts and minds beneath its shade!

Chapter 42

The Dividing of the Raiment

The scene we are about to contemplate is remarkable even for those who are either unable or unwilling to share in our belief. It represents the taking possession of an inheritance, in which – at least in some respects – we ourselves are interested. A dying bed presents itself to our view – an individual at the point of death – a legacy, and the heirs. Happy is he who is justified in numbering himself with the latter! Let us approach near, and direct our attention, first, to the Testator, and then to His legacy and heirs.

A testator, as you are aware, is one who bequeaths an inheritance. We find such a One in that part of the Gospel narrative which we are about to consider. The place where we meet with Him is indeed the last where we ought to seek Him. We are standing on the summit of Mount Calvary. The company by whom we are surrounded are certainly, in part, of high rank – senators, priests, and centurions meet our view. We might suppose that if there was a Testator here, He could be found only among these dignitaries. But such is not the case. Look up, and behold the bleeding Man upon the accursed tree between two companions in suffering. This is real degradation, misery, distress and pressure, and is death in the most complete and horrible sense of the word.

But how will you be astonished, when I inform you that this Man, the poorest of the poor, is the very One whom we went forth to seek. 'What!' you exclaim, 'not the Testator?' Yes, incomprehensible as it may seem, it is He and no other. Look at the inscription over His head. Pilate caused it to be written; but, believe me, God has had His hand in it, however seemingly it may stand in contradiction with the bleeding form to which it has reference. It is no bitter scoff, but actual truth: 'Jesus of Nazareth the King of the Jews.'

'What!' you exclaim again, 'that Man a King?' O, my friends, something still more and greater than that! The lines there do not say enough. We will strike them out and put in their place 'Jesus of Nazareth, the King of kings,' But even this title is too vague. Let us place another in its stead: 'Jesus of Nazareth, the Son of the living God.' Nor does this title satisfy us. We blot it out and write, 'Jesus of Nazareth, the Alpha and Omega, the First and the Last, the Creator and Preserver of all things, God blessed forever.' This epitaph may remain, for the description is most firmly and irrefutably founded.

It was He, it is He, even amid the horrors of such a death; all things are His, heaven and earth, the bliss of paradise and the trees of life by the river of the city of God, and the crown of honour on its pillars. But that which He possessed from the beginning, He possessed only for Himself, or at most, only for the holy angels that had remained faithful. Not the least glimmer of His glory could He bestow upon us sinners, without trenching upon His honour and majesty. Divine justice, which necessarily condemned us, decidedly protested against every impartation of the kind; likewise His divine holiness, which blesses only those who are free from sin.

Now, if the rich Lord of heaven was nevertheless desirous of bequeathing some part of His property to us, it was first of all necessary that He should satisfy these exalted opponents of our fallen race, in a holy and divinely appointed way. And to this He agreed, when He undertook to yield, in our stead, that obedience which we owed, and to endure in His own person, the curse inflicted upon us. And both these He accomplished at the moment in which we now find Him; and by His vicarious endurance of our misery He builds a bridge for us unhappy mortals, by which we are enabled to reach His own felicity.

But because, by His rendering this satisfaction, He acquires the power to receive us sinners into the fellowship of His blessedness, we shall do well to remove the inscriptions we have just attached to His cross, however well founded they may be, and leave the first and original one, 'Jesus of Nazareth, the King of the Jews.' It is the most characteristic in its place; for why did the Lord suffer and die, but because He was not merely the Son of the living God, and regent of the world and those upon it; but also because He became the King and the beatifying Prince of Peace of a spiritual Israel, gathered from among sinners.

We are now acquainted with the great Testator – the Man who is bleeding on the cross. And it is because He hangs there that He acquires the power to restore the justly disinherited children of Adam to their lost possessions. But in what does the legacy consist? Its noblest part will be seen in that portion of the narrative we are about to consider. In it a jewel glitters, with which is combined the pledge that no good thing will be withheld from us. From the summit of the cross cast your eyes down to its foot. Four assistant executioners are seen cowering down together, busily engaged in a peculiar manner. They inherit all that the Man possessed whom they have nailed to the cross – His clothing. They are occupied in parting the wide upper garment, and dividing it among them. But on more closely examining the underclothing, they see in it a singular piece of art, for the dress is without a seam, woven entirely in one piece. This vesture, they think, ought not to be cut; and hence they agreed to cast lots for it. They do so, and he who is so fortunate as to win becomes possessor of the whole garment, from that moment on.

Scrutinize narrowly this gambling group beneath the cross; for what they are doing is extremely significant. At first sight we would suppose that this was far from being the case; but the fact that the whole of the four Evangelists, including the beloved disciple, mention, on the dictate of the Holy Spirit, this division of the raiment, is a pledge to us of its symbolical importance and divine meaning. Besides this, the executioners, without any idea of it, are fulfilling, by their division of the garments, and their casting the lot for the unseamed vesture, a Scriptural prophecy almost a thousand years old. We read that 'this was done that the Scripture might be fulfilled,' and know that it is the twenty-second Psalm which is here referred to. In that sacred song, which may be regarded as a prophetic effusion of the suffering Lamb of God, the Redeemer utters beforehand by the mouth of David, the thoughts and feelings by which He would subsequently be affected during His crucifixion. It is there said, 'Dogs have compassed me: the assembly of the wicked have inclosed me. They pierced my hands and my feet; I may tell all my bones: they look and stare upon me.' Then follow the words, 'They part my garments among them, and cast lots for my vesture.'

What do you say to this passage? Must not expressions of this kind from the spirit of prophecy surprise and astonish even the most unbelieving? David could not have uttered these words with reference to himself. The description only suits the Sufferer, in whose life we now see it actually interwoven. He who bleeds on Calvary is therefore the mysterious Individual who announces Himself in the Psalm as the Redeemer of the world. But while it adds great importance to the trivial act of the division of the raiment by making known the Lord Jesus as the true Messiah, we shall find that something of a still more momentous nature is included in the passage.

We must first inquire for what reason the Lord caused these words to be inserted in the prophetic lamentation of the Psalmist: 'They parted my garments among them, and for my vesture they cast lots.' He certainly did so not merely with the intention of recording a circumstance trifling in itself, from the subsequent fulfilment of which it should be evident that He was indeed the promised Messiah. Consider that they are rather His own feelings and sentiments which are there expressed. They are, in part, complaints and expressions of suffering; but also comprise a heart-cheering view of the incomparable results which would accrue to sinners from His sufferings. In the latter class must be included the words, 'They parted my garments, and for my vesture they cast lots.' The Lord in them encourages Himself by the blessed consequences of His blood shedding. But in what does He perceive them? Naturally, not in the fact of His earthly garments being divided among sinners. He evidently takes this outward division of His raiment as symbol full of meaning, and regards it in a sense incomparably higher and more spiritual. And what is that? Thus we might ask if there was no mention in the Holy Scriptures of a garment which Christ had acquired for us. But you know that it is frequently alluded to. This spiritual legacy of a robe is there sensibly represented. Such is the object of the transaction on Mount Calvary.

What we read respecting Adam is worthy of our most serious consideration. Before he gave way to sin, he shone in the white and honourable robe of perfect innocence. He was treated as a beloved child in his Father's house. He was permitted to approach Him, and cast himself upon His bosom, when and wherever he pleased. Every thing was put under his feet, and his happiness flowed in an inexhaustible stream. The holy angels were his comrades, and the peace of God his food, early and late.

But scarcely had the unhappy fall occurred than his situation was entirely changed. We now behold him fleeing and even hiding himself from the face of God, and hear him reply to the inquiry, 'Adam, where art thou?' with the lamentable confession, 'I was afraid, and hid myself, because I was naked.' what was expressed in this confession but our own state by nature? Adam's nakedness is ours. We also, as the apostle says, are 'destitute of the glory we ought to have before God.' We are naked. Not a thread of that righteousness which avails in the sight of God is left us. Sin has banished the last gleam of the radiance of our original beauty.

But this fact is dreadful and momentous beyond degree. Does not even sound reason tell us that we dare not appear naked and unadorned before a holy God? Cain felt that he was thus naked in the sight of God, and became a prey to despair. The same feeling prompted Judas Iscariot to destroy himself. This truth smote the conscience of the Philippian jailor, and he was upon the point of throwing himself upon his sword. And what efforts do we see made on dying beds, to lay hold of something wherewith men may appear clothed before God!

As true as a holy God lives in heaven, so surely shall we be excluded from His fellowship if we have not a holiness to place in the light of His countenance, which shall reflect the purity of His own perfections. But where are we to procure such attire? Not from our own looms. It is elsewhere provided for us. Hear what the apostle says, 'Put on the Lord Jesus Christ.' These words direct us to that which leads to a most blissful discovery.

We return to the soldiers under the cross. They are busied in dividing among themselves the upper garment of the dying

Jesus. They are not prohibited from parting this. The upper garment symbolizes the outwardly operating fullness of the Saviour's power and life; and in a second signification, the spiritual endowment intended for us. This is divisible, and it also appears divided in the assembly of the faithful. One had more, the other less of this legacy. To one, the gift of knowledge was allotted, to another the gift of prophecy by the same Spirit; to a third the power to work miracles; to a fourth, the discerning of spirits (1 *Cor.* 12). A distinct measure of these gifts of the Spirit was not required in order to be saved.

But there was one kind of legacy which was quite indispensable to every one who desires to stand in the judgment. Its emblem you find in the hands of the mercenaries under the cross. Beside the Lord's upper garment, another prize has fallen to them, and it is this which forms the peculiar capital of their inheritance. It is the vesture or body-coat of the Man of Sorrows, which He used to wear under the mantle; therefore such a dress as the high priest was obliged to put on when he entered into the most holy place on the great day of atonement. That such a priestly garment is found on the body of Jesus, that it is inherited by one of His murderers, and falls to him wholly and undivided, is extremely significant. A child must be conscious that he is here standing before hieroglyphics which conceal something important and profound. But what is the marrow of this sacred symbol?

Beneath the resplendent robe of His wonderful and active life, the Saviour wore another, the garment of a perfect obedience which He yielded, even in distress and death. Nothing was wanting in Him. Many eyes – human, angelic, and satanic – have scrutinized it, but all have been filled with wonder at the sight. Even the eyes of God beheld it with delight, and a voice from heaven declared, 'This is my beloved Son, in whom I am well pleased.' It was a garment wrought entirely of the golden threads of the purest love to

God and man, without spot and without a seam, and woven in one piece. You see it is the robe of righteousness of the Son of God, which is symbolized by the coat without a seam, for which the lot is cast at the foot of the cross.

But you ask in surprise, 'Did this also belong to Jesus' legacy to sinners?' Without a doubt. Hear what the Scripture says: 'As by one man's disobedience many were made sinners; so by the obedience of one shall many be made righteous.' And again, 'As by the offence of one, condemnation came upon all men, so by the righteousness of one, the free gift came upon all men unto justification of life,' or which procures life (*Rom.* 5). Not merely was forgiveness intended for us, but also something further and greater. Paul testifies that the Lord assured him that His people should receive 'forgiveness of sins and inheritance among them which are sanctified' (*Acts* 26:18).

Here, therefore, are two things mentioned. Forgiveness would only secure us against deserved punishment, and bestow upon us the negative blessing of being uncondemned. But according to the counsel of a merciful God, we were to be positively exalted, blessed, and beatified; and for this purpose we required a righteousness which commanded us not only to the sparing magnanimity, but also to the loving good pleasure of a holy God. Christ acquired this for us also. While fulfilling the law as our Surety, He placed that incomparable obedience before the eyes of His heavenly Father which, being mercifully imputed to us on the part of God is on our part laid hold of by faith, and after being appropriated by us, causes us to break forth into the song of the prophet, 'I will greatly rejoice in the Lord, my soul shall be joyful in my God, for he hath clothed me with the garments of salvation; he hath covered me with the robe of righteousness, as a bridegroom decketh himself with ornaments, and as a bride adorneth herself with her jewels. For as the earth bringeth forth her bud, and as the garden causeth the things that are sown in it to spring forth; so the Lord God will cause righteousness and praise to spring forth before all nations' (*Isaiah* 61: 10, 11).

From the inheritance, let us now cast a cursory look upon the heirs. Who is it that inherits the costly attire? Only think, one of the murderers who are sitting beneath the cross is the fortunate man. This circumstance tells us that, according to the divine intention, no wickedness, however great, excludes unconditionally from the inheritance.

First, these men know how to value the preciousness of the seamless vestment. Next, they perceive that only in its undivided whole it was of value and a real treasure; and, finally, they are satisfied that they shall obtain possession of the costly garment entirely gratuitously, by a cast of the dice, and therefore without any merit of their own. Do you now understand these hieroglyphics? Become poor sinners, learn to understand the demands of God upon you, and be content to be justified by grace. The symbol under the cross will then find in you its actual antitype.

How the heir of the seamless garment will have rejoiced at the prize he won! We have inherited the robe, which makes us objects of the divine good pleasure, and shall the chords of our harps be silent? Doubtless the fortunate man immediately put on his legacy and wore it thenceforward. Let us avail ourselves of the hint thus given us, to 'put on the Lord Jesus Christ.'

Even the earthly dress of the crucified Jesus will have exercised a manifold influence on the mind of the mercenary, and have at times affected him, made him shudder and feel ashamed, and doubtless have caused the image of the Man from whom he inherited it never to be effaced from the mirror of his remembrance. Reflect, therefore, with what powerful and salutary influence the substance of that shadow, the righteousness of Christ Himself, must be accompanied, as regards the heart and life of those who are able to appropriate it by a living faith.

The soldier might – as regarded his upper garment – have occasionally gone about poorly clad; and yet, if one looked deeper, it would not be denied that he was more richly attired than many a king. Is not the case similar with the children of God, whose external dress is often, especially in the days of trial, any thing but splendid? and yet the eye of all heaven rests upon them with pleasure; and the words are applicable to them, 'The king's daughter is all glorious within.'

Let us congratulate ourselves, therefore, on the incomparable inheritance left us by Him who expired on the cross. Let as many of us as have reason to number ourselves among the heirs of Christ maintain the conviction, lively and fresh within us, that we are already justified in Him before God; and that the love of God is not measured out to us according to the degree of our personal holiness. Let the watchword of our faith, 'Jehovah Tsidkenu,' the Lord our righteousness, with which we overcome the world, be more and more fluent on our lips.

Chapter 43

The Inscription

Let us lift up our eyes to the inscription, which beams from the cross of the divine Sufferer. We there read, 'Jesus of Nazareth, King of the Jews', written in three different tongues – Greek, Latin, and Hebrew – the three theological languages, that all the world may read and understand. Pilate had so ordered it, induced partly by an obscure and reverential presentiment, and partly in order to give the hated Jews a final blow. No sooner had the latter read the inscription, than they angrily hasten to the governor, and say to him in an imperious tone, 'It must not be as thou hast written. Down with that inscription from the cross of the blasphemer. Write that He presumptuously said that He was the King of the Jews.' But Pilate briefly and resolutely replied, 'What I have written, I have written!' And thus, Pilate, it ought to be. What thou didst write was not from arbitrary choice, for Another guided thy hand. Thou has prophesied as did Balaam of old; and with thy inscription, art ignorantly and involuntarily become a witness for the truth.

Wilt thou behold the King of Israel? Come, friend, and follow me to Calvary's bloody hill. Seest thou that Man on the cross, dying the death of a malefactor? 'What?' sayest thou, 'Is this a King?' Do not shake thy head, but know that thou art wanting in discernment, not He in majesty. Retrace the ancient Levitical service, and behold in the sacred songs and prophetic language of the Old Testament that which shall throw light upon the appalling scene. Light thy torch in the psalms of David, in which thou hearest a great King say, 'They pierced my hands and my feet. They gave me also gall for my meat, and in my thirst they gave me vinegar to drink'; and yet He remains a King. Listen to the prophet Isaiah speaking of One who though He was 'bruised for our iniquities,' yet 'the government was upon his shoulder, and of his peaceful kingdom there shall be no end.' Read the words of Zechariah, 'Awake, O sword, against the man that is my fellow!' and hear the forerunner in the wilderness, exclaiming, 'Behold the Lamb of God, that taketh away the sin of the world!' Return with these lights to Calvary, and say if thou art still so much astonished at finding the inscription on the cross, which stands between the other two, bearing the words, 'Jesus of Nazareth, the King of the Jews?' A cloud of holy witnesses adoringly surround the cross, venerable figures, tried saints, patriarchs and seers, poets and prophets, kings and priests. The figure of the bleeding King did not mislead them. Reverentially, and far from starting back with surprise, they read the inscription, 'Jesus of Nazareth, the King of the Jews.'

Dost thou inquire, Where is the majesty of this King? Be not offended at the gloomy cloud which frowns around Him. The eye of faith penetrates through it, and perceives a rainbow-garland of angels' heads and seraphic faces. And who, in the further distance of the heavenly world, compose the brilliant host that, sunk in adoration, lie on their faces beneath the trees of life? They are the saints of God, who inherited the kingdom before the Lord of Glory descended to the earth. They now behold him paying the promised ransom for them and supporting the blissful abodes they inhabit with the pillars of justice. And look still further in spirit. The multitudes of people out of every age and nation, their eyes attentively directed to the cross, and their faces expressive of sacred peace and silent blessedness – who are they, who, in the interminable circles, surround the fatal hill? It is His Church, His redeemed people, including the best and noblest of mankind in every age. See the censers in their hands. They desire only to hear and know respecting the Lamb that was slain.

Such are the sights which faith beholds. And on beholding such a representation, the cross before it changes to a throne, the crown of thorns about the brow of the dying Man becomes a diadem, and Pilate's inscription is read with reverence and adoration, 'Jesus of Nazareth, the King of the Jews!'

Yes, it is He! Thou mayest recognize Him by the victories He achieves, even on the fatal tree. He is assailed by powerful temptations which rise up in the shape of the scornful revilings of the people, who exclaim, 'He saved others, himself he cannot save. If he be the King of Israel, let him now come down from the cross, and we will believe him,' a powerful assault of the wicked one. How much did the taunting advice to come down correspond with the necessities of His suffering human nature! If He had followed it, not only He Himself would have been delivered at once from His torment, but the host of blaspheming adversaries would have been driven from the field in an unexampled manner, convinced of His divinity almost more plainly than was afterward the case by His resurrection from the dead.

Alluring thought, at one blow to strike the raging multitude dumb, and bend their knees in the dust! But far be such an idea from Him! It is a snare, a trap of the artful fowler, a rock under water, to wreck the project of the atonement just before its final accomplishment. Jesus surveys the infernal toils, and says in spirit, 'Get thee behind me Satan; I will not come down, but bleed, sacrifice myself, and pay the wages of sin.'

In sublime silence He rejects the call and bears the torment; nor did He deviate from His path a single moment. Come, let us interweave an olive-branch in His crown of thorns and wreath about with the laurel of victory the inscription, 'Jesus of Nazareth, the King of the Jews.'

Yes, while hanging there, He is still a royal conqueror. Thou mightest think that no one was more overcome than He. But the prospective glass of faith will show thee something different. A conflict of desperation has commenced, and the human race is its object. The hostile parties are the captain of the Lord's host and the infernal powers. How the demons of the pit rage and struggle! The prey is to be taken from them and the captive delivered; the sceptre to be wrested from their hands, and the right they had acquired over us by the divine decision again torn from them.

And it is the Man in the crown of thorns who threatens their dominion, and is trying to overturn it. Nothing in the arsenal of hell is left untried, which may afford any hope of victory. The Lion of the tribe of Judah bleeds; but His blood is the enemy's overthrow. He falls into the hands of His adversaries; but this is the means of rescuing us out of their hands. He suffers Himself to be fettered by the bands of Belial; but His claims beget our liberty. He empties the cup of wrath; but only that He may fill it with blessings for us. He suffers Himself to be wounded in the heel, but at the same moment breaks the head of the old Serpent, and conquers the enemy, like Samson, by His fall.

Such are the achievements of the dying Jesus. To us He would not seem more glorious were He to descend in majestic splendour from the cross amid the music of angelic harps, than He appears to us yonder in His bleeding form. We see Him decked with victorious insignia, and, while sounding the trumpet of triumph, we exclaim, 'Jesus of Nazareth, the King of the Jews!'

A third victory is gained at the cross, the greatest and most wonderful of all. I call it the victory of the lawgiver over the law. There was no want of wish and will in heaven to save us. They existed abundantly; but the right to undertake the great work was wanting. The holy and inviolable law was the bolt which fastened the door of the treasury of divine mercy. The law put in its protest against our redemption. Its language was, 'No salvation for sinners till their guilt is expiated;' and even eternal Majesty felt bound by the protestation.

But divine wisdom was able to loose their fetters. The Eternal Son descended upon earth to change the negative of the law into an affirmative. He suffered Himself to be 'made under the law,' and fulfilled it, as our representative, in such a manner as to enable Him to stand forward, and say, 'Which of you convinceth me of sin?' But this did not remove the barrier from the sluices of divine mercy. The curse had to be endured, to which we had become subject by a breach of the law. He submitted to this likewise and drank the cup of wrath. Did a drop remain? 'Not one,' was the law's decision. And when the voice of mercy was heard from heaven, the law had nothing to object. Divine justice resigned the sceptre to its august sister, Love, without infringing its glory in the slightest degree. We admire the victory over the law in the way of justice, and adoringly read the inscription, 'Jesus of Nazareth, the King of the Jews.'

Yes, He is a King! But where is His kingdom? He is founding it while hanging on the cross. The drops of blood which trickle down, are the price He paid to ransom His people, and the dying groans which issue from His breast, the joyful peal which announces the birthday of His Zion.

He did not found His kingdom when gathering the people around Him, and addressing them from the mount of the beatitudes. Nor when He cast out the spirits of darkness, and by His miraculous aid won the eternal gratitude of hundreds of the weary and heavy-laden. Had He left the world after these triumphs, all would have remained upon earth as before, and He Himself have been without a kingdom and a people. Teaching, preaching, and example could not effect it. The new city had to be founded on the blood of the covenant; and it was done. The hands that were nailed to the cross overcame the world, and founded, in the midst of the kingdom of darkness, the kingdom of light and peace. O wonder beyond compare! What Pilate wrote remains forever true, 'Jesus of Nazareth, the King of the Jews.'

The Jews did not imagine it was He. They ventured to cry, 'His blood come upon us and upon our children!' You know that their imprecation was fulfilled in the manner they desired. 'Woe!' exclaimed the blood, and cried to heaven for vengeance upon them. Behold the result! A heavy storm gathers over Jerusalem. The torch of war is lighted in the land. A forest of hostile lances begirds the holy city. The temple sinks in flames. The walls fall down. Not one stone remains upon another, and the blood of the children of Abraham flows in torrents. Those who escape the sword must flee into the wide world, far from their beloved hills and the graves of their forefathers, into the barren and inhospitable waste. And Israel remains to this day a subjugated people. In their wretchedness they are a lasting memorial that He, whose blood they had invoked over them, was and is a King, and does not suffer Himself to be mocked with impunity. But we wait for a time in which the Lord will make it evident in another and more gratifying manner in these His ancient covenant people that He is their real and true King. When they shall eventually come with weeping and lamentation and He shall gather them out of the land of the north, and lead them in a plain path by the rivers of water, and shall say to them, 'I am Israel's father, and Ephraim is my first-born;' then the most obstinate unbelief shall no longer rebel, but reverently fold the hands on reading the inscription, 'Jesus of Nazareth, the King of the Jews.'

Yes, He is our King! He reigns from the cross. From thence to this hour He carries on the government in the city of peace. True, He no longer hangs there, but when He presents Himself to the eye of faith, He appears, as before, in His bleeding form, and hanging on the tree. It is from thence He takes the spoil from the strong, and produces repentance in the sinful. From thence He humbles the lofty looks, and melts the stony heart in the fire of His love. From thence He comforts the anxious soul, and dries the weeping eyes of the contrite. O how variously does He daily make it manifest that He, as the crucified Jesus, is the true King of Israel! Yes, in His crown of thorns, He governs the world of spirits and of hearts; and the greatest marvels by which He glorifies Himself upon earth, He performs with His pierced hands. Hence Calvary continues to be the place where we pay our homage, and where we cease not adoringly to cry, 'Jesus of Nazareth, the King of the Jews!'

Thus, in fact, no human hand ever wrote any thing more true and well-founded than the inscription which Pilate, under divine direction, wrote and placed on the cross. Yet a little while, and signs from heaven, angelic appearances, falling stars, and graves opening at the trumpet's sound will confirm it.

My friends, the time is at hand when we shall no longer read it on the cross, but in the radiant letters on the flowing robe of the returning Conqueror. O that then none of us may be forced to say to the rocks, 'Fall on us,' and to the hills, 'Cover us!' but each of us meet Him with joyful acclamations, and hail Him Lord of all!

Chapter 44

'Father, Forgive Them'

Our visit to the darkness which reigns on Calvary has this time reference only to the ray of compassion which flashes through it, than which none more beatifying ever shone upon the sinful earth. This ray displays its effulgence in the intercession of Him who hangs bleeding on the cross. In it, the divine Sufferer throws down from His cross the first-fruit of His passion into the lap of the human race, whom He came to redeem.

Horrible is the tumult on Calvary. A choir from the pit of hell precedes the chorus of angels. The powers of darkness exhaust themselves in vomiting forth rage and blasphemy; and alas! the very men whose vocation it is to be keepers of the sanctuary, yield themselves up to be the most zealous instruments of hell. Without being aware of it, these men of Belial entirely fail of their object. Their intention is to degrade the Man on the cross, and yet they are obliged to glorify Him. They are anxious to tear from His head the last remnant of His crown; but they only lift the veil from off His majesty. Listen to the taunts which they pour forth upon the Holy One; but remark at the same time how these outbreaks, viewed in the light, contain only the most honourable confessions respecting Him. 'He saved others,' say they, 'himself he can not save.' Truly, this plain confession on the part of His adversaries is of high importance, since it confirms anew the historical account of the saving acts of Jesus recorded in the Gospels.

'He trusted in God,' they continue. Infer from hence how evidently His heavenly and devotional frame must have impressed itself on His entire outward deportment, so that it did not remain concealed even from such worthless characters as these.

'He said, 'I am the Son of God;' let him deliver him now if he will have him!' Can it be otherwise than extremely welcome to us, to hear it confirmed, even by His most furious opponents, that the Lord had declared Himself to be the Son of God, and had therefore made no secret of His heavenly descent?

'Thou that destroyest the temple,' they exclaim further, and buildest it up in three days, save thyself!' Observe how they confirm what He had so decidedly announced concerning His resurrection from the dead. In the same manner, by their taunting words, 'Let Christ the King of Israel descend now from the cross,' they establish the fact that the Saviour had repeatedly applied this significant title to Himself.

The Saviour hears the envenomed taunts of the crowd below. He knows from whence they proceed, and whom the blasphemers serve as instruments, without being aware of it. In their infuriated language, He hears only a ruder echo of those temptations with which the prince of darkness once assailed Him in the wilderness. But now, as then, He is conscious of being on the path pointed out to Him by His heavenly Father; and this serves Him as an impenetrable shield, with which He quenches all the fiery darts of the adversary. O that we could now cast a look into the Redeemer's soul! But profound silence conceals it from us, like the veil in the temple.

But, see, His lips are moving. He is about to speak. What shall we now hear? Look, He opens His mouth. But – can we believe our ears? 'Father,' says He, 'forgive them!' Surely not the servants of Satan who have nailed Him to the cross – the heartless brutes, who are even still rending Him with their poisoned fangs? Yes, it is even they to whom His intercession refers. It is for them He requests mercy and forgiveness. We bow our heads and adore. What language, 'Father, forgive them!' and, in the words, what an act, greater than the most splendid miracles with which He marked His radiant path through the world. Christ was admirable in His transfiguration on Mount Tabor; but here He shines in superior light.

'Forgive them!' Is it possible! With these words, as sincerely as they sound, He covers the guilty heads of His murderers with the shield of His love, in order to secure them from the storm of the well-deserved wrath of Almighty God. With these words, which must have produced adoring astonishment even in the angels themselves, He takes these miscreants in the arms of His compassion, and bears them up the steps of His Father's throne, in order to commend them to His mercy. For the words, 'Forgive them,' mean, in Jesus' mouth not merely, 'Do not impute to them the murderous crime they have committed upon Me.' No, when He utters 'Forgive,' it comprehends something much more, and embraces the whole register of sins. In His mouth it means, 'Plunge their whole sinful life into the depths of the sea, and remember no more their transgressions, but consider these sinners henceforth as dear in Thy sight, and act toward them as such.'

There are individuals upon earth for whom no one feels inclined to pray, because they are too depraved. There are those who even dare not pray for themselves, because their consciences testify that such worthless creatures as they are cannot reckon upon being heard. What a prospect is here opened to people of this description! Ah, if no heart beats

for them on earth, the heart of the King of kings may still
feel for them. If among their friends, not one is to be found
to intercede for them, yet possibly the Lord of Glory is not
ashamed of bearing their names before His Father's throne.
O what hope beams on Calvary for a sinful world! And if the
great Intercessor appears there for a transgressor, how does
His intercession succeed! Though a whole world should
protest against it, His prayer saves whom He will. His voice
penetrates the heart of the eternal Father with irresistible
power. Mountains of sin vanish before His intercession. How
highly characteristic and deeply significant is the fact that
the Lord with this prayer commences the seven expressions
He uttered on the cross. The words, 'Forgive them!' show us
not merely the heaven of loving-kindness which He carries
in His bosom, but it also darts like a flash of lightning through
the gloom of the entire night of suffering, and deciphers the
mysterious position which the Holy One of Israel here
occupies as Mediator and High Priest.

'As High Priest?' you exclaim. Certainly, you must feel that
He could only venture to offer up such a prayer in that
capacity. Apart from this His peculiar divine office, such a
petition would have been an attempt to overturn the
foundations of God's throne, which are justice and judgment.
How can the holy God deal with sinners? Can He say
anything else than, 'Depart from me, ye polluted beings?'
How can the God of justice act toward transgressors? Must
He not, if He will not act contrary to His nature, reward every
one according to his works? Can He, who is the true God,
make laws and denounce threatenings against transgressors,
and yet pardon those who have actually trodden His law
underfoot, without breaking His word, and withdrawing His
threatenings?

Yet the prayer for forgiveness raises its wings from the
mount of suffering and passes apparently through all those

eternal statutes and limitations. It puts aside even Mount Sinai and Ebal. It soars with seemingly unheard-of boldness above the brazen walls of the manifold menaces of the divine maledictions which inexorably close against sinners the entrance to the mansions above, and requests forgiveness and even admittance into the habitations of the blessed children of God for rebels, blasphemers, and murderers.

'Does the Saviour's prayer do so much, and yet continue legitimate?' Yes, it is legitimate, well-founded and entitled to be heard. The mercy of interceding love on the cross is a law which is, at the same time, subject to all the ordinances of God. Its seeming boldness is only in appearance. It knows what it does, while crying for forgiveness to Him with whom is no variableness nor shadow of turning. It is well aware of the properties of the house of God, while desiring blessing and liberation for those whom the law condemns and sentences to the prisons of darkness. It does not direct its petition to an arbitrariness in God, which does not exist, but appeals to both the divine justice and mercy. Its prayer sets aside no divine ordinance, but leaves them all uninfringed upon. It is so far from desiring that the Almighty should deny Himself or His Word, that it has, on the contrary, the glory of God as its supreme and final aim.

'But can God continue in the exercise of all His perfections, if He rewards murderers with His favour?' Yes, He can; and it is just this which is the greatest mystery of godliness, of which the Gospel opens the seals, but which is accessible only to faith. Jesus, who here prays for His murderers stands in the very place of those men as their representative. If they have broken the law, He, the Surety, has fulfilled it in their stead. Are they worthy of death? He is the Lamb who lets Himself be made sin for them, that sin might be no longer imputed to them. If they drew down upon them the curse of the law, He is the Mediator of whom it is written, 'Christ

hath redeemed us from the curse of the law, being made a
curse for us.' If, according to the judgment of God, they are
consigned to the powers of darkness, He gives Himself up as
a voluntary sacrifice to their fiery darts.

Therefore, satisfaction, atonement, and mediation are the
momentous words which express the ground of justification
for the intercession of Jesus. The whole world must now be
mute and hell likewise, when God Himself receives into His
favour blasphemers and murderers, for whom Jesus appeared
in the breach. For complete satisfaction is rendered to all the
statutes of the eternal sanctuary, and divine justice can no
longer object when eternal love presses sinners with blessing
to its breast.

We now fully comprehend the tone and perfect certainty,
firmness, and confidence with which the words, 'Father,
forgive them!' are uttered. The High Priest pronounces them
from the most holy place, and that too at the very moment
when He is paying the debt of the guilty. That He really does
this, and that the true meaning of His sufferings is to be
sought in this, He once for all evinces to a sinful world from
His elevation on the cross; and hence, while bleeding on their
behalf, He sends up to heaven this unconditional petition
for mercy in favour of the vilest sinners, His murderers.

'But how could the Lord commend these hardened rebels
to divine mercy?' Observe that those whom He had in view
were by no means hardened. For such as have committed
the 'sin unto death' there is certainly no longer any deliverance or salvation, and according to the apostle's directions,
we ought not to pray for such. But the Lord well knows what
He is doing. Although He says at first, 'Forgive them,' which
is certainly very general, yet he immediately limits His words
so that Judas, for instance, and doubtless many of the heads
of the people, are excluded from the influence of His intercession.

The addition of the words, 'They know not what they do,' defines its bounds. By this clause the Lord selects from the multitude which surrounds Him those to whom the majority of them that crucified Him probably belonged.

Now observe first, the sublime self-possession which the Lord here again manifests in the words, 'They know not what they do.' For what other meaning lies concealed beneath them than this, that if they had known it was the Lord of Glory, or even some innocent and just person, they would not have done it? For in the words, 'They know not what they do,' the idea is included that while offering up the Lord Jesus, they unconsciously pay the ransom for themselves, and thereby render it possible for God to have mercy upon them, without detracting from His justice.

Finally, the words, 'They know not what they do,' contain a veiled prediction of the future repentance and conversion of those for whom Christ prays. For even by this petition a powerful impulse to repentance is given them, and a direction to a change of mind. Only look forward a little, and you will already see, first in the Roman centurion under the cross and his shield-bearer, the commencement of the fulfilment of that prediction. Mark then the crowds who, returning from Calvary to Jerusalem, smote upon their breasts, and at least in part gave evidence of sincere repentance. Assuredly among them were some to whom the petition, 'Father, forgive them,' applied. But if they were not among these, they were decidedly among the three thousand who were pierced to the heart by the apostle's words on the day of Pentecost. For listen to the address of Peter: 'This Jesus,' says he, 'whom ye have crucified, hath God made both Lord and Christ. Now, when they heard this,' the narrative states, 'they were pricked in their hearts, and said, Men and brethren, what shall we do?' Yes, it was these who knew not what they did, but now it became evident to them. O how did the remembrance of

the words, 'Father, forgive them,' smite humblingly and over-
whelmingly upon their hearts! How did the love which was
manifested in those words melt their souls! Alas! alas! they
had nailed to the cross their only Deliverer and Saviour! Thus
did the petition, 'Father, forgive them, they know not what
they do,' neither overthrow the statutes of divine justice, nor
the method of grace, once for all established by the Lord.
Justice retained its splendour by virtue of the satisfaction of
the only-begotten Son, and the plan of salvation was
preserved entire in the repentance and conversion of them
to whom the petition applied.

Let us then rejoice that the most desirable and indispensable of all blessings, the forgiveness of sins, is acquired
so fully and legally for us. What do all the treasures in the
world avail, if we do not know that our names are written in
heaven, and that we have an inheritance there? But reflect
that the forgiveness acquired on the cross, although always
an entirely free gift of grace, is forever withheld from those
who know what they do, while refusing to give their hearts
to Christ. Awake therefore, from your deadly sleep of security;
bid farewell to pharisaic deception, condemn the sin that
besets you, and then hasten penitently and believingly to the
cross of Christ, and devote yourselves, body, soul, and spirit,
unto Him who loved you, and gave Himself for you; for this
is the road that leadeth unto life.

Chapter 45

The Malefactor

Again we direct our eyes upward. The three crucified
individuals form the centre of our present meditation.
The dying men are alike in their situation, in so far as each
of them has now arrived at the last stage of his earthly
pilgrimage, and is hovering on the solemn and awful brink of
a momentous eternity. He who hangs in the midst, although
exposed to a raging storm, takes in the sails for a peaceful
entrance into the haven of repose. We see the other two, on
the contrary, almost shipwrecked, and threatened with the
most dreadful ruin, struggling with the billows. They had
opened their hearts to delusion; had pursued temporal
enjoyments, and were carried along unrestrainedly from sin
to sin, till arrested at length as murderers, they were crucified
as an atonement to public justice. Pleasure is short, repentance long. O folly and madness, to devote themselves to the
service of the devil instead of to that of the Most High God,
while the most costly rewards of the former are only
Belshazzar's feasts and the hands of the executioner!

Yet immense is the number of those who, like the herd into
which the unclean spirits entered, do not cease to plunge themselves into the gulf of destruction after their deluded forerunners.

The two malefactors have hung there for a while in silence;
but have been unable to turn away their eyes from the

wonderful Man who welters in His blood by their side, and in whom the vital and bodily appearance of a superhuman sanctity was by no means hidden from them. At length the one on Jesus' left begins to speak. Joining in the blasphemous speeches which rise up from the crowd below, he says to the Man in the crown of thorns, 'If thou be the Christ, save thyself and us!'

The meaning of these words is doubtless manifold. The malefactor has evidently received the impression respecting the Man at his side, that if He only would, He could both save Himself and them; and his speech to Him was an attempt, though a desperate one, to lay hold of Christ by His honour, and thereby to induce Him to an act of rescue. But the mistrust he placed in the willingness of Jesus to perform such a miracle far exceeded the hope in Him, and hence the words proceeded from him in a tone of vexation and bitter railing against Christ.

But who inspired him with the idea that the Lord, supposing He had the power, would still not save him? His conscience testified it. The spotless purity of the mysterious Sufferer threw a bright reflection even into the dark mind of the malefactor, and condemned him in his inmost soul by the mere display of its brilliance. Hence the words proceeded from him like the bite of the poisonous adder – 'If thou be the Christ, save thyself and us.' Wretched man, how should He who by a word could have burst the bonds of hell and of death, not have been able to save Himself, if higher considerations had not induced Him to act otherwise!

'Save thyself and us!' O unparalleled audacity, to degrade the Lord of heaven to a level with himself a son of Belial, and besides this, to claim His help, although his heart was hardened against Him! Yet echoes of these taunting words of the malefactor still very frequently reach our ears. How often do we hear people say, while biting their lips, 'Say no more about your God; for if He be God, why does He leave us in our wretchedness?' First humble thyself in the dust, and submit without reserve to His sceptre, and then wait and see if He will not let mercy take the place of justice.

No answer is returned to the malefactor on the left. There would still have been help for the robber and murderer; but there is no deliverance for the impenitent scoffer and hardened child of unbelief. The Lord is obliged to leave the wretched man to his fate – yes, the Lord, the only Saviour in heaven and on earth. Who does not tremble? But God is a God of order, and even His mercy is never arbitrarily bestowed.

Turn your eyes now to the right of the divine Sufferer. Here a spectacle is preparing, at which our souls may recover from the horror which took possession of them at the preceding scene. A refreshing contrast is presented by the other malefactor, whom, though equally guilty with the pitiable companion of his fate, and on the verge of hell, we behold rending and casting away the fetters of Satan, just in time, and then ascending a path which is not trodden too late even from the station which precedes the pit of destruction.

We are not expressly informed what it was that principally exercised such a blessed and transforming influence on the heart of this individual, who, as may be inferred from the Gospel narrative, had joined shortly before in the raillery against Jesus. It might have been the Lord's heart-affecting prayer for His murderers, and the full splendour of dignity and holiness in which He shone. Suffice it to say that the change which was wrought in the soul of the poor criminal was evidently thorough and decisive, and appears as the commencement, at least, of a complete regeneration and renewing of the Holy Spirit.

There he hangs silently on the cross; but every feature in his face, which is turned toward the divine Sufferer, unfolds and displays to us the world within him. We clearly see how the evil spirits have departed from him, and a solemn train of holy thoughts and emotions passes through his soul. The taunting attack of his companion in tribulation on Jesus' left loosens his tongue, which had been silent from contrition and reverence. He feels compelled to object against being included in the blasphemous appeal, 'If thou be the Christ, save us!' He is constrained to renounce all participation in such insulting language. He knows the importance as well as the awfulness of the moment, which places an opening eternity before him, and feels no longer any fellowship with his companion in crime as regards the Man who is crowned with thorns.

The horror which seizes him at the impious words of his fellow-sufferer is indescribable; and he begins to say to him, 'Dost thou not fear God, seeing thou art in the same condemnation?' Ah, he himself trembled at the thought of the judge of quick and dead! O how moving and heart-affecting is this call to repentance from one delinquent to another! But hear him further: 'And we indeed justly, for we receive the due reward of our deeds!' O hear this language of sincere abasement before the majesty of the law. Listen to this self-accusation in which as far as regards criminality he places himself on the same footing with the other malefactor! It is the language of manly self-deliverance from the net of delusion – of courageous homage offered to truth – and of a resolute return from the way of darkness to that of light and salvation.

Let us listen further to this malefactor. 'But this man,' continues he, 'has done nothing amiss.' What a fresh and pleasing testimony this is to the innocence of Jesus. O how evident it must have been from the Saviour's whole deportment, that, as the apostle says, 'He knew no sin.' From all the clouds of ignominy and accusation which covered Him, the light of His divine spotlessness and beauty shone so victoriously forth that the blindest shrank back from it in amazement; and every moment His well-known prediction was almost literally verified, 'If these should hold their peace, the stones would immediately cry out!' Something really astonishing now succeeds. The work of grace in the heart of the malefactor throws off its last veil. Who would have expected that we should have witnessed any thing of the kind on that awful hill! After the malefactor has rebuked his blaspheming fellow-sufferer, he turns his face again to Him, who increasingly became his only hope and the object of his affection, and says to Him, unpresumingly, humbly, devoutly and confidently, 'Lord, remember me when thou comest into thy kingdom.'

Here is divine illumination in midnight darkness. Even the enlightenment of an apostle scarcely reaches to this malefactor's height of faith. 'Lord,' says he, not Rabbi, not teacher, or master, no, in the word 'Kyrie,' he applies to him the title of Majesty. By this expression he brings out of the appearance of a worm that is trodden upon, the heavenly King of Glory.

'Remember me,' continues he, with a boundless reliance and confident childlike supplication. O how much is implied in this ejaculation! It is the expression of the most vital conviction of the existence of a future world; for it is not help from the bodily distress in which he languishes; but the malefactor desires something very different and superior. It is further a loud testimony to the necessity of a mediation, if sinners are to be saved. 'Intercede for me,' he means to say, 'speak a kind word for me a sinner; put in a word of entreaty on my behalf.' Yes, it is a frank confession that the Man in the crown of thorns is the Mediator, and therefore he flees to Him with the confidence that His intercession with the Father, and that only, can save him from eternal death.

To the supplication contained in the words 'Remember me,' the malefactor adds, 'when thou comest in (not into) thy kingdom.' What does he mean by this? Does he mean, 'Thy undertaking has not failed. Die, and from Thy prison of death Thou shalt again come forth triumphant? Thy kingdom shall come, and Thy throne exist forever?' Certainly he means nothing else. He intends to say, 'To thee belongs the world; the banner of Thy peaceful kingdom will wave from pole to pole. When Thou shalt have established Thy throne, then grant that I, a poor criminal, may be received among the meanest of Thy servants.'

What a herald of Christ in the midnight darkness of the crucifixion! What a bright and guiding star for all who seek a haven of rest on the stormy sea of life! We feel astonished at the great and penetrating faith of this malefactor. But here convince yourselves anew how rapidly the profoundest mysteries of heaven display themselves to the awakened feeling of the need of salvation. O if thou ever becomest powerfully conscious of thy estrangement from God, and dost feel that thou needest nothing so much as mercy, truly the spirit of illumination from above would soon descend upon thee, and thou wouldst be aware that in the Gospel and its plan of salvation, there is the only conceivable way of escape for beings who come short of the glory of God. Yes, we should then soon hear from thy lips the words 'Lord, remember me in thy kingdom!'

The malefactor has spoken. Now listen to the Lord's reply. It will reveal something very astonishing. The high and lofty One, whom the criminal discovered beneath the thorn-crowned bleeding form by his side now comes actually forth in His glory. Calvary becomes a palace, the cross a throne of the Judge of all worlds. The Man in the crown of thorns accepts the prayer which the poor criminal addressed to Him, and impresses the confirming seal upon his distinguished faith. There is no rejection, as if he were mistaken in his hopes – no reproof, as if he were an enthusiast and expected too much from Him, but rather an encouragement to hope still more boldly, since he was not mistaken in Him. With the full conviction of being the only-begotten Son of the Father, which He was, as well as the true and only Mediator between God and man, the Lord says, turning to the malefactor with a look full of grace and mercy, and loud enough for those who stood around Him to hear, 'Verily, I say unto thee, to-day shalt thou be with me in paradise.'

Here you have the great and majestic words which, if they were the only testimony Jesus had given of Himself, would forever decide the question who He was – the words which, bursting the bonds of death, and opening a heaven of consolation, have sounded like a peaceful chord of paradise in the ears of millions on their dying beds; the words which comprehend the whole result of the sufferings and death of Christ, the Bridegroom of our souls. O attend well to these words! They are the most precious boon which Christ has thrown into our lap from His cross.

Let every syllable of them be well weighed by us. 'Verily,' says our Lord at the commencement, and this is the confirmation of His words. How important is this assertion, uttered by such a mouth, at such a time, when on the threshold of eternity! How suited to dispel all our doubts. Unspeakably elevating is the fullness of confidence and certainty manifested in our Lord's speech to the dying criminal. The fact is firm as a rock, that He is the Way, the Truth, and the Life – immutably firm; that He bears the keys of hell and of death; that He will conduct the penitent sinner through the night of death into eternal life; and how greatly does this His own assurance tend to confirm and animate our faith in Him!

That which so highly ravishes us in His words, next to His confidence, is the repetition of the poor criminal's request in a superior degree. To his appellation of 'Lord!' the thorn-crowned Jesus replies with the words, 'I say unto thee.' And what else does this imply, but 'I am so; thou art not mistaken in Me. Thou canst not think too highly of Me.' Upon the petition, 'Remember me,' follows the Lord's words, 'Thou shalt be with me' – that is, 'I shall not need first to think of thee;' for we think not of those who are present, but of those who are absent. The period indicated by the word 'when,' the Lord responds to by the assertion, 'this day' – not at some distant period, but this day shall be the happy day of thy deliverance and redemption. To the criminal's appeal, 'when thou comest into thy kingdom, or appearest in thy regal glory,' the Lord replies: 'I am a King already. I will take thee with Me into paradise. With this bleeding hand will I open to thee the gates of the world of blessedness.'

The words addressed by the Sufferer to the malefactor produce lastly, such a beneficial effect upon us, because they bear in them an infallible testimony to the perfection and all-sufficiency of the redemption accomplished by Him for us. For on what ground is it that Jesus so confidently promises instead of the curse, salvation to a sinner? He promises paradise solely on the ground of His ever valid work of mediation and atonement.

The three crosses on Calvary present to us a very important subject for consideration. They afford us an image of the world, Christ in its midst; but to the one He is set for the rising, and for the falling of the other – a savour of life unto life to the one, and of death unto death to the other. You behold a sinner on His right hand and another on His left; but He is so little ashamed of their society that on the contrary, He then feels in His element and at home, because He can there exhibit His love to man – there heal and save.

You see in the three crosses, further, an actual exposition of the Saviour's words, 'I am the Way, the Truth, and the Life. For who is it that serves the malefactor on His right, in opposition to His fellow-sufferer on the left, as a bridge on which he may pass from a state of curse to that of grace? Who is it that enlightens him by that marvellous light, whose rays penetrate into his inmost soul, and expel all the phantoms of delusion from him? And lastly, who is it that takes from his bosom the consciousness of a state of death, and replaces it with the most blissful and vital hope? – yea, that imparts to his soul, even on this side eternity, a new life of peace, supernatural joy, divine consciousness of adoption, and the most heartfelt longing after heaven? Is it not the thorn-crowned Sufferer there who is the author of it all?

Finally, the scene on Calvary affords us a representation of the boundless power and wonderful efficacy of the merits of our great High Priest. For even as the word 'to-day,' in our Lord's announcement, represents all future purging and purifying fires as forever extinguished in His blood, as regards His believing people – so the expression, 'This day shalt thou be with me in paradise,' affords us a stupendous proof that Christ's vicarious satisfaction perfectly suffices for the sinner's justification and beatification. Certainly we must duly observe that the malefactor was in a state of true and thorough repentance, and that after breaking with sin by penitential grief, and opening his heart to Jesus by a living faith, he had received into himself all the germs of a subsequent sanctification – germs which immediately began to unfold themselves in the compassionate love in which he took to heart the critical state of his companion in crime.

Anticipate the next few moments, and what do you see occur above the summit of Calvary? The three who were crucified bow their heads, and the great separation is accomplished. Alas! he on Jesus' left descends also to the left; and the powers of darkness will have received him who, even in death, could insult the Lord of Glory. The criminal to the right, on the contrary, soars heavenward, at the side of the Prince of Peace, and received into His triumphal chariot, passes amid the acclamations of angels through the gates of paradise. He was the first herald who by his appearing there brought the glorified spirits the intelligence that Christ had won the great battle of our deliverance. As the first-fruits of the sufferings of the divine Surety, as well as of the blessed human harvest which should spring up from the wondrous seed of His blood, he may still be especially embraced by the worshippers of the Lamb in the realms above as a particularly dear citizen of the heavenly kingdom. To us he remains both an incomparable monument of the all-sufficiency of the blood of Christ, and a lofty candlestick on which the free grace of God beams as a flame, and an extremely significant beacon, yea, a light-house established by God for us on our passage through life. O, be assured that the spiritual footsteps of the dying malefactor, with the words, 'Remember me!' on his lips, point out to us, to this day, the only path that leads to Zion.

Chapter 46

The Legacy of Love

A pleasing scene presents itself to our view beneath the cross. He who was 'fairer than the children of men' does not die unlamented. In the midst of rage and fury, love stands near Him in His dying moments and lifts up to Him its tearful and affectionate eye. Look at the little mournful group yonder, and behold a lovely little company in the midst of the bands of Belial – a hidden rosebud under wild and tangled bramble-bushes, a splendid wreath of lilies around the deathbed of the Redeemer.

It is thus that the cross is surrounded even to this day. Though the infuriated hosts of hell rage around it, yet it is still encircled by the most estimable of the earth. For if we seek for sacred grief, for love which has emanated from heaven, for patience which never tires, and gratitude, which gives up every thing – where do these beautiful and heavenly flowers flourish except beneath the cross?

We know the faithful company there, who form a living commentary on the words of the Song of songs. 'Many waters can not quench love, neither can the floods drown it.' What do they care about hazarding their lives! Their life was the Man on the cross. What do they trouble themselves about the scorn and contempt of the world! They desire nothing else and nothing better from a world which crowned their

King with thorns. Had they been nailed to the cross with Him, they would have pushed away the earth from them as a rotten and worthless plank, and have triumphantly cast their anchor in the clouds.

Look at the courageous group a little more closely. Of whom does it consist? Strangely enough, with one exception, all of them are women. The strong are fled – the weak maintain their ground; the heroes despair – the timid, who did not presume to promise any thing, overcome the world. This was because they poured out their hearts before God, saying, 'Hold thou us up, and we shall be safe!' and speaking thus, they leaned firmly on the divine arm. God's strength was then mighty in their weakness.

Among the beloved women beneath the cross there is one who especially demands our sympathy. It is the blessed one who bore the Man that bleeds on the cross – the deeply stricken Mary. Though it was grievous for Eve to stand at the grave of her favourite son Abel, and still more so for the patriarch Jacob to behold the bloody garment of his son Joseph, yet what was their grief compared with that of the mother of our Lord at the foot of the cross? O think *where* she is standing, *what* is the cause of her grief, and *who* it is she mourns! Think what a Son, and what a kind of death! One thing, however, we may be assured of, that the deeply wounded Mary did not despair. Even through this, her night of weeping, the words of her Son respecting the necessity of the sufferings that awaited Him, and the glory that should follow, gleamed like some distant light.

Although leaning on the disciple whom Jesus loved, she still stands upright under the cross, and only a gentle shower of tears bedews her cheeks, but no cry of agony proceeds from her lips. Her earthly Son dies, with all the earthly connection in which she had hitherto stood toward Him, as well as the earthly ideas of Him and His kingdom. In opposition to these, she has now to receive Christ by faith, as from His ashes, in a very different capacity – as One hitherto not known by her – as a Lord and Prince of Peace of an incomparably higher kind and order than human; nor did she attain to this without great pain and conflict.

At Mary's side, and serving as her support, the Apostle John meets our eye. He sees himself surrounded by problems which he is unable to solve. But where his understanding beholds only an empty desert, he has, nevertheless, an inward presentiment of infinite and hidden riches. He again introduces himself here, as he is so gladly wont to do, as 'the disciple whom Jesus loved.' In these words he indicates to us what was his pride, his crown, and his highest boast. At the same time, they point out to us the source from whence he derived all his consolation, all his hope, and all his strength. This source was love – not the love with which he embraced the Lord, but that with which the Lord embraced him. Nor do I know any thing more precious or desirable than the lively, fresh, and well-founded consciousness of the Saviour's love and affection. He who with John can sign himself the disciple whom Jesus loves, has, in this appellation, a sure guarantee for all that he needs, and for all that his heart can desire.

While the little company stand mourning together below, the mighty Sufferer hangs silent and bleeding on the cross. He is in the sanctuary performing His high-priestly office, while bearing upon His heart the sinful race of Adam. 'Oh,' might the mourning Mary think, 'if he would but once more open His gracious lips to me, and give me one parting word!' But in the sublime situation He is now occupying will He still be able to attend to what is passing at the foot of the cross? Scarcely should we think it possible.

But what occurs? O when did any thing happen more generous and affecting than this? Truly, till the end of time His filial tenderness will be spoken of. In the midst of His dying agonies the divine Sufferer all at once directs His eyes to the little faithful group below; and he that is able to read in His eyes reads a sympathy and a degree of consoling, cheering, encouraging love, such as the world till then had never beheld. However much He may have to think of and attend to, He never loses sight of His children for a moment. However great and boundless may be the objects of His supervision and vigilance in His government, yet there will never be a moment when the eye of His love will not rest upon every individual whom the Father has given Him. They are His primary care, although in number and outward appearance, in comparison with what He has otherwise to superintend and provide for, they may be as the drops in the wide rolling ocean, and as flowerets in the immense and gloomy forests in which they stand.

The Lord first fixes His eyes on His beloved and sorely-tried mother. By means of the words He had spoken to the malefactor respecting being with Him that day in paradise, He had elevated her looks and thoughts above death and the grave. Yet still she would have to remain for a season alone in the world, which had now become so desolate to her, and lo! for this consideration, the Man of Sorrows on the cross still finds room in His heart, amid His anxieties for the world's redemption. He looks, in the kindest manner, at the weeping Mary, opens His mouth, and says in sublime tranquillity, self-possession, and serenity, referring to the disciple on whom His mother was leaning, 'Woman, behold thy son!' and then to John, 'Behold thy mother!'

Though the words are few, yet who is able to exhaust the fullness of tender affection which is poured into them? How consoling must it have been to Mary's grieved heart, the almost cheerful manner in which her dying Son made His last bequest. The sound of His voice and the peaceful look which accompanied His words were as much as to say, 'Mary,

thy Son is not lost. He is only returning to His Father's happy
abode in order to prepare a place for thee.' And then the
contents of the words themselves – how tenderly did He
clothe in them His last farewell to His beloved parent! How
delicately did He arrange it that by the hint given to John,
she who had been so severely tried, should not also be a
witness of His last and hardest struggle! And how providently
does He enter at the same time into all, and even the most
trifling necessities of His bereaved mother for the residue of
her life upon earth! Truly when was ever the divine command
to honour father and mother so deeply and comprehensively
fulfilled as it was on Calvary?

It has been considered strange that the Saviour, in speaking
to Mary, should have made use of the distant word, 'Woman,'
instead of the tender name of mother. In reply to this, it is
certainly true that He did so, partly because He would not
still more deeply wound her bleeding heart by the sweet title
of mother, and likewise lest He should expose His mother to
the rudeness of the surrounding crowd. But the chief reason
why He used the more general term 'Woman,' lies much
deeper, both in this and the well-known scene at the marriage
in Cana. He certainly meant His mother to understand that
henceforward His earthly connection with her must give way
to a superior one. As though He had said, 'Thou, My mother,
wilt from this time be as one of My daughters, and I thy Lord.
Thou believest in Me, and shalt be blessed. Thou layest hold
of the hem of My garment, and I appear in thy stead. Thou
adorest Me, and I am thy High Priest and King. Mother,
brother, and sister, henceforward, are all who swear allegiance
to My banner. The relationships according to the flesh and
the manner of the world have an end; other and more
spiritual and heavenly take their place.'

It was this that the Lord intended to suggest to Mary's
mind; and hence the word 'Woman,' which at first sounds

strange, instead of the more tender and affectionate term, 'Mother.' But while endeavouring to elevate Mary's mind above the sphere of merely human conceptions into a higher region, He does not forget either that He is her Son, or that she is His dear and sorely-tried mother. The Lord is desirous, in His filial forethought, and as far as is practicable, to fill up for Mary the void which His decease would leave in her life, and give her, instead of Himself, a son to assist her, in whom she might place entire confidence, and on whose shoulders she could lean in all her distresses, cares and sorrows.

And in this new son He bequeaths to her His favourite disciple, the faithful and feeling John. It was thus He loved to the end; thus delicately does He provide for all the necessities of those He loves. And as He formerly did, so He does still. He is to this hour the compassionate High Priest. He enters most feelingly into the wants of those who confide in Him, so that every one, whether they be widows, orphans, poor and infirm, or to whatever class of the weary and heavy-laden they belong, they may rely on His providential care.

After saying to Mary, 'Woman, behold thy son!' He says to John, 'Behold thy mother!' O what a proof does the Saviour here give His disciple of the affection and confidence which He reposes in him! He imposes a burden upon him, but He knows that John will regard it as the highest honour and felicity which could be bestowed upon him on earth. Nor is the Saviour mistaken in His disciple. John understands his Master's wish, looks at Mary, and his whole soul says to her, 'My Mother!'

'From that hour,' we are informed, 'that disciple took her unto his own home.' John possessed therefore a house of his own, doubtless in Jerusalem, which Mary did not. Joseph had evidently already fallen asleep. The expression, 'That disciple took her into his own home,' implies, however, according to the original, much more than that he only took care of her in his habitation. He received her into his heart. It may easily be supposed what love he felt toward her from that time, and with what tenderness and fidelity he accompanied her through life. And because John's love was in reality no other than a sacred spark from Jesus' own breast, Mary was beloved by John, as before, with the love of her divine Son.

'Woman, behold thy Son!' 'John, behold thy mother!' O attend carefully to these words. They contain nothing less than the record of the institution of a new family fellowship upon earth. In this fellowship Christ is the Head, and all His believing people form unitedly one great, closely-connected family. Begotten of the same seed, endued with the same spirit, they are all called to one inheritance, and eventually, though now scattered abroad through the world, one city with shining walls will embrace them. They soon know each other by their similarity of sentiment, bias, speech, and joyful hope, and love each other with one love – that love which overflowed into them from the heart of Christ their Head. As long as they linger here below, their habitation is under the cross, and their daily bread the Word of God; their breath, prayer, and the peace of God the atmosphere in which they freely and blissfully move. The inmost and most essential family feature of this spiritual fraternity is, that self in them is crucified, and Christ is the centre of all their doing and suffering.

Let him who would envy John the pleasing task of being a support to the mother of Jesus know that the way to the same honour lies open to him. Let him reflect on a previous expression of our Lord's, 'Who is my mother, and who are my brethren? and stretching forth his hand toward his disciples, he said, Behold my mother and my brethren! For whosoever shall do the will of my Father which is in heaven, the same is my mother, and sister, and brother' (*Matt.*12: 48–50).

If thou art really desirous of the privilege enjoyed by John, thou now seest it may be thine. Be, from love to the Lord, a faithful help to His children; feed the hungry, give drink to him that is thirsty, and especially visit pious widows in their loneliness, and thou wilt perform a service which is well-pleasing to Him. Apply to the heavenly Prince of Peace to open eyes that thou mayest recognize His household; and even as He will then say to the latter, who constitute His spiritual Church, while suing for their love to thee, 'Woman, behold thy Son!' so He will also say to thee, with reference to some troop of weary and heavy laden beloved ones, 'Behold thy mother!' Think what it would be if every one exhibited a living mirror of 'the fairest of the sons of men,' and loved God and the brethren as He did.

Chapter 47

'Eli, Eli, Lama Sabachthani?'

Once a voice spoke from heaven to the people who were assembled around Jesus and the evangelist relates, 'some said it thundered; others, that an angel spoke to him.' No one exactly knew what to make of the wondrous sound, although all were affected, amazed, and thrilled by a secret awe. Such are our feelings on the present occasion, on hearing the echo of the cry, which sounds down from the cross; and I confess that my soul trembles at the idea of approaching the unfathomable depth of suffering, from whence the cry of 'Eli, Eli, lama sabachthani' proceeded. How much rather would I lie prostrate on my face in silence before this awful incident, than write or speak upon it! You know what happened to Luther, when he plunged himself in profound meditation on this most enigmatical and affecting part of the whole of our Saviour's sufferings. He continued for a long time without food, and sat wide awake but as motionless as a corpse, in the same position, on his chair. And when at length he rose up from the depth of his cogitation, as from the shaft of a mysterious mine, he broke into a cry of amazement, and exclaimed, 'God forsaken of God! Who can understand it?' Yes, who is there that is able? We find ourselves surrounded by an impenetrable darkness. But if the understanding has here reached the boundary of all human comprehension, yet faith finds a path amid these mysterious shades. A holy light precedes it, and that light is derived from the Saviour's Mediatorship. Enlightened by it, let us now contemplate, more closely, the awful cry of the Redeemer.

It is about twelve o'clock at noon that we again meet on Mount Calvary. The Saviour has hung bleeding on the tree for nearly three hours. No change has meanwhile taken place in His vicinity, except that, in the little faithful group, we miss the disciple John and the mother of Jesus, the cause of which we know. A momentary silence has ensued in the crowd surrounding the place of execution. We may suppose that even on them the sublime behaviour of the divine Sufferer under His torture has not failed in producing feelings of emotion and shame. They look up to the cross with silent seriousness. The moaning of the two malefactors in their agony strikes their ears, and the trickling of the blood of the dying men is heard as it falls to the ground. From time to time, also, the grief and half-stifled sobs of the little faithful group is heard, whom we now, in spirit, join, asking with anxious hearts if the Father will continue forever silent con-cerning His Son, and not at length make it known by some sign, which shall be obvious to all the world, that He, who was apparently rejected both by earth and heaven, was no transgressor, but in reality the Holy One of Israel, and His, the Father's elect and well-beloved Son.

Lo, a sign appears! But what kind of one? Who could have anticipated any thing of the sort? Our surprise increases to horror, our amazement to dismay. The sun, just arrived at the meridian, withdraws its beams, as if the earth were no longer worthy of its light, and begins visibly, in a clear sky, to grow dark. First twilight commences, as at the decline of day; and this is followed by the obscurity of evening. Gloomy night at length spreads itself like a funeral pall, not only over the land of Judea, but over the whole of the enlightened part of the earth. The animal creation are terrified. The herds of the field crowd bellowing together. The birds of the air flutter, alarmed, to their retreats, and the masses of the people who surround the place of execution hurry back with loud outcries to Jerusalem, wringing their hands and beating their breasts. Trembling and lamentation extend into palaces and cottages, as if the world were menaced with destruction. The primitive fathers, as for instance Origen and Eusebius, were acquainted with heathen records, some of which were from distant countries, such as that of Phlegon a freedman of the Emperor Adrian, which mentions an eclipse of the sun at the same time with the crucifixion of Christ, and that one so entire, terrific, and wonderful had never before been seen in the world. An ancient tradition also states that Diogenes witnessed, in Egypt, the solar darkness which preceded the death of Jesus, and exclaimed, 'Either the Deity Himself suffers at this moment, or sympathises with one that does.'

We also stand amazed at this terrific phenomenon, in which even the blindest can not mistake the finger of the Almighty. But what does this gigantic hieroglyphic on the pillars of the world denote? Some have supposed it to convey a symbolical manifestation of the wrath of God against the murderers of Jesus. But such an interpretation is not in accordance with the event that is taking place on Calvary, and in which God, by the giving up of His only-begotten Son, evinces not merely His judicial severity and avenging justice, but especially His compassion for the murderers. The inference has also been drawn from the darkness that nature must have suffered in the death of Christ. But there seems little ground even for this explanation, since Christ, by His vicarious death, became, in an especial manner, the Renovator of nature.

It has also been supposed that the nocturnal darkness typified the fact that with Christ, the Light of the world was extinguished. But it was just in Christ's vicarious death that the Light of consolation and of real life rose upon the world. A sympathy also of the irrational creation with the pangs of its Lord and Master has been spoken of; but there is no room here for such poetic speculations. The sun did not obscure itself, but it was the Almighty who clothed it in that mourning-dress.

The import of the sudden darkness lies incomparably deeper than the attempts at explaining it. Even the mournful cry of the Sufferer does not leave us for a moment to doubt that the darkness stood in immediate relation to His sacred Person, and the situation in which He was at the time. It is true, indeed, that the miraculous event, according to the purpose of God, was intended to intimate to the world the wondrous nature of the fact about to be chronicled in its history, that the eternal Son the source of all life, became Himself a prey to death. But the chief object of the appalling phenomenon was to shadow forth by a stupendous figure, the mysterious position and inward state at the time, of Him who bled on the cross. The Lord withdrew Himself from the eyes of men behind the black curtain of appalling night, as behind the thick veil of the temple. He hung there full three hours on the cross, His thorn crowned head drooping on His breast, involved in that darkness. He is in the Most Holy Place. He stands at the altar of the Lord. He performs His sacrificial functions. He is the true Aaron, and at the same time the Lamb.

That which, during this time, passed between Him and His Father, lies for the present sealed as with seven seals, hidden in the depths of eternity. We only know that behind that veil, He was engaged in the most ardent conflict, gained the most brilliant victory, and adorned His representative obedience with its final crown. We know that the grave of our sins was then dug; the handwriting that was against us taken out of the way; the curse which impended over us blotted out; and the wall which separated us from our God removed. Call the sight of the Redeemer weltering in His blood, and in total darkness, heart-rending if you will; we know not a more delightful scene in heaven or on earth. The Man on the cross is to us the fairest star in the horizon of the world. We behold it, and feel delivered from every evil. When Moses came forth from the darkness in which God dwelt, his face shone in such a manner that the astonished Israelites could not bear the sight. The radiance which we wear upon our brow from the darkness of Calvary, as far as we enter believingly into it, is milder and more pleasant; for it is the radiance of a peace of which the world is ignorant, and the reflection of an inward and triumphant joy of which even the angels might envy us.

But I hear you say, 'Explain to us the meaning of the awful darkness; decipher the terrific and ambiguous hieroglyphic, and unfold to us the state it indicates.' Listen, then. The phenomenon signifies the withdrawing of another Sun than the earthly one – the obscuring of an inward world. It shadows the going down of a day of comfort and joy. It points to a night of the soul, in which the last bright star is about to disappear. Imagine to yourselves, if possible, a Man free from sin, holy, nay, of divine nature, who calls the Almighty His light, God's nearness His paradise, and God's love His bliss. Imagine Him deprived of all this, no longer refreshed with any experience of the gracious presence of His heavenly Father, and although exclaiming, 'Whom have I in heaven but thee?' banished into dreadful and horrifying visions of hell, and surrounded by nothing but images of sin and death. Imagine such a One, and then say if His state is not strikingly depicted by the midnight darkness which overspreads the earth.

The third hour of this appalling and universal gloom is drawing to a close. The sun again begins to cast off his obscuring veil. The Sufferer then breaks His long and anxious silence, and, like some cry of distress from the shaft of a mine, but at the same time, like a trumpet-sound of victory, the incomprehensible and heart-affecting exclamation breaks forth, 'Eli, Eli, lama sabachthani!' Under the influence of reverential awe, the evangelists give us this cry in the same language in which it was uttered by the divine Sufferer. It is as if they were apprehensive lest a rendering of it into Greek might detract somewhat from its import.

Like us, all believers for eighteen hundred years have stood amazed and astonished before these words, and have sought in vain to fathom their depth. You are aware that the words, 'My God, my God, why hast thou forsaken me!' form the commencement of the twenty-second Psalm, in which David, impelled and guided by the Holy Spirit, describes, while connecting with it his own sufferings, the lot of a righteous One sojourning in a sinful world. His description, however, expands in the sequel so much, that the Psalmist's personal state and circumstances lose themselves in it; and a child must perceive that more stupendous and important events than those in the life of David mingle in the expressions made use of by him. The portrait of a guiltless Sufferer gradually increases to a sublimity which has found its perfect antitype in the life of the holy Jesus. In the picture features appear of which we meet with only slight traces in David's history, and which, therefore, call upon us to seek the literal fulfilment elsewhere. For the Sufferer in the Psalms is not only represented as the offscouring of the whole world, not only do those who see Him say to Him, 'He trusted in the Lord that he would deliver him; let him deliver him, seeing that he delighted in him' – not only must He agonizingly exclaim, 'I am poured out like water; my bones are out of joint; my tongue cleaveth to my jaws, and thou hast brought me into the dust of death' – but He must also see what David never experienced, that His hands and feet were pierced, and that His enemies parted His garments among them, and casts lots upon His vesture. Besides this, His passion ends in such a manner as no other man's sufferings; for a glorious crown of victory at length adorns the head of this tried and faithful One, yea, He receives the testimony that His sufferings shall result in nothing short of the salvation of the world, and the restoration, enlightenment and blessing of the Gentiles.

Who is so blind as not to perceive that this just Man, who is so sorely tried, and who comes forth so triumphantly from the conflict, as depicted by the Spirit in this twenty-second Psalm, is no other than the promised Messiah in the person of Jesus of Nazareth? This is beyond a doubt, even if the New Testament had not expressly given that Psalm such an application. Even one of the champions of modern infidelity, prophesying like Balaam, has called the twenty-second Psalm 'the programme of the crucifixion of Christ'; and another, against his will, is carried away to use these words, 'One might almost think a Christian had written this Psalm.'

We will not entirely reject the idea that our Lord, in His distress of soul, bore this Psalm in mind. But if He uttered His exclamation with a conscious reference to it, He certainly did not do so simply in order that the words might be fulfilled; but only because that prophetic Psalm was now being fulfilled in Him. That mournful cry, as it proceeded from His lips, was the genuine expression of the most perfect personal reality and truth. 'But was Christ really forsaken of God while on the cross?' How could He be forsaken of God, who was essentially one with Him, and when just at the moment of His unconditional obedient self-sacrifice on the cross, He was the object of His supreme and paternal good pleasure? But in the depths of suffering into which He had then sunk, and through which His cry of 'Eli, Eli, lama sabachthani!' darts like a flash of lightning – such distress overpowered Him, such horrible and death-like terror appalled Him, and such infernal temptations roared around Him, that a feeling came over Him, as if He were exiled from the fellowship of God, and entirely given up to the infernal powers. Not only did all the horrors which were produced in the world from the dreadful womb of sin expand themselves before Him, but He also entered, with His holy soul, in a manner incomprehensible to us, into the fellowship of our consciousness of guilt, and emptied the whole of the horrible cup of the wages of sin – that is, of the death involved in the curse, which was threatened in paradise.

And no one stood by Him. No greeting of affection descended toward Him from heaven. No vision of angels refreshed Him in His great agony. The Father had really withdrawn Himself from His inward consciousness. If the trials in Gethsemane brought the Lord Jesus to the extreme boundary of obedience – those of the cross brought Him to the utmost extent of faith. Not a step, no, nor a line more was between Him and despair. According to Psalm 69:15, the idea entered His soul as with a vulture's claw, that these floods of suffering might swallow Him up, and the pit shut her mouth upon Him. It was then that the cry of 'Eli, Eli, lama sabachthani!' was wrung from His agitated breast.

But be very careful, in explaining this expression, that you make no mistake. It is not a charging God with having forsaken Him, but rather a powerful defence against infernal incitement to such an accusation. By the repetition of the words, 'My God,' He makes it evident that solely by means of His naked faith He had struggled through all opposing feelings; and that God was still His God. Does He not, in these words, still cling with filial fondness to His heavenly Father, and say – although the words, 'My God,' instead of

'My Father,' leave us to infer a superiority of inward reverence in the presence of the Eternal Majesty – 'Between Thee and Me there can never be any separation!'

Perhaps some one may say, 'But we hear Him inquire why God had forsaken Him.' That is true; but consider that the words do not, in the first place, ask the reason of His passion in general. Of this He was clearly conscious every moment on the cross. The question rather refers exclusively to the personal bearing of His heavenly Father toward Him, especially during the three hours of darkness; and the inquiry is a filial one, synonymous with 'Why art thou so far from Me, and hidest Thy face from Me?' But at the very moment in which He is threatened with the horrible idea that the hell which blazed around Him might close over Him, and when the nameless misery of being eternally rejected entered, as far as it was possible, into His consciousness, He fled from this horrible mental phantom, and from the fiery darts of the wicked one, holding the shield of faith against them, into the arms of God; and hence the following results as the real meaning of His mournful cry, 'My God, why dost thou forsake Me, and withdraw Thine aid from Me? Have I acted contrary to Thy commands? Am I not still Thy child, Thy only-begotten Son, in whom is all thy delight? And Thou art still My God; for how shouldst Thou be able to forsake Me? Thou canst not; Thou wilt help me out of this distress. Thou wilt cause Thy face again to shine.' Thus, complaint – not accusation – a cry for help, and a victorious child-like confidence are the three elements which mingle in the exclamation, 'Eli, Eli, lama sabachthani!'

But let this suffice respecting a subject which, inaccessible to human comprehension, discloses, even to believing presentiment, only a small part of its sublime signification. But so much must be dear to every one, that without the doctrine of mediation, Christ's mournful cry on the cross would be altogether inexplicable. But, viewed in connection with it, the words become the solemn announcement of our eternal redemption. May God in mercy grant that as such they may find a mighty and increasing echo within us!

Thus, as far as it was possible – and with reference to the mysterious connection into which Christ as the second Adam, entered with our race, we must not imagine the limits of this possibility too narrow – the Lord tasted the bitterest drop in the accursed cup – the being forsaken of God. The words, 'My God, why hast thou forsaken me?' were certainly the Warrior's cry, with which He overpowered and victoriously overcame the inward feeling of abandonment. But nevertheless, it was a manifest proof that Christ had really to endure an arduous struggle with this feeling.

If we now inquire what fruits have resulted to us from this conflict, the fact itself is encouraging and consolatory for us that in our Lord's inquiry why He was forsaken, the consciousness of His perfect righteousness before God is so clearly manifested. For in default of it, how could He have ventured the bold question to the thrice holy God, why He had forsaken Him? But the most essential benefit which we derive from His conflict is a very different one.

It was not of Himself that He thought, but of the sinners whom He was representing, when He exclaimed, 'Eli, Eli, lama sabachthani!' For if God forsook Him, He had also forsaken them whom He represented. If God rejected the Surety's work as insufficient, the redemption of the whole world was frustrated. It was chiefly this consideration which forced from our Lord the cry of 'My God, My God, why hast thou forsaken me?' and hence His question contains this meaning in it also – 'No, Thou dost not forsake Me, thou acceptest My work, and I, therefore, cleave firmly to Thee as My God, and consequently, also, as the God of those whose cause I have undertaken.'

But His heavenly Father did not suffer the cry of His Son to remain without His 'Amen.' He uttered it symbolically, by immediately dispelling the darkness, and restoring to the sun its full mid-day splendour. The being thus forsaken essentially belonged to the cup which our great High Priest was obliged to empty for us. Hence there can be no idea that those who are united to Christ by the bonds of a living faith can be really forsaken of God. Even as for us no sombre cloud any longer darkens heaven, and as we at all times behold the face of God unveiled, and every moment may enjoy free access to His throne of grace, so God will never more depart from us, whatever else may forsake us.

Though we may be abandoned by the world's favour, the friendship of men, earthly prosperity, and the bodily strength, though we may even be bereft of the feeling of God's nearness and the freshness of the inward life of faith; yet God Himself always continues near and favourably inclined to us in Christ. However strangely He may sometimes act toward us, into whatever furnace of affliction He may plunge us, however completely He may withdraw Himself from our con-sciousness, yet in every situation the blissful privilege belongs to us, not only courageously to approach Him, and say, 'Why dost thou forsake me, Thy child, for whom Thy Son has atoned?' but also to say to Him with still bolder confidence, 'Thou wilt not, canst not, and darest not forsake me, because the merits of Thy only-begotten Son forever bind Thee to me.'

Chapter 48

'I Thirst!'

That portion of the history of our Saviour's passion which will form the subject of our present meditation, does not apparently belong to the more important and edifying parts of it. But let us not be deceived by the mere appearance, for if we dig sufficiently deep, we shall here find also the water of life abundantly springing forth from the inexhaustible well of salvation, which was opened for us on Calvary.

It is about the ninth hour, or three o'clock in the afternoon. The awful cry of 'Eli, Eli, lama sabachthani!' has just been uttered. The sun again shines forth from its gloomy covering, and heaven again looks kindly down upon the earth. But you would be under a mistake in supposing this to be a sign that the agonizing darkness which reigned in the Redeemer's soul, was now over. It continues even till the moment of His decease, although essentially diminished by the clearness of faith, and even the words, 'I thirst!' reach our ears from the midst of that darkness. To doubt this would show little acquaintance with the sixty-ninth Psalm, the expressions in which receive their final fulfilment in this last stage of our Lord's crucifixion.

It is true that Jesus knew, according to the express declaration of the evangelist, that His passion was drawing to its close. He clearly saw that the cup of suffering was emptied, with the exception of the last drops; but these last drops still remained, and they did not yield in bitterness to those already tasted. Ah, see, He already drinks them! The woes of that death which was threatened in paradise seize Him. He enters into that state in which the spirit of prophecy represents Him in the abovementioned Psalm, as saying, 'I am weary of my crying, my throat is dried, mine eyes fail while I wait for my God. Draw nigh unto my soul and redeem it. Reproach hath broken my heart, and I am full of heaviness. I looked for some to take pity, but there was none, and for comforters, but I found none.' And these complaints conclude with the remarkable and prophetic words, 'They gave me also gall for my meat, and in my thirst they gave me vinegar to drink.' This had to be realized in the progress of His passion; and as a proof that this was really the case, or, as the Gospel expresses it, 'that the Scriptures might be fulfilled,' our Lord exclaims from the cross, 'I thirst!' Yes, these words tell of complaint, distress, and agony. This, the sixty-ninth Psalm, which portrays a succession of trials, places beyond a doubt.

But of what nature was the distress expressed by the cry? First, it was certainly of a physical kind. How wounded and exhausted was the Saviour, even when He reached Mount Calvary! and He had already hung nearly six hours on the cross. The blood vessels of His sacred body are almost dried up. A dreadful fever rages through His frame. His tongue cleaves to His jaws. His lips burn, and a drop of water seems a great refreshment to Him. There is scarcely a greater torment than that of insatiable thirst. Travellers who have experienced it in the burning steppes of the East give us descriptions of it which fill us with horror. They assure us that when thus situated, if they had possessed all the gold in the world, they would gladly have resigned it for a few drops even of the muddiest water of our brooks. Only think, the Saviour of the world was no stranger to this torment also!

Even to this depth of destitution and wretchedness did He, who was so unspeakably rich, descend. And all this for us, 'that we through his poverty might be made rich!' Who is able to comprehend and worthily to praise such amazing love?

But the cry from the cross, 'I thirst,' refers to something worse still than bodily torment. Does it not remind you of the awful representation from the invisible world, which the Lord once portrayed to our view in one of His parables? Does not the remembrance of the rich man present itself to you, who, while on earth, clothed himself in purple and fine linen, and fared sumptuously every day; but after inexorable death had swept him away, wrung his hands despairingly, being in pain and torment; and agonized by a nameless inward thirst, he called upon Abraham to send Lazarus, that he might dip the tip of his finger in water and cool his parched tongue, but whose request was refused without mercy, however suppliantly it knocked at heaven's gates from the habitations of eternal night?

'No;' I hear you reply, 'we did not think of this parable here. How should the rich man in torment remind us of the holy and righteous Sufferer? We should deem it impious to compare the thirst of the guiltless Jesus with that of this child of hell. By such a comparison we think we should be acting worse than the Jews in numbering Him with the transgressors. So you say; but know, my friends, that only those can speak thus who do not believe what the Scriptures state of the vicarious enduring of the curse by Jesus Christ. But he to whom the light of the Holy Spirit has risen upon the words, 'the chastisement of our peace was upon him, and with his stripes we are healed,' would be indeed astonished if the Mediator did not actually experience the lot of the man in the parable – that is, if He had not tasted, as far as was possible, all the torments of the damned. And He actually did so! The bitter scorn and ridicule which reached His ear

from below, and was also expressed in the words, 'Let us see
if Elias will come and help him,' was only a faint and human
representation of the assaults which He had to endure behind
the veil of that which was external.

There, unseen, He was surrounded by the bands of Belial.
There the powers of darkness aimed at Him their most
dangerous missiles. From this appalling host of adversaries,
from this horrible desert, from this 'pit in which there was no
water,' and in which He could only believe that God was His
God, without feeling Him to be so, rose, like the prayer of
the lost man to send Lazarus, the cry, 'I thirst!' To spare us
sinners the thirst of an infinite absence of comfort, He submitted to such torment in His mediatorial capacity! O what
a well of consolation has He opened for us by His thirst!

'I thirst!' For what did He thirst? I think the answer now is
plain. It was not only for earthly water that He languished,
but for something greater, higher, and more essential. He
longed for the termination of His redeeming toil, and the
completion of His great work of mediation. When this object
was attained, He would again be restored to the full beatifying
fellowship of His heavenly Father. He would not then have
laboriously to struggle for the consciousness that God was
kindly and paternally inclined toward Him, but would again
taste it, for He would then rest as formerly in His Father's
bosom, and instead of the horrible images of sin, the curse,
and death, the radiance of a spotless purity and holiness
would beam upon Him anew from every side. Peace and joy
would then return. The viperous hissing of the powers of
darkness around Him would be silenced. He would hear only
the hallelujahs of angels and the blest above. Every discord
would be dissolved in blissful harmony, and the atmosphere
which He breathed would again be love, entirely love.

Yes, He thirsted after the full restoration of His Father's
countenance, and after His Father's renewed and plain

declaration, 'Thou art my beloved Son, in whom I am well pleased,' as well as after the paternal confirmation of His work of redemption, as being spotlessly perfect. That He thirsted chiefly for this is no arbitrary supposition, but is derived from those passages of the sixty-ninth Psalm which belong here, and which represent Him as saying in His agony, 'Save me, O God, for the waters are come in unto my soul. My prayer is unto thee, O Lord! hear me in the truth of thy salvation. Turn unto me according to the multitude of thy tender mercies. Hide not thy face from thy servant, for I am in trouble. Hear me speedily; draw nigh unto my soul, and redeem it.' Hence His thirst is an expression of desire toward His heavenly Father.

But think not that in this complaint He had only Himself and what belonged to His peace in view. It was not for His own sake that he hung upon the cross. He longed to be again received into fellowship with God, because His reception into it would be a pledge of theirs, whom He bore vicariously upon His heart. As the second Adam, He experienced their fate in what He endured, and by that means acquired a legal claim to prepare their future inheritance. After taking their place as their Representative, He could not be justified, exalted, and crowned without their participating in it. But how did He long for the moment when He could appear before His Father and say, 'Here am I, and those whom Thou hast given Me! I have redeemed them, have bought them with My blood, and now present them before Thee unreprovable. Henceforth they are Thine and Mine, and worthy to enter into Thy courts.' It is to this desire of His heart, and to this especially, that He gave utterance in the symbolical words, 'I thirst!' O with what rich garlands of love has Jesus adorned the accursed tree!

But we do not fail to perceive that the words, 'I thirst,' not only expressed the Saviour's longing after God His heavenly

Father, but likewise a request to mankind, whom He saw represented at Calvary by those who crucified Him. Even from them He solicited a charitable act. He requested of them a drink of cooling water for His parched tongue. Do not overlook this circumstance. However trivial it may seem, there is something great concealed under it. Who, even if he had been the noblest of his race, would in Jesus' situation have uttered those words to his scoffing foes, and have besought of them a manifestation of kindness and charity? These men were deserving of proud contempt; but as a proof that He was so differently minded from His brethren after the flesh, and that nothing dwelt in His heart of all that is termed wounded pride, revenge, or angry feeling – He solicits from His adversaries an act of compassion and kindness, and says to them, 'I thirst.' What else did He intend to say by this, than, 'See, I do not break with you. I continue faithfully inclined toward you, and hold the bond firmly which connects Me with you.' Let him look here, who does not yet know what it is to heap coals of fire on his enemy's head! How does the holiness of your Redeemer again manifest itself! How does the pure golden grain of His divine nature here display itself afresh! Yes, light is His garment. But it was necessary that He who was willing to be our Surety and Mediator should be so constituted. A speck on the white robe of His righteousness would have sufficed to have deprived Him of the ability for the accomplishment of His great work.

It might be supposed that the words, 'I thirst,' must have filled those who crucified the Saviour with a confusion which would have scarcely permitted them to lift up their eyes any more. And it certainly seems as if it had not entirely failed of its conciliating impression, by producing in them milder sentiments. We see them immediately prepare to fulfil His request. One of them runs and fetches a branch of hyssop, and after they had dipped a sponge in vinegar, and put it on the reed, they held it up to His mouth that He might suck it. But even this miserable refreshment is mingled with the gall of renewed mockery. 'Let alone,' say they, 'let us see whether Elias will come to take him down!' But if I mistake not, there is more seriousness than jest in this speech, and that they really intended by it to disguise the better and gentler feelings of compassion – nay, even a certain inclining toward the dying Man, which they felt arise within them at that moment. If we wish to gain our opponents, we can not do so more rapidly or surely than by requesting them to do us a kindness, and thus oblige ourselves to thank them. This will immediately soften them. But in order to do this, a degree of humility and charity is requisite, which every one does not possess. But this charity and humility dwelt in the Saviour in unlimited fullness; and in order to place Himself in a position to owe the world His thanks, He gives the latter by saying, 'I thirst,' the opportunity of presenting Him with the last earthly solace of His life.

What an affecting and heart-winning thought is this! O that it may win our hearts also, if they are not already gained for Jesus! For that for which He chiefly thirsts is that He may gain us over to Himself. The principal object of His desire and longing is that transgressors may be freed from sin; they that are under the curse, absolved; those that are bound, liberated; and the prisoners set free. But that this great end of human redemption may be accomplished, He still thirsts for our love, the resignation of ourselves to Him, and for our childlike confidence in His saving Name. We therefore know how and with what we can still refresh the Lord of Glory. The first solace which He with desire awaits from us, is our tears of penitence and repentance. O let us bear them to Him! Shall the blood which flowed on the cross never succeed in softening the hard ground of our hearts, nor the love which died for us inflame our frigid souls with a reciprocal affection? O the abundance of awakening voices and attracting powers which urge themselves upon us from the cross! Will we ever resist them, as if the hardness of our hearts were altogether invincible? May God prevent it, and bestow upon us the humility of the publican, and the ardent desire of the dying malefactor!

There may be some of my readers whose eyes, from which a penitential tear never flowed, will soon close in death. O that they would melt before despair hardens them forever! There may be those who, from childhood up, have witnessed what many prophets and kings have desired to see and have not seen, and yet are far from recognizing the one thing that is needful. O that they would weep at length over their blindness, and their base and appalling ingratitude! There may be those also whose eyes require no light to reveal to them their misdeeds, and yet are nevertheless like sealed fountains which yield no water. O that you could weep as Peter wept, and like David, who watered his couch with his tears! Such tears are the drink-offering for which the Saviour still thirsts. God grant that we may approach His throne with them! As soon as this takes place, the actions change, the relations are reversed. It is then He who gives us to drink, and refreshes us, and we imbibe and enjoy. And blessed is he who experiences in himself the truth of His words, 'Whosoever drinketh of the water that I shall give him shall never thirst; but the water that I shall give him shall be in him a well of water springing up into everlasting life.' Who would not say with the Samaritan woman, with reference to such a draught, 'Lord, give me this water, that I thirst no more!'

Chapter 49

'It Is Finished!'

These are the greatest and most momentous words that were ever spoken upon earth since the beginning of the world. Who does not find in them a cry of victory? It is a shout of triumph, which announces to the kingdom of darkness its complete overthrow and to the kingdom of heaven upon earth its eternal establishment. How wonderful! At the very moment when, for the Hero of Judah, all seems lost, His words declare that all is won and accomplished! Our Lord's exclamation is like the sound of a heavenly jubilee-trumpet, and announces to the race of Adam, which was under the curse, the commencement of a free and sabbatic year, which will ever more extensively display its blessing, but never come to an end. Listen, and it will appear to you as if in the words, 'It is finished!' you heard fetters burst, and prison-walls fall down. At these words, barriers as high as heaven are overthrown, and gates which had been closed for thousands of years, again move on their hinges.

But what was it that was finished at the moment when that cry was uttered? The evangelist introduces his narrative with the words, 'After this, Jesus knowing that all things were accomplished.' Only think – 'All things!' What more can we want? But wherein did they consist? We hasten to lift the veil, and view in detail what was realized and brought about, and may the full peace be imparted to us which the words, 'It is finished!' announce to the world!

'Jesus cried with a loud voice, It is finished!' It would seem as if He had wished to drink only to make this victorious cry sound forth with full force, like the voice of a herald or the sound of a trumpet. The Lord has now reached the termination of His labours. He has performed the stupendous task which He undertook in the council of peace, before the world was, when He said, 'I delight to do thy will, O my God!' Death, to which He is on the point of submitting, formed the summit, but also the concluding act of His mediatorial work.

Only take into your hands the divine programme of His vicarious earthly course, as compiled in types and prophecies in the archives of the Old Testament, and be convinced how it has been most minutely carried out. The mysterious delineation of the Messiah, as it passes before us in increasing brightness and completeness in the writings of Moses and the prophets, is fully realized in its smallest and minutest traits in the person of Jesus. If you ask for the wondrous Infant of Bethlehem described by Micah, 'whose goings forth have been of old, from everlasting;' or for the Child born, and the Son given, with the government upon His shoulder, whom Isaiah brings before us; or for the meek and lowly King mentioned by Zechariah, who makes His entrance into Jerusalem on the foal of an ass – it meets you bodily in Jesus Christ. Do you seek for the Seed of the woman, who with His wounded heel bruises the serpent's head; or the second Aaron, who should actually bring about a reconciliation between God and a sinful world – look up to the cross, and there you will see all combined in One.

Do you look about you for the antitype of the brazen serpent in the wilderness, or of the paschal lamb and its delivering blood in Egypt; or for the exalted Sufferer who appears in the appalling descriptions given us in Psalms 22 and 69, which record a malefactor's awful doom, even to the mournful cry of 'My God, my God, why hast thou forsaken me!' – all is combined in Him who hangs yonder, and exclaims, 'It is finished!'

Then take a retrospective look into the writings of the ancient prophets, and what meets your view? The ancient types have put on flesh and blood in Jesus Christ. Their importance to us is henceforth limited to the testimony they bear that the divinely-promised Messiah is indeed come, and that no other is to be looked for. Every condition of the work of human redemption had been fulfilled at the moment when Christ uttered the words, 'It is finished!' with the exception of one, which was included and taken for granted in them, because it inevitably awaited Him, and actually took place immediately afterward – thus bringing the whole to a perfect conclusion.

That which still remained unaccomplished clearly proves that Jesus did not hang on the cross on His own account, but as our Representative. It was our death. The laws of nature forbade that a green and thoroughly healthy tree, which was rooted in eternity, should bleed and sink beneath the blows of 'the last enemy.' It was contrary to the divine government that One who had not with Adam tasted the forbidden fruit, should nevertheless fall under the sentence pronounced, 'In the day that thou eatest thereof, thou shalt surely die!' It was at variance with the express promise of the Most High – 'This do, and thou shalt live' – that One who did not leave unfulfilled one iota of the divine commands, should not live, but die. He Himself repeatedly declared that the universal law of mortality had no claim upon His Person. He asserted most pointedly that no one, not even His Father in heaven, took away His life, but that He laid it voluntarily down. Truly, the death of Jesus would have shaken the throne of the Almighty to its foundations, and violated all the statutes of the divine government, if it were not permitted us to carry the idea of it beyond the bounds of such a death as all experience.

These considerations compel us – irrespective of any revelation which the Scriptures afford – to regard the death of Christ as something extraordinary and unique in its kind. And certainly, it is a fact which stands solitary in history, and with which none besides can compare. He who, according to divine right, was exempt from death, freely submitted to it in our stead, as the last bitter drop of the accursed cup. Whether you believe this or not, the Scriptures most expressly affirm it in many and powerful words. They tell us that 'Christ tasted death by the grace of God,' and therefore not as the result of a natural necessity. They say, 'In that he died, he died unto sin.' And when they assert that, 'If One died for all, then were all dead,' it points out the vicarious nature of His death so plainly, that I know not how it could be more clearly expressed.

If, by His death, He paid the wages of sin for us, His death naturally could not resemble such a falling asleep as is granted at present to thousands of believers under the smile of heaven, and with the joy of redemption upon their lips. No; an eternal statute required that He should yield, as far as possible, to the stroke of the king of terrors, and taste the death to which the first Adam was sentenced. Under its horrors He bowed His head. Observe the continued silence on high concerning Him – the appalling restraint upon all the heavenly powers – the three hours' darkness in which He was involved – and the jeers and blasphemies which assail Him from below. Truly, in all this you perceive no cheering picture of the state in which He descends into the gloomy vale of death. No; He does not die on the downy couch of a pre-assumed blessedness, as many of the poorest sinners now die, at His expense.

Nevertheless, He dies in the crown of triumph. At the moment when His heart ceased to beat, the words, 'It is finished!' revealed the entire fullness of their meaning. He had now reached the final completion of His work of redemption. The exclamation, 'It is finished!' resounded in heaven and awoke hallelujahs to the Lamb which shall never more be mute. They reverberated through the abodes of darkness, like the thunders of God, announcing the termination of the dominion of their prince. But a more blissful sound on earth does not strike the ear of the penitent sinner to this hour than the words, 'It is finished!' It is as the sound of the great jubilee-trumpet, and the proclamation of an eternal salvation.

Yes, we are delivered. There is no longer any cause for anxiety, except in the case of those who refuse to acknowledge their sinfulness, and turn their backs on the Man of Sorrows on the cross. But if we are otherwise minded and, honouring truth, have judged and condemned ourselves in the presence of God, then come! No more circuitous paths – no fruitless efforts to help yourselves – no vain recourse to the empty cisterns of this world, whatever proud names they may bear! The voice of peace is heard on Calvary.

Oh, that we were solemnly conscious how much was done for us there! Great was our guilt; we were condemned to death, and the curse lay upon us; but all is done away in the words, 'It is finished!' If He has paid the ransom, how can a righteous God in heaven demand payment a second time? Know you not the assertion of the apostle, 'There is therefore now no condemnation to them that are in Christ Jesus!' Let us give our whole hearts to Him, and neither the multitude nor the heinousness of our sins need appal us. His closed eyes, His death-like visage, His pierced hands and feet oblige us, even for the glorifying of His name, to oppose not only the infernal accuser and the judge in our own breasts, but even the law of Moses, with the apostle's watchword, 'Who is he that condemneth, since Christ hath died?'

What invaluable fruit, therefore, do we reap from the tree of the cross! That which the Saviour accomplished by His death was not merely the work of satisfaction to divine justice, by which He removed the curse from our heads, but likewise His representative obedience, which is henceforth imputed to His believing people, as the righteousness which avails in the sight of God. Along with the sentence, 'Depart from me, ye cursed!' is also the 'Mene, Tekel,' erased from our walls, and in its stead we read the mighty words, 'Ye are washed, ye are sanctified, ye are justified in the name of the Lord Jesus.' And that we are so is confirmed to us by the fact that God now lovingly inclines toward us, breathes His Spirit into us, leads us in bonds of mercy and kindness, and as soon as we have finished our course, opens the gates of His heavenly mansions to us. But that condemned sinners are regarded as holy before God, without any infringement on His justice, holiness, and truth, is intimated by that which the suffering Saviour accomplished on the cross. Even the twenty-second Psalm asserts that this would be the consequence of His death, since in the last verse it is said, 'They shall come and shall declare his righteousness unto a people that shall be born, that he hath done this.' How just and well founded is, therefore, the victorious cry, 'It is finished!' with which the Lord, after performing His work, inclined His head to rest!

'With one offering he hath forever perfected them that are sanctified' (*Heb.* 10:14). Yes, by the one act of the offering up of Himself, He has so laid the foundation for all who believe in Him, of their justification, sanctification, and redemption, that they may now unhesitatingly rejoice in the first as an accomplished fact; that they bear in them the second; and that they have the third as surely and certainly in prospect, as Christ their Representative has already taken possession, in their names, of the glorious and heavenly inheritance. A creative act of a spiritual kind was accomplished on the cross; and when that which was there created shall have attained to its perfect development, and have laid aside all its earthly veils and coverings, the full truth of the triumphal shout, 'It is finished,' will become apparent, and its signification be revealed to us.

For know that the eye of the crucified Saviour, on uttering these sublime words, rested not merely on individual sinners, but also on the whole world at large. He had dissolved the ban that lay upon it – had snatched it from the curse which justice had impended over it, and had rent from the powers of darkness the desolate earth, which, by the divine decision, had fallen to them on account of sin, had conquered it for Himself, and consecrated it to be the scene of His future kingdom. The blood of Christ claims its transformation into an abode of righteousness – its renovation to a paradise – its renewed amalgamation with heaven; and the eternal Father who has solemnly sworn to His Son, saying, 'Ask of me, and I will give thee the heathen for an inheritance, and the uttermost parts of the earth for a possession,' will not refuse to listen to the claims of the blood of His only-begotten Son. Whatever confusion and desolation may yet come upon our world, its future is secure. On the cross, the ground of its inevitable transformation and glorification was laid, and the Holy Spirit was commissioned not to rest, till the great work of that new creation shall have been completed.

When the glorious representations which are here given us become life and reality, we shall then be truly conscious in what a stupendous and comprehensive sense the dying Redeemer uttered the words, 'It is finished!' At that moment, the entire fullness of deliverance and glorification there depicted, had been won by Him, and the new world, in all the preliminary conditions of its realization, was formed.

Let us avail ourselves, then, of the treasures of consolation and hope which he concealed for us in the words, 'It is finished!' Let us more closely encircle the cross, and derive from the death of the Redeemer, along with the blissful consciousness that our sins are forgiven us, strength to live henceforth only to Him who gave such an invaluable ransom for us. If we now wish to see what He has made of us poor children of Adam by the offering up of Himself, let us cast a look at the Church triumphant above. The just made perfect there were once people like ourselves. Among them are the malefactor, the publican, Magdalen, Zacchaeus, and a host of other poor sinners. Who recognizes them in their glorified state, their shining garments and unfading crowns of life before the throne of God?

In those saints the words, 'It is finished!' have, as it were, assumed a form. They display to us the entire greatness of the expression. They form its living and visible commentary. Let us therefore follow in their steps. No other banner but the cross accompanies us to the city of God. Let us join the band of travellers who follow this oriflamme, and let the full-toned echo, which resounds from the depth of our hearts, to the cry, 'It is finished!' be heard both now, and especially in our last hour, 'Who is he that condemneth, since Christ hath died?'

Chapter 50

'Father, into Thy Hands I Commend My Spirit!'

We are entering a sanctuary. Is there, generally speaking, any thing on earth more solemn and affecting than dying moments, in which time and eternity meet each other, and in the silence of which we seem to hear the striking of the hours of another world? What ought we then to feel at a deathbed, such as that we are now to contemplate, in which the Redeemer bows His head and expires! Lift up your eyes. O what a dying bed has been prepared yonder for the Father's beloved Son! No one wipes the perspiration from His brow. No one cheers Him with the words of life. Who ever left the world more forsaken and involved in deeper shades than He? Yet do not mistake Him. It is not a conflict in which we see Him engaged, but a sacrificial act. He does not yield to death like us, but devotes Himself to it after having previously invested it with the power over His life.

What is death? For thousands of years, as you know, has the gloomy and universally dreaded thing been in the world and carried on its dreadful work of destruction. It is the fate and destiny of our race. The young creation, as it came forth from the hand of the Almighty, knew not this monster. In consequence of the Fall, it entered upon the stage of reality, in order thenceforward, as the king of terrors, to subject every thing that breathed to its awful sceptre. Our first parents were the first who beheld it display its power and majesty on their beloved Abel. From that moment, death continued its dreadful sway over the earth, dropped its gall into every cup of joy, surrounded every loving bond with the certain prospect that sooner or later the hour of separation and dissolution would arrive.

The payment of the wages of sin is due only from sinners. The Holy One of Israel had nothing in common with death. What is it, then, that we witness on Calvary? Look up! After having uttered the great and triumphant shout, 'It is finished!' He again moves His lips to speak. What will follow? A mournful farewell? A painfully faltering out of the words, 'My senses forsake me. I succumb, and am going the way of all flesh?' Oh, not so! Listen! With a loud voice, and the strength and emphasis of One who does not die from weakness, nor dying pays a forced tribute to a mournful necessity; but as One who is Lord over death, and voluntarily yields Himself up to it, He exclaims, 'Father, into thy hands I commend my Spirit!' and after these words, like one whose labour is finished, He bows His bleeding head upon His breast, and resigns His spirit. But before we treat of the mighty results which proceed from His death, let us for a moment immerse ourselves in the consideration of the parting words of the divine Sufferer.

'Father!' He begins. He is therefore again conscious of His Father. The first word we hear from His lips on earth was His Father's name, and it is also the last. All His thoughts and deeds, desires and efforts, tended toward His Father and the glorifying of His Name. To accomplish His Father's will was His meat and drink; the love of His Father His delight and bliss; and union with Him the summit of all His hopes and desires. With the heraldic and conquering cry, 'It is finished!'

He turned once more to the world. It was His farewell to earth – a farewell such as beseemed the Conqueror of death, the Prince of life, the Governor of all things. He then withdrew Himself entirely into connection with His God, and turned His face to Him alone.

'Father!' This sound was the utterance of regained and strong filial confidence, but not the exclamation of One who had fully attained to rest in His Father's bosom. We must still regard the words, 'Father, into thy hands I commend my Spirit,' as the war-cry of a Warrior engaged in battle. Hell, which raged around Him, did not give up its cause as lost, but continued to assault Him in every way, and to distress Him; and the act of death cost Him, who was Life, no small effort.

We must, therefore, imagine to ourselves the Saviour's dying exclamation as that of one sorely oppressed, who is struggling to place His soul in a secure asylum, and flees from a horrid pressure into the hands of the Almighty; and that this taking refuge occurs with the peace and assurance of complete victory. The idea does not even remotely present itself to Him, that death could be any thing more than a transfer of the spirit into a different sphere of existence. He is exalted, high as heaven, above the miserable human inquiry, 'To be or not to be?' He knows that He falls asleep only to awake on the bosom of God; and in this consciousness, in which He already sees the arms of His Father lovingly extended to receive Him, He exclaims, 'Father, into thy hands I commend my Spirit!'

He takes these words from Psalm 31, except that He prefaces them with the word 'Father,' which gives the appropriate form to His position and dignity, and leaves out the words of the Psalmist which immediately follow, 'For thou hast redeemed me,' as not belonging to Him who, as the Redeemer of the world, hung upon the cross. But still how significant it is, that He left the world with a passage of Scripture on His lips! He was completely imbued with the Word of God, and even dying, gives us a hint respecting what ought to be the nourishment of our inner man.

His last cry is uttered. He then inclines His head, after His well and fully-accomplished work, and the most unheard-of event takes place – the Son of the living God becomes a corpse! We stand affected, astonished, and sink in adoration.

Where was the Lord Jesus after His departure from the body? Where else than whither His desires and longing carried Him – in the hands of His Father. Heaven celebrated His triumph; the music of angelic harps saluted His ears; the just made perfect before the throne shouted their adoring and rejoicing welcome.

But it is undeniable that mysterious passages of Scripture intimate that the Prince of Peace, after having laid aside His earthly body, had by no means concluded His mission. For the Apostle Peter says that Christ went in the Spirit – that is, divested of His bodily personality – 'and preached unto the spirits in prison, which sometime were disobedient, when once the long-suffering of God waited, in the days of Noah, while the ark was preparing' (1 Pet. 3:19–20). And supported by this passage especially, the Apostles' Creed asserts a descent into hell, immediately after the death of Christ. But the explanation of this passage requires great caution. If Christ entered the habitations of departed spirits, it was in order to announce His victory to them, as the words in the original expressly intimate. In every case we must be content with not having reached the conclusion of the exposition of these passages; and hence a veil of mystery continues to rest upon the sojourn of Christ during the interval between the moment of His death and that of His reunion with the body, as well as upon the correct and full meaning of the words, 'He descended into hell.'

But the reason of Christ's death stands, on the contrary, fully unveiled before us. Even a superficial consideration suffices to give us at least an idea of the cause of it. It must, first of all, appear extremely striking that an Individual dies who could testify respecting Himself that He was the Resurrection and the Life; who, at the grave of Lazarus, at the bier of the young man of Nain, and at the deathbed of the daughter of Jairus, manifested that He was Lord over death, and who had never committed a single sin by which He had forfeited His life. Still more does it surprise us that He becomes a prey to death, because according to His own assertion, no one took away His life from Him, and that this Man expires under circumstances which would lead one to suppose that He was a malefactor and a rebel, rejected both by God and the world, rather than a righteous Man, and even a universal Benefactor of mankind.

That He died voluntarily is evident to every one at first sight. But for what end did He die this voluntary death? Was it to give us the example of a heroic departure from the world? By no means. How do the words He spoke correspond with such an object? 'I have a baptism to be baptized with, and how am I straitened until it is accomplished!' Was it in order to show us that dying is an easy thing? Stephen has certainly given us an instance of this in his exit from the world, but not the Man whom we hear in the dark valley, exclaiming, 'My God, my God, why hast thou forsaken me?'

Many, again, suppose that He died to confirm His doctrine. But which doctrine did He seal on the cross? Was it this, that God is with the righteous? or this, that 'the angel of the Lord encampeth about them that fear him, and delivereth them?' or this, that 'godliness hath the promise of the life that now is?' I know not what fresh support these truths have found in the circumstances of His death; sooner should we think we found proof in them to the contrary. Besides, no one doubted these truths, so as to require a renewed practical confirmation of them. If Christ confirmed any thing by His death, it was His assertion on oath, with which He answered the high priest's question, 'Art thou the Son of the living God?' On account of this affirmation, they nailed Him to the cross. But that He continued firmly to abide by it, He testified by His sanguinary death.

The fact that He died as such certainly makes the mystery of His death complete; but the seals of this mystery are opened, and its depths revealed. Men enlightened from above stand ready to afford us every wished-for elucidation. They draw near to us at the cross, from the times of both the old and new covenant, and their statements illumine, like the candlestick in the temple, the darkness of Calvary. One of the divine heralds heads the phalanx with testifying that Christ 'restored what he took not away.' Another exclaims, 'He was wounded for our transgressions, the chastisement of our peace was upon him, and with his stripes we are healed.' A third, 'Behold the Lamb of God that taketh away the sin of the world!' A fourth, 'God made him to be sin for us who knew no sin.' And again, 'Christ hath redeemed us from the curse of the law, being made a curse for us;' and again, 'Christ hath reconciled us by the body of his flesh, through death;' and again, 'With one offering he hath perfected forever them that are sanctified.' And with the testimonies of these messengers of God are combined these of the Lord Himself. For instance, 'The Son of man came to give his life a ransom for many;' and again, 'Except a grain of wheat fall into the ground and die, it abideth alone, but if it die, it bringeth forth much fruit.' And more especially, the words of the institution of the sacrament of His body and blood, broken and shed for the forgiveness of sins.

But it may be said, 'We hear these words, but are they not themselves hieroglyphics which require deciphering?' They are so; and in order to understand them it requires a previous consecration, which however is not imparted by anointing or laying on of hands in temples of human erection, but in the privacy of the closet, amid grief and tears. Rouse yourselves, therefore, from your delusions, become conscious of your need of reconciliation and redemption, and in a short time, the words you have just read will burn like flaming torches before you. You will then behold in the Man of Sorrows, the Mediator between God and you, and rejoicingly embrace, in His death, the Sacrifice that outweighed all your guilt and justified you forever in the sight of God.

'Father, into thy hands I commend my Spirit!' O what did He not commend to His Father's hands when uttering these words! 'And being made perfect,' writes the apostle, 'he became the author of salvation to all them that obey him' (*Heb.* 5:9). It was therefore necessary that He Himself should be perfected as righteous, by fulfilling the whole law; as holy, by victoriously overcoming every temptation; as Surety, by the payment of all our debts; and as Mediator and Reconciler, by emptying the whole of the cup of curse allotted to us. In all these respects He was perfected the moment He expired, and thus He deposited in His Father's hands, along with His spiritual personality the basis of the new world, yea, His re-deemed Church itself, as purified in His blood, arrayed in His righteousness, a pleasing and acceptable offering in the sight of God.

Now, if we are obedient to the Son of His love, we know that there is a city of refuge for us in every supposable case. Into whatever distress we may fall, we need not be anxious as to its termination. If the world persecutes, or Satan tempts us, if death alarms us, or any thing else excites apprehension, we courageously exclaim, while relying on the merits of Immanuel, 'Because I have made the Lord my refuge, even the Most High my habitation, there shall no evil befall me.'

And we are sure that this high and lofty asylum is every moment open to receive and shelter us.

O the incomparable privileges which are granted us in Christ! Let us make good use of them, and cover the feet of Him, who acquired them for us, with reverential kisses. Let us peacefully go on our way, in the rainbow light which beams upon us from Calvary, and tune the strings of our hearts to gratitude and devoted love.

Chapter 51

The Signs That Followed

S carcely has the Lord of life and glory bowed His head and expired on Calvary, than the awful scene is changed. Heaven no longer withholds its recognition of the Man of Sorrows. The cry of the dying Mediator, 'It is finished!' receives the most brilliant confirmation; and in lieu of the hostile tumult which has hitherto raged around Him, a sublime celebration of His incomparable triumph ensues.

Follow me first into the temple of Jerusalem. It is three o'clock in the afternoon, the hour, therefore, when the Israelites assembled in its sacred courts for the evening sacrifice. The priests begin their customary duties, when at the very moment in which Christ on Calvary exclaims, 'Father into thy hands I commend my spirit!' who can describe the astonishment of the sons of Aaron! The thickly-woven heavy veil, without being touched by any human hand, is rent in twain, in the midst, from the top to the bottom, and the mercy-seat with the ark of the covenant and the golden cherubim, that sacred depositary which the high priest alone was permitted to approach, not without blood, and only once a year, stands suddenly naked and unveiled to the view of every one.

It was the Almighty at whose nod this event occurred. And what did it imply? First, a renewed intimation that the

Levitical service, though divinely ordered and prophetically significant, contained only types of a coming salvation, which, now that the latter was accomplished, were rendered void, even as the blossom is expelled by the fruit.

Secondly, a symbolical and obvious representation of the blissful effects which should attend the bloody death to which the Lord of Glory had just devoted Himself on Calvary. The most holy place in the temple was the shadow and type of the throne-room of heaven, from which we had been ejected and excluded by a divine decree. The veil which separated us from it was our sinful flesh. 'Who shall ascend into the hill of the Lord, and who shall stand in his holy place?' had not been the question hitherto; and the answer was, 'He that hath clean hands and a pure heart; who hath not lifted up his soul unto vanity.' But who could boast of being thus blameless in the sight of God? There was none righteous, no not one. 'Who among us,' was the inquiry, 'can dwell with devouring fire? Who can dwell with everlasting burnings?' And the reply was, he that doeth righteousness. But what remained for any one, except the mournful ejaculation of the prophet, 'Woe is me, for I am undone, for I am a man of unclean lips!' Righteousness had departed, sin reigned.

Suddenly the sign in the temple announces that our position, as regards the habitation of the Most High, had undergone a great and thorough change. That which hindered our access to the sanctuary of God was done away. That which elevated itself as a wall of separation between us and Him fell down. There is no longer any risk in casting ourselves into the hands of Him before whom even the angels are not pure. Put on the Lord Jesus Christ and then thou mayest boldly and with childlike confidence enter the Father's holy habitation which henceforward stands open to thee day and night. Wash thy robes in the blood of the Lamb, and then cast thyself with childlike confidence on the Father's heart, and pour every thing that harasses and oppresses thee into His bosom. O lay hold of the blissful idea, which in God's intention, and by His immediate arrangement, the rent in the veil of the temple portrays to thee! Thy Saviour by His death threw open every door and gate in heaven.

But wouldst thou still inquire whether we are really justified in giving that rent in the veil of the sanctuary such an encouraging meaning, know that we are fully authorized to do so. Read what the apostle says in Heb. 10: 19–23, 'Having, therefore, brethren, boldness to enter into the holiest by the blood of Jesus, by a new and living way, which he hath consecrated for us through the veil, that is to say, his flesh; and having an High Priest over the house of God; let us draw near with a true heart, in full assurance of faith, having our hearts sprinkled from an evil conscience, and our bodies washed with pure water.' Thou seest, therefore, that access to the holy place is opened to us, and that the way to our Father's house is prepared for us. 'By whom?' By Jesus Christ. 'In what manner?' By means of a rent in the veil. This veil was the flesh of the great High Priest. The veil was rent when He offered up His human nature on the cross for us, after taking, by imputation, our sins upon Himself. By this act of mediation, He answered and fulfilled every thing requisite for our justification in the sight of God, and, therefore, also for our admission before the throne of God. Hence at the moment when He expired, that took place substantially which the same moment occurred typically in the temple.

We leave the edifice at Jerusalem which has now lost its importance, and return to Calvary, where a second miracle meets us. 'The earth quakes, the rocks rend.' What does this imply? Something great and glorious. The death of the Mediator has decided the future of the old world. It is, with all its concerns, devoted to destruction, and awaits a great and comprehensive change. Hear what is said in Heb. 12:21,

26, 'Whose voice then shook the earth; but now he hath promised, saying, Yet once more I shake not the earth only, but also heaven. And this word, yet once more, signifieth the removing of those things that are shaken, that those things which can not be shaken may remain.'

The present creation is not what it was originally. Sin entered into it and overspread it with mortality and endless destruction. But after sin had been again put away through the satisfaction made by the Redeemer, its consequences must also naturally find their grave. The blood of the Lamb demands the restoration of the original state of created things. And the quaking of the earth to its very foundations, the tottering of the hills and mountains, the rending of the rocks which attended the Lord's death, all these are nothing else but an amen of Almighty God to the demand of the blood of His Son.

The third wonder ought to affect our hearts in the most powerful manner. Not only do rocks in the neighbourhood of Calvary rend, but ancient sepulchres of saints long fallen asleep are opened, and the corpses they conceal, invigorated by new life, after the resurrection of the Illustrious Sleeper, likewise go forth from their chambers, and appear unto many in the holy city.

What an event! It is certainly somewhat veiled in mysterious obscurity, and gives rise to a variety of questions. It seems to me that the graves only opened as a preceding intimation of what would afterward occur; while the reunion of the departed spirits with their bodies took place three days after, on the great Easter morning. But the fact itself is beyond a doubt, and would stand fast even without being confirmed by many of the inhabitants of Jerusalem, to whom the evangelists appeal for its historical truth.

But that which God intended by this miracle is sufficiently evident. The powerful effects of Christ's vicarious death reach down even to the domains of the dead. By the offering up of

His own life, He became the Prince of Life. Even in the appalling regions of corruption, He overthrew the throne of him who, according to the Scriptures, 'had the power of death,' and acquired the authority not only to conduct the souls He had redeemed to the mansions of eternal peace, but also to wrest their bodies from the bonds of the curse, and in due time to present His people to His Father in bodily as well as spiritual glorification. This truth the Almighty intended primarily to confirm by the miracle of the opening of the graves, connected with the death of Christ, and then by the actual resurrection of the bodies of the saints on the third day.

Who were these first trophies of the glorious Conqueror of the king of terrors? Was Abraham among them, to whom it was promised that he should see, in a very peculiar manner, the day of the Lord? Was Moses, of whom the apostle Jude relates that Satan strove with the heavenly powers about his body? The narrative leaves us without a reply, and is also silent as to the appearance presented by the risen saints, who were made visible to many in the holy city; and when, where, and in what manner they were afterward taken up to heaven. The mission of those who were thus called from the dust of the grave was limited to one thing, namely, to represent the death of Jesus as an event which operated with creative power, both in the past, the present, and the future, and not less in the depth than in the height, and to give actual proof of the exceedingly abundant and well-grounded cause we have to rejoice beneath the cross of Christ, and to say with the apostle, 'O death, where is thy sting? O grave, where is thy victory? The sting of death is sin, and the strength of sin is the law; but thanks be to God which giveth us the victory through our Lord Jesus Christ' (*1 Cor.* 15:55–57).

Thus the atoning death of Christ was solemnized in a majestic manner by divine signs and wonders which commenced immediately beneath the cross. He who first attracts our attention is the Roman centurion, the commander of the band of soldiers who watch the cross. Mute, and apparently lost in thought, he stands and looks up to the cross of the divine Sufferer. He has witnessed the whole course of the crucifixion. He beheld the admirable behaviour of the mysterious Man. He listened to the words which proceeded from His bleeding lips, and at the moment when the just One expired, he felt the earth tremble beneath his feet; and he saw also with his own eyes how the hills around tottered, and the rocks were rent asunder. The emotions which had till then affected his soul, compressed themselves into one powerful and appalling impression, and he gives vent to his feelings in the loud and unambiguous exclamation, in which he praised the true God, the God of Israel, saying, 'Certainly this was a righteous man, this was the Son of God!'

We must not be too anxious to know what the centurion meant by the later expression. He was certainly no dogmatician, nor a Jew instructed in the catechism, but only a poor blind heathen. But according to all that he had seen of the Man of Nazareth, he doubted not that He must be more than a Man, and according to the presentiment which had taken possession of his soul, he regarded Him as in fact, no other than the Son of God, foretold in the Jewish scriptures.

But see! Not only the centurion, but also several of his troops are overpowered by feelings similar to his own; and astonished and thrilled with a sacred reverence, join in his confession, or murmur something of the kind. What a pleasing and significant occurrence! A number of blind heathen, among them probably even those who had been the instruments of Jesus' crucifixion, give Him, in spite of a world of opponents, the glory of the candid confession that He is the Son of the living God.

You have seen and heard not merely that which those heathen saw and heard, but something infinitely greater and

more important. You are witnesses of the fact that Christ's
death on the cross not only rent the rocks and made the hills
to tremble, but lifted the whole order of the old world from
its joints and hinges, and pushed it into an entirely new path.
You saw from that death a resurrection-beam dart not merely
over a few bodies of sleeping saints, but the fiery stream of a
new and divine life pour itself over the whole graveyard of
the earth. You are not only aware of the rending of the veil
in the temple at the moment when the great Sufferer expired,
but also of the rending of a prophetic covering which had
existed for four thousand years, in order that what was
concealed under it might be realized in the world, even in its
minutest features. You not only heard the dying Saviour
majestically gladden the heart of a single malefactor with the
promise, 'This day shalt thou be with me in paradise;' but
are aware that to this hour no one under heaven attains to
thorough peace amid the darkness and storms of this life, till
he has lifted up the eye of faith to that thorn-crowned head.
All these things have been brought before you, and you are
daily conversant with them; and can you delay to detach
yourselves, resolutely, from an unbelieving world, and to
make the confession of those heathen soldiers your own?

The Roman mercenaries are not however the only individuals on Calvary who pay tribute of reverence to the deceased
Saviour. It is done more profoundly and fervently by the group
of weeping women who followed the Master from Galilee and
ministered unto Him. Even in death they can not leave Him.
They still cling to Him with their love and hope, like ivy to
the fallen tree. Duly mark the sacred fire which burns in the
centre of their hearts. It is the fire of the purest enthusiasm
for Christ and His kingdom. Beloved souls, do not despair of
this kingdom, even though the whole world should declare
it to be an idle dream. It alone is reality, and will have the
victory under all circumstances. Let us therefore all join

ourselves to it. Let us all address the crucified Redeemer, and say, 'We side with Thee, thou beauteous Morning Star!' Let us give our word and our hands, that we will walk in His paths, through whatever straits and difficulties they may lead us. Extend toward us Thy hand, therefore, Thou who are estranged from all that is low and vain, and teach us to elevate our nature by following in Thy steps!

Let these be the ejaculations which rise from our breasts beneath the cross. But know that the celebration of His death does not terminate in such enthusiasm for the Lord and His kingdom. The women had found in Jesus more than a model of humanity and a guiding star in the path of virtue. They felt their need, above all things, of a Surety, who should mediate their reconciliation with God, in order that the beginning of a new life might be made. And they believed that they had really found the object of their ardent desires in their great Master. But did they give up their belief at His death? It was doubtless deeply shaken by the sanguinary exit of their divine Friend out of this life; but the signs they had just witnessed, swelled the sails of their hope anew, and seemed to them nothing less than a voice of their heavenly Father, saying to them, 'Endure and wait, for He is nevertheless the Man whom you held Him to be.' And however weak might be their confidence, they celebrated their reconciliation through the blood of the Lamb, although more in hope than in clear consciousness. O let us enter into the fellowship with them! The only real, true, and full celebration of the death of Christ is that which is based upon the song of the blest above, 'The Lamb that was slain, is worthy to receive praise, and honour and glory!'

Let such be also our celebration of it. We read in the Gospel that many who had likewise been witnesses of the divine wonders at the cross, returned to Jerusalem, in great amazement, beating their breasts. The state of these people points out to you the preparation for a real 'Good Friday.' Be aware what enormous guilt apart from your other sins you incur, by refusing due homage and submission to a Lord and King so powerfully accredited as Jesus upon the cross. O that you would take deeply to heart, and now begin to humble yourselves before God!

Chapter 52

The Wound of the Lance

On our return to the scene of suffering on Calvary, we find a great change has taken place. Profound silence reigns on the three crosses. Death has spread his sable wings over the sufferers. The gazing crowd which surrounded the place of execution has dispersed – in part, deeply affected and conscience smitten. Even the little company of faithful women, almost ready to succumb with grief and sorrow, appear to have returned to the city. We therefore find only the Roman guard, and beside them the disciple whom Jesus loved, who after he had safely lodged Mary in his peaceful cottage, could not resist the urgent impulse to seek again the place where He that was all to him, hung on the cross. Who could we have wished as a witness to the last event on Calvary, sooner than this sober-minded and sanctified disciple? He relates to us, in all simplicity, what he there beheld.

The priests and scribes, accustomed to strain at a gnat and swallow a camel, think not of the heinous blood-guiltiness they had incurred, but only of the prevailing custom in Israel, to take down from the gibbets, where they had been exposed to public view, as a warning to others, the bodies of malefactors, and inter them before night. This custom was founded on an express divine command. We read in

Deuteronomy 21:22, 23, 'If a man have committed a sin worthy of death, and he be put to death, and thou hang him on a tree, his body shall not remain all night upon the tree, but thou shalt in anywise bury him that day; (for he that is hanged is accursed of God) that thy land be not defiled, which the LORD thy God giveth thee for an inheritance.'

This is a strange and peculiar ordinance, which we should scarcely have been able to account for, had not the Spirit of the Lord himself presented us with the key to it. The fact that God points out those that are hung as especially burdened with His curse compelled the more thoughtful in Israel to infer that there was something typical in it; because a wicked man, though not thus put to death, could not really be less accursed than one whose dead body was thus publicly exhibited. Thus the divine command to inter the body, and the promise connected with it, 'So shalt thou bury with it the curse that rests upon the land,' unfolded the consoling prospect that a removal and blotting out of guilt was actually possible.

But since it followed, of course, that it could not be affected by the mere interment of executed malefactors, the idea must have occurred to them that in the divine counsels, the re-moval of the curse would, at a future period, be actually accomplished by the death and burial of some prominent mysterious Personage. Now, when believing Israelites hit upon such thoughts, their ideas were in accordance with God's intention, who, in the ordinance respecting malefactors that had been put to death, had no other object in view than a prophetic symbolizing of the future redemption of Christ. The latter is clearly evident from Galatians 3:13, 14, where the apostle says, 'Christ hath redeemed us from the curse of the law, being made a curse for us (for it is written, Cursed is every one that hangeth on a tree) that' – instead of a curse – 'the blessing of Abraham might come on the Gentiles through Jesus Christ.'

Here Christ is undeniably set forth as the antitype of those who were hanged in Israel. On the cross He bore the curse for us, and in doing this, died the public death of a criminal. But after He had commended His Spirit as a voluntary offering into the hands of His Father, the curse that lay upon the earth and its inhabitants was actually interred with His body, since all that believe on Him are freed from the curse, and become heirs of an incorruptible and heavenly blessing.

Hence, how deeply significant does the scene on Calvary appear which we are now contemplating! The persons who are acting there do not indeed know what they are doing. But this does not prevent them from being led by the hand of divine Providence. Without reflecting further, they call to mind the letter of the Mosiac law, and believe they ought to hasten with the taking down of the bodies from the crosses, in order to bury them, both because the day begins to decline, and because it is the preparation for the great Sabbath – that of the feast of the Passover, and hence peculiarly holy. They, therefore, proceed in a body to Pilate, and request him to cause the legs of the three criminals to be broken, as was customary, then to be taken down, and afterward interred.

The governor does not hesitate to grant their request, and sends, at the same time, another guard to the place of execution to break the legs of the malefactors, and to convince themselves of their being really dead. It was considered an act of mercy to those that were crucified, to hasten their death by breaking their limbs with an iron bar, and then giving them a final *coup de grâce* on the breast. The beginning was made with the two malefactors, but when the turn came to the Lord Jesus, every sign of His being already dead was so apparent, that the breaking of His legs was thought needless, especially as one of the spearmen pierced His side with his lance, which alone would have sufficed to have caused His death, had the divine Sufferer been still alive.

In the abstract, this occurrence appears of extremely trifling importance; but the Evangelist John who so expressly states it, regarded it with other eyes. In the twofold fact of the Saviour's limbs not being broken, and of His side being pierced by the lance, he recognizes a divine interposition by which two ancient prophecies were fulfilled. 'These things were done,' says he, 'that the Scriptures should be fulfilled. A bone in him shall not be broken.' This was said in reference to the paschal lamb (*Exod.* 12:46), to which the evangelist here expressly attributes the significance of the type of the Lamb of God, offered up for the sins of the world. As a shadow of Him that was to come, the paschal lamb was to be a male, and in order especially to intimate the holiness of Him who was prefigured, it was required to be without blemish. But that not a bone of him was to be broken was intended to point out that Christ would offer Himself as an atonement to God, whole and undivided; and those who desired to become partakers of His salvation must appropriate Him to themselves entirely. The Lord also in that appoint-ment aimed at the establishment of an additional sign, which when the Messiah should appear, would contribute clearly to make Him known to every one. And John seems to say to us in his narrative, 'Behold here the predicted sign!' The fact that the sacred vessel of His body remained unmutilated impresses the confirming seal upon the deceased as the true atoning Paschal Lamb. He is the righteous One, of whom it is said in Psalm 34:20, 'He keepeth all his bones; not one of them is broken.'

In the wound with the spear the evangelist sees the fulfilment of another passage of Scripture. 'Again,' continues he, 'another scripture saith, They shall look on him whom they pierced.' The word of the Lord by the prophet presents itself to his mind, where it is said, 'I will pour upon the house of David and upon the inhabitants of Jerusalem, the spirit of grace and of supplications, and they shall look upon me whom they have pierced' (*Zech.* 12: 10). This passage was an inexplicable riddle to the Jews, on which account in the Greek version of the Septuagint the original word, without any ground for so doing, instead of 'pierced,' has been rendered 'despised.'

But the only true meaning of these prophetic words has, since then, been made evident to thousands, and will become so to thousands more – yea, even to the whole world, either in the day of grace or of judgment. Either they who have hitherto denied Christ the homage due to Him shall be enlightened by the Holy Spirit, and with weeping eyes and supplicating hearts shall look up to Him; or they shall experience what the apostle announces beforehand in the book of Revelation, 'Behold he cometh with clouds, and every eye shall see him, and they also which pierced him, and all kindreds of the earth shall wail because of him. Even so. Amen.'

Thus you see how the profound evangelist discovers, in all that occurs on Calvary, even in the most unimportant circumstance, a striking divine hieroglyphic, which has solely reference to the acknowledgment and glorification of Christ as the true and promised Messiah and Redeemer of the world. But who does not perceive that in all these various events the hand of a living God overrules and causes them to occur in such a manner that one passage of prophecy after another is fulfilled by them to the letter? How highly the evangelist estimates them as a means of strengthening our faith, he proves very impressively by the words, 'And he that saw it, bare record, and his record is true, and he knoweth that he saith true, that ye might believe.'

The narrative states that 'one of the soldiers with a spear pierced his side, and forthwith there came thereout blood and water.' It has been supposed that John laid so much stress upon this circumstance, because he believed it might serve to refute certain erroneous spirits of his day who assigned to Christ an imaginary and not a real body. It is certainly possible that, in giving his account of the matter, he was partly induced by such a motive. But it is the miraculous nature of the event that chiefly excited his interest in it. In dead bodies the blood always coagulates, while from the wound above mentioned, on the contrary, it flowed clearly and abundantly, unmixed with the water which burst forth from the pierced pericardium of His heart, and ran down from the cross.

That which most deeply affected the soul of the beloved disciple was the divine symbol he perceived beneath the wondrous event. In the water and the blood he sees represented the most essential blessings of salvation for which the world is indebted to Christ. We know that in his first epistle he points out the fact of His coming with water and blood, as well as with the Holy Spirit, as the most peculiar characteristic of the Redeemer of the world; and who does not perceive, in these words, that the wondrous event on Calvary must have been present to his mind?

But what do these three elements imply? Water chiefly symbolizes to the evangelist, in accordance with the figurative language throughout the Holy Scriptures, the moral purifying power of the word of Christ – yea, the atmosphere of His kingdom. Wherever the Gospel penetrates, it changes the moral aspect of nations, apart from regeneration and conversion, in the more limited and specific sense of these words. Decorum and mental culture expel barbarism. Discipline and order take the place of a licentious service of sin. Animal carnality finds its bound in the rising apprehension of a superior ideal of human life.

Even as justice establishes its claims in legislation and civil institutions, so does also love. Men become conscious of the obligation for mutual assistance and kind offices. Attention to the poor and the sick erects its hospitals, and opens to the destitute its places of refuge. There is nothing which is not cemented, ennobled, and transfigured, as soon as affected by the gentle breath of the Christian religion. Compare even the most degraded of the nations of Christendom with any of the heathen, and say if in comparison with these they may not, in a general sense of the word, be termed regenerated? It is in these effects that the water of Christ and His Gospel manifests itself.

Suffice it to say that by means of His Word, and the planting of His Church, a moral purification ennobling and transforming the human race emanates from Christ, and to these results the water which flowed from Jesus' opened side symbolically points.

But water alone would not have saved us. We are deeply involved in guilt in the sight of God; and though we might cease to accumulate fresh guilt, yet our former offences would not on that account be undone and blotted out. Besides, notwithstanding all the cleansing and ennobling of our lives by the Word – when measured according to the model of the divine requirement – we remain poor sinners as before, and exposed to the curse. We therefore need, besides a moral reformation, and more urgently than that, a deliverance from the sentence of condemnation which impended over us, and a being replaced in a state of grace.

For this necessity – the most urgent of all – that which is requisite is supplied by the blood we see streaming along with the water from the wounded side of Jesus. It points out the ransom paid for our guilt once for all before God, as well as the atoning sacrifice by means of which the reconciliation of divine justice with God's love to sinners is brought about. The blood flowed separately from the water; justification must not be mingled with, much less exchanged for, personal amendment. That which again recommends us to the love of God is solely the merit of Christ, and by no means the work of our own virtue. Certainly, union by faith and life with Christ is requisite on our part, but in Christ's righteousness and in that alone, do we receive the absolution from deserved punishment; even as, for its sake alone, we are reinstated in the privileges of divine adoption.

But we know that water and blood by no means exhaust the exhibition of the saving efficacy of Christ's merits. There are three, says the apostle, that testify for Him and of Him on earth – the water (the power of the Word), the blood (the atoning and peace-bringing effect of His vicarious sufferings), and the Holy Spirit, who not merely amends, but renews, not only prunes away the twigs from the tree of sin, but roots it up, and plants in its place an essentially new being and life. He who passes through the world adorned with the threefold seals of such powerful credentials must be the Redeemer and Messiah ordained of God. John regards it as scarcely possible that any one can mistake this, and ve- hemently urges us to swear fealty to Him along with himself, while most impressively exclaiming, 'He that saw it bare record, and his record is true; and he knoweth that he saith true, that ye might believe.'

Let us, then, also believe that we may likewise experience the Lord of Glory as Him who cometh with water, blood, and the Holy Spirit – that is, cleansing, reconciling, and regen- erating. Let us give our selves wholly and without reserve to Him, after He has thus given Himself up to death for us.

Chapter 53

The Interment

After all the scenes we have been witnessing, how beneficial to our spirits is the solemn stillness that now reigns on Calvary! It is the preparation for the Sabbath, and to us it seems just as if we heard the gentle sound of the Sabbath bells reaching us from a distance. The Gospel narrative which details to us the circumstances attending our Lord's being taken down from the cross – His being laid in the grave – and the watch which was set over it – produce in us a tranquil and peaceful feeling. It is our last meditation on the history of our Saviour's passion. May the peace of God, which passeth understanding, be the precious fruit that we shall derive from it! May it prepare our hearts for the wonder of His resurrection!

The crowd have vacated the summit of Calvary. The Roman guard, however, remains. Whether John was also there, we are not informed. Profound silence reigns around. The bodies of the two malefactors are taken down from their crosses, and their graves are being dug. The crucified Redeemer, with His head crowned with thorns and reclining upon His breast, still hangs solitarily between heaven and earth. Who is to inter Him? According to the law, it was the duty of the executioners to bury Him on the place of execution.

But God ordered it otherwise. After the great High Priest's atoning sacrifice had been offered up, He was not to be subjected to any further ignominy. This would have been contrary to the order of the divine statutes. If He had brought His cause to a successful and triumphant termination, honour and glory alone were henceforth His due. Such was also the judgment of Almighty God. A funeral was to be given to His Son, in the circumstances attending which even the blindest might perceive the overruling hand of Eternal Love. Two honourable men – honourable not only in the eyes of men, but also before God – are entrusted with the interment of Immanuel's corpse; and a company of tried female disciples are to be joined with them.

Let us not anticipate the narrative. We leave Mount Calvary for a few moments, and take our stand in the city of Jerusalem. Who is it that is walking so hastily up the street that leads to the palace of the Roman governor? The man seems to be the bearer of some important commission. His countenance expresses it, and his haste betrays it. Who is he? Jerusalem knows him, and numbers him among her principal and most estimable citizens. It is Joseph, surnamed of Arimathea, his birthplace which lay on the mountains of Ephraim – a man honoured with the universal confidence of his tribe, and at the same time a member of the highest Jewish court of justice – the Sanhedrin. As such, he had been personally present at the whole of the proceedings against Jesus; and in the course of them had acquired a vital conviction, not only of the perfect innocence of the Accused, but also something more. He 'had not consented to the counsel and deed' of his associates, but yet he had not had the courage to enter a strong and decided protest against it. Christ was led away to execution, and Joseph in spirit with Him, so far as he was severely judged and condemned by his own conscience.

The bloody execution took place. We know not whether Joseph beheld it from a distance, or learned its details from another. We see him sitting solitarily in his chamber at Jerusalem, and hear him say in broken sentences, 'He is therefore dead! They have slain Him whom they ought to have bound to the earth by a thousand ties of love. Woe to the murderers! They have extinguished, in His own blood, the fairest star that ever shone from heaven upon the world. They knew not what they did, but I knew. Why did I not appear in His behalf? Why did I not confess myself to be His disciple? I never bowed the knee to Him, and suffered Him to be slain without solemnly protesting against it!' Such was the language which we may suppose Joseph uttered to himself in his solitude, while with a grieved heart, he covered his face with his mantle. But suddenly rising up, he exclaims, 'Thou whom I ought to have honoured in life, let my homage in death be acceptable to Thee!' So saying, he leaves his chamber and his dwelling, and mingles with the crowd which throngs the streets.

What is Joseph's object? He is proceeding directly to the governor to ask his permission to take down the Saviour from the cross, and honourably inter Him in his own family sepulchre. He arrives at the Roman palace, and after having been announced, he appears in the presence of Pilate, and says with firmness and in plain terms, 'I am come to beg of thee one thing – that thou wouldst give me the body of Jesus that I may prepare an honourable grave for Him as He deserves.'

Pilate is not a little astonished at such a request from the lips of a Jewish senator. He immediately sends for the commander of the guard, and inquires most carefully respecting the three men that had been crucified. In spite of the quiet official mien which he seeks to put on, it does not escape us that he sympathizes with the deeply affected senator. Even in the surprise with which he hears the news that Jesus is already dead, I think I see reflected something of the powerful presentiments which his soul was unable to resist at the thought of Him who was crucified. Besides, his conscience accuses him respecting his conduct toward One whom he knew to be guiltless; and that He should experience now that He was dead, an honourable funeral such as Joseph intended, corresponded so entirely with his own wishes and feelings that he readily gives his permission, as if his own heart were relieved by so doing.

Joseph heartily thanks the governor, and hastens from him as joyfully as if he had gained a great treasure, in order first of all to purchase the finest linen he can procure, and at the same time the most costly ointment and spices. And if the whole world should wish to know for whom they were intended, he would have testified aloud that they were for his Lord and King. And though the Sanhedrin should warn, or go so far as to threaten him with a removal from office, or even something worse, Joseph will still more loudly exclaim that it is for his King, his Lord, and his Prince of Peace, that he is making these funeral preparations. The narrative states that 'he went in boldly to Pilate;' but to him it did not seem too bold. He would gladly have sacrificed any thing for Jesus, if by so doing he could have made amends for what he had neglected to do while He was living.

We leave him, and return to the place of execution. O see who has meanwhile arrived there! We recognize the man who is standing mute and motionless beneath the cross, and is looking up with devout and tearful eyes to the deceased Sufferer. Joseph finds in him a companion in spirit; for he has to repent of the same thing, and burns with desire, like him, to make amends for his fault. And who is this contemplative stranger? It is Nicodemus, Joseph's colleague in office, that Pharisee who came to Jesus desirous of learning and anxious for salvation, but by night; because in him also the fear of the Jews at least equated his love for the truth. He likewise has thrown aside the disgraceful fetters which bound him. Truly we see marvellous things occurring in the vicinity of the cross.

Who is it that has suddenly opened their eyes? It is the Spirit of the living God. The germ of faith which manifests itself so gloriously and so fully developed had long lain in their hearts, though bound, and as if under the sod. From out of the thunder-cloud that brooded over Calvary, abundant grace has proceeded, and hence it is that we see it so freely and powerfully manifested.

After Nicodemus has meditated awhile with unspeakable emotion at the sight of the cross, Joseph also reaches the summit of Calvary; and how cordially does he greet his associate in mind and spirit! Then after conversing a short time confidentially together, and making the soldiers acquainted with the permission they have received from the governor, they begin their mournful labours. Ladders are fetched, and planted against the cross of the Prince of Peace, and they reverentially ascend to the corpse, feeling at the same time as if they were mounting the steps of some sacred temple.

The two friends have just reached their departed Master's wounded feet. There they devoutly bow their heads, and cover them with kisses and tears, for He is worthy of it. They then ascend higher to His lacerated head. It is not tender sympathy, but something more, with which they behold His blood-stained countenance. They do not fail to perceive what lofty majesty sits enthroned on that pallid brow, and that over the closed eyelids something hovers like the dawn of resurrection. Their minds are deeply affected by the anticipation of what may still come to pass respecting Him; and they then begin, tenderly and gently, to draw out the nails from His hands and feet. The precious corpse reclines upon their shoulders, and after they have wrapped it in linen, they gently let it down from the cross to the ground.

Let us imitate their example. Jesus teaching at Nazareth, or preaching on the mount of the beatitudes, or even transfigured on Mount Tabor, will not suffice us. Christ crucified must be the object of our affections. Therefore ascend to Him on the spiritual ladder of sorrow for sin, longing for mercy, and belief in the efficacy of His sufferings and death. Detach Him from the accursed tree, and deposit Him in your hearts as your only consolation in life and death. That it is the real saving love to Jesus which burns within us, and not a mere caricature of it, may be best ascertained by its being first enkindled by the sight of Him, bleeding and dying on the cross, and then embracing Him as the ever-living One. He on the contrary who turns away from the dead Christ, and imagines that the living Christ, going about doing good, teaching, and setting an example, suffices him, miscalculates, and on the day of His coming, notwithstanding his greeting of 'Rabbi! Rabbi!' will hear from His lips the awful words, 'I know not whence thou art, I never knew thee!'

Let us return to our two friends. We see them descending the hill with their precious burden. The funeral is without pomp, but rendered distinguished by the tenderness and courageous conduct of the two who carry the corpse. No mournful peal accompanies the quiet procession, but in the future it is so much the more abundantly celebrated. From how many thousand towers in the present day do the solemn bells resound over the cross and grave of Jesus, on the annual return of the day which is sacred to the memory of His death and burial! No mournful dirge precedes it, no funeral torches flame. But what more costly flambeaux can there be than those of inextinguishable love and reverence, the offspring of heaven? And only listen; there is also no want of a burial-service. An inspired seer has chanted it nearly a thousand

years before, the prophet Isaiah in chapter 53:9, 'His grave
was destined to be with the wicked, but he found his resting-
place with the rich; because he had done no violence, neither
was guile found in his mouth.'

We have reached the place, and enter a quiet plot of
ground partly enclosed by rocks. It is Joseph's garden. The
sun is just casting its last rays upon it, and the twilight of
evening its first cool shades. In this peaceful seclusion the
Holy One is to find His last earthly resting-place. He who
had not where to lay His head possessed no grave of His own,
and therefore required that one should be lent Him for His
transient repose. But how happy Joseph thought himself to
have the honour of being permitted to prepare Him a
sepulchre; and how pleasing is the prospect to him of
eventually, when his last hour shall arrive, entering, in death,
into the closest fellowship with Him whom in life he had,
alas! so basely deserted!

When the two friends reach the rocky grotto with their
beloved burden, they perceive that there is no want of a
train of mourners. The faithful women, Mary Magdalene,
Mary Joses, and many other courageous female friends had
followed them at some distance; for they also were anxious
to see the place where the object of their entire hope and
love was to be deposited. Joseph and Nicodemus heartily
welcome them, and gladly accept of their services to aid
them in the interment. The sacred body is then gently laid
on the ground, and, while the women, almost more with
their tears than with the water they have brought, wash
the bloody spots from His head and breast, the men fill the
white linen in which the body is to be wrapped, with myrrh,
aloes, and other of the most costly spices, of which they
had brought a large quantity with them, Nicodemus even a
hundred pounds weight. Then, after having wrapped the
body in the customary linen bandages, they once more look

in silence at the pallid yet regal face of the dead, and spread the napkin over it.

The entire business of interment is, however, not yet ended; but the nearness of the Sabbath requires them to delay the actual embalming until the close of that festival, and, for the time, leave the corpse simply with those preliminary labours of love. If Mary, the sister of Lazarus, was also among the burial train, she would remember that no further work of that kind with the Master's corpse was necessary, since, according to His own express assurance, He had already received from her hands in Bethany the anointing for the day of His burial.

The friends now again lift up the beloved corpse and bear it, gently and solemnly, into the new, clean sepulchre in the rock, where they softly lay it down to rest, as though it were only asleep, in a large and high-arched niche. Once more they look at it deeply affected, then forcibly tear themselves away, leave the vault, roll a great stone before its door, and because the Sabbath lights are already seen glimmering from a distance, return to their dwellings in profound sorrow, but not without hopeful anticipations.

We leave them, and linger a few moments longer at the sepulchre, from whence a vital atmosphere proceeds, and the peace of God is breathed upon us. There He rests, the Lion of the tribe of Judah. How grateful is the feeling to us, after all the ignominy and suffering He has endured, to see Him at least once again honourably reposing, and that too upon a couch, which love, fidelity, and tenderness have prepared for Him! Who does not perceive that even in the circumstances of His interment, the overruling hand of God has interwoven for our consolation a gentle testimony, that His only-begotten Son had well accomplished the great task which He was commissioned to perform? How dearly the taking down from the cross, and the interment of the Redeemer before the setting in of night and the Sabbath, shows the fulfilment of the ancient ordinance of Israel respecting those who were hanged on a tree! And how distinctly are we convinced that the curse is now removed from a sinful world, and that the eye of God again looks graciously and well-pleased down upon the earth!

There He slumbers. Well for us that He was willing to pass through this dark passage on our behalf! Nothing hindered Him from taking up His life again on the cross, and returning from thence immediately to His Father. But had He done so, our bodies would have been left in the grave, and you know how much more we are wont to fear the grave, than even death itself. There, where corruption reigns, it seems as if the curse of sin still hung over us, and as if no redemption had been accomplished. In order to dispel this terror, He paternally took into consideration all our necessities, and suffered Himself to be laid in the grave before our eyes. He did not indeed see corruption, because He was not a sinner. 'Thou wilt not suffer thine Holy One to see corruption,' said David in Psalm 16: 10, impelled by the spirit of prophecy.

Our flesh, on the contrary, which is poisoned by sin, must necessarily pass through the process of the germinating seed-corn, and be dissolved into its original element before its glorification. But the difference between our lot and that of our divine Head is not an essential one. The chief thing continues to be that we know our bodies are not lost in the grave, but that they rest there in hope. This is confirmed and guaranteed to us by Christ. The way we have seen Him go we shall also take. That which His obedience merited for Him as the Son of man, it merited and acquired for us, because Christ yielded it in our stead.

If, therefore, the second Adam's rest in the grave was only a peaceful sabbatic repose, ours can not be any thing more. If, on the third day, He was called forth from the prison in which the king of terrors had confined Him and was crowned with glory and honour; the same thing, in due time, awaits our bodies, if we have entered into union with Him by faith and love. If, henceforth we say that Christ by His burial has consecrated and shed light upon the darkness of our graves, we give utterance to something incomparably more than a mere poetic mode of speaking.

The Apostle Paul writes, in 1 Corinthians 14:13, that our bodies will be raised again, that if this were not the case, Christ Himself would not have risen. Who therefore will deny that grave-yards may justly be termed, 'Resurrection fields'! Yes! those who are bought with the blood of the Lamb rest in their graves under the Almighty's wing, and over their remains a divinely sealed hope casts a radiant and trans-figuring light.

The Prince of Peace reposes in His sepulchre. A venerable man approaches it in silent devotion. It is Paul of Tarsus, and he writes upon the tombstone a mighty inscription. You may read it in Romans 6, where it is testified that we are not only dead with Him but buried with Him. But even as we are planted together in the likeness of His death, so shall we be also in the likeness of His resurrection. What is the meaning of this inscription? It asserts nothing less than this, that Christ has endured the curse of sin on the cross for us. 'There is therefore now no condemnation to them that are in Christ Jesus.' But even though regenerate, we still bear the remains of the old sinful nature in and upon us. This is our grief and cross, and impels us to utter the anxious inquiry, 'O wretched man that I am, who shall deliver me from the body of this death?' May God enable us to say, with him who uttered it, 'I thank God, through our Lord Jesus Christ!'

The first night which succeeded the great and momentous day is past. The body of the deceased Redeemer slumbers solitarily in the prison of the tomb. The morning at length dawns, and movements are heard about the sepulchre. They are no longer the beloved forms of His friends that we see hasting so early through the garden. The latter, accustomed to obey every commandment, remain quietly in their habitations during the great Sabbath. It is enemies whom we see so active and busy at the first dawning of the morning.

The previous evening, an anxious solicitude had seized their hearts. Their excited evil consciences saw visions. The remembrance of so many sayings of the Nazarene occurred to them, in which He had most clearly announced a resurrection by which His heavenly Father after His crucifixion would glorify Him before the whole world. The hypocrites pretended that they were far from supposing that such fanatical fancies would ever be realized; but they think otherwise in their hearts. Even in death the crucified Jesus asserts His regal influence on their minds, and in His grave terrifies them by His majesty. Careless about the Sabbath or the Passover festival, the high priests and Pharisees go in solemn procession to the governor's palace, in order to induce him to take measures for securing the grave of the crucified Jesus. They are admitted into the presence of Pilate, who is not a little surprised at such an early visit from the notables of Israel.

'Sir,' say they, 'we remember that that deceiver (Shame upon them to speak in such a manner of the Holy One of Israel, contrary to their better light and knowledge) said, while he was yet alive, After three days, I will rise again. (Thus they confirm it, that He had really asserted this.) Command therefore that the sepulchre be watched until the third day, lest his disciples come by night and steal him away, and say unto the people, he is risen from the dead, so the last error shall be worse than the first.'

Observe how cunningly these wicked men try to conceal their real thoughts and feelings. One would suppose that they were afraid only of a possible deception. But if they were merely anxious to repel the poor disciples, would any such measures as they demanded have been requisite? But the mighty acts which they had seen the murdered Man perform cause them to think every thing possible; and the terrific events which had accompanied His death were not calculated to dispel or alleviate their anxiety. They scent the air of Easter morning, and are afraid of a resurrection of the buried corpse. But if the latter were to ensue, of what avail would be a guard, or the lime and plaster with which they intended to fix the stone? So we might well inquire, and doubt whether any serious apprehensions of Jesus' restoration to life could have actuated His enemies.

But fear is foolish, and sin is blind, and gropes in the dark, however wise it may think itself. Pilate, who probably felt very peculiar emotion thrill through him while listening to what the rulers of Israel had to say, very willingly granted their request, and, pointing to a band of armed soldiers which he saw parading before the palace, says, 'Ye have there a watch, go your way, make it as sure as you can.'

Not a little pleased at having attained their object, the deputation, together with the Roman guard, repair to Joseph's garden. After having convinced themselves by inspection that the body still lay in its place, the heavy stone which they had rolled away from the mouth of the sepulchre is replaced, and the work of fixing and sealing commences.

The adversaries act as if they were the victors, but inwardly they are the vanquished. The slumbering Hero of Judah took from them the armour of careless confidence, and filled their souls with a cloud of terrific and oppressive forebodings. What do they mean by their extensive preparations? They are fighting for the cause of death against life; and would gladly establish and maintain the throne of death, and keep down and immure the throne of life. Let them do their utmost. An all-overruling God controls their designs, and permits them to assist death by still more strongly forging his fetters, in order that the bursting of them may appear so much the more glorious. And thus they are suffered to deprive life of all scope, and to wall up every outlet, that when it bursts through every barrier, it may the more evidently prove itself to be divine.

We depart from the sepulchre of our Lord – not in grief and sorrow, but full of joyful expectation of what is shortly to take place. We already behold in spirit the first glimmer of the dawning resurrection morn upon the rocky tomb. Only twenty-four hours more till the trumpet of God shall sound, and Joseph's garden present a different spectacle. Then every seal will be broken, not from the Redeemer's tomb only, but also, from the mystery of the whole of His passion. An 'Amen!' from on high, the most glorious and stupendous that ever resounded under heaven, will then announce to the world that reconciliation has been made, and that the Prince of Life, crowned with glory and honour, as the Conqueror of all the terrific powers which were opposed to us, offers the first Easter salutation of peace to the favoured race of man, from the ruins of His shattered tomb. Let us then tune our harps, and hold our festive garlands in readiness, while awaiting the mighty moment that shall put an eternal end to all the sadness and anxiety of the human heart.